ONLINE EDUCATION
Global Questions, Local Answers

Edited by
Kelli Cargile Cook and Keith Grant-Davie
Utah State University

Baywood's Technical Communications Series
Series Editor: Charles H. Sides

Baywood Publishing Company, Inc.
AMITYVILLE, NEW YORK

Baywood Publishing Company, Inc.
26 Austin Avenue
Amityville, NY 11701
(800) 638-7819
E-mail: baywood@baywood.com
Web site: baywood.com

Library of Congress Catalog Number: 2004050283
ISBN: 0-89503-295-3 (cloth)

Library of Congress Cataloging-in-Publication Data

Online education : global questions, local answers / edited by Kelli Cargile Cook and Keith Grant-Davie.
  p. cm. -- (Technical communications series)
 Includes bibliographical references and index.
 ISBN 0-89503-295-3 (cloth)
  1. Education, Higher--Computer-assisted instruction. 2. Distance
education--Computer-assisted instruction. 3. Internet in higher education. I. Cargile Cook,
Kelli, 1959- II. Grant-Davie, Keith, 1957- III. Series.

LB2395.7.O63 2004
378.1'758--dc22

                                                          2004050283

Table of Contents

SECTION 3: HOW SHOULD WE MONITOR
AND ASSESS THE QUALITY OF ONLINE
COURSES AND PROGRAMS?

Introduction

Keith Grant-Davie and
Kelli Cargile Cook

During the last decade, technical communication instructors and program directors have been discussing and experimenting with teaching technical communication from a distance using technologies such as audio, video, telephony, and wide-area networks. The first reports of courses taught from a distance appeared in the field's professional journals in 1994. Since then, developments in digital media have rapidly accelerated the growth of distance education, opening up possibilities unavailable just a few years ago. In the technical communication field alone, 22 U.S. colleges and universities currently offer courses, undergraduate degrees, and/or graduate degrees via digital media, and when we consider how many faculty members are now creating or planning to create online courses at institutions across the country, the need for information about best practices in online education is staggering.[1] It is also urgent because many of the scholar-teachers developing these online courses and degree programs are under pressure to act quickly. This pressure has three main sources: 1) institutional pressure to launch courses and programs rapidly in order to keep up with, or ahead of, the competition; 2) sales pressure from the developers of the hardware and software, who are anxious to suggest how and why we should use their products; and 3) pressure from the technology itself, which has developed in dazzling, tempting profusion, at a faster rate than the theory needed to guide our use of it.

Many of us now have access to a variety of technologies that allow us to teach students anyplace and anytime, but we are still discovering the implications of teaching with these new instructional media, and we have only begun to discuss

---

[1] By "online education" we mean computer-mediated, interactive instruction, currently characterized by such features as synchronous and asynchronous discussion boards, email, and other uses of the World Wide Web and Internet.

how best we should use them and why those uses are the best. Unless we promote this discussion, we run the real risk of allowing the technology and its creators to determine for us how online education should be done.

THEMES AND REFRAINS

One of the themes of this book is the importance of making sure that our use of technology is driven by our pedagogy, rather than vice versa. We should no more allow the way we teach online to be determined by the available educational software than we should allow the way we teach in a traditional classroom to be determined by the way the custodians think the chairs should be arranged (which at our institution is typically in tight rows, facing forward). Unless we discuss what constitutes effective online instruction, we also risk being lulled into the idea that teaching through electronic media is essentially the same as teaching in a traditional classroom, only easier (or harder). *Online Education: Global Questions, Local Answers* takes the position that teaching through electronic media is neither better nor worse but a different experience for teachers and students, that some aspects are harder and others easier than they are in a traditional classroom, and that before teachers can succeed with the new media they need to examine a range of issues and revise many of their own and their students' expectations that have been developed through decades of experience in traditional classrooms.

This book therefore focuses on the relationship between the best online education practices that have been developed and the theories on which they are founded. We believe online education in the early 21st century is at a theory-building stage, a stage at which we need not only to take stock of what we are doing with the new technologies, and what we might do with them, but also to examine and discuss our rationales for those practices. Building theories of good online education involves asking ourselves which of the principles and practices that have guided instruction in traditional classrooms can be transferred or adapted to work in the new electronic class spaces that have become available to us, which ones must be discarded or replaced, and what new practices must be developed for these new spaces.

Online Education: Global Questions, Local Answers brings together 24 college educators experienced in various aspects of online education to present and discuss those issues and to explain what they have done to address them. The book focuses on what we think are the most important questions that scholar-teachers and administrators need to address if they are committed to developing high-quality online education programs. We call these questions "global" because they transcend the particular situations of individual institutions. They are questions all of us involved in online education need to address: What are the issues to consider when first developing and then sustaining an online education program? How do we create interactive, pedagogically sound online courses and classroom communities? How should we monitor and assess the quality of online courses and programs? And how should recent developments and innovations in online education cause us to reexamine our roles and responsibilities as educators in technical communication?

While these global questions affect all of us in one way or another, we believe they demand the kinds of different local answers that the authors discuss throughout this collection. Readers will need to consider which of these local answers might apply to their own situations and how those answers might need to be adapted to reflect the particular needs of their own institutions. As we reflect on the contents of this collection, it becomes clear to us, even as we search for the best practices of online education, that there is no single most effective model for all situations. For example, Texas Tech and Utah State both began their online master's programs around 1997, addressing working professional communicators as their main clientele. Both programs include distance courses as part of professors' regular teaching loads, and both programs admit students through their Graduate School, but Utah State's program is administered and funded by an Extension office while Texas Tech's is administered and funded through its English Department. Another example where local solutions obviously differ is individual programs' choice of primary discussion technology. The graduate programs at Texas Tech and Mercer both use synchronous chat sessions as their primary discussion technology while East Carolina State University, Georgia Tech, and Utah State prefer asynchronous threaded discussions. Furthermore, programs that use the same primary discussion technology, such as Texas Tech and Mercer, may employ this technology differently, as illustrated by the chat protocols illustrated in Carolyn Rude's, Susan Lang's, and Helen Grady and Marjorie Davis's chapters. Extending this point one step further, it is even possible that instructors within programs may use the same technology differently, depending on pedagogical (course) requirements and student needs. These similarities and differences reflect some of the global questions that individual programs and instructors must address—How will the program be administered, and how will instructors and students interact within courses?—as well as the local answers specific programs have developed.

In some cases, our authors mention specific software that has helped them reach their local answers, but this book is not simply a celebration or promotion of any of today's software. We acknowledge that online education would not be possible without technological innovations and that the lure of what can now be done with technology is motivating many schools to begin offering online education. However, we have tried to keep the focus of this book from being on the features of particular software solutions that, in a few years, are sure to seem as quaint as five-and-a-quarter-inch floppy disks and daisy-wheel printers seem to us now. Documenting the software in use at this point in our profession's evolution has some historical value, but we hope the book will serve a more important purpose: to initiate and promote a meta-discussion about the issues of pedagogy and instructional design we think should continue to guide our choice of available software in the next decade—and, more importantly, ought to guide the development of new educational software during that time.

Two chapters in the collection speak to this purpose, Avery, Civjan, and Johri's discussion of VisOC in Section 3 and Faber and Johnson-Eilola's discussion of Crateware in Section 4. As possible directions that future applications may take, these are examples of technological innovations currently on the horizon that oblige us to reconsider our pedagogies in light of what might be done in an online environment. What we think is most interesting about these innovations is the global questions they raise: How should these applications be used in the future—for teaching or research purposes? How will they affect the online teaching environment in which they are used? What are the ethical, political, and social implications of these applications and future applications like them? The local answers to these questions found in this collection are just that—local answers. We anticipate that readers of this book will want to ask the same global questions and seek answers that best fit their local contexts.

Another theme running through this book is that online education and technical communication have a natural affinity for each other—that although not all teaching methods translate readily from traditional classrooms to online classrooms, technical communication teachers already tend to favor the kind of interactive, constructivist approaches to instruction that seem to suit online classes. The book might be said to have a dominant refrain that repeats in various forms: Both technical communication and online education allow participants to remove or cross traditional, restrictive boundaries of discourse and discipline, and the environments that result from such border crossings are rich, complex, diverse, messy, difficult to control or describe neatly, and full of variables, disconnections, imperfections, and contradictions. In such environments, we have the best chance of success if we accept those characteristics and learn not only to live with them and make allowances for them but also to take advantage of them, looking for the opportunities they provide for learning and growth. This theme appears notably in the chapters by Carolyn Rude and Susan Lang, where they describe the controlled frenzy of synchronous discussion; by Kristin Walker on activity theory; by Mark Zachry on paralogy; by Locke Carter and Rebecca Rickly on gaps; and by TyAnna Herrington and Yuri Tretyakov on the unpredictability and confusion of an intercontinental online education project.

FOUR GLOBAL QUESTIONS

The first section of the book addresses the global question, "How do we create and sustain online programs and courses?" Its four chapters identify the issues that teachers and administrators need to consider as they prepare to develop a new online program or course. Marjorie Davis opens by making the case that technical communication teachers are ideally prepared to be leaders in the field of online education, showing how the knowledge domains of technical communication equip them to guide the development of good online programs. Angela Eaton, in Chapter 2, asks who online students are and reports on a survey of these students, describing their demographics and the aspects of online education that they like and dislike, suggesting the survey's implications for the design and marketing of online programs. In Chapter 3, Kelli Cargile Cook argues that we need to notice the impact of technology on writing practices and on instruction and to adapt instruction to the new medium, but to avoid letting technology determine pedagogy. She provides a pedagogy-driven heuristic for developing online courses. The first section of the book concludes with Carolyn Rude's chapter, in which she reviews the issues and questions that a teacher or administrator should consider in order to set up a program that is supported by theory and driven by pedagogy rather than technology.

The six chapters in the second section of the book address the question, "How do we create interactive, pedagogically sound online courses and classroom communities?" They show how familiar elements of face-to-face instruction change, or must be changed, when teaching online and also describe innovative practices, not found in onsite classes, developed for the new online teaching environment. In Chapter 5, Nancy Coppola reviews the literature on faculty roles to explore ways in which cognitive, affective, and managerial roles change as instructors learn to teach online. Helen Grady and Marjorie Davis then draw on principles of instructional design to show how instructors can create an authentic interactive, collaborative learning environment online by providing students with visual, verbal, textual, and procedural scaffolding. In Chapter 7, Locke Carter and Rebecca Rickly discuss the ways in which space (physical, virtual, and cognitive) is transformed in an online classroom and examine how online instructors need to look out for the gaps or differences that can occur in this virtual space—gaps that can become obstacles if ignored or opportunities if given the right attention. Chapters 8 and 9 both discuss the translation of particular activities from traditional classes to online classes. Lee-Ann Kastman Breuch, in Chapter 8, shows how virtual peer review differs from peer review in traditional, face-to-face classrooms, arguing that, while the pedagogical assumptions remain unchanged, the practices need to be modified for peer review to work in the virtual classroom. In the next chapter, Susan Lang considers how the student-centered discussion that is typically the core activity of a face-to-face graduate seminar in technical communication can be recreated in an online class, arguing for the importance of synchronous discussion. Mark Zachry concludes this section of the book in Chapter 10 by arguing that graduate students in technical communication need to have their trust in principles of clear communication challenged by the discovery that real communication is not logical but rather paralogical, causing clarity of meaning to be unpredictable. Asynchronous online discussion, Zachry argues, is the ideal medium in which students can experience how easily their best attempts at clear written communication can fail.

The global question uniting the chapters in section 3 of the book is "How should we monitor and assess the quality of online courses and programs?" The first two chapters in this section assess and address the needs of students in online classes. Philip Rubens and Sherry Southard's Chapter 11 opens section 3 by recounting their early efforts to create an online classroom environment that could easily be accessed and used by all students, including the technologically impoverished. They discuss the problems their students encountered and ways they solved them. While almost all the chapters in this book discuss online education at the graduate level, Kristin Walker in Chapter 12 shares her experiences with undergraduates. Drawing on activity theory as a guiding principle, she reminds us to consider all the possible variables that might be in play in an online class and that might require teachers to make allowances or modifications. Keith Grant-Davie follows in Chapter 13 with the story of an attempt to create a research internship in a graduate technical writing program. Although the assignment was eventually shelved as too ambitious for the existing resources, he uses the story to demonstrate the importance of praxis—the practice of continually reflecting upon and improving instruction—as we continue to discover the best practices of online education.

Self-reflection is one of a number of methods of assessing online instruction that Kelli Cargile Cook and Keith Grant-Davie review in Chapter 14. They note the richness of the data available for assessment in online class archives and discuss whether online assessment should look for evidence of minimal standards or of excellence. The richness of online course archives is also the subject of the final chapter in this section of the book. Cassie Avery, Jason Civjan, and Aditya Johri describe the development and performance of a new computer application that creates a graphic representation of patterns of student interaction within the copious records of online discussion, helping instructors locate places in the archive where they might find evidence of particular kinds of interaction.

The three chapters in the final section of the book are united by the global question, "How is online education challenging our assumptions?" In Chapter 16, TyAnna Herrington and Yuri Tretyakov describe the Global Classroom Project, a jointly developed project in which students from the United States and Russia interact online. The authors draw parallels between the unavoidable "chaos, confusion, and disarray" that they have observed in this project and the inter-disciplinarity, lack of unifying theory or subject, and resistance to neat, tidy description that they see in the field of technical communication. They caution against trying too hard to clear up such conditions, arguing instead for the value of experiential learning—learning to cope with the mess—which may be the best method of achieving "contextual functionality."

Online Education: Global Questions, Local Answers concludes with two provocative chapters that openly challenge readers to reevaluate some accepted assumptions and practices. Brenton Faber and Johndan Johnson-Eilola in Chapter 17 ask us to rethink the ethical and political implications of turning educational technology developed at universities into profit-making enterprises.

They argue that open source software, in which users have access to the source code and can adapt it to their own purposes, is more consistent with the principle that knowledge developed in an academic environment should be freely disseminated rather than marketed for financial gain.

The book opens with Marjorie Davis's assertion that teachers of technical communication are ideally qualified to be leaders in the development of online education at their institutions. It concludes with Chapter 18, in which Billie Wahlstrom and Linda Clemens call on technical communication teachers to expand their leadership roles in another direction and set national standards for lifelong learning. They argue that online education can give us the means to remain in touch with former students, continuing to share new knowledge with students long after they have graduated and joined the workforce.

OTHER QUESTIONS IN SEARCH OF ANSWERS

Although it includes 18 chapters written by 24 authors, *Online Education: Global Questions, Local Answers* does not provide an exhaustive analysis of issues in its subject. We are well aware of some important aspects of online education that we were not able to address in detail in this collection. One such issue is the extent to which online education meets the needs of students with disabilities. Online education seems to render some disabilities invisible. For example, wheelchairs, speech impediments, and hearing disabilities need not be apparent in online discussions. On the other hand, students who are blind or have visual disabilities may have a harder time in an online class than they might in the oral environment of a face-to-face class. Those of us who have taught students with disabilities online have learned that we must consider accessibility when designing our online materials. And, although we can offer advice gained from experiences working with students with disabilities, as Carter and Rickly do in their chapter, accessibility remains a surprisingly under-researched area of online education in technical communication. We hope this deficiency will soon be addressed.

Although Eaton's chapter provides a profile of online students in technical communication, a subject that is not addressed in her chapter or in others in the collection is the status of online students relative to traditional students—and the increasing difficulty of making that binary distinction. This issue recently came to our attention at Utah State over a question of eligibility for the university's top recruitment fellowships for graduate students. The criteria for these fellowships are a telling indication of the kinds of student that an institution values and wants to attract and enable. Students applying to our master's program in Technical Writing, which is delivered online, have been ruled ineligible for the most valuable fellowships available to graduate students. The fellowships are to be reserved as enticements to recruit the best students to come to campus for their studies. The main reasons—or rather, assumptions—offered to justify this decision are that students on campus are more valuable because they enrich the intellectual life of their departments through extensive interactions outside class and that students who come to campus have more need of fellowship support because they incur greater expenses than students who continue to live at home while pursuing their studies online. While both assumptions may be true for individual students, we take issue with them as general principles that apply to all students. We believe students are capable of interacting outside class just as much online as when they are on campus and that students taking online classes from remote locations may have living expenses as high as, or higher than, those who live on or near campus.

More fundamentally, though, we take issue with the assumption that online students and on-campus students belong to two discrete groups and that their membership in either group is fixed from matriculation to graduation. Terms like "online," "remote," and "distance" may be valid descriptors of students and classes at any given moment, but they are questionable when used as qualifiers to label students when they matriculate. A few examples of our students at Utah State should illustrate how the categories "online" and "on-campus" can become confused. One of the students in our online Technical Writing program works on campus as a university employee and lives in Logan. She takes mostly online classes, but she has also taken a number of on-campus workshops and occasionally meets with us to discuss her work. Is she an "online student," and should she be ruled ineligible for a fellowship? Is she a significantly different type of student from the two who live in Bermuda and Okinawa, respectively, and take online classes in the same program but have come to campus in the summer for face-to-face workshops or from another student in Israel who has never met his instructors face-to-face? Then again, there is our graduate student in American Studies (a program in which all the classes are traditional, face-to-face seminars), who lives 85 miles away and commutes to our campus. She arrives just in time for each class and heads home to her family immediately afterwards. She is clearly not an online student, so she would be considered eligible for a fellowship, but is she contributing any more to the intellectual life of the campus by her brief presences than the students in our online program, who interact with each other several days a week on class discussion boards and through personal email?

Online education has already developed to the point where simple equations between online education and distance education soon deconstruct under examination, as do simple distinctions between on-campus education and online or distance education. We believe that students will continue to complicate and undermine these categories as online education becomes more pervasive, the students appearing as an integral part of an increasing number of traditional classes that meet face-to-face on campus but continuing their discussions online between class meetings. After all, students and instructors can interact online even when they are working side by side at computers in the same classroom, so physical separation or "distance" is neither a necessary nor a definitive feature of online education. Online education just happens to be a good way to overcome the communication barriers that distance might otherwise present.

Rather than trying to classify students once and for all as one type of student or another and attaching financial implications to that classification, we prefer to say that students may now find themselves in a number of possible instructional situations. Each of these situations might be described by the medium (or media) of instruction used in the class and by the student's and the instructor's locations (in an on-campus or off-campus classroom, or somewhere else), as illustrated by the matrix in Table 1.

Using the matrix, we can identify different instructional situations by combining items from each of the three columns in the table. For example, 1-A-a would describe a traditional class where students and instructor meet together in a classroom on campus at set times each week, and 1-B-b would describe an instructor traveling some distance to a remote classroom to meet face-to-face with students from the surrounding area. For a few combinations in our table, it is hard to imagine functional instructional situations—for instance, 1-C-a or 1-B-c. If students and instructor are remote from each other, face-to-face communication isn't possible. However, most combinations do correspond to familiar instructional situations. 1-C-c would be a field trip. 3-B-a describes some traditional extension classes on campus, where the instructor teaches from a studio on campus, using audio-visual media to conduct a lecture and demonstration that is transmitted to students who have gathered at a number of different remote locations around the state. At these centers, the necessary technology has been installed to allow students to see the instructor and ask questions. 2-C-c would describe classes taught in our online master's program in Technical Writing, where students and instructors can log in to the virtual class space from their workplaces, their homes, or any location that allows Internet access.

Table 1 lists only three options in each column, but it should be clear that they are only examples and that more might be added to give the table more fine-grained descriptive ability. Furthermore, we should point out that a class can include more than one combination of medium, student location, and instructor location and that multiple combinations can occur in parallel or serial relationships. For instance, 1-A-a and 2-A-a might both occur simultaneously in a course taught by an instructor in an on-campus classroom full of computers; or a class might start as a 1-A-a traditional class and then shift at some point in the term to become a 2-C-c class as participants stop meeting face-to-face and start interacting only online—a serial shift from one instructional situation to another. This kind of shift happened in our department when one of our faculty members had a baby in the middle of the semester and continued to teach her classes online from home. A similar shift can happen when an instructor goes away for a conference and, rather than cancel an on-campus class for a week, moves the class

Table 1. A Matrix Describing Instructional Situations

Class Medium	Student Location	Instructor Location
1. Face-to-face	A. On-campus classroom	a. On-campus classroom
2. Online interaction through Internet	B. Off-campus classroom	b. Off-campus classroom
3. Other media (e.g., correspondence, telephone, interactive TV)	C. Elsewhere (work, home, field trip destination, Internet café, etc.)	c. Elsewhere (work, home, conference, field trip destination, etc.)

online during his or her absence. Alternatively, an onsite class might include both 1-A-a and 2-C-c situations in parallel throughout the term, where online discussion is used as a supplement to face-to-face discussion.

In any case, the point of Table 1 is not to provide an exhaustive typology but simply to suggest a way of thinking about classroom space that recognizes the expanding variety of instructional situations, involving various kinds of technology, that are now available or becoming available. We still find ourselves using terms like "online student," "remote student," and "traditional student" out of habit and convenience, but we are becoming more wary of the ways that such labels can be used politically to privilege some students over others in ways that we don't think are justified. At any given moment in a semester, many of our students defy singular classification as they may be participating in several different instructional situations in their various classes, and those situations may well change from week to week.

Our thinking about ways to describe online classes and the students who take them was precipitated by a very local issue—the disagreement with some of our colleagues at Utah State about graduate fellowship eligibility—but we wonder whether this experience may be just one example of the kinds of skepticism, prejudice, or fear that many of us involved with online programs will need to engage and overcome at our individual institutions before online education can be fully understood, accepted, and respected across campus and beyond. Surely we aren't the only ones who have heard our more reactionary colleagues express suspicion and preconceptions about online education with remarks like these: "You mean you might never *meet* these students?" "How do you know they are who they say they are?" "How do you know it's their work?" On the other hand, even if this kind of resistance is as widespread as we suspect, we are reassured by Marjorie Davis's comments in Chapter 1 that technical communicators have the knowledge and persuasive skills needed to lead our colleagues in the development of online education.

Considering the distinctions between traditional and remote students has also led us to reconsider the distinctions and importance of institutional and programmatic identities commonly defined by faculty and disciplinary specializations. Online education has created opportunities for remote, adjunct professors who are experts in technical communication to teach remote students, creating situations in which neither instructor nor students are located at the course's institutional (geographical) home. Perhaps we should add a fourth item to the second and third columns of our table. 2-D-d or 3-D-d would indicate instructional situations where technological media are allowing classes at one institution to include students at another institution and to be taught by an instructor at a third. These remote, adjunct professors bring a richness of knowledge and experience to an institution's technical communication faculty and student body that was only possible in the past through visiting professorships, which few working professionals were able to accept or fill. An adjunct faculty member's presence can enhance a student's programmatic experience but, at the same time, it modifies the character of the program in general. However, see Davis and Rude (Section 1) for further discussion of the potential drawbacks of this practice. What is the effect, then, of employing remote professors on a program's identity, and how do remote or distant professors fit into a faculty's programmatic and pedagogical profile? Furthermore, how important are these institutional and programmatic identities for undergraduate and master's students' educations? Shouldn't students have the opportunity to take courses from the best in the field, wherever they are geographically located, and why should institutional boundaries, as Clemens and Wahlstrom refer to them, prevent online students from learning from the best professors available? Such questions have led us to reconsider our assumptions about programmatic identity and to begin to think seriously about the positive and negative implications of consortia, a concept suggested by several of our book's authors. Although we do not claim to have an answer for these questions, we hope that this book will promote meaningful discussions about them.

Collectively, the book's authors have considered many questions and issues that concern us as online educators and that, we believe, will concern others who are currently teaching technical communication online or planning to do so in the future. Each chapter, whether its focus is on concrete, practical matters or on the more abstract theories that underlie these matters, offers a possible map for the successful design, delivery, or evaluation of online courses. In addition, the authors model the kinds of reflective thinking they have employed to create and sustain effective online classrooms. Such reflection, we argue, is the hallmark of bold, new, and effective learning spaces, whether they are found in traditional or online classrooms.

SECTION 1

How Do We Create and Sustain Online Programs and Courses?

CHAPTER 1

Applying Technical Communication Theory to the Design of Online Education

Marjorie T. Davis

Whether you are talking about education in colleges or corporations, the trend toward online education is very strong and getting stronger. As technologies improve and become more affordable, schools and businesses are taking up the challenge to offer learning in electronic, nontraditional modes. The second study of distance education at postsecondary institutions conducted by the National Center for Education Statistics (data gathered 1997-98) reported that 78% of public four-year colleges offered at least some distance education courses, enrolling more than 1.6 million students [1]. The magazine *Business Week* predicted in the fall of 1999 that the number of people taking courses online would increase to 2.23 million by 2002 and would constitute about 15% of all higher education enrollments [2]. Businesses have long since surpassed colleges and universities in the amount of money spent on training and education. In a benchmarking study in 1999 by the American Society for Training and Development (ASTD), predictions were that about 27% of business training of all types would be delivered using learning technologies [3]. It's clear that online education is a booming business.

OPPORTUNITIES FOR TECHNICAL COMMUNICATORS

This strong growth in online education provides new opportunities for technical communicators. Businesses need people with online education skills to develop and run their extensive training programs, and colleges and universities need people with both content knowledge and online education knowledge in order to develop programs. The opportunities are there for those who want to develop online education systems for industries and for those who want to lead in academic online education efforts. While this chapter applies to both industry and academe, the primary emphasis is on the role of technical communication faculty in colleges and universities offering two-year, four-year, and graduate courses or degree programs. Its thesis is that technical communicators should accept the challenge to apply what they know to the development of online education because they are uniquely positioned to provide leadership to schools and companies who are designing instruction for online delivery. They have mastered the important concepts of audience, purpose, persona, and usability; they have the knowledge of the technology for online delivery (or can acquire it easily); they have a strong collaborative work ethic and experience in project management; and they usually have the strength in instructional design to create effective online learning. Applying the theories of technical communication to the design and delivery of online education—especially within the field of technical communication—can be a significant service to the department, to the school or company, and most importantly to the students. As schools or industries venture into the online education environment, they can benefit from the significant expertise and knowledge of technical communicators.

To assist technical communication instructors in moving toward leadership in online education, this chapter presents the theories from technical communication that may be profitably applied to the design of online learning programs. This theoretical application demonstrates that technical communicators are not only qualified to develop online education within their own specialties, but, through this knowledge, are also capable of leading and assisting others as they develop online learning programs. In the sections that follow, I'll discuss seven key knowledge domains of technical communicators that relate specifically to developing online education. From these knowledge domains arise both questions necessary for online program development and specific, local answers to these questions.

My own experience in developing online education comes from having helped start the first online degree program at Mercer University, the Master of Science in Technical Communication Management, offered entirely by online learning since 1996 [4]. For this reason, throughout this chapter, I emphasize *program* development, not *course* development. In most cases, providing a single course online is not a cost-effective endeavor in terms of time, effort, and technology. If students are to be attracted to online education, they must be able to derive substantial benefit from it—such as completing a degree or certificate. Further, the assumption is that these courses will be offered for credit from an accredited institution, and that they will be subject to evaluation by accreditation agencies. A further assumption is that the online learners will be truly adults—usually those with some work experience and enough maturity to be self-directed learners.

TECHNICAL COMMUNICATION KNOWLEDGE
APPLIED TO ONLINE EDUCATION

The diversity of knowledge required to teach technical communication provides a strong foundation for planning and delivering education online. The process of teaching and learning is always demanding, but when the element of online education is introduced, the cognitive demands on the teacher increase exponentially. As teachers, we all have good skills in research, analysis, and creation of coherent knowledge. When we initially begin to plan education for online delivery, however, we may at first feel overwhelmed with so many new design tasks. Unlike teachers in many other disciplines, however, technical communicators have a strong knowledge base that will provide excellent strategies for designing online education. This knowledge includes the following areas and their related knowledge domains:

- The broad dimensions of rhetoric as applied to all aspects of communication but especially the analysis of audience and purpose;
- The understanding of an iterative design process that includes prototype development and testing for usability;
- Familiarity with a broad range of tool technologies, along with a willingness to experiment and learn more; and
- An understanding of business environments involving collaboration, marketing, and project management.

The rest of this section explores how technical communicators can apply these key knowledge domains to online education and explains how they can use these domains to overcome its challenges.

Analyzing Audiences

The importance of the audience in any communication has been recognized since Aristotle's days. While modern rhetoricians have extended the theory and its applications, the basic principles are commonly known and used by technical communicators. Audience analysis is one of the strengths of skilled technical communicators, and this strength provides a solid foundation for planning education or training programs.

One of the first tasks that a program planner must do is to analyze the complex audiences involved in designing education for online delivery. This analysis is different from planning a course for in-house delivery in a number of ways, but especially because of the wider distribution of the materials. The audience will almost certainly be much larger and more diverse than students sitting in a physical classroom. Audiences who must be considered include the following:

- Local audiences—colleagues and administrators within one's own department, school, or company who will need to approve the programs;

- Distance audiences—the target audience of students or customers who will want to take the online education programs;
- Employers of the graduates or employees who will authorize tuition reimbursements or accept the college credentials;
- The competitors for the target audience—all those schools and corporate entities who are offering learning online already;
- Accrediting agencies who will evaluate the educational product; and
- Peers in the technical communication community who will evaluate the quality of the content, the educational process, and its products.

One of the best tools for performing complex audience analyses, the egocentric audience analysis chart, was developed by Mathes and Stevenson[1] and widely replicated in more recent technical communication texts [5]. Using the egocentric audience analysis chart will help technical communicators to identify the complex audience that their educational planning must address, whether for their own programs or for other programs they may be developing.

First, audiences must be identified in broad enough terms to include not only those to whom we are delivering our educational product but also those on the periphery. In writing to request approval of a new online education proposal in technical communication, for example, the audience must include not only the department chair and dean of the college but all those stakeholders who have opinions about online education and will have the opportunity to vote aye or nay. In a company setting, the audience analysis must identify not only the learners but also the many internal competitors and potential allies for the online education product. Using the egocentric audience analysis chart provides a visual representation to help keep all those audiences in mind.

Second, the planning must carefully and specifically describe the target audience. Is the program going to serve those with degrees in other fields who wish to enter the field of technical communication? Those who are already in the profession and need to acquire more advanced skills? Those who are seeking the PhD in order to teach or to lead corporate units? Are you targeting traditional-age students who wish to take asynchronous courses as a convenience, or non-traditional adults who do not wish to give up jobs and family life to complete a degree? Carefully and specifically describing the market niche will help to define and delineate the boundaries of the program proposal; additionally, it will help in writing the mission and purpose of the program.

Third, the audiences must include employers, parents, etc., who will evaluate the benefits of the knowledge gained in the online education program. In some cases the cost of tuition in online education may be less than the cost of travel,

---

[1] The "egocentric organization chart" is introduced in their text on pages 23 and following, with a full discussion of the breakdown of readers by their operational, objective, and personal characteristics. These concepts are ubiquitous now in most good technical communication textbooks.

lodging, and lost productivity for students or employees who now attend educational programs onsite. The program must be prepared to address any concerns of these audiences about the credibility of the online educational offerings and the applicability of the learning objectives.

Fourth, the audiences include competitors—those who are already engaged in online education. With every year that passes, more and more technical communication programs are beginning to offer courses, certificates, or degrees online. This accessibility to a number of education providers means that competition is no longer limited to the 100-mile driving radius of your campus. A separate audience chart of competing programs should help further to determine the target audience and to focus on the benefits the program must provide in order to be competitive.

Finally, the audience analysis should include those external audiences who will judge the value of the program. Every college and university must answer to boards of trustees, state regulating bodies, and regional accrediting agencies; a few have professional accreditation boards who must be considered. If you are planning to submit your program for accreditation, keep that audience in mind as you begin to design the program. Additionally, colleagues beyond your own campus will evaluate the quality of programs as they advise students or employers about the value of the degree program.

No single program can accomplish all the goals that all these audiences might wish. A well-considered audience analysis, however, can help to determine exactly whom you are trying to reach as you plan the program. Eaton's chapter, which follows this one, provides additional information about learners at a distance.

Analyzing Purposes

Once the complex audience analysis is completed, the statement of purpose or mission statement must be developed. Universities or industries may want to embark on online learning for a multitude of complex, often poorly defined, reasons. Many of these may be based on false assumptions. For example, a university chief academic officer may believe that online learning will be a cheap way to increase enrollments and revenues, seeing visions of the masses enrolling in courses unhindered by the pesky limitations of classroom size and concurrent time zones. In a recent survey of faculty from all disciplines who deliver instruction online, "forty-one percent of the respondents agreed with the statement that a primary motive behind online education was profit" [6, p. 6]. Perhaps companies are not as idealistic about financial returns as are universities; within the corporate setting, 44% of respondents recognized "the perception of high cost" as an obstacle to Web-based learning [7, p. 14]. (For additional discussions of the economics of online education, see Cargile Cook's and Faber and Johnson-Eilola's chapters later in this book.) From my experience and that of other colleagues, it should be abundantly clear that the profit motive is not a legitimate purpose for engaging in online education—it just won't happen. Online delivery will likely cost more than you will predict in your planning in terms of time, effort, and money. It's important to know exactly why you are committed to developing online education programs, and writing a clear purpose statement helps.

Another false assumption I have heard expressed is that a university or a corporation can "buy the best" world-renowned scholar, premiere in his or her field, who will be hired to develop the content, while lesser beings can do the daily work of grading quizzes and meeting with students who are having problems[2] [8]. Again, building a reputation on a big-name scholar will not, in my opinion, provide the kind of content your audiences want and need, nor will it meet the ongoing demands of maintaining a program. The same kind of vision was predicted for educational television several decades ago. If the mass media/broadcast mode could have worked, the ubiquitous television technology would have accomplished it. The truth is that learners of all kinds want a more personalized, customized, interactive learning experience than the broadcast model using star scholars can provide.

In spite of some misguided intentions, there are some excellent reasons to design an online education program. Those who do so have a set of complex reasons and purposes. One of the most difficult tasks is to state explicitly and in some detail exactly what your purpose is. Such a statement should address the following issues:

- Why the department, institution, or company wants to engage in online education;
- What the program will attempt to accomplish;
- Why the program is needed;
- What benefits the program will offer students and employers through online education;
- What specific target audience the program will reach;
- How you know that the audience wants or needs your educational program; and
- What benefits the faculty expect to gain from engaging in this effort.

Again, the audience analysis theories (especially Mathes and Stevenson's) related to clear statements of purpose are especially useful. Forcing yourself to

---

[2] In an interview with representatives of IBM's Media Center in Atlanta, one spokesperson asserted that only the very best faculty with international reputations would be sought to create content for digital delivery. In his view, the less prestigious "satellite universities" would handle the mundane chores of interacting with students and grading their papers. I encountered others in interviews who espoused this same master-slave educational model (which I obviously do not accept). One can occasionally still find advocates of a star system among those creating for-profit universities, though the fervor has waned in recent years.

move away from the easier and more pleasant planning activities (like planning readings and course assignments) and facing the hard questions about purpose will strengthen your grasp on the kind of program you want to build. Comparing your plan to all of the programs out there will further help narrow the focus and identify the distinctive mission. Here are some sample mission statements from just a few universities:

- **Mercer University's Master of Science in Technical Communication Management**—A Web-based graduate program directed toward working adult professionals in the field of technical communication. Students learn about knowledge management, multimedia and hypermedia technologies, online information design, and usability evaluation through electronic work teams in a distance education environment [9].
- **Bentley College's Master of Science in Human Factors in Information Design**—The Master of Science in Human Factors in Information Design (MSHFID) program prepares working professionals to meet the requirements of the changing marketplace for technology products, with the ultimate goal of improving product usability and promoting non-intrusive design [10].
- **Rensselaer Polytechnic Institute's Master of Science in Technical Communication**—The MS in Technical Communication is aimed at individuals who wish to work as information and writing specialists in industry or government. Technical communicators must be able to take the lead in every stage of the communication process, from the earliest efforts to plan, gather, and organize information, through the actual production of final copy and the analysis of user response. Students take coursework in theory, document and electronic information design, and analysis of communication systems and contexts. The program combines work in theory, writing, information design, and analysis of communication systems and contexts. The MS is a 30 credit professional degree program, the immediate goal of which is to help students acquire the knowledge and abilities to begin or enhance a career as a technical communicator [11].

Even more important than thinking well about your audience and purpose is finding out what *they* think. To find out what your program's targeted audience thinks, gather some reliable data from well-designed surveys, carefully selected focus groups, industry advisory boards, informational interviews with practitioners, and surveys of alumni and employers. There is no substitute for gathering real data to go along with brainstorming. In designing Mercer's Master of Science program in the early 1990s, we created several focus groups of employers of technical communicators who represented the best experience available in our area. We conducted interviews with several groups in well-planned but open-ended conversational meetings. Typical questions included asking employers what skills they could identify for the demands of their business in the future; what knowledge or competencies their employees had or needed to acquire; what future business trends would affect their need for technical communicators; and how they regarded technical communicators within their business structure. We tried to be open and alert to any ideas that seemed new or different from what we had been thinking. Additionally, we interviewed a number of other individuals (members of the target audience of potential students) who offered insights into what they would appreciate in a master's degree. This first-hand information was worth far more than the time and effort it took to gather it.

Developing and Testing a Prototype

Technical communication professionals are accustomed to developing prototypes and testing them with members of the target audience. Once you have carefully delineated audience and purpose, you are ready to sketch the vision of what the program will contain and to get feedback from members of the target audience.

Rude's chapter later in this section will describe several possible models for online education in technical communication and present criteria for choosing among them. Another source providing information about model programs (though not for online education, necessarily) is Michael Keene's *Education in Scientific and Technical Communication: Academic Programs That Work* [12]. Your own program for online education may follow one of the models already in existence, or it may be unique to your own institution. The critical issue is to design the model program (including the prototype of a course or unit) and to get feedback at this design stage.

In the preliminary design model, it is imperative to take the following steps:

1. Sketch a description of content—the boundaries and depth of the knowledge to be delivered;
2. Plan the instructional design—the learning objectives, materials, and methods of instruction and interaction;
3. Describe the different alternatives in delivery methods—the research on advantages and disadvantages of various media;
4. Forecast methods for dealing with evaluation and accreditation issues— the design for testing and evaluating the students' achievement of learning objectives and the instructors' delivery of educational services;
5. Describe the infrastructure of support needed for teachers, students, and administrators—the availability of 24/7 help and technical support, of instructional media or support staff, etc.

Once you have written a description of the program and a prototype of an instructional unit, return to your focus groups or potential audiences and conduct a paper prototype usability test to assure that they accept and can use the prototype successfully.

Usability theory and practice will provide helpful background information for testing the prototype. I find it especially helpful to use the kind of user and task analysis described by Hackos and Redish [13]. Conceptualizing the student on the other end of the instructional conversation will help assure that you remain learner-focused and not just content- or teacher-focused. An easy-to-use reference on setting up and evaluating usability tests is found in Rubin [14]. Barnum provides an up-to-date review of usability research. Since your website will be seen around the world, it is also a good idea to consider international audiences as you design the educational interface [15]. Del Galdo and Nielsen's book provides a conceptual overview of issues related to international interface design [16]. (Herrington and Tretyakov's chapter later in this book describes some cross-cultural issues in one international online education project; additionally, see Rubens and Southard's chapter for further discussion on how usability testing can improve interface design in online education environments.)

Evaluating and Selecting Technological Tools

Only after you have completed the prototype of the program should you begin looking at online education tools. In too many colleges or companies, Chief Executive Officers or Chief Technology Officers make technology decisions based on different criteria than technical communicators would use. Using the education model that has been designed and tested on paper, create the set of criteria that will assure the best delivery of instruction according to your design. Again, evaluating and choosing technology and tools are common skills of technical communicators. The challenge will be conveying your selection criteria in clear, understandable terms so that instructional support staff and budget managers can see the benefit of the expenditures. As Cargile Cook suggests in her chapter, the learning goals must drive the selection of the delivery technology—not vice versa.

In a university or in a company, technology decisions will be made with a number of users in mind. It is important to find those other users and to establish a common understanding of the needs, expectations, and performance criteria for the hardware and the software. Taking your plan and your prototype to meetings and asking to look over the plans of others will help assure that you build a common language and can reach acceptable compromises in technology selection.

Collaborating with Partners

Unlike college faculty from a number of other disciplines, technical communicators are experienced and skilled in creating collaborative partnerships. In creating an online learning program, you will need to work with many different groups on your own campus: with technicians and technical support staff, with instructional designers or trainers, with faculty outside your own school or department, and even with faculty outside your institution. The best programs can only be built, in my opinion, with true collaboration that seeks expertise wherever it is found. I suggest setting up a formal group of those planning the online education program and using good project management skills as you work together to achieve the goals. For example, Hackos provides an excellent overview of the process and life cycle of projects, including the phases of planning, specifying content and production, and evaluation [17].

Not all of the good collaborators out there will be local. Consider that there are a number of online learning practitioners around the country and the world. A short list of international organizations and resources is included at the end of this chapter to assist you in locating external partners or information.

In our experience at Mercer, the cognitive and creative demands of online education are much easier with a collaborative group of authors and designers. Some courses are co-authored; others are developed by a single author but carefully reviewed by several colleagues. Since we teach experienced graduate students online, we foster collaborative learning models in the courses and thus gain excellent feedback from our students about ways to improve our educational offerings; they see themselves as co-creators of the knowledge and thus feel some ownership in its continuous improvement.

An ideal collaboration may be possible among directors of online education programs in technical communication. One school may have a specialized course that yours cannot offer, and you may have a course that someone else cannot offer. Sharing some courses across institutional boundaries would seem to offer a win-win solution. Graduate programs have long made it a practice to accept one or two transfer courses; accepting a good online education course from another institution should be equally possible. A group of program directors associated with the IEEE Professional Communication Society is discussing the desirability of setting up a consortium to enable this kind of collaborative learning among students from different schools. Such a consortium could provide excellent vetting of comparable quality of content and student expectations[3]. (For more on the potential of consortia, see Wahlstrom and Clemens' chapter in the final section.)

The first five knowledge domains mentioned above should come easily to most technical communication faculty. Unless they have some business experience, faculty may find the next two domains a bit of a stretch. Marketing and managing online education programs, however, are essential skills. Just because you build it does *not* mean that they will come—and keep on coming!

Marketing an Online Program

While marketing is a familiar concept for those in business, those in academe may have little or no experience in recruiting students. For a program to be

---

[3] Contact the author for more information on developing a consortium of universities offering online education in technical communication.

successful, however, it must be marketed on many levels. Strategies and plans for recruiting students and faculty, avenues for advertising to potential students (including professional societies), networking with industries and managers of technical communicators, all will require some degree of marketing skills. Strategies such as direct mail and Web marketing are useful, but all have their limitations. The influence of contacts within professional societies cannot be underestimated.

The global potential for recruiting students is at once a blessing and a curse. When one of our Mercer colleagues began to offer software engineering courses online, he was inundated by hundreds of international inquirers, most of whom wanted a full time program and financial aid—which we do not currently offer since our programs are targeted toward professionals working full time. Setting admissions criteria carefully can help to weed out ineligible applicants. For example, applicants to our MS program in Technical Communication Management (MSTCO) must have excellent skills in English (TOEFL score if non-native speaker of English) and three years of work experience in addition to academic requirements. It is important to determine in advance how you will respond to the needs of potential students from many different cultures, time zones, and backgrounds. Communicating your program's mission and goals clearly will help both you and your potential students determine whether they would be a good fit for this online education program.

Advertising your program is a crucial marketing issue. Online education programs are most often found via Web searches, according to our survey of inquirers to Mercer's MSTCO program. Working with your university's Webmaster, list your site with a number of search engines and fine-tune the metatags to assure that the program can be found easily. A number of professional societies maintain lists of academic programs. In some databases, such as the academic database on the website for the Society for Technical Communication, inquirers may search for distance learning options in various programs. Another useful marketing tool to reach potential students is to advertise in the professional society journals or newsletters. Targeting is very important since this advertising can be costly. Discovering the journals read by your specific group of targeted students is more difficult than it would first appear and requires that you be familiar with a wide range of professional and trade publications. Using focus groups containing members from your target audiences will help to identify the publications they read most regularly. Professional societies and trade organizations often sell mailing lists for direct mail of brochures or information packets, though you must pay separately for each mailing sent to the list. Direct mail is costly because it typically takes about seven mailings to elicit a response (at least, that is what my marketing colleagues tell me).

Perhaps the best advertising is by word of mouth from currently enrolled students or graduates, and from faculty at other institutions. Students will tell the bald truth about their experiences in your programs, rather than repeating your marketing slogans. As a result, their testimonials are excellent advertising if indeed the program is good. When faculty teaching in the program present widely at professional conferences and publish regularly, they contribute toward awareness of the program. In our experience, it takes about five years for a program to become widely known unless you can invest significant resources in advertising. Keeping the faculty and students active professionally will provide good public awareness and an authentic image of what the program is like. For more in-depth discussion of marketing, see Eaton's chapter next.

Managing an Online Program

Technical communication skills are needed even after the planning is done and the program is launched. It is helpful to understand the life cycles of program development, the recurring cycle of recruitment activities, and the ongoing communication demands. It is important to define and gain acceptance on workload issues for faculty and administrators, to commit to providing total learner support online, and to secure budgetary commitments to keep technology current. Other management communication issues include working with industry advisory boards, maintaining continuous visibility for the program, performing frequent program reviews with input from students or clients, and making continuous quality improvements. For an example of how one program used its graduate director's contact with students to conduct such a quality review, see Grant-Davie's chapter in the third section of this book.

Various business models of a product development lifecycle typically use stages such as these: plan, design, procure, produce, deliver, service. Technical communicators are probably more familiar with Hackos's model of the publications development life cycle. Developing an online education program is similar in many ways, so these steps can help to manage the project:

1. Information Planning
2. Content Specification
3. Implementation
4. Production
5. Evaluation [17].

Recruitment activities have a similar life cycle and predictable repetitions. Regular communication demands include responding promptly to inquiries, providing print and online program information, processing and acting upon applications, responding to problems or concerns of students and faculty, planning course scheduling, advising, and evaluating courses and student learning—in short, all the activities associated with an on-campus program, except that there is much less face-to-face communication.

Managing student support online is a significant challenge. In a chapter elsewhere in this book, Grady and Davis discuss the importance of "scaffolding" to enable students to succeed in the online learning environment. Most first-time teachers underestimate the level of support that students will need and have a difficult time adapting to the lack of "face time" with the learners.

It is commonly accepted among colleges and universities providing online education that an online learning course requires more faculty effort than a face-to-face course. The additional challenges include preparing the entire course ahead of time, mounting all materials to the website, and dealing with a heavy email load throughout the term. In my informal surveys of colleagues, most schools count creating an online learning course as a two-course load. Once the course has been taught, the usual count in faculty load is one-and-a-half courses. There is a wide disparity among programs in enrollment limits on online learning students. While Mercer's MSTCO program generally runs below 25 students per class, colleagues elsewhere report having 75 or 100 students in a class. (In those cases they generally have the assistance of graduate teaching assistants, however.) This faculty load issue is one of the most difficult negotiations program directors will face, in all likelihood.

Establishing a technology plan that includes regular updates and revisions is an essential part of any management strategy. With luck, you can find a skilled university technology administrator who will be responsible for this activity; lacking that, you may wish to negotiate outside vendor contracts for technical services that can be provided 24/7. At any rate, you will need to build university (or corporate) support for the significant budget demands of online learning.

Good management skills will help to assure that the online education program is successful and students are well served. For experienced technical communicators, project management is probably second nature. These skills will transfer easily to managing online education programs.

CONCLUSION

Online learning has proven in the last decade that it is far more than a flash in the pan. As corporations continue to develop training for online delivery, the "corporate university" is emerging as a significant competitor with educational institutions [18]. Each year more and more universities enter the arena with online learning opportunities. Technical communication is an especially attractive discipline for online learning because of its subject matter, the skills and interests of potential students, and the extensive skills of technical communication faculty. Bringing our skills as technical communicators to the table, we can greatly enhance the development of online learning programs in our departments, across the university, and around the world.

Colleges and corporations are rushing to take advantage of opportunities to deliver education online. Professionals from many areas of study are developing materials and programs—not all of them as strong as they should be. Technical communicators are in an ideal position to assume leadership roles within their institutions as departments and schools venture into online education. We have the background, the strategies, and the technology skills that will make us strong contributors in this important new area. As we step forward into these leadership roles, the technical communication profession will be enhanced and our skills will become more widely recognized. We are positioned for leadership—let's accept the challenge.

REFERENCES

1. National Center for Education Statistics, U.S. Department of Education, *Distance Education at Postsecondary Education Institutions: 1997-98,* NCES 2000-013, 1999.
2. *Business Week*, p. 168, October 4, 1999.
3. L.J. Bassi and M. E. Van Buren, Sharpening the Leading Edge, *American Society for Training and Development* http://www.astd.org/CMS/templates/index.html?template_id=1&articleid=209401999, May 21, 2002.
4. D. C. Leonard, Using the Web for Graduate Courses in Technical Communication with Distant Learners, *Technical Communication, 43*:4, pp. 388-401, 1996.
5. J. D. Mathes and D. W. Stevenson, *Designing Technical Reports; Writing for Audiences in Organizations* (2nd Edition), Macmillan Publishing Company, New York, 1991.
6. C. J. Bonk, *Executive Summary: Online Teaching in an Online World*, http://www.jonesknowledge.com/higher/resources_research.html, May 2001.
7. C. J. Bonk, *Executive Summary: Online Training in an Online World*, http://PublicationShare.com, January 2002.
8. M. T. Davis, *Sabbatical Research Report,* Mercer University (unpublished), 1996.
9. *Mercer University's Master of Science in Technical Communication Management Web Site,* http://www.mercer.edu/mstco, February 21, 2003.
10. *Bentley College's MS Program in Human Factors in Information Design Web Site,* http://www.bentley.edu/graduate/academics/ms_programs/.
11. *Rensselaer Polytechnic Institute's Language, Literature, and Communication Web Site,* http://rpi.edu/dept/hss/swf/grad.swf.
12. M. L. Keene, *Education in Scientific and Technical Communication: Academic Programs That Work*, Society for Technical Communication, Arlington, Virginia, 1997.
13. J. T. Hackos and J. C. Redish, *User and Task Analysis for Interface Design,* John Wiley & Sons, Inc., New York, 1998.
14. J. Rubin, *Handbook of Usability Testing: How to Plan, Design, and Conduct Effective Tests*, John Wiley & Sons, Inc., New York, 1994.
15. C. M. Barnum, *Usability Testing and Research*, Longman, New York, 2002.
16. E. M. Del Galdo and J. Nielsen, *International User Interfaces,* John Wiley & Sons, Inc., New York, 1996.
17. J. T. Hackos, *Managing Your Documentation Projects*, John Wiley & Sons, Inc., New York, 1994.
18. R. Paton and S. Taylor, Corporate Universities: Historical Development, Conceptual Analysis and Relations with Public-Sector Higher Education, *The Observatory on Borderless Higher Education*, http://www.obhe.ac.uk/products/reports/, July 2002.

ONLINE INFORMATION SOURCES

The American Center for the Study of Distance Education: http://www.ed.psu.edu/acsde/
The American Distance Education Consortium: http://www.adec.edu/
Association of Teachers of Technical Writing: http://www.attw.org/
Asynchronous Learning Networks (The Sloan Consortium): http://aln.org
Council for Programs in Technical and Scientific Communication: http://cptsc.org/
The International Review of Research in Open and Distance Learning:
    http://www.irrodl.org/
The Open University: http://www.open.ac.uk/
Peterson's Distance Learning:
    http://iiswinprd03.petersons.com/distancelearning/default.asp
Society for Technical Communication: http://www.stc.org

CHAPTER 2

Students in the Online Technical Communication Classroom

Angela Eaton

In the previous chapter, Davis made the argument that technical communication instructors are well qualified to lead online education efforts; this chapter will discuss whom these instructors will be teaching. Specifically, this chapter provides the demographics and motivating factors of online technical communication students, traits we should consider when designing courses for these students, and the best methods of marketing online technical communication programs.

The demographics and other results provided in this chapter were taken from a survey of online education technical communication students conducted between March 14th and April 20th of 2002. Respondents who took classes via videostreaming and tape delay have been removed from the data set, leaving 37 respondents who took classes online ($N = 37$)[1]. The respondents came from six institutions: Indiana University Purdue University at Indianapolis (IUPUI) (1 respondent), Mercer University (4), Rensselaer Polytechnic Institute (2^2), Southern Polytechnic State University (1), Texas Tech University (12), and Utah State University (17). Although the sample in this survey isn't very large, neither is the population from which it is taken. Previous surveys of the online technical communication education population have been performed

---

[1] Unfortunately, because I depended on the kindness of instructors to forward the email announcements of the survey to departmental or class listservs, and I do not know the memberships of those lists, I cannot determine the response rate.

[2] Rensselaer Polytechnic Institute has a well developed Master of Science in Technical Communication degree offered via distance education, but it is not entirely online. As a result, only the responses of online students in RPI's program were included.

by individual institutions, usually through course evaluations, and aren't generally available to the field. This survey, though based on a small sample size, is perhaps the first that combines respondents from multiple institutions, shares information publicly, and can serve as a baseline from which more extensive research can depart.

WHAT TYPES OF STUDENTS CAN YOU EXPECT TO TEACH IN ONLINE TECHNICAL COMMUNICATION PROGRAMS?

Participants in the survey were asked demographic questions. In this section, the degree they pursued, their ages and genders, workload, the number of online classes they have taken, and the number of semesters they have been an online student will be reported. From the survey results, generally, online technical communication students are primarily graduate students pursuing master's degrees, most frequently female and most frequently in their thirties, who work more than 30 hours a week while taking one course per semester.

Degree Pursued

Survey respondents were by far primarily graduate students. Of the respondents, 54% were pursuing or had completed a Master of Science degree, 38% were pursuing a Master of Arts degree, and only 5% were pursuing a Bachelor of Science. One student was concurrently pursuing an MA and a PhD in Natural Science. Overall, fully 95% of respondents were pursuing a master's degree.

Ages and Genders of Students

The mean age of respondents was 36.03 ($N = 36$ [one student did not provide an age], $SD = 8.79$). Eleven students were aged 20-29, 14 were 30-39 years old, 9 were 40-49 years old, and 2 were 50-59 (see Figure 1). Ten respondents were male, and 26 were female. Whether this age distribution is typical is difficult to determine—the National Center for Education Statistics places every student 35 and older in the same age group [1, p. 208]. This larger number of female respondents is supported by statistics kept by the National Center for Education Statistics on post-secondary enrollment. Since 1984, women have outnumbered men in post-secondary education [1, p. 197]; in the total fall enrollment for degree-granting institutions in 1999, enrollment of female students was 128% of enrollment of male students [1, p. 206].

Student Workload

Perhaps the most salient characteristic for instructors and administrators to consider is the workload of online technical communication students: fully 60%

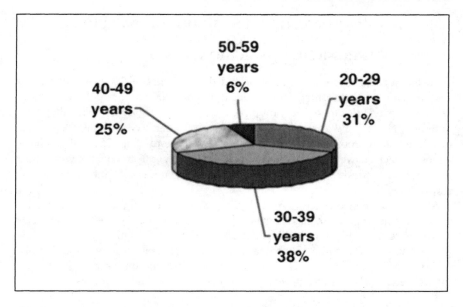

Figure 1. Percentage of respondents by age range.

of respondents work more than 40 hours a week in addition to coursework (the question asked students to include work inside or outside the home). More than 90% work 30 or more hours a week.

Number of Online Classes Taken

With the heavy workload that most students report, it's not surprising that most students take one online class per semester (68%). Some vary between one and two online courses a semester (24%), and only a few take two online classes each semester (9%). Most students take classes only through one delivery method—86% take only online courses, and 14% mix in traditional courses with online courses. The heaviest course load any student reported was four courses, with a mix between online and traditional.

Length of Program of Study

Each respondent was asked how many semesters he or she had taken online classes ($N = 36$ [one student did not reply to this question]); the responses were well distributed, indicating a mix of new and experienced students. Eleven students had taken one or two semesters. Ten students had taken three or four, six had taken five or six semesters, and finally nine respondents had taken seven or eight semesters of online courses.

WHY DID THESE STUDENTS CHOOSE TO PURSUE ONLINE EDUCATION FOR A TECHNICAL COMMUNICATION DEGREE?

In the survey, respondents were provided with a list of 10 possible reasons why they might be pursuing online education and a text box to enter additional responses; students could select multiple answers (see Figure 2). "Fit schedule," "improve skills," and "participate in a distant program" were the most popular categories for choosing online education, with more than 75% of students choosing each answer. Saving the commute and working from home or work were also frequently chosen reasons, chosen by 64% and 61% of the respondents, respectively.

Students were also asked to provide their *primary* reason for choosing to take technical communication classes via online education (see Figure 3) (as opposed to *all* the reasons they took online education courses, see Figure 2). By far, their primary reason was to be able to participate in a program not available locally ("participate distant program"), followed by the fact that online programs fit in their schedule. These two answers make up 76% of the total responses.

WHAT DO STUDENTS LIKE ABOUT THE ONLINE CLASSROOM?

In addition to asking the students why they chose to pursue online education, the survey also solicited answers about the features of online education that the students liked (see Figure 4). They could select every answer, and they could also add information in a text box. Unlike Figure 2, which identifies the many reasons students choose online education in the first place, Figure 4 identifies all the reasons students liked their online programs after matriculating. After matriculation, students identified flexible schedules as the most popular feature of online education. The second most popular feature, selected by nearly 80% of respondents, was the lack of a commute. Diverse classmates, the ability to prepare in advance, and the convenience of working from home or work were also selected by more than 50% of respondents. Few students chose to add comments in the textbox. One student specified that he or she liked having classmates from all over the world, not just from around the country.

Respondents were then asked to choose their *primary* reason for liking online education. The most frequently cited primary reason for students liking online education was the convenience of working from home or work, with 35% of respondents choosing this as their primary reason (see Figure 5). Another 27% chose the flexible schedule as their top reason for liking online education. And finally, the only other answer that received a double-digit response was the lack of a commute, with 19% of respondents choosing this as their primary reason.

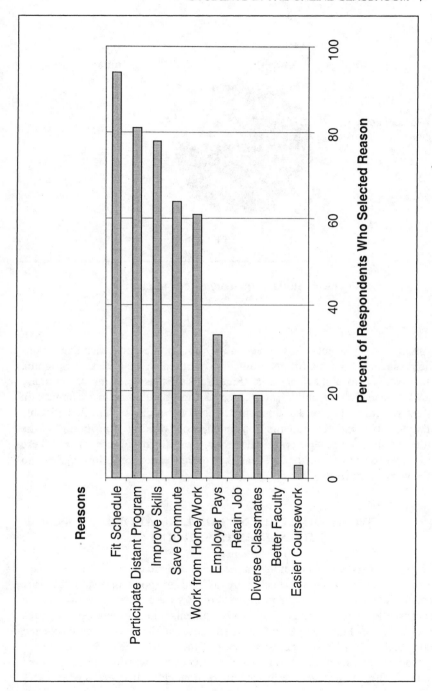

Figure 2. Reasons students chose online education (multiple responses allowed).

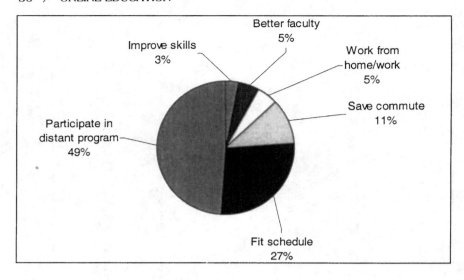

Figure 3. Students' primary reason to pursue
online education.

In summary, applicants chose their online programs because these programs fit their schedule, the applicants wanted to participate in a distant program, and they wanted to build their skills (Figure 2). Of these reasons, the primary reason applicants chose online programs was the opportunity to participate in a distant program (Figure 3). Upon matriculation, students identified flexible scheduling, no commute, and the convenience of working from home as the qualities of their online programs that they most liked (Figure 4). Of these qualities, the one they liked most was that online education allowed them to work at home or at work (Figure 5).

WHAT DO STUDENTS DISLIKE ABOUT
THE ONLINE CLASSROOM?

The two least-liked features of the online classroom are the lack of face-to-face interaction with classmates (selected by 59% of respondents) and the lack of face-to-face interaction with professors (65%; see Figure 6). However, in contrast to the response rates about what students like, these response rates were much lower. For example, two of the features students liked were selected by more than 70% of respondents; not *one* of the disliked features had such a high response rate. Even the feature that is so frequently worried about in online education— that there is no face-to-face interaction, either between the professor

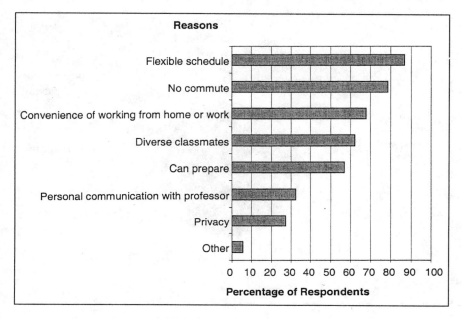

Figure 4. What respondents like about online education
(multiple responses allowed).

and student or between students—was not mentioned by approximately 1/3 of the respondents.

Also revealing were the "other" answers that students typed into the text box. Three commented specifically that they didn't dislike any of the proposed features; one added, "I love this experience." Two respondents mentioned that they dislike the lack of recognition of the program as a serious academic program, that people mistake it for a correspondence course. Four respondents had concerns about course structure and time.

WHAT ADVICE DO ONLINE EDUCATION STUDENTS HAVE FOR CURRENT AND FUTURE INSTRUCTORS?

Based on the demographic data, responses from the students, and on student advice for "instructors who are designing or who are considering designing distance technical communication courses," there are a few rules of thumb that should be kept in mind when creating a course (or program, for that matter) for online technical communication students.

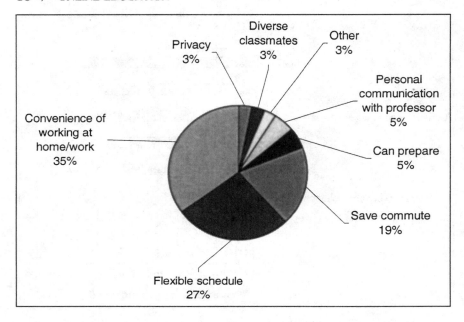

Figure 5. Students' primary reason for liking online education.

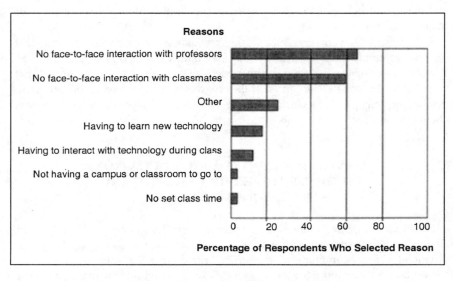

Figure 6. Least liked features of online education.

Respect Students' Time

This particular population has a very limited amount of time, as shown by their work schedules, their choice of online education to save them commuting time, and direct comments from the students themselves. Instructors should be careful to make sure that the work for the course does not exceed what is fair for the course credits.

Be Careful about the Time Demands of Course Features

New online instructors are sometimes surprised with how much time an activity can take up online. Particularly with posting to a bulletin board, the amount of reading and writing can increase exponentially. For example, in a class of 25, if an instructor decides to require two posts from each student per week, requires each student to read every post, and adds a requirement that each student respond to five of the posts per week, that assignment becomes 50-100 pages of reading per week (depending on whether the posts are one or two pages) and 5-10 pages of writing. Instructors should make sure that time is accurately budgeted for all activities.

Be Explicit about the Benefit of the Course Activities

Due to their workloads, and perhaps their maturity, this population does not have much patience for busywork. At least two students specifically suggested eliminating required responses to classmates' posts because they thought it wasn't useful. Explicitly stating the benefit of course activities can help motivate students. Also, solicit students' opinions regularly; activities that students aren't learning from can be reshaped or replaced. (See Carter and Rickly's chapter in this volume for more information on explicitly stating the importance of assignments.)

Structure Course Due Dates Fairly

Strive to place due dates on the same day or two days of the week, so students can better predict and maintain their schedules. When choosing dates and times, keep in mind that students may live in different time zones.

Be Involved

The most frequent suggestion, made by 17% of students, was for instructors to be involved. Many students complained that instructors would not participate in group discussions, respond to posted messages, or even return email.

Provide Feedback Regularly

A related suggestion, made by 14% of respondents, was a plea for timely feedback from instructors. Many students mentioned that timely feedback helps assure students they're understanding the concepts. When online students are confused, one student pointed out, "Unlike onsite students, we can't 'camp out' at an instructor's office until s/he returns." What this means is that instructing an online course takes regular, consistent, and timely feedback. Instructors should anticipate participating *at least* as often as a regular course—once or twice a week—and the better instructors participate much more frequently, as frequently as many times a day. For example, online instructors might consider sending confirmation emails to students when a paper has been received with an estimate on when the student might receive feedback. This confirmation will reassure the student, and it will also preclude student emails asking if the file "came through."

Be Personable

Instructors were also encouraged to be personable; one student wrote, "Remember that students can't see your facial expressions, so be personable in email and chats. I believe a lot of insecurities can be heightened in this type of environment, and it helps if a student feels their instructor is 'human' and approachable." To become more personable, instructors can use student names and give explicit compliments. Good online instructors will use every technique good traditional classroom instructors use but will use them more frequently and perhaps more consciously. (For more suggestions and examples of how instructors have used such techniques in their online classes, see Section 2 of this volume.)

Structure Courses Carefully

Course structure and features strongly influence the quality of the students' experience. When advising instructors about how to structure courses, the most popular comment (11%) was for instructors to make online education courses the same amount of work as traditional classes (also voiced as a request for a realistic workload). One respondent noted, "Just because there is not a set class time where discussion is limited to one hour, remember that we don't have any more time. Some classes I have had required more reading and participation than traditional classes might have." Another stated, "Instructors should take into account that combinations of assignments that require more than 10 hours per week of coursework for the students will put severe strains on their ability to complete all of the assignments."

Choose Technology to Serve Pedagogy (Not the Other Way Around)

In the survey results, pedagogical suggestions were fairly specific, and only once was the same suggestion made twice. Examples of the pedagogical suggestions provided by respondents include "repeat information," "demonstrate, give examples," and "consider practitioner point of view." To support these pedagogical activities, students suggested that instructors use multiple delivery methods, methods such as "phone, email, chatroom (MOO), and NetMeeting with video and audio," primarily to maintain student interest. Smart instructors choose to incorporate only the technology they need to help students learn. Adding bells and whistles without strong pedagogical rationale will only annoy this population of students. See Cargile Cook's chapter for discussion of this issue.

Be Careful with Hybrid Courses

Some instructors, when designing online courses, consider having students come to campus for face-to-face contact once or perhaps twice a semester. That the lack of face-to-face contact with professors and fellow students were the two least-liked features of online education might seem to lend credence to the hybrid course idea. However, none of the respondents to the survey were in hybrid classes, and when given the opportunity to give instructors advice, *not a single student* suggested adding a face-to-face component. Attending face-to-face elements of a course is also impossible for geographically separate students. The survey results do not indicate that students desire hybrid elements.

Be Aware of Departmental Advertising and Student Expectations

If an instructor's department advertises its online classes as being flexible and able to fit into any schedule, requiring weekly MOO sessions or NetMeeting meetings may seem contradictory. By no means should instructors eliminate sound pedagogical activities because they might conflict with departmental advertising, but the instructors should realize that students may have different expectations. Instructors should make expectations clear early on, in the syllabus, and in initial class meetings, so students can plan accordingly. (For further discussion of marketing issues, see Davis' chapter, and for a discussion of differences in programmatic and student expectations and the value of clarifying these expectations, see Zachry's.)

HOW DO WE MARKET TO THESE POTENTIAL STUDENTS?

Now that the demographics, preferences, and implications for course structure have been explored, where can potential students be found? Perhaps the first question is *where* a program should look for potential students. Should they be sought out in remote areas, areas that are free of competing colleges or universities? Or should they be sought out in populated areas, with more potential students per square mile? When survey respondents were asked, "Are traditional courses (courses which take place on a college campus with the instructor and students in the classroom at the same time) in technical communication available to you?" 46% of respondents reported that there were no local classes available, 11% responded that they didn't know whether local classes were available, and 43% reported that there *were* local classes available.

If there were local courses available, why did these students choose to pursue online education? By looking only at the responses of the online students who knew of local classes or who didn't know if there were local classes, and by examining the reasons for these students listed for pursuing online education, it becomes evident that 44% of the respondents chose online classes because they fit their schedule (see Figure 7). Another 21% of respondents chose online classes in order to participate in a program not available locally. Equal numbers of respondents chose the convenience of working from home or work and saving commuting time as their primary reasons for choosing online classes.

As a result of this information, instructors and administrators seeking to recruit students can recruit from areas without technical communication classes *as well as* areas that have existing programs. If a program chooses to seek students in an area with local classes, however, it should stress that online courses fit into schedules that traditional courses can't. That program should also be able to articulate and highlight its strengths compared to other local or online programs.

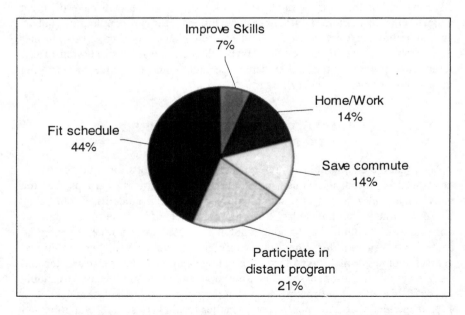

Figure 7. Reasons for taking online courses when local programs exist.

WHAT METHODS SHOULD BE USED TO ADVERTISE AN ONLINE TECHNICAL COMMUNICATION PROGRAM?

When technical communication instructors or administrators think about marketing programs or courses, it's very likely that they think of sending advertisements through direct mail or placing advertisements in industry journals. The results from the survey, however, show that only 11% of respondents heard about their programs through methods that might be thought of as traditional marketing—contact with the university, such as a course catalog or pamphlet picked up in an office, or a direct mail advertisement (see Table 1). Only one respondent heard about his or her program through a magazine or journal.

If traditional methods haven't been responsible for most of the respondents learning about their programs, what methods might be more promising? Surprisingly, methods that could be characterized as "word of mouth"—information received from their employer, friend or co-worker, or professor or advisor—were responsible for 30% of respondents learning about their programs. Professional organizations were responsible for 22% of students learning about their programs, and only one of those eight respondents specifically chose a magazine or journal as the source. The final group of methods through which respondents learned about their programs should come

Table 1. How Online Technical Communication Students
Learned about Their Programs

Marketing method	Number of respondents
Traditional marketing	11%
Contact with university (phone, catalog, pamphlet in office)	3
Direct mail	1
Word of mouth	30%
Friend or co-worker	5
Professor or advisor	4
Employer	2
Professional organizations	22%
Professional organization	7
Magazine or journal	1
Electronic marketing	38%
Web search	10
Listserv or newsgroup (ex: Techwr-l mentioned twice)	3
Website (not sure if through Web search or direct access)	1

as no surprise—electronically. Fully 38% of respondents learned about their programs by using a listserv or newsgroup, through a Web search, or on a departmental webpage, with the Web search by far being the most popular method reported.

Determine If Your Websites Can Be Found in a Search

First, instructors or administrators should make sure that the websites that describe their program are found in a Web search. They should run tests in a number of different search engines, using terms prospective students will use, such as online education, online classes, technical communication, technical writing, and distance education. If the instructor or administrator finds out that the page isn't found in a search, he or she may need to register it. Registration can be done at no charge at each individual Web search homepage (such as http://www.google.com/addurl.html) or a professional company, such as www.submit-it.com, will register the page with multiple engines for a small fee. Professional Web designers know the importance of registering a page with the various search engines, and will include the cost in the original proposal or will offer it as an additional service near the end of the project. However, in academia, which frequently depends on over-worked instructional technology staff or graduate students for Web design, registration might be overlooked. And considering that the cost is so very low ($49 for www.submit-it.com), and that Web searches alone have been responsible for 27% of the survey respondents learning about their programs, it may be worth registering the page through a professional service simply as insurance.

Be on the First Page of Search Results

Also, instructors or administrators should make a note of where the website comes up on the list of search results. Is it on the first page? While writing this chapter, I searched Google™ for "online classes technical communication" and received approximately 299,000 results. How far will prospective students have to scroll, or how many pages will they have to click through before they see the program's page? If a site is listed too late in the results, students may not see it, or may see a competing program's information first.

Websites can be moved up in search results by reworking the keywords. Search engines locate webpages by keywords, and pages that have higher numbers of the desired keywords are nearer the top of the search results. By increasing the accuracy and number of the keywords associated with a department's website, the link to the page might be boosted to a higher position in the search results.

Use the "Word of Mouth" Technique

To capture the word-of-mouth advertising, which was responsible for 30% of respondents finding out about their programs, instructors and administrators could take just a few simple steps. To encourage employers to tell employees about the program, brochures could be provided to selected Human Resources departments to be placed in appropriate orientation packets. To keep costs down, particularly in larger companies, brochures could be provided to the managers of technical communications departments to be given to new or existing employees.

In the "word of mouth" category, the largest number of respondents learned about their programs through a friend or co-worker. Instructors could also be asked to make an announcement to their classes when the application period begins, asking students to encourage friends and co-workers to apply. If a program chooses to be really aggressive, it might even send existing students brochures about the program with a request that they be given to interested friends or co-workers. To recruit through instructors directly, the second most cited method in the "word of mouth" category, administrators might encourage instructors to tell their traditional classes about the online programs and class offerings.

Recruit through Professional Organizations

To recruit through professional organizations, which were responsible for 22% of students learning about their current programs, programs might consider a number of options. Respondents who chose this answer did not provide additional information about how the professional organization let them know about the program they entered, and only one respondent answered that he or she learned about the program through a professional magazine or journal. Students may have learned about their programs through national organizations' websites or conference booths or through meeting students or program graduates in local chapters. Programs might try to take advantage of this method by maintaining a booth at a national conference, by encouraging student and faculty activity in local professional organization chapters, or by sending information to chapter members.

WHAT MARKETING MESSAGES WILL BE EFFECTIVE WITH ONLINE TECHNICAL COMMUNICATION STUDENTS?

From the survey results, the same benefits of online education are noted by students repeatedly. By comparing all the reasons students provided for joining online education classes with the primary reason they provided, a list of the most important online education benefits was created. By using these benefits as marketing messages, we can persuade students to join programs based on what has been important to other online distance education technical communication students. These benefits, beginning with the most important, are that online students can participate in a program not available locally, online courses fit into students' schedules, online courses are convenient, and online students save the commute.

Message 1: "Participate in a Unique Program not Available Locally"

By far, the most important marketing message points out the benefits of participating in a program not available locally—and more specifically, the message distinguishes the advertised program from its competitors (see Table 1). While geographic flexibility enables online programs to obtain students from nearly anywhere in the world, it also forces programs to compete against each other. For a program to succeed, it needs to have a feature the other existing programs do not have—it needs to have a specialization, a certificate, a degree, a focus, a faculty that other programs can't offer. More than 80% of students marked the ability to participate in a program not available locally as a reason for pursuing online education. Nearly half of all respondents listed the ability to participate in a distant program as the *primary* reason for participating in online education. The differentiating strength of the program should be well articulated and highly visible to any prospective student, and it should be well known to instructors and administrators in the department, to help in "word of mouth" recruiting efforts. This marketing message is particularly important when advertising in an area that has local traditional technical communication classes. The survey results show that nearly half of respondents will take online classes even when there are local technical communication classes, but their primary reason for doing so is participating in a program they cannot access locally. To recruit these students, the advertised program must be better in some way than the local one.

Message #2: "Fit your Busy Schedule"

The second most important marketing message, based on survey results, is that online education fits students' schedules. This benefit was actually chosen by the most respondents—92%—as a reason why they chose to participate in online education, but only 27% chose it as the primary reason, so it is ranked second. More than 80% of respondents marked "flexible schedule" as a reason they like online education, and 27% of those ranked it as their favorite feature of online education.

Message #3: "Experience the Convenience of Learning from Home or Work"

The third most important marketing message is the convenience of learning from home or work that online education provides. More than 60% of respondents listed it as one of the reasons they chose to pursue online education, and a small percentage of them (5%) chose it as the primary reason. When listing features they like about online education, nearly 70% of respondents noted the convenience, and 35% chose it as the feature they like best about online education— the largest percentage of any feature.

Message #4: "Save the Commute"

The fourth most important marketing message is that online education enables students to save the commute. More than 60% of students cited saving the commute as a reason they were pursuing online education; 11% chose it as their primary reason for pursuing online education. Nearly 80% of respondents marked saving the commute as a feature of online education that they like, and nearly 20% rated it their favorite feature of online education. Particularly in urban areas with chronic traffic congestion or rural areas with long commutes, this message might be emphasized. Expanding on this message, programs may note that online students don't have to pay parking fees or possibly health care or campus activity fees.

Additional Messages

Other marketing messages are possible. Any of the features or reasons for pursuing online education that the survey respondents have mentioned—being able to prepare comments, having classmates from all over the world, experiencing increased personal communication from the instructor—may be persuasive to potential students. Smart administrators and instructors might survey their own students to help identify program strengths, determine how their own students learned of their program, and identify other factors that might help in planning or improving an online technical communication education course or program.

HOW MANY POTENTIAL STUDENTS ARE OUT THERE?

How big is the potential market for online technical communication education? We can use recent Society for Technical Communication publications to give us a rough estimate. Of respondents to the 2001 STC Salary Survey, 65% hold only a bachelor's degree [2, p. 4]. If that percentage is multiplied by the total number of STC members—18,989 [3, p. 4]—the total number of possible students for an online master's degree is 12,342 students.

While more than 12,000 students is an impressive figure, it is highly unlikely that every STC member who holds a bachelor's degree will pursue a master's. However, with careful analysis of student traits and needs, and marketing efforts that target student benefits, more online education students can be recruited.

Online education for technical communication has grown greatly and still has not reached its full potential. As the cost of computer equipment falls, the number of Internet connections increase, and bandwidths widen, new pedagogical techniques become possible and educational opportunities become available to more and more students. With careful planning based on research, technical communication programs can reach and educate many of them.

REFERENCES

1. National Center for Education Statistics, *Digest of Education Statistics, 2001,* National Center for Education Statistics, Washington, D.C., NCES Number 2002130, pp. 197, 206, 2002.
2. Society for Technical Communication, *2001 United States Salary Survey,* http://www.stc.org/PDF_Files/2001_Salary_Survey.pdf, p. 4, 2002.
3. Society for Technical Communication, *STC Membership Count,* http://www.stc.org/Word_Files/Counts/2001_06.rtf, p. 4, 2001.

CHAPTER 3

An Argument For Pedagogy-Driven Online Education

Kelli Cargile Cook

The increasing importance of distance education in our university was brought home to me in what seemed an unusual place: an evaluation form for candidates for our dean's position in the College of Humanities, Arts, and Social Sciences. The fifth of 10 items on which we were asked to rate the candidates was "distance learning experience, philosophy, and strategies." This item underscored the importance upper administrators at our university are placing on the growth of distance education.

My university administration's attitude toward online education mirrors that of many other land grant universities and postsecondary institutions, as Davis describes in Chapter 1. The most recent survey of distance education in postsecondary institutions by the National Center for Educational Statistics was published in December 1999. This survey projected that by the year 2000 approximately 2,670 (54%) of all U.S. two-year and four-year postsecondary institutions would be delivering or planning to deliver distance education courses [1]. Of the institutions planning to deliver distance education by 2000, as many as 82% reported that they intended to use Internet technologies and other digital media to provide instruction to their distant students. With such interest, it is no wonder a 2001 survey of American college and university employees who manage or use technology-based information resources identified "funding IT [instructional technology]," "faculty professional development and training," and "distance education" among the top five issues most important for their campuses to resolve for strategic success [2].

By all accounts, a variety of causes—economic, technological, educational, and psychological—are driving administrative emphases on the online education movement. Economically, administrators see the online movement as a way to increase enrollment (and enrollment dollars) while, at the same time, reducing the need for additional physical facilities to house a larger student population. As buildings age and available classroom space diminishes, the possibility of growing the university enrollment, without placing higher demands on deteriorating physical facilities, becomes even more attractive. Davis, however, counters this argument in Chapter 1. Concurrently, the availability of technology to deliver courses online and the enthusiastic marketing of this technology have encouraged administrators to migrate university instruction to the Internet. Another compelling force behind this movement is the market for online education itself—a workforce whose educational needs continue to grow. Within this workforce are individuals who must update their skills and increase their knowledge to remain in their current jobs or to move on to new ones. (For a specific discussion of life-long learning and technical communication, see Wahlstrom and Clemens's chapter at the end of this collection.)

In response to this shift from static to episodic educational needs, one corporate provider of distance education noted: "Static education is a thing of the past. You can't fill up your tank at age 25 and then coast without needing to refill" [3]. The competition for this market of lifelong learners has further intensified administrative pressure to move courses online and to do so quickly. Describing these pressures and the sense of competition that often accompanies them, Christine Dalziel, executive director of the Instructional Telecommunications Council, identifies a final motivational factor: "A lot of colleges are really rushing to put courses together, and they're very afraid of the competition from other states. That's really what's driving it in a lot of cases: fear" [4].

While some faculty at American colleges and universities, viewing themselves as pathfinders in a new instructional frontier, have embraced and even pioneered this movement toward online education, many others are concerned that administrators, not faculty members, are spearheading the online movement. These faculty members worry that administrators are encouraging the movement to online instruction for all the wrong reasons and, in doing so, are disregarding important pedagogical questions and concerns that should be driving university instruction. Compounding these concerns is the often wholesale institutional adoption of delivery technologies for online courses. In other words, instructors have found themselves with mandates to develop online courses using x technology within y months. In these cases where delivery technologies are mandated, the technologies themselves may drive the decisions instructors make about their courses, with instructors attempting to "fit" their courses into prescribed templates and use common technological features to communicate with their distant students, no matter who these students are or what they are learning. Such an approach assumes that all teaching and learning can be delivered online in the same way, not taking into account differences in individual subject matters, instructors' teaching styles, or teaching and learning requirements.

Faced with institutional pressures and technological mandates, concerned instructors find themselves struggling with a variety of questions, anxieties, and fears about how they will teach with online technologies. At the same time, many of these faculty members feel a good deal of trepidation at, and resistance to, the prospect of shifting from the familiar face-to-face classes to some combination of the many possible forms that online instruction can currently take. They wonder how they will shift their teaching from the known face-to-face classroom to the unknown online classroom, and they are uncertain about the support they will need or receive as they make this move. Because answers to these questions are not easily or quickly found, some instructors, under pressure to move online as rapidly as possible, are adopting the familiar and simple, although not always popular, correspondence model of instruction, typified by traditional correspondence courses. This model, a mainstay of campus extended learning services as well as third-party technology developers, provides a quick and easy, if not optimal, technology-driven solution to the pressures of online course development and delivery.

The rest of this chapter examines the history and assumptions of technology-driven distance education and contrasts these assumptions with pedagogy-driven online education. Like technology-driven online education, pedagogy-driven online education has its own set of underlying assumptions and values, which require instructors to re-evaluate and articulate their theories of learning, their instructional strategies and course activities, and their assessment strategies before choosing delivery technologies and moving a course online. Although this articulation process is time-consuming, it can produce intellectually rigorous online learning experiences that are not weak replicas of onsite courses. Furthermore, pedagogically driven distance courses, as opposed to boilerplate technology-driven ones, begin with what effective instructors do best—teaching students—and, in the end, may better satisfy both instructors and their administrators by sustaining the student market's interest in online education.

THE HISTORY AND ASSUMPTIONS OF TECHNOLOGY-DRIVEN ONLINE EDUCATION

Technology-driven distance education using the correspondence model is not a new educational solution. In fact, its origin can be traced to the early correspondence study first used to provide distance education to rural populations in Sweden in 1833. In this and other early instances of distance education, the printing and postal services of Sweden, England, and Germany provided the necessary technologies for course delivery. Considered the first generation of distance education, these early correspondence courses delivered via print and post set the standard for nearly a hundred years. First-generation distance courses provided students with access to secondary and post-secondary educational opportunities—opportunities that were theretofore unavailable to them, especially in geographically remote regions. The technologies through which these courses were delivered restricted pedagogical strategies to activities such as reading course materials, responding to these materials through lessons or assignments, and receiving written feedback on these assignments from the instructor. Early instructors, consequently, were forced to confine their course goals and activities to those that could be directed and assessed within these technological boundaries, and correspondence courses, for the most part, were limited to independent self-paced study. The technology available thus constrained curricular possibilities.

Of course, first-generation distance instruction would probably not have gained such popularity had instructors' and administrators' theories of learning not supported this type of instruction. The objectivist learning theory that grounded early courses is characterized by teachers' tendency to use declarative instructions (lecture, recitation, drill, and practice) and highly structured activities. Objectivist activities typically fragmented tasks and teaching units into building block modules and required students to accomplish simpler tasks first before moving on to more complex ones. Instructors who hold this theory of learning believe that they or the textbooks from which they teach possess the knowledge students need to learn and that their job is to impart this knowledge to students. The objectivist theory of learning suggests that print course materials can be trusted to transfer or deliver critical course knowledge from the expert course developer—the instructor—to the novice learner. Another important assumption of objectivist learning theory is that the expert instructor can adequately assess novice learning through summative evaluation of their final written products or test results. Printed textbooks, course manuals, and test banks used to deliver and assess instruction, therefore, complement and support this learning theory and the epistemological assumptions behind it.

While delivery technologies have changed dramatically since the inception of distance education, many technologies currently employed (and mandated by some institutions) to deliver online instruction still privilege objectivist learning theories underlying early correspondence courses. Popular third-party online delivery applications, such as WebCT and Blackboard, for example, can easily be employed to deliver a correspondence-type class in which students read course materials, complete self-paced activities and pretests, and then take final tests to assess their learning. To use the delivery technologies in this way, instructors divide their course materials and assignments into "learning paths" or study modules. They develop test banks of possible test questions for each module; from these databanks, the delivery technology generates individualized tests for students. The technology also allows instructors to determine when to test students and for how long, and it checks roll, records how long and where students have worked on the course website, and averages grades. These easy-to-use features promote a lecture-style classroom and student self-paced activities as well as testing, all mainstays of objectivist learning theory. Given these features, it is not surprising that instructors who teach courses based in objectivist pedagogy and who need a fast and relatively easy means for online course delivery have turned to these popular technological solutions. Other instructors, however, find revamping their courses to rely entirely upon objectivist pedagogical strategies both difficult and undesirable.

No matter how easy to use a delivery technology is, for some instructors, among them many writing and communication instructors, teaching solely through objectivist learning activities, such as textbook readings, lectures, drill-and-practice exercises, and tests, is not sufficient to promote the pedagogy and learning theory they have adopted and used for years in their onsite writing classrooms. While some objectivist activities continue to be used in onsite writing classrooms (asking student to read from handbooks, for example), writing instructors commonly employ other activities that are more dialogic or discursive in nature. Such dialogic activities in which the teacher is facilitator and students work together as collaborators to create and share their knowledge are more difficult to implement with the more popular online delivery applications. Consequently, instructors who base their pedagogies upon constructivist and social theories of learning have sought additional online teaching and learning features that support the kinds of activities and assessment opportunities that they employ commonly in their onsite classrooms.

Pioneering technical communication instructors noted these problems—disconnections between available online delivery applications and their preferred teaching theories and pedagogies—in their first reports of online distance classes, appearing as early as 1994. Their accounts describe how they worked to resolve these problems, searching for technological solutions and online activities that support the pedagogies and activities with which they were comfortable. Among these pioneers were technical communication instructors: Elizabeth Tebeaux,Texas A&M University; David Leonard, Mercer University; Raymond Dumont, University of Massachusetts-Dartmouth; and Linda Jorn, Ann Hill Duin, and Billie Wahlstrom, University of Minnesota [5-8].

What is interesting about these earliest accounts of distance education courses in technical communication is each author's attention to the reciprocal relationship of theory, pedagogy, and technology. Tebeaux's final analysis of her course faults the goals she established for her courses, goals shaped and constrained by the technologies to which she had access. To achieve the collaborative goals and projects that Leonard set for his students, the students added face-to-face meetings to the activities required in the class. Dumont cobbled together four technologies (email, FTP, Web pages, and chat rooms) to achieve the interaction he set as a goal for his students' learning; and Jorn, Duin, and Wahlstrom de-emphasize technological issues as a primary concern, encouraging instructors to think first about their pedagogical goals then choose technologies that support course activities. All four of the arguments illustrate how distance educators in technical communication have begun to solve the theoretical, pedagogical, and technological puzzles of their online courses. While none of these first attempts was reported as completely successful, they do suggest that, as in the traditional onsite classroom, online instructors' underlying learning theories and pedagogical goals may vary, but the better the fit between the instructors' theoretical foundation, pedagogical goals, and available technologies, the more easily attainable pedagogical goals will be.

THEORETICAL, PEDAGOGICAL, AND TECHNOLOGICAL VALUES IN WRITING INSTRUCTION

Another assumption questioned in these early accounts of distance teaching is that familiar and successful onsite practices can be transferred directly and easily to online practices. In these early cases, for example, teaming activities did not always work as they should have, face-to-face meetings were added to supplement online collaborations, and distant team members felt isolated. In spite of instructors' best efforts to promote success in online collaborations, what worked online was often less successful or, at least, different from what worked in prior onsite collaborations. Consequently, what instructors can learn from pioneering online instructors is that they must carefully examine their pedagogical goals, activities, and technologies before moving online. In other words, the practice of teaching is changed when one moves into the online environment; therefore, instructors should not blindly expect that their traditional teaching strategies will directly transfer into successful online teaching scenarios.

Historically, this is not the first occasion when instructors have re-examined their traditional teaching practices in light of changes in learning theory or technologies. In fact, transitions from one predominant learning technology to another have often accompanied and frequently required changes in learning theories, practices, and activities. Similarly, shifts in learning theories underlying instruction have also motivated instructors to rethink their pedagogical goals, activities, and technologies used within classrooms. Two brief historical examples illustrate how the values embedded in learning theories and technologies influence or shape what goes on in the writing classroom and explain, in broad terms, why it is risky to consider onsite and online teaching as analogous.

Technological Shifts

Among the first technologies for writing instruction were chalk, slates, and later, when available, paper and pencil. In eighteenth century writing instruction, textbooks were rare and costly, so class activities were restricted to lecture and note-taking. To provide students with texts for their subjects, professors dictated their lectures, typically in Latin, to students who dutifully copied them, often word for word. In Scottish universities at this time, according to Horner, "The custom of 'dictates,' where the professor spoke slowly enough so that the student could take down the lecture word for word, provided accurate textbooks for the students" [9, p. 142]. In addition to listening to lectures, students completed grammar exercises, first writing and then correcting their exercises with chalk on slates. After their instructors orally evaluated these exercises, students copied their corrected work into more permanent notebooks, including in their notes explanations of rules they had broken in their first incorrect attempts [9, p. 144]. Through the processes of lecture, dictation, note-taking, and drill and practice, early writing instructors provided students with writing models and activities that promoted learning of formalized grammar and style rules. All of the technologies used—lectures, chalk, slates, pencils, and paper—supported and encouraged an objectivist pedagogy in which expert instructors transferred their knowledge of rules, principles, and forms to novice, inexperienced students.

By the nineteenth century, the technologies available for instruction began to change the way writing instruction occurred. Paper became less expensive; printing became more readily available and less costly; and pens and pencils were less cumbersome and more efficient to use. Less expensive paper and enhanced printing capabilities also meant greater textbook availability [10, p. 169]. With the use of these new technologies, class time was no longer needed to dictate rules to students (rules were now printed in textbooks), and professors "[exploited] the potential of the new writing tools to some extent by having students write often and much" [10, p. 171]. More class time was thus devoted to practice in the forms of drills, exercises, and composition.

Increased emphasis on practice affected the way writing instructors viewed and evaluated students' written communication: evaluation shifted away from primarily oral examinations of students' final products between student and tutor or instructor. New evaluation methods allowed tutors or instructors to read and respond to student work by writing comments on it without the student being physically present. Although some instructors supplemented this more removed evaluative method with in-class tutorials or workshops and provided formative evaluation during these sessions, in most writing instruction the two-way inter-actions of earlier chalk and slate evaluations were eliminated and the new evalu-ative interactions between student and tutor were made primarily with written rather than spoken words [11]. Using this new evaluative method, instructors more frequently viewed writing and commented upon it; consequently, words and their appearance on the page took on a new importance. Specifically, "this writing communicated through the eyes of readers rather than through the ears of an audience, and so visual metaphors had to be invented for understanding style and structure. Important among these were words, sentences, and paragraphs understood as 'elements' of discourse; the outline format . . . ; and the very notion of 'structure,' which suggests a quasi-architectural three-dimensional ordering of parts" [10, p. 173].

In a sense, from the shift in technologies for teaching writing, a new vocabu-lary of visual structure and form emerged. Combined with the eighteenth century emphasis on grammar and style, this structural vocabulary helped to codify the accepted appearance of writing on a page. Writing that did not meet this codified standard was less favorably evaluated. The structural vocabulary of page and paragraph was used not only to instruct students as they learned to compose but also to evaluate their efforts once they had finished.

In this way, by the nineteenth century, the production of inexpensive paper appears to have had a dramatic effect on instructional practices. Readily available textbooks eliminated the need for students to write their own texts from dictated lectures, freed instructors from delivering these lectures, and created more class time for students to write and practice their skills. As writing instruction focused more on student writing rather than lectures and evaluative tutorials, assessment methods also began to change from primarily oral to primarily written critiques. These technological changes and the teaching strategies and methods that developed from them also sparked the growth of a new vocabulary for the printed essay and introduced a visual component to writing evaluation.

The change in technology not only affected how instructors taught but also what they taught. Indeed many of these eighteenth and nineteenth century innovations are still applicable in writing courses today. Many instructors direct their students to textbooks, such as grammar handbooks, to substitute for extensive lectures, and practice through drafting and writing workshops is still valued in many writing classrooms, whether the emphasis is on academic or workplace writing. In addition, the structural vocabulary for page and paragraph developed from this movement continues to shape how instructors of writing and their students discuss what appears on the written page.

Theoretical Shifts

In the late twentieth century, a theoretical shift accompanied by technological changes transformed onsite writing instruction yet again. At this time, constructivist theory diverged from objectivist theories of learning, breaking with the objectivist belief that learners come to knowledge entirely through experts. In contrast, constructivists viewed learning as emergent and driven by the student's own quest for knowledge and application of learning strategies. By the 1990s, constructivists described learning as a construction of new knowledge from contexts, not a reproduction of already known facts. In the traditional writing classroom, constructivist learning theory was often wed to and expanded by collaborative (or social) learning theory. Simply put, in this convergence of theories, individuals construct knowledge within social contexts or communities. Knowledge, in this view, is antifoundational, contingent, and local or individualized. Individuals create their own knowledge through interaction and collaboration with others, and language plays a key role in knowledge development.

Although students writing in socially constructed traditional classrooms still used textbooks for grammar review and traditional pen and paper technology to share drafts of papers and write critiques, one interesting change that social construction theory promoted was teachers' rearrangement of the physical classroom itself. Social constructivist teachers rearranged their students' desks, which traditionally were organized into rows facing the teacher's desk or blackboard, into writing circles so students could better face each other as they discussed their work before, during, and after they wrote. Later, with the advent of the computers in the classroom, instructors reconfigured their classroom layouts again. These configurations, however, were made in electronic spaces, not physical ones. Computer-classroom instructors first organized their student writing groups and communities using local-area networks (LAN) and then later through wide-area networks (WAN). The LAN writing software they employed provided students with both synchronous and asynchronous communication features that allowed them to meet electronically to critique and respond to one another's ideas. Other features included text-creation (writing), text-sharing (reading), and text-response (critiquing) capabilities. These new software innovations not only supported students working through the writing process in the computer classroom but also, with the development of WAN networks, provided students with collaborative opportunities to work with others when their traditional classrooms were not in session. These changes reconfigured what students did to learn writing (through collaborative activities); where and when they performed these activities (almost anytime and anyplace); and how they practiced their writing (via computers in classrooms or computers connected through the Internet).

Making the Invisible Visible

Using technologies to teach writing might be as simple as showing students how to hold a pencil or crayon, or it can be as complex and, at first, as strange as asking students to meet online, not face to face, for class. Yet, historically, even the most dramatic changes eventually become commonplace or mundane in the classroom. When used everyday, technologies become transparent until they are virtually invisible or unrecognizable as technologies. Everyday writing technologies often become so transparent, in fact, that their uses are regarded simply as facts or means of production, not as experiences tied to theory or a practice open to inquiry. The use of pens, chalk, and textbooks exemplify such transparency.

No matter how commonplace these technologies become, however, they are cultural artifacts of writing pedagogy and both permit and constrain the teaching activities for which they are used: "The heritage of any given practice is carried in its technologies. Technologies and other artifacts 'encode' the knowledge of a community and allow for certain kinds of cultural activity and not others" [12, p. 45]. For example, pens and pencils promote somewhat different writing practices: one easily allows erasure and revision while the other typically does not. In a more technologically advanced example, presentational technologies in the traditional classroom, such as electronic slide shows, allow instructors to present information quickly to a group. They do not necessarily encourage discussion, although students might interrupt the slide show by raising their hands and asking the presenter questions. Online, these same electronic slide shows can be employed similarly to present information to students, but interrupting the slide show and asking or answering questions is much more difficult even if the show is being presented synchronously to the class. Interruptions and questions require a different delivery technology (a chat, MOO, or email, for example), and getting the instructor's or other students' attention with the secondary technology will be much more difficult than simply raising a hand. The simple act of asking a question during a slide show can thus become a complicated procedure and a problem in need of a solution when instructors move courses online.

As these examples show, even mundane writing and teaching technologies are neither neutral, transparent practical instruments, simply allowing users to teach or practice writing, nor are they technological equivalents of one another. Because of our familiarity with them, however, the differences between these mundane technologies only become apparent or visible during periods of transition, such as the current movement toward online distance instruction. Not recognizing these differences can result in problems, especially when instructors or their administrators conflate writing technologies, such as those used to teach online and those used to teach onsite. They may mistakenly assume that one writing technology equals the other, when, in fact, the technologies' embedded values and applications may be quite different. Furthermore, technologies that work in onsite activities may simply not exist online, or they may exist or be used in such a way that their instructional impact is dissimilar.

During transitional periods when technologies become more visible and, therefore, more easily studied, instructors should carefully consider the values embedded in their traditional onsite pedagogies, activities, and technologies and compare these values with those embedded within the online technologies they are considering. Recognizing that practices and technologies have embedded values and articulating how these values differ from one another can help instructors to understand and explain why teaching onsite is different from teaching online. An articulation of these differences can also assist instructors in making an argument for the time needed to make a smooth transition from onsite to online teaching. When making this transition, instructors will need to reflect upon their own pedagogical values (and theories of learning) and to consider how these values as well as those embedded in their preferred and projected teaching technologies will shape their online curricula. The final section of this chapter provides some guidance for instructors as they reflect upon their teaching practices in preparation for the move to online instruction.

PLANNING A PEDAGOGY-DRIVEN
ONLINE COURSE

To promote a good fit between instructors' values, learning theories, and technologies, this final section outlines a five-step reflective process for designing pedagogy-driven online courses, a process that begins with careful articulation of instructors' preferred pedagogical theories and practices. By beginning with pedagogical assumptions, this process de-emphasizes the search for technological solutions and emphasizes instead online instruction that places effective teaching and learning, not delivery, as its primary concern. This process is designed to be open to multiple teaching styles, practices, and assessment strategies, assuming as it does that online teaching, like onsite teaching, will have a variety of successful models, depending upon the instructor, the subject matter, and the goals and descriptors of student achievement.

To serve as extended examples in this process description, two models of instructional delivery are presented here: a presentational delivery model and an interactive delivery model. In the onsite classroom, the presentational model is most similar to lecture-based classrooms, in which the instructor provides all class materials through oral and written presentations. Typically, the presentational model accompanies objectivist pedagogies. The interactive model, however, employs constructivist pedagogies as found in dialogic onsite classrooms, in which students interact with each other, with reading materials, and with their instructors to learn course materials. Table 1 further compares the presentational and interactive models.

Table 1. Comparison of Presentational and Interactive Delivery Models

Presentational Delivery	Interactive Delivery
• Similar to lecture-based onsite courses	• Similar to dialogic onsite classrooms
• Instructors and/or textbooks provide all course content	• Instructor and students provide course content
• To meet course goals, students work independently at their own pace, with little, if any, interaction with other students	• To meet course goals, students must work with other students through a variety of activities, including discussions, document-sharing, and collaboration
• Student/instructor and student/ student interactions are infrequent	• Student/instructor and student/ student interactions are frequent
• Only instructors assess student work through summative evaluations	• Both instructors and students assess student work through formative and summative evaluations

In practice, neither model exists purely in any classroom, even in writing classrooms where instructors tend to privilege the interactive design. In fact, many hybrids exist that incorporate both presentational and interactive elements. For example, an editing course might include class discussions of social and technological issues related to editing practice (interactive model) while, at the same time, requiring students to demonstrate their abilities to use copyediting or proofreading symbols through a variety of practice exercises (presentational model). In another example, a highly interactive writing course that primarily employs workshops in which students talk and collaborate may occasionally have short presentational interludes in which instructors dictate assignment guidelines, grammatical rules, or documentation practices. Given that most classroom activities fall somewhere between the presentational and interactive models, few actual classes will be entirely presentational or interactive in design. Nevertheless, these two designs can give instructors a means to describe their predominant instructional model as well as to situate their activities as relatively presentational or interactive. With this information, instructors can then choose technologies that best fit their courses' theoretical and pedagogical needs. Considering theoretical and pedagogical needs prior to choosing technologies results in courses that are pedagogically, rather than technologically, driven. The rest of this section outlines the five-step process for developing pedagogically driven online courses.

Step 1: Define Course Goals and Delivery Models

To begin this process, instructors should articulate their courses' pedagogical goals and identify the delivery model that best fits these goals. When making this list of goals, instructors should not think about whether the class is being taught onsite or online. Rather, the focus should be on the goals of study: what should students know or be able to do after taking the course?

For some courses, these goals may be statements of specific, observable outcomes, or they may be more general or abstract statements of goals; courses may also have a combination of goals that fit into both categories. For example, an editing course might have this specific observable goal or objective— "Students will be able to evaluate a document's needs and state specific editing objectives"—as well as this more general course goal—"Students will consider ethical, social, and technological implications of editing and act responsibly given these implications."

After articulating course goals, instructors then need to consider how they will ask students to accomplish these goals: will students be able to accomplish the goals alone and working at their own pace; will students be required to work with others to meet this goal; or can some course goals be accomplished alone while others require interaction with other students or the instructor? If students can meet the course goals by independently interacting with course materials, learning specified skills or datasets, and demonstrating their knowledge through tests, then these goals can be accomplished using the presentational delivery model. On the other hand, if the instructor wants students to interact with others to achieve these goals, the interactive delivery model will best fit their course goals, as Rude describes in the next chapter of this book. When some goals require interaction while others do not, then instructors may need to develop their courses using both presentational and interactive delivery models.

Step 2: Define Activities for Goal Achievement

With course goals and their corresponding delivery models articulated, instructors can then identify activities that will promote student achievement of the course's pedagogical goals. To identify these activities, instructors may start by listing activities they ordinarily use in their onsite courses. With this list, instructors can then consider how these activities might be translated into online instructional activities.

When students need to access course materials, read or study these materials, and test their knowledge at varying stages throughout the course, then presentational activities will best meet their needs. Online activities that support these needs include the following:

- Referring to an online class calendar;
- Using textbooks, webpages, electronic slide shows to access course materials;
- Listening to audio clips or lectures;
- Viewing videos, art/graphics, simulations, or presentations;
- Reading and completing assignments; and
- Taking examinations.

Interactive activities, in contrast, promote interactions or exchanges among students and between instructor and students. Interactive course goals often require students to create course materials and to interact with the instructor and other students about what they are creating or learning. To promote exchanges, interactive activities can include the following:

- Asking and answering questions through various communication tools, such as chat rooms, MOOs, discussion threads, or email;
- Sharing/exchanging writing, presentations, and other materials using text-sharing or file-transfer technologies;
- Meeting in small groups in chat rooms or MOOs to discuss readings, other course materials, or student postings; and
- Meeting in large groups to discuss readings, other course materials, or student postings in chat rooms, MOOs, or through discussion threads.

When both presentational and interactive activities are needed to accomplish course goals, instructors may incorporate both kinds of activities into their online courses. For example, activities for accomplishing a specific course goal might include reading online course materials (presentational), writing a short individual response to these readings (presentational), sharing this response in a small group discussion thread (interactive), and reporting and discussing the small group's findings in a synchronous classroom chat session (interactive).

After identifying which activities best promote the course goals, instructors can begin to consider assessment opportunities that allow course activities to be evaluated. The evaluation of assessment opportunities is the next step in course planning evaluation.

Step 3: Evaluate Assessment Opportunities for Course Goals

To evaluate assessment opportunities, instructors should determine how many and what kind of assessment opportunities they have integrated or can integrate into their curricula. Specifically, instructors should analyze and consider how much formative and summative evaluation they want to provide to students, and they should consider how much formative evaluation they expect students to provide to one another. Given this information, instructors can then determine how and when they will assess their students online.

Presentational course goals typically require summative (final product) instructor-provided assessments. An assessment strategy that is primarily summative is optimal for courses with large enrollments where instructors have time to assess only final products or tests. Summative assessment can be administered in several ways online: students can submit final drafts and even portfolios through file-sharing or email; they can take objective tests directly online; or they can take essay examinations and submit them through file-sharing or email.

In contrast, an interactive assessment strategy typically requires formative and summative assessments with students. Using an interactive strategy, instructors or students can offer others formative feedback and critique throughout the assessment activity. Formative assessment can be provided online though file-sharing, uploading into discussion forums, and use of email attachments.

Such a strategy is optimal for small class enrollments because instructional contacts are frequent. Given the number of interactions in an interactive strategy, however, instructors should consider the time commitments and course load constraints they will face as they deliver the distance course; both considerations may affect how much and what kind of assessment opportunities they can successfully offer their distance students.

Step 4: Choose Instructional Technologies that Support the Course's Pedagogical Goals, Activities, and Assessment Strategies

After instructors have identified their curricular goals, the activities for goal achievement, and its assessment opportunities, the fourth step in the course planning process is determining what technology is available for course delivery and considering if and how technology choices can enhance learning and goals.

Presentational designs can be delivered with the simplest and smallest cadre of technology choices. Minimally, Internet-based presentational designs require a textbook or Web-based course guide and a website for course policies, assignments, and submission policies. Other more technological tools that can enhance presentational learning are calendars for identifying deadlines and test dates, bulletin boards for posting assignments and announcements, presentation areas for slide shows, email for exchanging any written assignments, streaming audio and video for content presentation, and self-testing, testing, and survey tools for assessment of student learning.

Interactive designs require additional access to and layering of technologies. In addition to a textbook or course guide, a website, and email capabilities, interactive designs may also include chat rooms, bulletin boards, text-sharing applications, and, as bandwidths expand, more advanced synchronous conferencing and networking. Using a combination of these technologies will provide many opportunities—through chat room discussions or text-sharing applications—for students to receive both formative and summative evaluations from other students and their instructors.

Step 5: Consider Student Needs in Terms of Goals, Activities, and Technologies

After instructors have determined their courses' pedagogical goals, evaluated course activities in terms of these goals, considered how best to assess student literacy achievement, and chosen technologies that support the literacies, activities, and assessment options they have chosen, the final phase of course planning is to reconsider all these choices from students' perspectives. When reconsidering the curricular and design choices in terms of students' needs, instructors should try to determine how students will perceive their need for instructional support. Presentational designs, for example, create an independent, self-paced learning environment, while interactive designs are best for collaborative, group-situated learning environments. (For a more detailed discussion of student instructional support in online courses, see Grady and Davis' chapter on scaffolding.) Other important considerations include the following:

- Student motivational factors (How will students' grades be reported? What kinds of grades will these students expect to earn?);
- Student self-efficacy about writing (Do they consider themselves effective or ineffective writers?);
- Student self-efficacy with technologies (How much computer and Internet experience do they have? Are they comfortable using Internet-based technologies?);

- Students' desire for independent versus cohort learning (Do they prefer to learn alone or with others?), and
- Student access to technologies.

All of these questions can help instructors to be certain that the curricular and technology choices for their courses will serve students effectively and satisfyingly.

Such student-centered questions are important considerations in course planning. For a course to be successful, students must enroll in it. They must see the course as valuable and convenient, and they must have access to the technologies necessary to take it online. Reconsidering planning decisions from students' perspectives can help instructors to ensure that students will desire to take the course, will be able to participate in the course, and will be satisfied with the goals they achieve at the course's end.

THE BENEFITS OF A PEDAGOGY-DRIVEN ONLINE COURSE

This discussion of the process for designing a pedagogy-driven online course is not intended to suggest that all technical communication instructors should use a single design or a specific set of technologies for distance course delivery. To the contrary, a variety of effective designs is not only possible but also desirable, depending on course goals and student needs. The variety of possibilities suggests a continuum from most presentational design to most interactive. Since both designs have their strengths and weaknesses, instructors should carefully consider their situational needs as they choose the design that best fits their purposes. After assessing their courses' goals, activities, assessment opportunities, delivery technologies, and student needs, instructors should then be able to hybridize their pedagogical designs to fit specific course requirements. As more instructors employ these hybridized designs, our understanding of these designs and their advantages and disadvantages will become even clearer, and the continuum of course designs should become even more defined.

Clearly, using this reflective process for designing an online course may result in very different courses, but that is the point of the process—to produce courses that work with and for individual instructors, their subject matter, and their student needs. While this process is most likely more time-consuming and perhaps expensive than some solutions provided by technology providers, it is, without question, more faithful to what successful onsite instructors know—how to teach their subject matter effectively in their own classrooms. By encouraging local solutions to online teaching problems, rather than boilerplate solutions, this process also responds to the competitive fears and pressures that administrators may be feeling—individual faculty members create their own courses based on their expertise, their subject matter emphases, and their students' needs. As Eaton suggests in Chapter 2, such courses will be distinguishable from the competition because faculty members bring their individual strengths and expertise to these courses. Such strengths and expertise are the differences between one onsite institution and another; they should also be the hallmark of online institutions.

In addition, the variable course designs suggest that many solutions are possible but steps toward solutions are often similar. These similarities might be considered an agenda for online distance education:

1. Distance education courses need not be weak or impoverished replicas of traditional classroom courses; rather, such courses should be rich, stimulating, and nourishing learning spaces in their own rights.
2. At the same time, distance education courses must be as rigorous as their onsite counterparts, incorporating the same course goals and requiring students to use their intellects and demonstrate their knowledge and skills through adequate and appropriate assessment opportunities.
3. Finally, to achieve these goals, distance education courses must be pedagogy-driven, not technology-driven—courses wherein instructors plan and implement pedagogically sound goals and appropriate activities that are supported by technology choices.

With such an agenda, online instructors can move forward with more certainty that the courses they develop online meet the same high standards that they expect from their onsite courses. Maintaining this agenda should also allow instructors to challenge the pressures, both temporal and economic, placed on them by those who adopt and promote technology-driven distance education and allow instructors to demonstrate that distance education requires forethought, research, and reflection. Courses, therefore, should not be designed and implemented too quickly. With these steps in place and agenda established, distance educators can, however, meet at least one of their administrators' primary goals for moving courses online: they can provide lifelong learning and enriched learning environments to individuals in need of them. Indeed, meeting this need is perhaps the most important of all.

REFERENCES

1. L. Lewis, E. Farris, K. Snow, and D. Levin, *Distance Education at Postsecondary Education Institutions: 1997-98,* National Center for Educational Statistics, Washington, D.C., http://nces.ed.gov/pubsearch/pubsinfo.asp?pubid=2000013, December 1999.
2. R. Lembke and J. Rudy, Second Annual EDUCAUSE Survey Identifies Key IT Issues, *Educause,* http://www.educause.edu/issues/survey2001/responses_by_question.asp, 2001.
3. Y. J. Dreazen, Student, Teach Thyself: The Classroom of the Future Won't Have Much in Common with Today's Version; For One Thing, There Probably Won't Be a Classroom, *The Wall Street Journal Millennium (A Special Report): Politics &*

Society, http://www.wsj.com/millennium/articles/SB944517850742359260.htm, December 31, 1999.

4. J. R. Young, Web Site Tracks Statewide Virtual University Projects, *The Chronicle of Higher Education*, http://chronicle.com/free/2001/06/2001061301u.htm, July 13, 2001.

5. E. Tebeaux, Technical Writing by Distance: Refocusing the Pedagogy of Technical Communication, *Technical Communication Quarterly, 4*, pp. 365-393, 1995.

6. D. C. Leonard, The Web, the Millennium, and the Digital Evolution of Distance Education, *Technical Communication Quarterly, 8*:1, pp. 9-20, 1999.

7. R. A. Dumont, Teaching and Learning in Cyberspace, *IEEE Transactions In Professional Communication, 39*:4, pp. 192-204, 1996.

8. L. A. Jorn, A. H. Duin, and B. J. Wahlstrom, Designing and Managing Virtual Learning Communities, *IEEE Transactions on Professional Communication, 39*:4, pp. 183-191, 1996.

9. H. B. Horner, Writing Instruction in Great Britain: Eighteenth and Nineteenth Centuries, in *A Short History of Writing Instruction: From Ancient Greek to Twentieth-Century America*, J. J. Murphy (ed.), Hermagoras Press, Davis, California, pp. 121-149, 1990.

10. S. M. Halloran, From Rhetoric to Composition: The Teaching of Writing in America to 1900, in *A Short History of Writing Instruction: From Ancient Greek to Twentieth-Century America*, J. J. Murphy (ed.), Hermagoras Press, Davis, California, pp. 151-182, 1990.

11. K. H. Adams, *A History of Professional Writing Instruction in American Colleges: Years of Acceptance, Growth, and Doubt*, Southern Methodist University, Dallas, Texas, 1993.

12. C. Haas, *Writing Technologies: Studies on the Materiality of Literacy*, Lawrence Erlbaum, Mahwah, New Jersey, 1996.

CHAPTER 4

Strategic Planning for Online Education: Sustaining Students, Faculty, and Programs

Carolyn Rude

Texas Tech University offered its first online graduate class in technical communication in the fall of 1997, enrolling eight students including two resident students. From that modest and even precarious beginning, we have developed a robust and selective online degree program. The Master of Arts in Technical Communication (MATC) was approved for online delivery in 1998. In the spring of 2003, we had 27 students admitted to the degree program and currently enrolled. We offered three distance classes in that semester with a total of 34 enrollments. We could have filled a fourth class with qualified students if we had had the faculty resources to offer the course. We no longer advertise the program for fear of raising false hopes of admission for limited spaces. (Information is available at the website and through Extended Studies for potential students to find.) Online students perform at a slightly higher level than their onsite counterparts as measured by their grades. They evaluate the online courses as equal to or higher than resident graduate courses in rigor and quality. Faculty are eager to teach online courses. Program growth confirms the demand for online graduate education in this field and the feasibility of offering Internet-based courses. The performance and satisfaction of the students and positive experience of faculty suggest that online courses may offer high-quality graduate education.

The rhetorical concept of *kairos* helps to explain program development: the time is right for this pedagogy in this field. But success also follows from planning with emphasis on pedagogy and sustainability. Planning strategically for the long term enables sustainable programs that encourage students to continue to enroll in courses, that produce degrees of value to the students who invest in education, and that excite and inspire faculty. These outcomes are not inherent in online education, which, if poorly planned, may trivialize courses and exhaust faculty without offering students substantial value. Sustainability refers not just to attrition. It also represents the potential of renewal in teaching and in the discipline.

The focus of this chapter is the planning and administration of online programs. The chapter uses the example of Texas Tech's online graduate program to illustrate and analyze the planning with emphasis on the impacts of choices. While the chapter describes features of the program (a local answer to global questions about online education), its purpose is to suggest the connection between pedagogical, technical, and administrative choices and program outcomes rather than to represent the Texas Tech program as the model for all online education.

VARIABLES IN ONLINE EDUCATION

A starting point in planning an online program is to determine what is meant by online education in the local setting. The education will take advantage of the Internet or CD-ROMs, but other variables relate to whether the course features independent study or a class organized on the semester schedule, whether the instructor leads the class or provides materials to be used independently, whether the pedagogy emphasizes transfer of knowledge and mastery of content or whether it encourages student participation in constructing knowledge, whether the online materials constitute the entire course or supplement a traditional course, who is qualified to teach, who is qualified to take the courses, whether the course is delivered in a university or by a private corporation, and what constitutes satisfactory completion of requirements and credit. These variables are discussed in the section of this chapter on planning for quality, but planners should understand that their own sense of online education may differ from understanding by administrators in other units and by prospective students. Online education does not have a simple and uniform definition.

Predictably, people have tried to understand something new by comparing it to something familiar, whether to the classroom as a physical space led by an instructor, to independent studies courses offered by correspondence, to online tutorials available for software and other products on the Internet and CD-ROM, or even to the products of course development programs, such as WebCT and Blackboard. So much emphasis has been placed on the materials and technologies that the dominant sense of online education in higher education seems to be independent study with a diminished role for the professor except as he or she develops the content of materials. The self-contained online course, also called a CBT (computer-based training) course, is somewhat analogous to the first distance technology, the textbook: it is developed by the professor but able to stand alone. The CBT course, better than the textbook, however, builds in feedback and evaluation so that learning can presumably be measured through the technology.

Independent study and self-contained courses appeal to students because of the "just-in-time" nature of the instruction and flexible timelines for completion. They appeal to administrators because they offer the promise of more students and some economies. Self-contained courses may be expensive to develop, requiring subject-matter knowledge as well as technical knowledge, and it is likely that a team of course developers will work on a course, including at least a content expert (professor) and a technical expert. Once they are developed, however, they are relatively inexpensive to deliver as class sizes are not determined by physical space, nor, in some instances, by the need for instructors. So long as there is a server with space to deliver the course via the Internet, the number of students is potentially limitless. Self-contained courses are probably the main growth area of online education, especially in corporate training.

Developers of an online course or degree program should expect that many decision makers will expect some variation of independent study or courses that minimize instructor involvement and should be prepared to justify any variations from these defaults. However, the particular goals of technical communication courses and the level at which they are offered may point to different methods, as they did at Texas Tech, which chose an administratively risky alternative to these models: the instructor-led, Internet-based course offered on the semester schedule with a synchronous weekly class meeting. This model in many ways replicates the methods of the physical classroom. This choice was administratively risky for several reasons: it requires the same commitment of faculty time as the resident courses and limits class size, thereby negating any cost savings over resident courses; because it contradicts some default expectations, it needs to be explained and justified both to administrators and to some prospective students; because the courses are offered on-load and supported with state funding, a tuition surcharge applies to out-of-state students; and the synchronous meeting time is difficult for students several time zones away from Texas. However, except for the tuition differential and inconvenience to international students, the administrative risks equate, we believe, to pedagogical strengths, measured by student interaction with other students and faculty, student quality, and faculty commitment.

PEDAGOGICAL VARIABLES

Pedagogy is more important to the quality of the course and long-term success of the program than materials and technologies. (See Cargile Cook's chapter for an extended explanation of this priority; see also Blythe [1] for a discussion of user-centered design of online courses.) There are competing priorities, especially costs (to the university and to students) and established schemes of online education in the university (program designers will have incentives to follow patterns already established in a particular setting). However, a pedagogically driven course and program design is more important in the long term for sustaining programs than short-term efficiencies. When students are satisfied with the quality of what they are offered, they come back for more; when faculty find the teaching exciting intellectually, they seek additional online teaching experiences.

Independent study tends to be objectivist in pedagogy: a body of knowledge is available for students to master. The course is a means of transferring information to the student. The organized class may also embody objectivist pedagogy, but if it emphasizes interaction among students and with the professor and if students are encouraged to construct their own knowledge and meanings, the pedagogy is constructivist. (See Hillocks [2] for a comparison of objectivist and constructivist pedagogies in writing instruction.)

Writing courses have their own pedagogical requirements that differ from requirements from an introductory course in, say, psychology or geology. Writing courses emphasize performance as well as content mastery. Writing ability cannot be tested adequately through automated feedback any more than ability to play a musical instrument can be tested with a quiz. Some components of an online course might be developed as self-contained units. For example, if the course requires sophisticated computer skills that the students do not possess, they might be sent to an online tutorial. They might be quizzed over textbook content. However, their writing will require expert evaluation and commentary.

The assumption of much of the literature in writing instruction is that pedagogy should be constructivist, encouraging students to take an active role in learning and performance and to work in collaboration with peers and the instructor. Contemporary theories of writing instruction emphasize document exchange and peer review, pointing to some need for student-to-student interaction. The tradition of graduate-level courses includes discussion, the ability not just to consume ideas but to articulate them, complicate them, and adapt them. Multiple perspectives of a class of students encourage these goals. These instructional goals favor the class or the cohort over a purely independent model of teaching.

THE VISION:
DEFINING THE LOCAL ANSWER

Program designers need a clear vision of their goals and target student group. The vision statement is a variation of the "audience and purpose" question that is so familiar to technical communication. Will the program serve undergraduates, master's students, or doctoral students? Will it serve majors pursuing degrees or serve other fields in which writing is important? What qualifications for study are important?

At Texas Tech, we targeted working professionals who had moved into technical communication without formal education in the field and who sought professional development. The master's degree is an optimal level at which to offer online distance classes. Students have proven their academic ability in their undergraduate degrees, and they are mature and experienced. The degree is shorter and less complex than either the undergraduate degree or PhD, and completion of the degree does not stretch over an unreasonable period of time. At Texas Tech, there was also a university imperative to develop the graduate program. Indeed, the growth in the online program is one basis on which the technical communication program successfully argued to the provost for four new faculty lines. The distance program has given the Department of English the visibility of having the largest graduate enrollment of any department on campus.

We have chosen the organized course model and on-load teaching to make the program and the courses central to our mission and the same priority for faculty time and energy as an onsite course. The program is administered by the department and Graduate School, not by Extended Studies. Students must be admitted to the Graduate School as well as to the program. An assignment to teach an online class is equivalent to an assignment to teach a resident class. Class sizes are limited as they are for onsite classes to a maximum of 15 per class but with an ideal enrollment limit of 10 to 12. Students provide the same course evaluations as onsite students, and the teaching of online courses counts in merit reviews the same as the teaching of resident courses. There are no time or money incentives to shortchange the distance classes.

Most instructors use a variety of technologies, including a bulletin board for asynchronous discussion, a course management program, and a website archive of course materials. Learning these technologies is not very demanding. The synchronous component of our classes (a weekly online meeting) distinguishes this program from some others. The meeting is inconvenient for students several time zones away, but as will be discussed later, it is highly valued by both students and faculty for the intensity and depth of discussion, for its opportunities for interaction, and for the way it makes the experience of online education personally fulfilling. (However, for a different perspective on the utility of synchronous discussions, see Rubens and Southard's chapter in Section 3.)

Although the students and the delivery methods are new, the goals, the faculty, the curriculum, and the pedagogies all closely replicate the comparable components of the onsite program. In that sense, the program design is conservative. But those choices have proven to be sound for an experiment in higher education. They are reassuring at a time when students, faculty, and administrators are getting used to online delivery. They link the new to the familiar. In 1996, when Texas Tech administrators were curious but resistant as well, they made the program feasible. In time, as universities accept and embrace the idea of online education and as new technologies enable new pedagogies, the vision can expand.

What we did not predict in our vision statement was how much the online program would give back to existing programs. The online students are smart, lively, interested, and informed. They provide an excellent way for the faculty to connect to and understand the corporate workplace. When the online classes are joined to resident classes, the online students help introduce the resident students to the discourse of the field and to the kinds of issues that professional technical communicators confront. These students are admirable human beings, with many of them active in professional associations and in social service. If sustainability means in part renewal, the online students are responsible for a new energy in the onsite programs.

PLANNING FOR QUALITY: CRITERIA FOR PROGRAM AND COURSE DESIGN

If a program is to be sustainable, both as it encourages and attracts students and rewards faculty for their efforts, it must first of all offer quality education. The quality question is especially important for online education given some faculty and administrative skepticism about quality. Skepticism derives from association with correspondence courses (perceived as second class and second rate), from concerns about impersonality, and perhaps to concerns about academic honesty (are the students getting the credit the ones doing the work?). Commercially developed and delivered courses also raise academic skepticism. Prospective students as well as faculty and administrators want to be assured that their investment of time and money will be rewarded with a quality education and a credential that has recognized value. To compensate for these concerns, the quality of an online course may have to be even higher than the quality of a conventional course for it to be considered equal to the benchmark.

Quality depends on a match of the pedagogy with course goals, faculty who meet qualifications for teaching, students who are qualified for the study, and course and degree requirements that are equivalent to those for a campus-based program. In short, program design needs to build in assurances that online students will receive the same considerations that their onsite counterparts take for granted.

Quality: Match of Educational Goals with Delivery Model

The method has to be right for the course material and expectations for students. Planning questions include these: Who are the students? Why are they taking the course or enrolled in the degree program? What do we hope that they will gain from taking these courses? What strategies will help them accomplish these goals? These questions, like those suggested by other authors in this section, should drive course decisions more than questions of technology. Courses should be defined as "writing courses" or "technical communication courses" that happen to use a variety of online technologies, not as "WebCT courses" or "CD-ROM courses" that happen to address writing.

Quality: Faculty

The faculty must be qualified for teaching (or for graduate teaching if courses are at the graduate level); they must be committed to this teaching and not regard it as peripheral to their primary work. These qualifications are more important than their ability to work with technology. Who will develop the courses? Who will teach them? How will faculty be compensated (as part of their regular salary or with supplementary stipends or by the piece)? What is the impact on faculty workload? What is the impact on sustaining faculty interest in the online program, including the motivation to develop courses and to teach them over the long term? How will faculty be prepared (and encouraged) to teach online?

Correspondence courses have often used graders other than the faculty member who develops the course to respond to student assignments. Faculty may moonlight from their regular jobs to grade correspondence assignments. Online courses may use adjunct faculty, saving the regular faculty for the resident courses. Because faculty may be hired at a distance, this option extends the faculty and makes experts beyond the regular faculty available to students. Adjunct faculty can enrich a distance faculty, but if the entire faculty is adjunct, the program is likely to be adjunct to the university's mission. The risk of a separate faculty that does not necessarily qualify for the regular faculty is the risk of a second-rate program. If the incentives for teaching online relate primarily to teaching, the instructor is likely to develop a commitment to this particular type of teaching. If the incentives are primarily financial (extra compensation for extra work), faculty may lose interest as the fatigue of overwork overcomes the need for material rewards.

Issues of faculty quality relate not just to who is teaching the course but also to the perception of the online program's significance to the department or university mission. When courses are taught on overtime or mostly by adjuncts, the program by description becomes peripheral (and second class in perception even if not in reality). In addition, overtime work steals time from faculty research. The extra income is seductive, but extra work can divert energy from the research and teaching that develop a career.

Questions about faculty technical expertise can be distracting in planning online education. The concern that the online instructor be a computer wizard recalls the now-obsolete assumption that the best technical communicator is the one who knows the most equipment and software, not the one who knows the most about writing. The online teacher, like the campus teacher, offers knowledge of the subject matter, ability to plan and organize learning experiences, and ability to evaluate student work. Learning to use technology, such as a bulletin board or a chat room, is like learning to use audiovisual equipment in the classroom. It may take a mentor (or pleasure in figuring out technical things), but the learning of the technology is much quicker than the learning entailed by a graduate degree in a subject area.

One good reason for matching the delivery method to the methods of the onsite course is that the time to prepare for teaching online is lower than if the instructor is expected to develop elaborate CD-ROMs with substantial pro-gramming to build in quizzes and other feedback. The faculty in the writing programs at Texas Tech have taught online courses successfully whether they have well-developed computer knowledge or mainly use computers as tools to complete ordinary tasks like writing articles and keeping course records. Some have been supported in course development materials by the university's Teaching, Learning, and Technology Center, and when faculty have wanted help developing websites, the program has provided it through a student assistant.

When the online courses are similar to campus courses, the hesitation faculty may feel about online teaching diminishes. When possible, Texas Tech pairs an online class with an onsite class. The instructor has one preparation. This plan offers possibilities for interaction of distance and resident students, and it also helps to maintain parallel standards and expectations for the courses. An additional benefit because of the way course load is calculated is that this plan reduces the number of courses an instructor teaches. Each graduate course is worth 1.5 undergraduate courses. Thus, someone teaching two graduate courses in a semester can fulfill the three-course load with just two courses. It is unlikely that a faculty member would be assigned to two onsite graduate courses in a semester, so the online program assists directly in faculty load management.

Quality: Students

Students must be qualified for study and able to complete the work. One way to ensure this goal is to use parallel admission standards for an online program as for a resident program. Students must also, of course, have the special skills necessary to complete an online course, including computer knowledge, ability to troubleshoot problems, and ability to work independently. The online master's degree program at Texas Tech has faced few student problems, probably because a student who qualifies for a master's degree has already proven the ability to succeed academically and because technical communication in the workplace requires a high level of computer proficiency. A student assistant has helped the occasional student whose computer skills were not sufficient to work effectively. The qualifications of undergraduate students for online education might not be so apparent.

Although review of online and onsite applicants is parallel in most respects, we have modified the application requirements for online students to eliminate the letters of recommendation. Many of the online students have been out of college for several years or more, and even if they can find faculty who remember them, the information the faculty member can provide about likelihood of success in a graduate program is out of date. Relevant work experience seems to be a good predictor of success, making the letter of recommendation less useful than it is for students who enter graduate school directly after completing an undergraduate degree.

Can students cheat their way to a master's degree? The odds are against it. Each course requires about 150 hours of work (10 hours per week for 15 weeks). There are 12 courses in the degree program. That's a lot of time to buy if one were inclined to try. The students' voices and work are very apparent in the weekly meetings and in the bulletin board. The students reveal more about themselves through their writing style and content of comments than their physical features would reveal in a classroom, where there are also no guarantees that the one in class is the one preparing the assignments.

Quality: Course and Degree Requirements

If the degree is to be credible and valuable, these requirements must be comparable to those of the benchmark campus-based program. In some ways Texas Tech did not have a choice about these criteria. The Graduate School and accrediting body hold any online degree program to the standards established for the campus program as a condition of accreditation. But as we began teaching online courses at Texas Tech, the faculty were all conscious that it would be possible to dumb down the courses for the online students. Perhaps the attitude was driven by academic snobbery: the suspicion that workplace writers would not be interested in theory or ideas but only in production. Fortunately, our students have disabused us of any such idea. They eagerly embrace the theory we offer and in fact several have prompted us for more. Some courses are more production oriented than others, and the assignments emulate workplace documents (a manual, a style guide). But through the 12 courses required for the master's degree, we also include opportunities for academic papers: theoretical, analytical, research based. Such work is one way to distinguish a master's level program from an undergraduate program, and should any of the graduates eventually pursue a PhD, they will be prepared for the coursework at the advanced level.

WORKING WITHIN THE SYSTEM: ADMINISTRATIVE DECISIONS

All programs exist within larger systems: the department, the university, the discipline, corporations that employ the students and graduates, society as a whole. Programs are influenced by the available technologies. Expectations and goals for online education may differ among these groups, and decisions made in one system may constrain the options for program development, especially as programs are funded and as technologies are available. Program administrators can often strategically manage the systems in which they work and not be constrained by them. Knowing the system is a way to keep the system from determining the course and program. But first they have to understand and articulate what they want to accomplish in online education.

Administrative Authority and Accreditation

Online education as it is part of the campus program is probably administered by departments and colleges. The real question emerges when online education is also distance education. Depending on university structure, distance education may be administered by the department and college, or it may be administered by a unit set up particularly for extended studies or correspondence courses.

As one of the first distance degree programs at Texas Tech, the technical communication online master's degree would have been easier to administer through Extended Studies than through the Graduate School. Extended Studies has its own procedures for admissions and enrollment, fee payment, and marketing. This division also works with the state Coordinating Board and accreditation body to register online courses. Still, the separation of administration of this graduate program from campus programs was metaphorically troubling, and we opted to be administered through the department and the Graduate School. That decision helped to make the online MATC equivalent to the resident MATC. Students must meet the Graduate School's standards for admission, faculty must qualify for graduate faculty status, courses are taught as part of the regular faculty load, and class sizes are limited. Because the online program requires the same courses and credits as the resident program, it was not considered a new program and could enjoy the accredited status of the existing program. The transcripts of distance students look the same as the transcripts of resident students, and their credits should transfer if they choose to pursue a degree at another university. The courses count in the state's formula funding. The department can boast growth in graduate enrollment because the students are counted the same as campus students though they are not in residence.

These benefits of status and accreditation were worth the struggle of helping the university system adapt procedures for students who are not in residence. The procedures did not accommodate online students in several funny but frustrating respects. For example, this university requires that every student have a measles immunization. Online students are routinely prevented from their first registration because they have not turned in their verification of immunization, but Health Services now knows what to do when I phone to request a waiver. I have had to work with administrators to get the fees for the recreation center and athletics waived, but finally that has happened. A draft of the university-wide student evaluation form for distance courses omitted reference to instructors, and a course registration form has asked for identification of the course "owner." These university procedures were based on the default concept of the self-contained course. Because of initiatives from the technical communication program, the course registration and evaluation forms have been modified to accommodate the MATC pedagogy.

Opting for conventional administrative authority will probably increase demands on the time of the program administrator. Because Texas Tech is a public university, this conventional authority also increased the costs for out-of-state students (because they pay tuition at out-of-state rates). A university will need to weigh the time costs and student costs of working within a conventional university structure against the benefits of credentialing and of embracing the online program as central to the mission. If out-of-state students pay at higher rates, will there be enough in-state students to make the program work? Might those out-of-state students benefit from tuition-reimbursement programs? Is scholarship support available? Because university governance and policies vary, it will be important to investigate opportunities within the local setting.

Impact on Existing Programs

An online program that enrolls new students will affect existing programs. Thus, program designers must anticipate what those impacts may be and how to ensure good impacts while minimizing negative ones. Additional courses in the schedule may divert faculty from existing courses; one of the feasibility questions is whether faculty resources are sufficient to begin a new program while maintaining existing programs. Distance online courses might compete with onsite courses. It may be desirable to shift from an onsite to an online program, but if both onsite and online programs are desirable, competition between the programs (costs, admission standards, degree value) should be minimized.

The Technology Question

A criterion for course and program design has to be what technology options are available. These options refer not just to hardware, such as remote classrooms for interactive video, but also technical support for course development and for maintaining the software and hardware. Knowing these options may stimulate some creative thinking about course design. However, as argued throughout this chapter, the primary design question is not how to adapt a course to the technology but rather how to find technological solutions to pedagogical needs.

DELIVERY AND EVALUATION: THE TEXAS TECH EXPERIENCE

This section provides information on the online MATC program, including student enrollment patterns, the synchronous discussion, and student perspectives. The information answers some questions about the impact and nature of online education at least as it has been experienced in this context.

Student Enrollment Patterns

Student backgrounds and enrollment patterns differ from those of students in the onsite program. Online students may be less interested in the degree than in the professional development offered by a few courses. They may drop in and out of the program because of personal or work schedules whereas resident students usually start and finish their degrees without a break. Anticipating such patterns will help administrators plan for an online distance program. One of the tasks of the program administrator is to help redefine program "productivity" and "success" for the Graduate School, which tends to look at number of graduations in comparison with number of admissions.

Of the 20 students enrolled in the fall of 2002, 19 were admitted to the degree program. The other one was a doctoral student from the College of Education enrolled as a professional courtesy to that program because of course availability. Of the 19, 14 were Texans; others were from Arizona, Massachusetts, Washington, Wisconsin, and Germany. Three of the five out-of-state students received tuition reimbursement from their employers, minimizing the impact of the out-of-state tuition surcharge.

The GRE scores and the grades of the online students in the Master of Arts in Technical Communication are parallel to those of onsite students. For example, in the fall of 2002, average GRE scores of online students admitted and attending were Verbal 542, Quantitative 580, and Analytical 561 (combined = 1,683). These scores compare well with scores for resident MATC students in Fall 2002: Verbal 561, Quantitative 582, and Analytical 565 (combined = 1,708). The grades of distance students are somewhat higher than those of onsite students, probably reflecting their work experience and maturity.

Enrollment is more volatile than enrollment in the onsite program: students may not enroll every semester in sequence, they may take a few courses for professional development without intending to pursue a degree, and the economy affects their ability to enroll more than it affects resident students. For example in the fall of 2001, four students had significant job reassignments after the September 11 terrorist attack, including one who was called up by the National Guard. These four students withdrew from their classes. In the spring of 2002, one student lost his job during downsizing and withdrew. Otherwise, enrollment within specific classes is stable: when working students commit to a class, they tend to turn in their work on time and to complete the class. Still, the attrition rate is higher than in resident classes. From fall 1997 through fall 2002, not counting resident students who took an online class, 52 students took attempted online courses, but of these, 26 took one to four classes and then no more. Of these 26, 16 were admitted as "temporary" students, without GRE scores. Because the attrition rate is so high for this class of students, we no longer enroll students unless they are admitted to the degree program. That policy should help us achieve a better graduation rate and also make spaces available for those students who are most committed to this field. However, when the program was new, it seemed fair to let students try out online education before committing to a degree.

Of the 36 who have been admitted to the degree program, 15 are temporarily or permanently inactive, though five of these declare their intent to return once personal and work obligations enable study (two are having babies, one is caring for an elderly parent, and two have major work projects). Of those 10 who have been admitted and will probably not return, some will pursue PhD degrees in other fields—3; job situations have changed (a new employer who does not value a master's degree, a layoff, a reassignment)—3; they may have met their education objectives (a course or two in a specific subject)—3; or career opportunities may seem geographically limited in technical communication—1. Other reasons explain attrition: students' personal situations may change (a new baby, a move); graduate study may be more demanding than they had imagined and they don't have time; the synchronous meeting is inconvenient (especially for international students); or they may not like the distance environment or technical communication.

The attrition rate is declining as we learn more about how to evaluate applicants and how to describe the courses for prospective students. Work experience in the field will probably become a requirement, though this policy will limit access of the program to career changers unless we interpret "work experience" broadly. But because of the nature of online education, it is likely that patterns of enrollment will always be more uncertain than they are for resident students. Strategic planning should accommodate these patterns and not try to make them match the patterns of an onsite program, in which completion of a degree is likely to be the top priority. But maintaining interest in continued enrollment is necessary for program sustainability.

Because students are usually working fulltime and taking a course in addition, fatigue is a factor in continued enrollment, even for those students who are committed to the field and to the degree. Although we offer at least two courses in the long terms, only two students have managed to take two courses at a time. This means that the 12-course degree takes four years to complete or longer if a student does not take summer courses. A cumulative fatigue can make it hard to keep going, especially because most employers do not require the degree. Although the program attracts potential career changers, most of the students who continue beyond two courses are working professionals in the field. The odds of continuation are strengthened by a strong identification with technical communication. The personal relationships students develop in classes seem to encourage continued enrollment. Students like their classmates and are motivated to join them. Under discussion is the possibility of offering a six-course certificate to give students something more tangible than course credits if they do not want to complete the entire master's degree. The credits earned for the certificate would apply to the degree requirements if the students continued beyond six courses.

The Synchronous Component in Instruction

Texas Tech includes a weekly, scheduled synchronous discussion in a MOO in its courses along with asynchronous discussion through a bulletin board and email contact. (The MOO—"multi-user domain object oriented"—is a sophisticated chat space accessed through an Internet browser.) The English Department MOO is based on the enCore Xpress database, available as freeware from Lingua Moo (http://lingua.utdallas.edu). This MOO enables display of "slides," served as html files, in the right pane of the screen so that the group can look together at a meeting agenda or sample text, much as they might study a slide on an overhead projector or on a webpage in a classroom. Conversations may be recorded so that a transcript is available for review after the meeting has ended. Guests may log on to explore the options at http://MOO.engl.ttu.edu:7000.

The MOO enables student-to-student interaction. It satisfies the discussion part of a lecture-discussion course. The discussion is likely to begin by following up on reading responses posted during the week at the bulletin board. The discussion, in the Texas Tech experience, is more intense than the face-to-face discussion of a classroom. Charlotte Kaempf, a distance student who has formatted and threaded the topics in the MOO transcripts for her classmates, reports that the typical one-hour MOO session with 8–12 participants generates 350–450 comments. (She bases this conclusion on courses taught by Professors Baake, Carter, and Rude.) Another larger class (15 participants) taught by Professor Dragga using three separate and simultaneous discussion groups for 30 minutes with whole-group discussion for 30 minutes generated about 600 comments in an hour. It takes one or two class meetings for students and instructors to get used to the fast-paced discussion, both reading and writing. A transcript of the discussion is emailed to the class, and students report reviewing it to catch up on comments they have missed.

Kaempf has determined that instructors generate about 25% of the comments, many of them questions or prompts for expanding the discussion. All of these instructors prepare possible discussion questions in advance and have them ready to copy and paste into the MOO at the appropriate time. Like a good classroom discussion, an online discussion benefits from planning and direction, as Lang discusses in more detail in Section 2.

The MOO enables a playfulness, and characters can be aliases, but at Texas Tech the convention is for participants to use their first names, as they would in an onsite class or in another setting with a serious purpose. Casual conversation is encouraged before and after class, but the meetings themselves are focused on the course topic. Most of the comments are substantive. There are so many because students may respond simultaneously to a prompt whereas in a classroom, there is usually one comment at a time, offered sequentially as students take turns. But the level of participation (and interaction) is substantially increased with this online technology because of the potential for multiple students to respond to any one prompt. That many comments would constitute chaos in a traditional classroom because people would be speaking at the same time. The MOO enables more people to actively engage in learning. A single comment in a traditional classroom may be taken as representative of what everyone in the classroom understands and thinks whereas multiple comments reflect different perspectives and understanding.

The developers of enCore Xpress (Holmevik and Haynes) provide good online help, and their book, *MOOniversity* [3], provides good details of how to use a MOO. Texas Tech distance students have developed some information for new students and faculty on how to perform various MOO functions, including communicating but also building rooms and recording sessions. These procedures are not difficult to learn. A student assistant creates MOO characters and passwords for the students, and the department technology assistant maintains the hardware.

The synchronous discussion is pedagogically sound according to constructivist pedagogy. Multiple voices contribute to the understanding of an issue, and the odds of this understanding developing in fruitful ways are increased because of the different perspectives. The synchronous discussion also helps faculty and students to develop interpersonal relationships and a sense of each other as people. It provides a space for interpersonal sharing as well as serious discussion. Students tend to gather before each class meeting to exchange comments that engage all in the class. My students shared their favorite vacation spots, anecdotes about pets, and responses to movies. We knew about anniversaries and births. Everyone could listen in if not participate, so there were no private conversations in one part of the room. Students may be intuitively aware of the need to use words to bridge the distances and to compensate for inability to nod heads or smile or frown. A few students took on the role of drawing out reticent students, just as some in a classroom setting will draw out classmates. If someone missed a MOO meeting, at the next meeting they were welcomed back with "missed you last week." They often complimented each other's statements in the MOO with "Good comment." Classes typically ended with explicit statements of satisfaction, "Great class. Thanks." "I can't believe the class is over already. Time goes so fast." These comments are ordinary exchanges of polite society, but they are often not articulated in a physical classroom because students are afraid their classmates or instructor may misinterpret their intent. Writing opens the possibility for expression that face-to-face encounters may discourage, and such comments take on a sincerity in writing. My own experience in teaching is that the online courses permit an intimacy that is not typical in face-to-face courses. The synchronous discussion enables that intimacy.

In course evaluations at Texas Tech, all of the students have rated the MOO as very valuable or valuable among the course technologies. This positive response is one reason why Texas Tech retains the synchronous component in spite of the time problem for people who are removed from the U.S. central time zone. Three European students have enrolled in classes, logging on to the MOO at 1 A.M. their time; two of them have endured for multiple classes. However, students one or two time zones away from central time seem able to work within the schedule. The only other MOO problem we have had is that some company firewalls prevent access to the MOO port. The technician has been able to resolve these problems.

In short, synchronous discussion in the MOO works for faculty and students. It supports constructivist pedagogy, and it enables active and extended participation by everyone in the class. The intensity and speed of the conversation are intellectually stimulating. The discussion also builds a sense of community that helps to sustain the interest of both students and faculty in the online courses.

Student Voices

As various writers in the field remind us (Blythe [1], Johnson [4]), design for uses of technology should be user centered, and users should participate in the design. At Texas Tech, instructors mostly designed the original program, but the plans were based on experience in the onsite program that included student feedback. Prospective students were surveyed (by Kelli Cargile Cook, then a doctoral student) about their interest in audioconferencing, which they declined, and that technology was not implemented.

Student participation in the ongoing program development includes course projects involving the program, suggestions during the courses, and course evaluations. Projects have included suggestions about the program website, development of a student resource center, and MOO instructions. During courses, students may negotiate deadlines, modifications of assignments, and reading materials. Through email to the program director, they have suggested course topics and the shape of the program as a whole.

The course evaluations provide sustained and substantial information on student responses. We have developed an evaluation form to supplement the university evaluation form and designed to explore responses to the pedagogies as well as to gather demographic information on students. (This form may be accessed at http://english.ttu.edu/disted.) Some parts are quantitative. Students rank the technologies (MOO, bulletin board, website, email) on Likert scales, of which the MOO gets the best response. The method that gets the most mixed reviews is collaborative projects, especially when projects involve both online and onsite students. Students comment on their professors and on their classmates. "I respect my classmates" gets a very strong affirmation. No one has ever requested a change from the scheduled courses to independent study, though perhaps some students who have inquired with the expectation that "online" means "independent study" have not pursued applications. Most students report working 10–15 hours per week on a course. When asked how the quality and rigor compare with those of graduate courses they may have taken in residence, they overwhelmingly respond either "about the same" or "higher."

The open-ended questions give some insight into their responses to online education:

- The dialogue with other grad students in your class has so often given me insight to training and strategic issues I'm dealing with at xxx. Granted, I am gaining a lot of knowledge, but I'm able to see the immediate or long-term application of the knowledge to our goals at xxx. That has multiplied the value of the distance learning program for me. I'm eager for more of the same next year. Just thought you'd want to know how valuable this has been.

- I did not know what to expect when I first signed up for the class. At best I thought I would find a "pared-down" version of a post-graduate class. I was most happily wrong. These classes are every bit as rich and robust as their onsite versions. In fact, in the Technical Manuals class I am taking now, both the on-siters and we distancers meet together.
- Even if I lived in Lubbock, I would take the distance courses. We have a very rich environment due to the experiences of the students—both in industry and also from their geographic locations. Additionally, the majority of the professors treat us like peers. . . . Our feedback is seriously considered and our work schedules acknowledged. We are building a knowledge community—and it won't expire after we get our degrees.

One open-ended question asks, "What do you most like about distance graduate courses in technical communication at Texas Tech?" Some responses are these:

- The one-on-one interaction with faculty. I don't feel distanced from TTU.
- Excellent integration of theory and practice.
- High quality professors who are *very* accessible.

For more on course evaluations and their uses, see Cargile Cook and Grant-Davie's chapter in Section 3.

PLANNING FOR SUSTAINABILITY AND GROWTH

A number of experiments in education over the past several decades now seem like fads of the day. Two examples using technology were programmed instruction and televised lectures in classrooms. Is online education the fad of the early 21st century, or will it become a permanent part of higher education, perhaps changing some concepts as well as methods of education?

Some differences between online education and past experiments with technology in education predict that online education will be central in higher education well into the future. One is that the Internet is so readily available to students and to universities. The digital divide is narrowing, and an increasing number of homes have Internet access. Access for people with sensory disabilities is technologically manageable with options for large print and audio versions of text and graphics. Like programmed instruction and televised lectures, the Internet offers excellent possibilities for presentation of information. But its real strength, unavailable through the other technical experiments, is in the possibilities for interaction and for the constructivist pedagogy that interaction enables. Discussion, collaboration, and review of work in progress engage students as active participants in learning. They also build a sense of community and a sense of the uses of information in a context, among people. The learning experience is richer when the goal is more than mastery of a body of content. The teaching experience is richer when students tug at the ideas the teacher offers, challenging or reshaping them, and when the teacher engages with the students in learning, not just measuring what they have mastered. Exchange is not just one way or even two way. Multiple voices negotiate and contribute and challenge until what was simple and mundane develops complexities and realities that were at first unimagined. New knowledge is constructed. Strategic planning for sustainable online learning will exploit these possibilities for exchange, perhaps not in every class and for every subject but as part of the program of courses.

In technical communication, the opportunities for online education are especially promising. The need is apparent: both the workplace and the academy seek people with academic, not just experiential, preparation. Not all colleges offer courses in technical communication, especially courses beyond the introductory course. The colleges that do offer advanced courses need to reach beyond their usual student populations. Because many potential students are already employed, campus-based degree programs cannot always offer what the students need. Employed people are likely to be comfortable with online learning in a corporate setting. And the field values and encourages innovative uses of technology in education. The match between the needs of students and the people who employ them and the options universities have for meeting those needs points to online education.

Some established trends in teaching, especially the use of computers in writing instruction, find their natural extension in online learning. Since the 1980s, computers have developed from a vision into a necessity in the teaching of writing. Investment in online education, both commercial and academic, indicates that many people have a stake in the success of online education and will do what it takes to make it succeed. John Chambers, CEO of Cisco Systems, predicts that "the next big killer application for the Internet is going to be education. Education over the Internet is going to be so big it is going to make email usage look like a rounding error" in terms of the Internet capacity it will consume (qtd. in [5]). Chambers has in mind mostly e-learning in industry, but he also includes higher education.

The most compelling reason to believe that online education is a substantial part of the higher education of the future is that the teaching is rewarding, and the students who commit to it are enthusiastic as well. I am always glad when the course schedule enables me to teach an online class. The students stretch me intellectually and experientially, the class meetings are intense and exciting, and the relationships that develop feed the sense of doing something worthwhile. The students raise the bar of achievement in the graduate classes. In my career of 20+ years, online teaching is one of the experiences that has best energized me and made me think in terms of potential for the future rather than yield comfortably to repetition of the past. My Texas Tech colleagues in technical communication and rhetoric have similar responses. We like this teaching. As the student comments in the previous section reveal, they find the courses rigorous and interesting, not just convenient.

Yet this kind of response on the part of the faculty and students is not a certain one. Some online teaching fails; some teachers would prefer not to repeat their experiences. Likewise, some students will commit to one or two courses and abandon online education. There is no formula for a happy outcome, just as there is no one model of online learning that fits all situations. Strategic planning, with careful consideration of the students and their needs, pedagogical goals and methods, and administrative options, as well as an emphasis on educational quality dominating concerns for costs and technology, can increase the chances of success and sustainability.

REFERENCES

1. S. Blythe, Designing Online Courses: User-Centered Practices, *Computers and Composition, 18,* pp. 329–346, 2001.
2. G. Hillocks, *Ways of Thinking, Ways of Teaching,* Teachers College Press, New York, 1999.
3. J. R. Holmevik and C. Haynes, *MOOniversity: A Student's Guide to Online Learning Environments,* Allyn & Bacon, Boston, 2000.
4. R. R. Johnson, *User Centered Technology: A Rhetorical Theory for Computers and Other Mundane Artifacts,* SUNY Press, Albany, 1998.
5. T. L. Friedman, Foreign Affairs; Next, It's E-ducation, *New York Times,* November 17, 1999, www.nytimes.org.

SECTION 2

How Do We Create Interactive, Pedagogically Sound Online Courses and Classroom Communities?

CHAPTER 5

Changing Roles for Online Teachers of Technical Communication

Nancy W. Coppola

In 1994, when I developed and offered my first course in distance learning, *Advanced Professional and Technical Communication,* I had the benefit of basic training and instructional technology survival skills offered by New Jersey Institute of Technology's (NJIT) media services group and learning network practitioners. We spent many hours videotaping lectures to develop content for this technical communication graduate course. Also, I had the advantage of a residential asynchronous learning network called Virtual Classroom® developed by the NJIT Hiltz-Turoff research group in 1986. With good support and content, I felt ready and eager to take the course online. The technology issues were challenging, and the amount of time to maintain the course was prodigious, as many experienced online teachers had warned. However, as the semester progressed, I was unexpectedly frustrated by my inability to transition my face-to-face teaching presence into the online environment. I found myself in a position where I needed to change my teaching style, and I did not know how to do that. I was not alone. A colleague, who began teaching technical communication online during the same period, described the change in persona: "I felt that a lot of my skills, the things I would traditionally rely on, I didn't have anymore. I don't have my body language; I use a lot of body language. So you use a lot of exclamation points. But smiley faces are not my thing. It took awhile, thinking about all that good stuff and wondering, how do I get that back?"

How do faculty roles change in online teaching? How do we translate "all that good stuff" to the virtual classroom? How can we prepare for the inevitable feeling of displacement that comes from transition to online teaching? Fortunately, since those early days of distance learning, researchers have looked at the changing roles of online professors. So that teachers may understand role changes as they move their courses online, this chapter will present information on role theory and distance learning as well as research on the changing nature of online faculty roles.

ROLE THEORY AND DISTANCE LEARNING

We all play many roles in our lives, and these roles change over time. Roles are concerned with the expected behavior of a person in a particular social status or position within a social system. We all arrive at higher education with an understanding of clearly defined roles that have been formed by our common educational background as students and/or teachers. Role theory, which offers perspectives from social psychology, sociology, and anthropology, gives us a framework for understanding these behaviors and characteristics. Organizational role theory purports that role expectations are developed through a combination of organizational and individual factors [1]. When the organizational context of instruction shifts dramatically, as it does in the change from the traditional classroom to the online classroom, then we should expect shifts in role enactment from the instructor. When roles change, the instructor must cope with shifts in self-perception and thus must find strategies for coping with the situation [2].

A different body of research has demonstrated that distance learning is not a distinct learning process [3]. Those factors (knowledge, attitudes, course design, communication, and interaction) that influence learning in the traditional classroom are present in the online distance-learning situation. However, the media for transmission of these factors change from direct contact to contact via telecommunication or the Internet. Given this fundamental change, we need to understand how professors modify their various teaching roles to accommodate the new medium and how these modifications are expressed.

A review of research suggests roles that are enacted by instructors in face-to-face settings [4-6]. Among the many roles mentioned are cognitive role (conveying content knowledge), affective role (influencing the relationships between students, the instructor, and the classroom atmosphere), disciplinary role (enforcing policies, resolving conflicts, and controlling student behavior), managing role (organizing, planning, and setting up the course), evaluative role (measuring learning outcomes), performing role (presenting material in a dynamic manner), facilitator role (promoting active student learning), gate-keeper role (setting standards and evaluating progress), and boundary-spanner role (making connections between disciplines). Underlying the enactment of all roles is the critical factor of communication. In the traditional classroom, the instructor has both verbal and non-verbal communication available to enact the various roles. The shift to online learning changes the nature of verbal communication from spoken to written and diminishes available paralinguistic cues, as other authors in this section will discuss. To the extent that some of the roles require affective expression, the diminution of non-verbal communication could prove problematic to enacting the affective role. Given so fundamental a change in communication medium, how do these roles get enacted, do all get enacted, and does the priority attached to any of the roles change?

REVIEW OF RESEARCH IN ONLINE
TEACHING ROLES

Henrietta Nickels Shirk identifies new roles for technical communicators that are analogous to the role changes described in this chapter. As Shirk points out, "Changes in technology require concomitant role changes for technical communicators whose job it is to assist users of technology in using technology" [7, p. 361]. We might consider that observation in light of teaching technical communication with new technologies as well. Technology changes our teaching.

While there are quite a few studies about students' response to online courses, relatively little research has been published that documents exactly how the technology changes the teaching process and the role of the university faculty member. An earlier in-depth study of an online course at NJIT that includes observations based on faculty experiences is the Hiltz study of the late 1980s implementation of the Virtual Classroom® in a variety of courses [8]. This included a chapter on faculty experiences and perspectives, based on participant observation and on standard post-course reports completed by six faculty members. All except one of the six were enthusiastic volunteers who were early adopters of what was then a new technological innovation.

As so often happens in times of technological innovation, the new technology is framed in terms of its predecessor. Examples of past technological innovation that extended the more familiar traditions are automobiles that first resembled horse-drawn carriages and early photography that reflected the conventions of painting. Thus, the teacher's role in brick-and-mortar classrooms is often the analog for describing the online role. Gillette reminds teachers of technical writing that, of the pedagogical shifts they will make, they are architects and builders first, teachers second, "When teaching online, you step into the multi-faceted, continually shifting roles of architect, building administrator, departmental secretary, postal worker, custodian, security officers, grounds keeper, equipment purchasing officer, maintenance supervisor, and overall technical ombudsman" [9, p. 25]. Anderson, Rourke, Garrison, and Archer also use an architectural metaphor as they compare the teaching roles in a "pioneering" virtual learning environment with those of an earlier pioneer era [10, p. 2]. They liken the online teacher to the teacher in the one-room school who provided several functions, including instructing, maintaining the facility, and creating a community of learners who could teach one another when the teacher's presence could not accommodate all students at once.

We often hear the change in instruction characterized as moving from the "Sage on the Stage" to the "Guide on the Side" [11]. This analogy sets up an unfair comparison that suggests onsite teachers stand at a podium in front of a class and deliver lectures, while online teachers need only sit on the sidelines and wait for the miracle of learning to take place. Of course, faculty who are accustomed to being performers in the classroom will need to adjust their role expectations and behaviors to suit a different instructional environment. Other researchers, who report on their own experiences with online teaching, described their role shift from facilitators of student acquisition of knowledge to moderators of student activity in collaborative groups [12]. Lang and Breuch, in this volume, make similar arguments about changing teaching style to facilitate students' self-directed learning.

Researchers who have investigated the changing roles of teachers working in virtual classrooms generally assert that teachers have three main roles. Anderson et al. assess the teaching role as teaching presence in online courses that use text-based computer conferencing [10, p. 2]. These researchers identify indicators for the three teaching roles by summarizing the literature and then analyzing computer conference transcripts for two online graduate university courses. Using content analysis, the researchers coded message units in the conferences. Zane Berge presents collected practical experience in his work that describes the roles and functions of the online instructor in computer conferencing [13, p. 22]. Berge, who has long been researching and writing about teaching with new technologies, believes that, regardless of the level of technology, the three teaching roles must be enacted for successful learning. Coppola, Hiltz, and Rotter designed, conducted, transcribed, and coded 20 semi-structured interviews with 14 male and female professors who have prepared and delivered at least one online course [14, 15]. The courses ranged from undergraduate to graduate courses in computer science, engineering, humanities, social sciences, and information systems. The researchers captured faculty observations about how faculty perceive the teaching and learning process to have been altered by using online communication as the primary mode of communication with their students. Table 1, Onsite and Online Teaching Roles, summarizes the three main roles identified by these researchers; these roles are cognitive or pedagogical, affective or social, and managerial or organizational.

Cognitive Roles in Online Teaching

The primary role of the teacher in any context is to construct an environment whereby students gain content knowledge. Teachers provide a framework for interaction with content that allows students to analyze, synthesize, and evaluate. How do teachers provide this intellectual leadership online?

Berge categorizes the cognitive role as the pedagogical role and the instructor as moderator [13]. Berge reports that the pedagogical role requires the moderator to use questions and probes for student responses that focus discussions on critical concepts, principles, and skills. By modeling cognitive processes,

Table 1. Onsite and Online Teaching Roles

Onsite	Online		
	Berge	Anderson et al.	Coppola et al.
Cognitive	Pedagogical	Direct instruction	Cognitive
Affective	Social	Facilitating discourse	Affective
Managerial	Managerial	Instructional design and organization	Managerial
	Technical		

instructors can encourage reflection about thinking as well as promote cooperation and teamwork.

Anderson et al., who refer to the cognitive role as direct instruction, believe that a subject matter expert, not a moderator, should lead online learning [10, p. 7]. They found that providing intellectual leadership in online teaching is accomplished through these tasks: present content/questions; focus the discussion on specific issues; summarize the discussion; confirm understanding through assessment and explanatory feedback; diagnose misconceptions; inject knowledge from diverse sources; and respond to technical concerns.

Coppola et al. report on the cognitive aspect of instruction that deals with mental processes pertaining to perception, learning, information storage, memory, thinking, and problem solving [16, p. 176]. Faculty in this study reported that they learned from student's experiences and that online learning became more obviously a two-way process. Online instructors, who engage in interactive discussions, observed that they were more reflective and deliberate in crafting their questions and responses to questions.

In discussing the mental manipulation of information, instructors mentioned that online teaching also helped extend students' ability to analyze information because instructors could easily guide students to other sources of information on the Web to assist in their analyses. One instructor commented:

> I tell them what they should be doing, just to keep them on track. And then I give them things to think about. So for leadership, I'll ask them to think about what a transformational leader is, is there a moral dimension to leadership, if there is what is it or is it just about making money and looking good in Forbes. I give them four or five questions and I just throw them out. Sometimes they answer them and sometimes they don't. Sometimes they bring up other issues. But I do require that the bulk, not all of it, but the majority of the discussion deal with the topic for the week. I get an awful lot of stuff from their personal experiences, their worklives [16, p. 177].

lty in this study also noted the increased flow of questions from students. In an onsite class, when a question is asked, only a few students may respond. Ideally, everyone in the onsite class would engage in mental rehearsal even though the instructor has no clue whether all students attempted an answer. However, in the online course, all students are frequently required to respond. This added effort helps students engage in rehearsing information and retrieving information. The more actively information is processed, the more connections it makes to other information and the better it is stored. Faculty frequently spoke of being more reflective or carefully crafting their own responses and also mentioned the increased flow of questions from students. Several devised exercises to assist students in reflecting on material they were assigned.

Affective Roles in Online Teaching

In carrying out tasks related to online pedagogy, one instructor role deals with the affective domain. The affective role, which includes developing online community and social presence, is especially important in a virtual classroom where the medium for communication is textual. In fact, concern for instructors' ability to support social process in an online environment goes back to Daft and Lengle, whose work on organizational communication showed that electronic communication was "information lean" and could not provide for the facial expressions and spontaneity needed for complex communication [17]. The media richness theory predicts that computer-mediated communication loses its socio-emotional context.

Berge describes the affective category in terms of facilitating social activities and a friendly environment [13]. According to Berge, the social role suggests promoting human relationships, developing group cohesiveness, maintaining the group as a unit, and helping members to work together in a mutual cause. He sees this changing role as lessening isolation for instructors who move from being the solitary teacher to a member of a learning team.

Anderson et al. expand the social or affective role from facilitating a friendly environment to facilitating social discourse that creates a positive learning environment [10, p. 6]. These researchers describe the instructor's role in facilitating discourse with the following tasks: identifying areas of agreement/disagreement; seeking to reach consensus/understanding; encouraging, acknowledging, or reinforcing student contributions; setting climate for learning; drawing in participants, prompting discussion; and assessing the efficacy of the process. Anderson et al. stress that the instructor's role here differs from facilitating social activities, such as chat rooms; rather, the teacher's role is to promote social processes that stimulate learning.

Coppola et al. were particularly interested in learning how faculty members were coping with this emotionally lean communication channel [16, p. 178]. Faculty reported in their interviews that their affective role changed in terms of non-verbal communication, intimacy, and energy/humor. They noted the absence of non-verbal cues, such as facial expressions, eye contact, voice qualities, and body movement that are used in the traditional classroom to support and encourage students on both conscious and unconscious levels. For example, one faculty member said, "When you and I are talking face-to-face, the manner, the way we go about discussing things, how we say things, how we look each other in the eye, how we gauge things that we say based on how you react to what I said. . . . If I get the impression that you are uncomfortable I may adjust and so on. This isn't there with the keyboard" [16, p. 179]. In spite of the lack of non-verbal expression, faculty found that their relationship with the students online was more intimate, more connected: "I have more of a sense of some of the issues and problems that students face in their work lives. They tell me about it in VC [Virtual Classroom]. They are having all these problems in work and all these stresses in their lives. They don't tell me about it in the classroom for obvious reasons. I've become more sensitive to some of the issues they face" [16, p. 179].

Faculty members also noted that their interactions were characterized by more formality and less humor. But they commented that they were trying to find new tools to show energy and humor, as illustrated by this quote: "I'm more reserved online. I don't know why. In the classroom I tend to be energetic and I use humor a lot. I use energy a lot. Online, I tend to be more reflective and introspective. It has driven me to be more intellectual, to write well-crafted answers, to ask better questions, to think more abstractly and to think about the total implication" [16, p. 180].

However we describe and explain the affective role, students expect the online teacher to facilitate community learning, and they recognize when the role is missing. In a comparison of two online graduate courses, Tangri analyzes the facilitator's role of teaching presence in terms of Desmond Keegan's "reintegration of teaching acts" in distance learning [18]. Keegan reminds us that interactive communication between instructor and student is a key tool for reintegrating the learning experiences for students [19]. In describing the class in which complex learning did not take place, Tangri writes: "The instructor's own comments about the class discussions, her encouragement to work together, would have made the XHTML class more interesting and educative. There were so many instances when my questions went unanswered. One had to simply wait for a response, which didn't come sometimes." Similarly, in her chapter in this volume, Lang describes a situation in which some discussions in her graduate seminar were left open-ended, rather than neatly closed.

Managerial Roles in Online Teaching

Cascio, describing challenges for managers of the virtual workplace, notes that managers will need better supervisory skills for the online environment [20]. In a parallel fashion, research suggests professors using the virtual classroom will need more attenuated managerial skills, including communication, organization, and motivation. Collis et al. define management tasks as the activities of the instructor outside of content-specific aspects of a course [12]. The managerial role encompasses all class and course management and includes course planning, organizing, leading, and controlling. Course planning deals with the effort involved in getting the course online. Organizing deals with establishing relationships between the instructor and others in administration, between students and the instructor, and among students so that course goals can be achieved. Leading deals with instructor behaviors that reflect motivation and coordination of students, and controlling deals with monitoring and evaluating student learning outcomes. The management role is one that is most widely described as requiring substantially more time and effort than in classroom-based teaching [12].

Berge describes the managerial role as organizational, procedural, and administrative. The tasks for this role include setting the teaching agenda by defining the objectives of the discussion, the timetable, procedural rules, and decision-making norms. Berge advises online instructors to have a high profile in the interactive conferences: "Managing the interactions with strong leadership and direction is considered a sine qua non of successful conferencing" [13, pp. 23-24].

Anderson et al. define the managerial role as design and organization, a role that is more extensive and time consuming than its analogous role in onsite teaching [10, p. 5]. They note that building a course in digital form requires teachers to plan ahead and predict the process, structure, evaluation, and interaction components of the course. The responsibilities for the management role include setting curriculum, designing methods, establishing time parameters, utilizing the medium effectively, and establishing "netiquette."

Coppola et al. report that faculty found they had to plan and structure a course for online delivery much more tightly than for classroom-based courses [16, p. 180]. They spent a great deal of time gathering, organizing, and digitizing materials. Faculty needed to manage the path of students into the online classroom and then through the content. In addition, instructors needed to interact with other administrative units such as instructional technology and the distance learning office. These authors concur with Berge on the importance of leading discussion. Faculty reported that they monitored student progress by being online frequently to answer student questions and to guide them in the right direction regarding assignments. Addressing the time spent online, one faculty member noted:

> It is still much more time then I ever spent in a classroom, obviously. . . .
> Managing the discussion will take time, somewhere from 3 to 6 hours a week,
> where with a normal classroom, it will take a hour. With a normal classroom
> you have a discussion and it's over. But if you're monitoring people and
> keeping track of how many comments they do and deciding which ones
> you want to answer and deciding which ones you want other people to
> answer, to keep track of that would take three or four hours a week. . . In
> a traditional classroom it is an hour. Plus the fact that you were "expected"

to be on-line for an hour a day. Although I didn't do it on weekends, I was there four or five days a week . . . [16, p. 181].

In a metacognitive way, faculty in the Coppola et al. study described their teaching persona and were able to articulate the stance they take, the sense of acting, or mask they wear in teaching, as being differentiated in online and face-to-face modes. They characterized the differences in this overall teaching persona primarily in four ways: formality, Socratic method, accessibility, and authority. The most frequent response characterizing change in teaching style was formality (11 times). Formality was interpreted as relating to: a) precision; b) intimacy; and c) lack of humor. Precision was described by instructors in terms of tasks such as posting specific and unchanging schedules, avoiding extemporaneous activities, and considering connotation and denotation of words when writing in the conferences. A frequently reported characterization of changes in teaching style was the increased use of the Socratic method, typified by a give and take between instructor and student with questions leading to learning.

EVOLVING ROLES IN ONLINE TEACHING

As the instructor's institution itself transforms, new faculty roles and behaviors will evolve. A key concept in role theory is role evolution, which suggests that role shifts are a process that occur over time with dynamics by which a role is adjusted and modified. But sometimes, role expectations can change quickly and dramatically. Experienced instructors in the classroom become novices online. Understanding the shift in teaching roles should assist instructors as they change classroom venues from traditional onsite to online. While universities plan expansion of eLearning by increasing bandwidth and by training the instructional staff in Web design, there has been little attention paid to changing professorial roles. Although there may be informal transmission of role information, instructors tend to get their training on the job. The information regarding professorial role enactment in an online course can be used to provide instructors with realistic expectations for ways their role behavior may change.

This chapter suggests that the roles enacted by instructors in traditional settings are also enacted in online environments, though each of these roles is transformed. This analysis shows that the specific faculty roles related to cognitive, affective, and managerial activities do change. The cognitive role, which relates to mental processes of learning, information storage, and thinking, shifts to one of deeper cognitive complexity for virtual professors. The affective role, which relates to influencing the relationships between students and the instructor and the classroom atmosphere, required instructors to find new tools to express emotion, yet they found the relationship with students more intimate. The managerial role, which deals with class and course management, requires greater attention to detail, more structure, and additional student monitoring.

Anticipating evolving overall role changes is perhaps the best advice for new teachers in online environments. One professor in the Coppola et al. study captures this evolution: "It takes time. An online professor is not born; they evolve from this and it takes a long time" [16, p. 183].

ACKNOWLEDGMENTS

I am grateful to my colleagues Naomi Rotter and Roxanne Hiltz for their contribution to the original study and to the Alfred P. Sloan Foundation for its support.

REFERENCES

1. D. Katz and R. Kahn, *The Social Psychology of Organizations,* John Wiley & Sons, New York, 1978.
2. V. L. Allen and E. van de Vliert, *Role Transitions: Explorations and Explanations,* Plenum, New York, 1984.
3. E. Kirby and M. Driscoll, *Facilitator and Students Roles and Performance in a High School Distance Education Course,* paper presented at the Annual Meeting of the Association of American Education Research Association, Chicago, Illinois, March 1997.
4. P. A. Kahlich and J. J. Dorminey, *Role Perception of Early Childhood Teachers,* paper presented at the Annual Meeting of the Association of Teacher Educators, Los Angeles, California, February 1993.
5. C. Colbeck, *It's All in How You Look at Things: Alternative Constructions of Professors' Undergraduate Education Role,* paper presented at the Annual Meeting of the Association for the Study of Higher Education, Orlando, Florida, November 1995.
6. J. I. Tallman and J. D. van Deusen, Collaborative Unit Planning: Schedule, Time and Participants, Part Three: The 1993-94 AASL/Highsmith Research Award Study, *School-Library-Media Quarterly, 23,* pp. 33-37, 1994.
7. H. N. Shirk, New Roles for Technical Communicators in the Computer Age, in *Computers and Technical Communication: Pedagogical and Programmatic Perspectives,* S. A. Selber (ed.), Greenwood Publishing, Greenwich, Connecticut, 1997.
8. S. R. Hiltz, *The Virtual Classroom: Learning Without Limits via Computer Networks,* Human-Computer Interaction Series, Ablex Publishing Corp., Norwood, New Jersey, 1994.
9. D. Gillette, Pedagogy, Architecture, and the Virtual Classroom, *Technical Communication Quarterly, 18*:1, pp. 21-36, 1999.
10. T. L. Anderson, D. R. Garrison Rourke, and W. Archer, Assessing Teacher Presence in a Computer Conferencing Context, *Journal of Ssynchronous Learning Networks, 5*:2, http://www.aln.org/alnweb/journal/Vol5_issue2, 2001.
11. N. Coppola, Sage on Stage or Mentor in MUD: Changing Roles for Teachers of Technical Communication, *INTERCOM,* January 1997.

12. B. Collis and G. G. Nijhuis, The Instructor as Manager: Time and Task, *The Internet and Higher Education, 3,* pp. 75-97, 2000.
13. Z. L. Berge, Facilitating Computer Conferencing: Recommendations from the Field, *Educational Technology, 15*:1, pp. 22-30, 1995, http://www.emoderators.com/moderators/onteach.html.
14. N. Coppola, S. R. Hiltz, and N. Rotter, *Becoming a Virtual Professor: Preliminary Results of Semi-Structured Interviews,* presentation at the Fourth International Conference on Asynchronous Learning Networks, New York, November 1998.
15. N. Coppola, S. R. Hiltz, and N. Rotter, *Becoming a Virtual Professor: Pedagogical Changes and Asynchronous Learning Networks,* presentation scheduled for the Fifth International Conference on Asynchronous Learning Networks, University of Maryland, October 1999.
16. N. Coppola, S. R. Hiltz, and N. Rotter. Becoming a Virtual Professor: Pedagogical Roles and Asynchronous Learning Networks, *Journal of Management Information Systems, 18*:4, pp.169-189, 2002.
17. R. L. Daft and R. Lengel, Organizational Information Requirements, Media Richness, and Structural Design, *Management Science, 32*, pp. 554-571, 1986.
18. A. Tangri, *Collaboration in Online Classes: Restoring Communication,* paper presented at Southwest/Texas Popular and American Culture Associations Conference, Albuquerque, New Mexico, 2002.
19. D. Keegan, Reintegration of the Teaching Acts, in *Theoretical Principles of Distance Education*, D. Keegan (ed.), Routledge, London, pp. 113-134, 1993.
20. W. F. Cascio, Managing a Virtual Workplace, *The Academy of Management Executive, 14*:2, pp. 81-90, 2000.

CHAPTER 6

Teaching Well Online with Instructional and Procedural Scaffolding

Helen M. Grady and Marjorie T. Davis

Once we have committed to begin delivering instruction or training online, we naturally begin to consider ways to translate what we do face-to-face, with a live class, to what we do in a virtual learning environment. The most significant challenges are not, in fact, choosing the technology or deciding upon content—those decisions will be constrained by a number of boundaries that will make it relatively simple to decide. What is most challenging is developing an authentic interactive learning environment online. To develop such an environment online, our chapter argues for the importance of founding online instruction on sound principles of instructional design, particularly the issue of supporting the learner in creating a virtual collaborative learning experience.

Whether we should be teaching interactively is not typically a question to technical communicators. Unlike some faculty in disciplines still wedded to the "sage on the stage" model, most technical communication faculty are grounded in the theories and practice generally known as constructivism. Jone Rymer said it well a number of years ago: "[W]e are transforming our classrooms into communities. Instead of attempting to transmit knowledge to students, we are inviting them to become co-learners with us" [1, p. 180]. Nearly everything we technical communicators teach is grounded in a strong sense of community: document design, writing, speaking, audience analysis, communication purpose, usability, visual communication, international communication, and instructional design. Most of us have evolved methods of teaching to bring that interactive, collaborative, people-focused commitment into the classroom in significant ways. We have studied the impact of the computer on teaching and learning [2], and we are starting to understand ways to use technology to support a collaborative learning environment. As we have moved into distance learning or online teaching, we have struggled with ways to keep the interactive, collaborative model intact. A central issue in course design is the challenge of creating a virtual environment that recreates the best qualities of face-to-face interactive teaching and learning.

Our local experience with the problem of designing interactive, collaborative learning online is gained through delivering our Master of Science degree in technical communication management (MSTCO) online since 1995-1996 at Mercer University [3]. Our population is a diverse set of graduate students primarily from the United States but also Europe and Asia. They are all practicing technical communicators with a minimum of three years' experience in the field. The program is designed to prepare them to assume leadership roles within their technical communication organizations—a very practice-based learning goal. The program is delivered primarily asynchronously via the Web, with most classes holding at least occasional synchronous meetings online. We do not assert that our model is perfect nor perfectly delivered; however, we do believe, based on student and employer feedback over the years, that we have established a valid and engaging method of creating interactive, collaborative learning environments online. Though we expect to continually refine and improve our process and our product, this chapter presents what we are currently doing to achieve our learning goals.

SCAFFOLDING FOR LEARNERS

Face-to-face teaching involves a number of strategies to encourage the process of learning. For example, watching and reacting to what we see students doing as they learn creates a responsive, student-centered style of teaching that looks for the "teachable moment"—that time and place where learners are ready to leap from one stage of cognitive mastery to another [4]. What teachers do to promote that leaping has been called "scaffolding."

The idea of scaffolding was introduced by Wood, Bruner, and Ross [5] when referring to the kind of personal tutorial interactions that occur when an adult is coaching a child in a learning task. These interactions help the child master a task that, when attempted alone, the child cannot master. Palincsar's [6] seminal work on scaffolding included the notion of reciprocal teaching, in which the teacher initially models and guides the students in acquiring cognitive strategies. Reciprocal teaching occurs when a teacher presents a skill, strategy, or process; shows students how to achieve it; and then guides the students as they attempt it. The scaffolding is gradually withdrawn as the student becomes more competent with the task at hand.

Dialogue is a critical element in Palincsar's scaffolding metaphor. As noted by Wertsch [cited in Palincsar]:

> When children engage in problem solving, they display the kind of behaviors that are characteristic of dialogue, posing and responding to their own questions, essentially internalizing the dialogue they have experienced in the initial stages of problem solving when they are collaborating with a more expert individual. It is this dialog, occurring with initial instruction regarding the strategy, that enables learners to participate in strategic activity even though they may not fully understand the activity and would most certainly not be able to exercise the strategy independently [6, p. 75].

This type of scaffolded instruction is by its very nature interactive, with the student and teacher actively involved in the joint completion of a task.

In other words, scaffolding can be defined as those strategies that a teacher uses to help learners span a cognitive gap or leap a learning hurdle. (See also Carter & Rickly's chapter following this one.) These strategies evolve as the teacher watches and listens closely to what the learner is doing. In these early studies, scaffolding occurred primarily in oral, face-to-face learning situations. In traditional classroom interactions, scaffolding may include modeling behaviors, coaching and prompting, thinking out loud, dialogue with questions and answers, planned and spontaneous discussions, and so forth—any device that structures assistance to help the learner bridge a cognitive gap.

Some recent studies have focused on other forms of scaffolding, such as non-verbal or textual scaffolding [7]. Other studies have examined procedural scaffolding, such as written guidelines that help learners manage their learning process, as well as scaffolds embedded in the computer technology, such as pull-down menus that act as metacognitive tools [8]. Using technology in this way is beginning to uncover both the extraordinary challenge and the powerful potential for creating scaffolding in other ways than in face-to-face teaching.

Exploring the Scaffolding Metaphor

If we think of what we are building when we design online instruction, we can see it as a body of shared knowledge (including both theory and practice). We can begin to envision the purpose of scaffolding in a way that can help us develop strategies. Consider, for example, all the uses for scaffolding in constructing a building:

- To hold pieces together; to lay out the boundaries true and straight;
- To support the structure while it is being built;
- To support the workers, especially in the early or difficult stages of the project; and
- To raise workers up so that they can reach high places.

The scaffolding is never the important part of the building—it is removed when no longer needed. While in place, however, it is critical to the strength and integrity of the construction. It's this image of a structural support system that provides help, strength, assistance, protection, guidance, and capability to the learning community as it works to build the shared knowledge that is the online course.

Scaffolding Cues and Their Expression

Providing scaffolding in a face-to-face, personal classroom is both like and different from providing scaffolding for distance learners in online teaching environments. We believe that scaffolding involves four major types of structure and cues: verbal, visual, textual, and procedural. Table 1 shows a comparison of how these types of structure and cues work in a face-to-face and an online classroom.

As Table 1 (pages 106-107) shows, when we teach students who are not physically present, we are forced to adapt to an environment where face-to-face interaction is usually absent. A different kind of scaffolding must thus be constructed to replace the traditional face-to-face expressions we take so much for granted if we are to be successful in constructing an interactive, collaborative learning environment for distance learners. This new form of scaffolding consists of two elements: 1) instructional scaffolding to facilitate the interactive nature of teaching and learning described in Palincsar's metaphor; and 2) procedural scaffolding that helps students manage the online learning environment.

INSTRUCTIONAL SCAFFOLDING FOR ONLINE COURSES

Historically, instructional design models have been used as the underlying theory to help us develop face-to-face instruction, either in a traditional educational classroom or for training purposes. Instructional designers are now struggling with how to apply these models to a whole new genre of instruction—online education and training. It is not our intention here to review these instructional design models, but rather to look at special design considerations related to what we are calling scaffolding for interactive online learning environments.

However, we feel it would be useful to briefly review the instructional design process to provide the context for the first part of this chapter. Essentially, instructional designers must answer three questions:

1. Where are we going? (learner and task analysis);
2. How will we get there? (instructional strategy and medium); and
3. How will we know we have arrived? (assessment and evaluation) [10].

During the learner and task analysis phase, designers gather information about the students and the learning tasks, determining what the students should be able to know or do when they finish the tasks [11, 12]. To answer the question "How will we get there?" designers evaluate what must be taught, in what order, how to best teach it, and what media are most appropriate [13, 14]. In the last phase, designers select the assessment tools to determine how well the students learned and what changes need to be made before teaching the course again [15]. These three phases are not actually separate and linear, but rather looping and interactive. The design of instruction is iterative, just as in most other kinds of design. For the purposes of this discussion, however, we will take each of these three phases in order to show how they apply to online courses and how instructors can build scaffolds in these phases to better support their students' learning.

Learner and Task Analysis

Before beginning to design any course, instructors should conduct a learner analysis to collect data about who will be taking the course. While this may seem self-evident to technical communicators who are familiar with the concept of audience analysis, it is an important step that is often overlooked by many instructors. This analysis is similar for both traditional and online classes but may be more difficult for online classes due to the diverse nature of students enrolled in these classes. (Angela Eaton's chapter in Section 1 provides an insightful analysis of the types of students who enroll in online technical communication courses.)

In our MSTCO program, for example, we know our students are full-time working professionals who have an average of 5-10 years of experience. They are in low-to-middle management positions in their organizations and are enrolled in the program with the expectation that completing it will enable them to move to a higher position within their organization. All students have at least a bachelor's degree and are an average age of 35.

Since our students are adults, the characteristics of andragogy (adult learning) [16] shape how we design the instruction. For example, adult learners are usually highly motivated, self-directed, and independent learners; seek courses that are relevant to their personal/professional goals; want clearly specified course goals; bring extensive experience to the classroom and expect to participate in the learning process; and must be able to complete their learning tasks in the small "chunks" of free time between their professional and personal obligations.

What design implications are driven by these characteristics of our student population? We know we will have to have clear learning goals and objectives, the course must be organized into discrete units that can be completed in a short amount of time, the assignments must be authentic and relevant to the students' work, and the learning environment will be most effective if it is collaborative with carefully designed mechanisms for student input and feedback. Many of these design implications can be addressed through carefully laid scaffolding.

An important part of learner and task analysis is identifying the learning goals and outcomes for the course, i.e., what the instructor expects the students to be able to do or know by the time they finish the course. In the traditional class-room, instructors often include the overall learning outcomes on their syllabi. For

Table 1. Scaffolding in the Classroom

Scaffolding Cues	Expressing in Teaching Environments	
	Face-to-face	Online
Verbal (Oral)		
Oral feedback—instructor to students; student to student; student to instructor	Dialog, discussion between and among present participants	Absent unless in telephone conferences or 2-way Interactive Compressed Video (ICV) exchanges
Clarification of instructions, giving examples	Presentation, dialog, question-answer	Absent unless in telephone conferences or ICV exchanges
Social interactions, personal greetings	Chatting before and after class, personal exchanges	Absent unless in telephone conferences or ICV exchanges
Tone of voice, humor, personality expressed orally and spontaneously	Conversations, presentations, dialog	Absent unless in telephone conferences or 2-way ICV exchanges (where nuances are lost)
Visual		
Non-verbal body language	Immediately perceived by visual means	Absent unless in 2-way ICV exchanges (where resolution and gaps interfere)
Showing of physical objects	Perceived visually; can be manipulated, touched, passed around	Visual representations (lose dimensionality, texture, weight, etc.)
Use of graphic elements	Limited by capacity to show in classroom setting (lighting, computer projection, etc.)	Unlimited in theory, but may be limited due to download time and student equipment.
Facial expressions, reactions of instructor and other students	Perceived immediately, depending upon where students are sitting	Usually absent unless in ICV; limited to the views chosen by operator

Textual

Handouts such as syllabus, instructions, etc.	Unlimited in theory, but usually constrained by copy costs	Unlimited in theory, but constrained by online readability
Instructor's written comments, corrections	Received individually on own papers	Received individually through embedded comments
Student produces exams, papers, quizzes, homework	Received on paper, usually (though online sometimes)	Received online; information may be captured as document, database entries, etc.

Procedural

Timeframes for class interactions	Discrete time limits (50-75" classes); synchronous	Asynchronous time with no prescribed limits
Environmental constraints	Students in same or similar physical classroom	Environment unique to each student
Course sequencing	Linear, structured by length of classes and prescribed calendar intervals	Nonlinear; may appear simultaneously if not structured by calendar
Information to be mastered	Textbook(s) as core information, supplemented by readings (paper or electronic), lectures	Information may reside in multiple online sources accessible simultaneously
Methods of class discussions	May be student centered, but usually instructor controlled, limit of class time	Chat rooms, listservs, threaded discussion with no time limits; may be moderated by instructor
Who students are and what they are to do	More homogeneous population (age, background) due to geographical limits; prototype of traditional group class led by teacher	Diverse due to geographical freedom; prototype may be individual learning alone

example, our school requires each syllabus to include the words "Upon completion of this course, the student will be able to" followed by a list of the learning outcomes. Specific learning objectives for each class session are sometimes, but not always, stated verbally at the beginning of the class, and often in a very informal manner. These verbally stated learning objectives must be translated into written form for online courses, not only because they identify the skills and knowledge the student must master but because they provide the rationale for the course activities. Not providing online students with clearly written learning objectives is equivalent to asking them to board a bus, not knowing where it is going, and telling them, "Trust me, you'll like it when you get there." Students physically present in the classroom and operating under the teacher-directed paradigm probably are more accepting of this lack of stated objectives than are adults learning at a distance; distance learning students, as our own teaching experiences and Eaton's survey demonstrate, want to know explicitly what they will be learning as well as the benefits of learning activities.

Instructional Strategy and Medium

Teaching online requires course designers to implement a much more rigorous instructional design process than is required for face-to-face instruction. Prior to starting the course, online course designers must write the learning outcomes and learning objectives and define the sequence of instructional events to reach those outcomes for the entire course. In terms of our scaffolding metaphor, this planning is analogous to building the framework for each room (instructional objectives), arranging the rooms into floors (grouping objectives from lowest to highest cognitive level), creating a pathway from room to room and floor to floor (sequencing objectives), defining the activities that occur within each room (instructional events), and making this entire structure visible to the students (through the design of the "physical" environment). Simply uploading all the course materials and handouts for a traditional course without a framework that defines how all the pieces of the course are related results in overwhelming confusion for the students.

Regardless of their teaching environment, all instructors must decide what content to include in their courses, how to best present that content, how much material to include in each lesson, and how to sequence the instruction. Many excellent textbooks and articles contain information on this, the instructional strategy phase of the design process. While the process is similar for traditional and online courses, online course designers have the added task of making these design decisions explicit because they provide the scaffolding for the rooms and floors of the course being built. In this next section, we discuss some of these design decisions and how we make them explicit in our online course's syllabus, instructional unit design, discussion of assignments and deliverables, and course environment design.

The Syllabus

In our MSTCO program, we use the syllabus to provide the framework or scaffolding for the entire course (building). For example, a typical syllabus used in a face-to-face course answers questions, identifying course goals and objectives, the instructor, the reading and assignments schedule, and course requirements.

Unlike a static, hard-copy syllabus that is normally handed out on the first day of the traditional face-to-face class, the online syllabus takes advantage of the features of the Web. The various elements of the syllabus contain links to all the learning events, activities, and assignments that constitute the course. Following these links provides pathways to the various rooms and floors that constitute the course. Additionally, the syllabus is instantly revisable to allow for more detail and explanation, updating of schedules, and adapting to student feedback as the course progresses. With its clearly marked links and connections to other parts of the online course, the syllabus becomes a kind of scaffold that works as a blueprint or map for students to follow from the course's beginning until its end. In addition to this mapping scaffold, the syllabus also contains sections that further support student learning.

Course introduction. In our syllabi, the introduction (what is this course all about?) and the instructional goals and objectives define for the student the shape of the building. It is important to provide more content and explanation in an online course in order to replace the natural interactions and explanations that occur in a face-to-face class. The sample introduction in Figure 1 is from a course titled Instructional Design. It includes the rationale for the course, forecasts the course content, previews the assignments, and explains why the course is relevant to our MSTCO students.

This course was developed in response to a growing awareness of the need for instructional design in education and training. Due to the explosion of information and technology in today's workplace, many companies are investing significantly in training and professional development of their employees. The course was designed to introduce you to the process of systematic instructional design, which includes analyzing learners, contexts, and instructional tasks; generating and sequencing learning goals and objectives; determining assessment methods; developing instructional strategies; and planning formative and summative evaluations. You will design a unit of instruction specifically for your organization by applying this process. Ultimately, a better understanding of the instructional design process will help you design, manage, or evaluate the training and professional development activities in your company.

Figure 1. Online syllabus introduction.

Overall goal and learning objectives. Drawn from the learner and task analysis phases, the instructional goals and objectives for this course include one learning outcome, which is "to design a unit of instruction by applying systematic design, tools, techniques, and procedures," and five general learning objectives, each of which has four to six specific objectives (see Figure 2 for the goal and sample objectives).

Course schedule. Within the context of the scaffolding metaphor, instructors need to provide several pathways for students to navigate from room to room and floor to floor. Another tool we have found useful is the course schedule, which is a pivotal element in the syllabus. The schedule provides an overview of all the instructional events and activities for the course, arranged in chunks of time—usually weekly (see Figure 3). Using hyperlinks, students can access each of the instructional units, their assignments, additional resources, and chat transcripts, which are posted within 24 hours of each chat session. The schedule is updated weekly, and changes to assignments or due dates are highlighted in a different color.

Instructional Unit Design

Another significant design decision that must be made for online courses is how to "chunk" the instructional content and activities. In traditional classrooms, this decision is profoundly influenced by the length of the class period, usually 50 to 75 minutes. However, there are no such constraints in an online class. Instructors must analyze the instructional activities associated with each learning objective and cluster these activities into logical instructional units. It has been

---

Goal: To design a unit of instruction by applying systematic design tools, techniques, and procedures.

Objectives:
1.0 Define your educational philosophy by examining your personal assumptions related to teaching and learning.
2.0 Analyze an instructional situation.
    2.1 Conduct a context analysis of an instructional scenario in your organization.
    2.2 Conduct a learner analysis to identify key characteristics of the potential target audience.
    2.3 Prepare an instructional goal statement.
    2.4 Identify key components of the instructional goal by performing an information processing analysis.

Figure 2. Sample learning goal and two of its objectives.

Week	Topic	Readings	Assignments
1/7-14	Unit 1 Intro to ID	Chapter 1 & Additional Readings	Post response to discussion question Online chat — M, 1/14; transcript
1/15-21	Unit 2 Educational Philosophies & Learning Theories	Chapter 2	Post assignment 1 Post peer reviews Provide link to your homepage Online chat — M, 1/21; transcript

Figure 3. Course schedule. Hyperlinks are underlined.

our experience that we usually underestimate the amount of time it takes students to complete a unit, particularly in a collaborative learning environment where students help shape and build the course content. This is where we find the idea of the instructional unit, or "room" to be helpful. Each unit is shaped by the learning objectives and contains specific instructional events. However, we often find that we modify these units, both in terms of content and activities, based on the input of our students. (Eaton's survey of online students corroborates our findings and points to the importance of formative feedback to determine how much time students are actually spending on assignments. For more information on using formative assessment, see Cargile Cook and Grant-Davie's chapter in Section 3.)

In our MSTCO program, we typically organize a 15-week semester course into 15 instructional units. A typical instructional unit for the Instructional Design course is shown in Figure 4. The overview of this instructional unit shows the relationship of the unit to the complete learning module on learning strategies, which encompassed a total of six instructional units. These six units had an overarching learning outcome, which was defined in the syllabus and in the assignments that related to that outcome. The overview also contains scaffolds or assistance to help students focus on the important concepts, to provide prompts to guide learning activities, and to relate what is being learned to their professional or personal interests.

Note that smaller, specific learning objectives for the instructional unit are clearly defined, as are the procedures for completing the various instructional events, such as the assignment, discussion board, and chat. Links to the assignment and discussion board provide additional help in navigating.

Assignments and Deliverables

Finally, instructors must decide on the type of assignments and deliverables they will use to assess student learning. Because our program has practice-based learning goals, assignments are project-based and often team-based. Each

Topic: Cognitive and Psychomotor Learning Strategies
Overview: This week we will concentrate on the final two learning strategies: cognitive and psychomotor.
- verbal information (declarative knowledge)
- intellectual skills (procedural knowledge)
  - discriminations
  - concepts (concrete and defined)
  - principles (relational rules)
  - problem solving (higher order rules)
  - procedures (procedural rules)
- cognitive strategies (conditional knowledge)
  - organizing
  - elaborating
  - rehearsing
  - monitoring comprehension
- attitudes
- psychomotor skills

Learning how to learn is the goal of cognitive learning strategies. If you were lucky as a student, you had a teacher who explicitly taught you some of these learning strategies. Do you remember any of them? Do you currently practice any of the learning strategies discussed in Chapter 13? If you are a parent, talk to your children about *how* they are learning, not *what* they are learning. You might be surprised by what they tell you. Obviously, the learner's level of cognitive development has a direct impact on which cognitive learning strategy is being used or being taught, particularly in the area of metacognition (see article by Hacker for more information on this intriguing topic). Note that journaling is one metacognitive tool. Give some thought as to how you could incorporate a cognitive learning strategy into your instructional unit. The important concept to understand about psychomotor skill learning is that it involves learning new muscular movements, which have a cognitive basis (usually a procedural rule). Figures 15.1 (p. 274) and 15.3 (p. 276) are useful summaries of elements in psychomotor skill learning.

Learning Objectives:
- Define cognitive learning
- Describe specific strategies for teaching cognitive learning
- Given a cognitive learning objective, design strategy plans for that objective
- Define psychomotor learning
- Describe specific strategies for psychomotor learning
- Given a psychomotor learning objective, design strategy plans for that objective

Required Reading: Chapters 13 and 15
Additional Reading:
Cognitive strategy - Excerpted from Chapter 9 of Biehler/Snowman, *Psychology Applied to Teaching,* 8/e, Houghton Mifflin Co., 1997
Concept Mapping as Cognitive Learning and Assessment Tools - Jonassen et al.
Metacognition: Definitions and Empirical Foundations - Hacker, U. of Memphis
Assignment:
1. Post assignment 3.3 for peer review to the deliverables folder (you know the drill by now . . . smile).
2. Final version of 3.3 due by 4/3.
3. Designer's journal due 3/31.

Discussion Board: Post response to Unit 11 discussion question. Discussion closes 3/30.

Figure 4. A typical instruction unit design.

assignment begins with an overview describing the assignment goals, followed by specific learning objectives. Scaffolding that would normally be provided in the form of verbal directions from the instructor is replaced in the online course with more information and specific procedures for completing the assignment. This type of scaffolding supports the students by keeping them focused on the tasks to be accomplished. For example, the procedure for completing an assignment on formative evaluation plans is listed in Figure 5. (Note that in WebCT there can be hyperlinks to the named readings and student folders to provide easy and immediate navigation.)

Course Environment Design

In a brick and mortar building, the classroom environment is not usually the responsibility of the traditional classroom instructor. Teaching online, however, requires that we design and construct the "classroom" or learning space. In designing the homepage and other pages, for example, instructors must contend with issues such as page layout, color, graphics, typeface, and type size; or technical considerations such as load times, passwords, server size, procedures, and space to upload student assignments. Dealing effectively with these issues can place an enormous burden on the online instructor. In some institutions there may be staff skilled in instructional design and delivery or in programming; in others, the burden falls upon the instructor to create the space. However it gets done, though, the instructor has the ultimate responsibility to create the look, feel, and usability of the course.

---

1. Read Chapter 16.
2. Read the excerpt from Kemp, Morrison, and Ross on formative evaluation, which is adapted from D. D. Gooler (1998), Formative Evaluation Strategies for Major Instructional Development Projects. *J. Instruct. Development, 3,* 7-11.
3. Write a general formative evaluation plan using Gooler's eight-step approach.
4. Write a specific formative evaluation plan.
5. Use the grading rubrics as guidelines for important elements to include in the plans.
6. Post Assignment 4.1 or the Assignment 4, Peer Review folder.
7. Ask a fellow team member to peer review your assignment. Revise your assignment as needed, then post it to the Assignment 4.1 & 4.2, Final folder in the Student Deliverables area by 4/25.

Figure 5. Guidelines for online assessment.

The homepage is an important part of the course environment. We have designed the homepage to create automatic links to some resources outside the WebCT platform, thus making the homepage operate somewhat like a portal. The homepage for the sample MSCTO course, shown in Figure 6, organizes the various course elements so that they are easily accessible by the students.

Making use of some hierarchical design features on the homepage can help establish clear, functional navigation for the students. While course management systems include a navigation bar as a feature, they do not automatically organize the course information so as to make the course structure and content visible and useful. Creating a homepage with links to outside resources, groupings of information in content modules, and one-click access to frequently used course sections will enhance the student's ability to see how the course environment works. These strategies also allow students to access more easily instructional supports found within the syllabus, instructional units, and assignments and deliverables explanations.

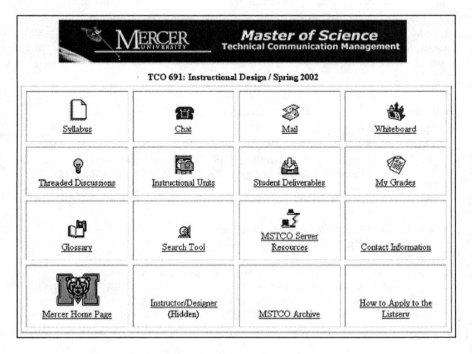

Figure 6. Online portal to course.

Assessment and Evaluation

The last phase of instructional design deals with assessing student learning, as well as evaluating the effectiveness of the instruction (both formative and summative). Formative and summative evaluations are beyond the scope of this chapter, but see Cargile Cook and Grant-Davie's chapter in Section 3. The critical task for the course designer is to create frequent feedback mechanisms so that the instructor gains a clear sense of what is happening at every step of the student's learning process. Using chats, asking for email responses, and posting feedback questions on the discussion board are all useful tools for formative and summative evaluation.

Grading online work is not very different from grading work received face to face. The primary added difficulty is in providing enough feedback and explanation so that a student, working alone without hearing the questions and answers of other students as graded assignments are handed back, will understand the evaluation of the learning. An easily transferable scaffold from the traditional to the online class is the grading rubric. It should be no surprise to technical communicators that rubrics were originally created as a means of assessing the quality of student writing [19]. Grading rubrics, unlike a scoring sheet alone, provide an explanation of performance at each level of competency. Students thus gain not only a grade but also a description of what would constitute a better, more effective effort. We continue to practice this means of authentic assessment in our online classes by using rubrics to provide feedback to the students on most assignments.

PROCEDURAL SCAFFOLDING WHEN CONDUCTING THE ONLINE COURSE

In addition to all the design efforts needed to create the course online, we must pay careful attention to creating a sense of community online. Good interactive classrooms require a personalized environment and strategies that foster sharing. In this section, we describe the important task of creating a true community of learners, sharing some of the procedural scaffolding techniques we have found to be useful. These procedural scaffolding techniques are not related specifically to *what* students will learn (course content); rather they focus on *how* students will interact and learn the course content.

Without meeting face to face, students can feel isolated and disconnected from others in the course. Establishing an effective learning community online requires intentionality and effort. We have found these tools effective in breaking the barriers of distance and invisibility.

Personal Homepages

Personal homepages create an initial support for social interactions among students, and most course management systems (such as WebCT or Blackboard) have the capability of relatively simple uploading of student homepages. We tried assigning individual homepages initially as a kind of novelty, but then became convinced that instructors and students relate much better to each other when there is a photograph and some personal information available about each student. Students are in control of how much information they wish to divulge, and access is limited to those who are enrolled in the class (unlike an open server where anyone on the Web might access it). Students universally evaluate these personal homepages as very helpful as they engage with one another.

Class Listserv and Personal Email

As everyone who has taught online can attest, there are frequent occasions when a student or the instructor needs to contact the others in the class to give or request information, share relevant discoveries, ask for clarification, and so forth. We establish a class listserv on the local Mercer server to allow for simultaneous distributions. Students have the advantage of subscribing to the listserv as many times as they wish; a number of them use their home email address, their work email, and perhaps a travel email account they can access easily when away. Instructors have the advantage of never having to keep up with all the different email addresses; once we get everyone subscribed during the first week, maintenance is not a problem. Using this class listserv, students and instructor can print out the subscriber's list as well. That way, when a student needs to contact a specific team member or resource person, personal emails can be sent only to one or a selected few class members.

Instructors should be prepared for a very heavy load of email traffic from the listserv—after all, this piece of scaffolding is replacing a great deal of the face-to-face interactions that would occur in a live classroom. Additionally, they may need to remind people how important it is to be courteous and thoughtful in using email. A few students will initially use curt and impersonal communications, and the instructor may wish to correct (privately) the affective impressions the emails are giving. Emails become the lifeline of interconnectivity, forming a large part of the trust necessary for a learning community. (See Coppola's chapter earlier in this section on establishing trust.)

Scheduled Online Chats

Though it is certainly possible to have no synchronous activity, we have discovered that weekly Web chats provide an important part of the scaffolding for online classes. We have developed the following useful guidelines for making Web chats an effective, powerful part of the learning community.

Weekly Meeting Time

Even with students scattered around the globe, there is usually a time when most students can get online together for an hour or so each week. Setting this meeting is usually possible only after all students are enrolled and the instructor can identify the time zones. We usually find that chats can occur at 8:30 or 9:00 P.M. EST, though occasionally we must work very hard to accommodate a student who is in a very different time zone.

This weekly meeting helps to structure learning events, fosters continuous progress on readings or tasks, provides accountability to each other and to the instructor, and enables the teacher to get a sense of how students are reacting to their work. Chats thus serve an important role in scaffolding, replacing some of what is lost in the face-to-face environment. (See Lang later in this section for more discussion of how to reproduce dialog online.)

Also important is planning some free time each week when the professor announces that "the chat room is open" just for students. Social chit-chat, humor, and sharing are important in creating rapport and a sense of community. While the professor cannot force this, he or she can provide the occasion simply by creating a structured place and time, usually right before or right after class. Several of our professors announce that they'll stay after class for students to ask more questions or have a more private conversation with them.

Planned Agenda and Discussion Timing

Students have their readings and research prepared prior to coming to the chat session. Agendas are sent out in advance, so that everyone has a chance to think about meaningful contributions to the discussion. The instructor estimates the number of minutes each topic should take; sometimes we ask a student to be the timekeeper for each topic segment, announcing "time's up" at the appointed time. The instructor can decide to alter the timeframe, but having a framework for conversation helps keep conversations focused and fairly intensive.

Moderated Discussion

While those who advocate purely constructivist learning would find this too directive, we prefer a moderated discussion instead of a free-wheeling one. In a moderated discussion, there is an agenda announced in advance and a discussion leader who calls on "speakers" and keeps track of the time. For each chat, there are specific learning objectives and goals; this structure is a part of what the instructor designs in order to help assure that students' time and efforts are well spent. The purpose of the chats is to extend, deepen, and apply the knowledge students are gaining from their readings, projects, and research. The insights that emerge within this collaborative learning space are truly beneficial and often quite surprising.

Additionally, we find that a moderated discussion helps to assure that all students will participate. Once the instructor has modeled successfully how to manage an online discussion a few times, student moderators can be assigned from week to week. Having to moderate the discussion and keep aware of the communication process is excellent experience for the class members. Not only do they really appreciate the effort it takes, but they assume part of the responsibility for the learning community's success. They also report that their skill in managing both live and online meetings in the workplace improves!

Interaction Protocols

Over several years of moderating and managing chats, we have developed a set of simple protocols to make interacting online smoother and more equitable. The HU (hand up) and E (end) protocols allow students to virtually raise a hand to ask a question or make a comment without interrupting the flow of thought. When posting a longer paragraph response, the "speaker" should post it in short installments, ending each installment with an ellipsis (. . .) to indicate that there is more to come. This keeps attention on the screen without long waiting periods. This protocol can be particularly important when working with synchronous technology that imposes character number restrictions in chat dialog boxes. Typing E (or <e>) at the end helps others to know that another person can speak [20].

Chat Logs

Occasionally a student or instructor may miss a weekly chat session due to travel, illness, or work demands. Most course management systems such as WebCT provide the instructor with the capability of retrieving the chat log so that it can be posted on the course website. Students are free to review the log in order to revisit a topic or make up for lost time.

Since student teams often meet in one of the chat rooms, students can capture their own chat logs by copying and pasting into a document. We try to make it very clear that the instructor has access to all chat logs in the system, so that students will not be embarrassed by some communication they thought was private. Personal, private comments that could offend someone in the class should be restricted to personal emails and not shared in chat rooms. (And even emails should be kept professional. A great rule of thumb: how would you feel if that email showed up in the newspaper tomorrow?)

Discussion Boards

In addition to the weekly live chats, we find it very useful to post topics for asynchronous discussion in a threaded discussion board. In this format, students can think about, respond to, and react to concepts and practices. All comments are visible to everyone else in the class. Dialogs and opposing views can find expression without the strict limits of real time. These discussions remain as part of the course materials and are open for student review at any time.

While voluntary, unassigned student postings could be seen as ideal for a collaborative learning environment, we find that it is most effective for the instructor to design structured ways to incorporate threaded discussions into the learning design. For example, perhaps one person is assigned each week to pose the Question of the Week that everyone will respond to. Or, the instructor may post a question or two requiring interpretation, comparison, or evaluation of some of the materials being read. Discussion boards thus provide a valuable part of the scaffolding for shared learning within the class.

Teams and Leaders

In our course design we emphasize the collaborative nature not only of our learning environment, but also of the technical communication workplace. It is true that not every technical communicator works daily with a team; there are many lone writers out there. On the other hand, our MSTCO is designed to prepare leaders for organizations. They need skills in project management, team motivation, leadership, negotiation, crisis management, and strategic planning that they can get best through working with a team. Thus, our courses usually involve at least some degree of team effort. We use teams for the following kinds of activities.

For learning tasks. Assigning every new student to a team with an experienced student provides an important part of the scaffolding for learning. Mentoring and being mentored are significant activities in creating a working community of learners. While the instructor can do a great deal to assist new students, the best help usually comes from a colleague who has recently been in the same situation. Assigning teams who are to gather knowledge and report it back to the whole class provides excellent opportunities for students to contribute significantly, to get feedback on the quality of their own study, and to gain an appreciation for the knowledge of their classmates. These tasks can be graded or ungraded, team or individual grades, but the important goal is to establish effective means of creating shared knowledge in the class. Teams thus become an effective scaffolding device, especially to initiate new students into the learning community.

For peer reviews. As discussed earlier, peer reviews are regarded as a central part of the professional role of learners in a community. Peer reviews also form an essential part of the scaffolding for creating a learning community, since responding to each others' work necessitates attention and respect for what someone other than the instructor is contributing. Additionally, peer reviewing is a professional skill that requires practice and coaching; providing these opportunities is part of our learning design. Peer review teams may be pairs or larger groups; they may remain constant throughout the term or be rotated; they may work on many smaller projects or only on the major assignment. In every case, however, peer reviews provide an essential kind of feedback that enriches everyone's experience. (See Breuch later in this section for more discussion of peer review.)

For team progress reports. Appointing a team leader helps to assure that teams will meet regularly and will report their work in helpful ways. We ask teams to meet in a chat room at their convenience, or to hold an asynchronous meeting through emails. Either way, the team leader is responsible for reporting on the team's efforts and progress to the professor and others in the class.

Occasional Telephone Contacts

From time to time, instructors find it useful to pick up the phone and talk with a student. When someone has become frustrated or confused or angry, a person-to-person conversation is the best way to resolve the issues. Additionally, a phone call can be particularly effective whenever students are in the decision-making stage for developing a major project or paper idea. Occasionally, several people need to meet in a phone conference call. In all these cases, students and instructor must be mindful of the demands of their homes and workplaces, allowing a great deal of flexibility in setting up convenient times to call. Employers may not allow personal calls, or students and instructors may have small children to get to bed in the evenings. One of our instructors always posts several days during which he is able to call students and asks them to sign up for times and to provide the number where they can be reached.

Sometimes there is no substitute for hearing the tone of a voice and speaking directly to another person. In these times, telephone conversations can provide extraordinary benefits.

Using all these tools and procedures is time-consuming and often challenging to the instructor designing the online course. We find, however, that these kinds of procedural techniques provide an important part of the scaffolding for students in a virtual learning community. They provide depth, interaction, structure, and texture to what could otherwise seem to be a one-way, passive way of learning.

CREATING CONTEXTS FOR LEARNING

As technical communicators, we work within a context of the real world and real tasks to be accomplished. This context makes us more pragmatic than some pure constructivists, since our goal is not knowledge sharing and knowledge creation alone, but rather knowledge put to some applied use. We would be remiss if we did not close our chapter with a strong recommendation about the necessity for situating online learning for technical communicators within real-world contexts.

Technical communication as a discipline exists within the real world of practical application. Here at Mercer, where our setting is within the School of Engineering, we fit very comfortably into the professional environment where knowledge is applied to solving real-world problems. Our students in MSTCO are working professionals, seeking to improve and enhance their knowledge and skills in order to advance and to make more valuable contributions to their companies. Though there is an important role for theory and "purely academic" study, we believe that the most authentic learning for technical communicators is situated within the work environment. Accepting this premise and applying it is part of the "coming of age" of our discipline [21].

The assignments we give and the learning we orchestrate need to be focused on the wider world, and not solely on the "private" discussion from student to teacher, and vice versa. As Duin and Hansen put it, "In its focus on getting something done, nonacademic writing [technical communication] subordinates the role of the writer and the status of the text to the job at hand . . ." [22, p. x].

Furthermore, the creation of documents themselves comes under scrutiny. No longer is the single-authored text the primary thing in most settings; the document in the workplace is often collaborative, usually digital, continually updated, and even ephemeral [22, p. xi]. The important thing for technical communication faculty to teach is that knowledge is applied. It is collaborative for a purpose. It does not exist for its own sake, apart from some need or application. We are trying to model this authentic context as we teach graduate students in technical communication. As we design, guide, and facilitate these learning communities, we are living out what we hope are best practices in developing sharing and creating knowledge together. We hope that what remains, once the scaffolding has been taken down and the course has disappeared from view, is not only a body of relevant and usable knowledge, but also a way of learning and working that will last for a lifetime.

REFERENCES

1. J. Rhymer, Collaboration and Conversation in Learning Communities: The Discipline and the Classroom, in *Professional Communication,* N. R. Blyler and C. Thralls (eds.), Sage, Newbury Park, pp. 179-195, 1993.
2. S. A. Selber (ed.), *Computers and Technical Communication: Pedagogical and Programmatic Perspectives*, Ablex, Greenwich, Connecticut, 1997.
3. D. C. Leonard, Using the Web for Graduate Courses in Technical Communication with Distance Learners, *Technical Communication, 43*:4, pp. 388-401, November 1996.
4. M. T. Davis, Teaching Well Online: Part II, Session 2158, in *2002 ASEE Annual Conference Proceedings.*
5. D. Wood, J. S. Bruner, and G. Ross, The Role of Tutoring in Problem Solving, *Journal of Child Psychology and Psychiatry, 17*, pp. 89-100, 1976.
6. A. S. Palincsar, The Role of Dialogue in Providing Scaffolded Instruction, *Educational Psychologist, 21*:1 and 2, pp. 73-98, 1986.
7. K. J. Brown, What Kind of Text—For Whom and When? Textual Scaffolding for Beginning Readers, *Reading Teacher, 53*:4, pp. 292-307, December 1999/January 2000.

8. B. A. Greene and S. M. Land, A Qualitative Analysis of Scaffolding Use in a Resource-Based Learning Environment Involving the World Wide Web, *Journal of Educational Computing Research, 23*:2, pp. 151-179, 2000.
9. K. L. Gustafson and R. B. Branch, *Survey of Instructional Design Models* (3rd Edition), Clearinghouse on Information and Technology, Syracuse, New York, 1997.
10. P. L. Smith and T. J. Ragan, *Instructional Design*, Prentice Hall, Inc., Upper Saddle River, New Jersey, 1999.
11. R. M. Gagne, L. J. Briggs, and W. W. Wager, *Principles of Instructional Design* (4th Edition), Harcourt Brace & Company, Orlando, Florida, 1992.
12. W. Dick, L. Carey, and J. O. Carey, *The Systematic Design of Instruction*, (5th Edition), Addison Wesley Longman, Inc., New York, 2000.
13. C. M. Reigeluth (ed.), *Instructional-Design Theories and Models*, Volume II, *A New Model of Instructional Theory*, Lawrence Erlbaum Associates, Mahwah, New Jersey, 1999.
14. D. H. Jonassen and S. M. Land, *Theoretical Foundations of Learning Environments*, Lawrence Erlbaum Associates, Mahwah, New Jersey, 2000.
15. J. E. Kemp, G. R. Morrison, and S. M. Ross, *Designing Effective Instruction* (2nd Edition), John Wiley & Sons, New York, 1999.
16. S. Imel, Guidelines for Working with Adult Learners, *ERIC Digest,* No. 154, 1994.
17. N. E. Gronlund, *How to Write Instructional Objectives* (6th Edition), Merrill Prentice Hall, Upper Saddle River, New Jersey, 2000.
18. M. D. Merrill, *Suggested Self-Study Program for Instructional Systems Development*, http://www.id2.usu.edu/MDavidMerrill/IDREAD.PDF.
19. J. W. Popham, What's Wrong and What's Right with Rubrics, *Educational Leadership, 55*:2, pp. 72-75, 1997
20. G. Hayhoe, An Experiment in Meeting Virtually, in *IEEE Professional Communication Society Newsletter*, pp. 3-4, May-June 2001.
21. K. Staples and C. Ornatowski, Introduction to *Foundations for Teaching Technical Communication: Theory, Practice, and Program Design*, Ablex, Greenwich, Connecticut, 1997.
22. A. H. Duin and C. J. Hansen, *Nonacademic Writing: Social Theory and Technology*, Lawrence Erlbaum Associates, Mahwah, New Jersey, 1996.

CHAPTER 7

Mind the Gap(s): Modeling Space in Online Education

Locke Carter and Rebecca Rickly

As technology becomes more and more accessible and affordable, institutions of higher learning will increasingly utilize it both in and outside of the classroom. While many teachers and students have experience with computer classrooms in more traditional settings, e-learning, or online education, is predicted to overtake classroom-based instruction as the primary method of delivery in both educational and service-oriented industries by 2004 [1, p. 11]. In a recent editorial in *T.H.E. Journal,* Sylvia Charp noted that electronic learning courses are particularly powerful because they are

- **Portable**—They are available on the Web, at any time, from any place;
- **Modular**—They consist of multiple units, making it easy for learners to digest the material; and
- **Interactive**—Learners must respond, and students are able to chat with their peers and teachers [1, p. 12].

Yet many educators will note that these same descriptors might well be used for traditional face-to-face (onsite) classroom instruction as well as e-learning. Since most educators who find themselves in an e-learning environment have, at one time or another, taught in a face-to-face classroom, it might be beneficial to begin with some sort of comparison of e-learning and traditional face-to-face learning, if only to see how we might learn from one and apply it to the other. However, if we make such a comparison, even as a starting place, we must also be wary of re-creating problems, of trying to take pedagogies that work in one medium and apply them to another uncritically and without reflection, and not considering how the content of the course, the delivery, and the audience (class members) might interact.

All good teachers—both online and onsite—*do* think about how they might make their courses better in terms of learning from the past, critically considering context, and considering how the learners, the course content, and delivery might be best matched. Yet, often instructors begin without prior knowledge of the learners; in fact, we might call this missing information *gaps* in what we know, and only through identifying, understanding, and "minding" these gaps can we truly become better teachers, regardless of the media we use to teach with. Some of these gaps are visible—age, gender, ethnic origin, and, to a lesser extent, socio-economic status—but others reside below the surface: learning style, personality preference, gender identification, past experiences, and so forth.

The goal of this chapter, then, is to explore what we mean by gaps, discuss the importance of gaps in learning, and suggest ways to mind them, specifically in terms of online education. Those of us who teach at a distance must take care to identify the gaps, then take steps to "mind" them in how we construct, deliver, and assess learning at a distance. In order to begin this discussion, we must offer a preliminary definition of gaps. A gap involves dissonance or incongruity between a "theoretically perfect" situation and the actual situation in which we find ourselves. The obvious gap regarding online education is the incongruity between having all students in the same place at the same time and having them spread out over the globe. Or we can apply "gap" to preparedness: ideally, all students enrolling in a class have not only taken the prerequisites but also have matured cognitively to the point of both "getting" the main ideas of the course and also contributing to class discussion. Upon further consideration, however, it occurs to us that all learning assumes the presence of gaps. We learn about the richness of humanity through the gap of not sharing identical backgrounds, genes, educations, and experiences. Homogeneity has no gaps, offers few possibilities of intervention. Ultimately, we have come to realize that gaps are inherent to human experience and are key to good educational experiences. So let us revisit the definition of "gap" and remove words like "perfect" and "actual," for they suggest that gaps are undesirable. Instead, let us define a gap as the difference between homogeneity and the diversity/heterogeneity that we encounter every day in our brick-and-mortar classrooms, in our online communications with distance students, and in all other facets of our lives.

When we think of the classroom (and its participants) online in an e-learning situation, we become mindful of space first and foremost, because it is the most obvious difference, or "gap," between the brick-and-mortar classroom and the online education classroom. Yet face-to-face classrooms have been dealing with space issues for decades; think about how delivery of course content has changed from the podium-based lecture in a large hall, to a smaller classroom of bolted-down desks, to a more modern classroom in which the desks can be moved so that class members might form circles or small groups so that peer-to-peer interaction might occur. Technology comes in many guises—not only have high tech devices like computers and projectors affected classroom space, but so have devices like whiteboards, air conditioning, and movable partitions. Similarly, techniques and theories about what we should be doing in the classroom have affected its concept of space; Cargile Cook (Chapter 3) describes how theoretical shifts in writing instruction transformed the configuration of and technologies used within writing classes.

SPACES IN WHICH WE FIND GAPS

In online education, it is tempting to call the distance gap the primary "problem." However, as we argue below, this distance gap is but one of many observable (and unobservable) gaps in *both* the online and face-to-face classroom. In fact, "gaps," as we are using the term, come in all forms: physical, personal, social, curricular, and cognitive. Think about the gap between the London Underground platform and the actual train; if there were no gap, the train would be unable to move; if there were too much of a gap, passengers would not be able to board the train easily. Other options might be a temporary or movable bridge, but such constructs are simply not cost-effective. The solution? Customers are merely told to "mind the gap" as they board. How they choose to mind it is up to them. Similarly, we want to stress that identifying and examining gaps doesn't always mean that these gaps must be filled or bridged or mended; often, they merely need to be minded. Participants need to be mindful, adjust to things observed, and adapt proactively.

However, as long as we approach online education as a site of merely spatial difference, our notions of gaps will be simplistic. One of our goals in this chapter is to propose a more thorough model of space, one that accounts for unique qualities of the distance course as well as the brick-and-mortar course, the lecture hall, and the seminar room. For the purposes of this chapter, we can distinguish gaps that occur among and between three different kinds of space—the physical, virtual, and cognitive. By examining each of these spaces individually and then in a complex overlay, and by identifying gaps that might affect teaching and learning, we will better understand how space affects communication in online education, particularly in terms of knowledge-making/sharing, team building, and goal-based communicative activities. When we enrich our categories of space to include the physical, cognitive, and virtual, we suddenly see that gaps may occur along any boundary in any combination with other gaps. And when we recognize this fact, then we can also see that distance is the least of our problems; it is simply the most visible. Although this chapter ostensibly explores how we in online education courses might reduce or at least minimize gaps, one of the conclusions we will reach below is that not all gaps should be minimized; indeed, exaggerating gaps may be one of the most effective techniques for facilitating knowledge-making and communication practices.

Physical Space

The physical involves space, bodies, gestalt, distance, and context. This space is clearly involved in online classes, but also comes into play regarding the position of bodies, desks, and classrooms in brick-and-mortar classrooms. Maybe your classroom is near a squeaky hallway water cooler that distracts you and your students, or perhaps students have to race from the Engineering building to make it to your classroom to avoid being tardy. Consider the physical space in which you work, teach, and learn, including the temperature, the lighting, color scheme, physical proximity, body language, textures, feng shui, and "flow," all of which impact communication. Physical space includes not only the building in which the class is situated but also all physical cues (visual, aural, oral cues) that participants share.

One of the problems with treating distance as the main issue in online education is that while physical space is certainly different, it doesn't go away. It is represented by the personal spaces of the individual student experiences instead of the shared physical space of the classroom. When we participate in our distance courses, we still have our bodies. Our fingers type furiously over the keyboard during an intense discussion. Our adrenaline builds over the excitement, we shift around in our home or office chairs, and so on. In a face-to-face seminar, students sometimes pass notes while others are talking, or exchange looks or raised eyebrows. These gestures clearly operate within the physical space of the class-room. But these unofficial, possibly subversive "subcommunications" also represent contact points with the virtual world that is always present. It is the world of society, class, cliques, family concerns, and job worries, among other things.

Virtual Space

Indeed, virtual space involves one's representation of the physical, even when there is no "physical" to adhere to. When a student "zones out" in remembering last night's dance, we might suggest that he has called into being the virtual space of that dance. And by allowing that space to take the forefront of his mind, he makes the virtual space the main mode of existence, at least until the teacher or classmate says something to foreground the physical. When things are going well in the classroom, in fact, one would hope that everyone's virtual space is closely aligned with their physical space, which is to say that everyone is both physically and mentally present. The "underlife" that Robert Brooke writes about in the classroom is a factor here as well [2]. While passing notes and having sidebar, tangential conversations in class are physical activities, they add a dimension to the physical and cognitive spaces students reside in as part of the class which can, in effect, create a virtual place—a place of shared understanding—in the traditional classroom.

Focusing specifically on online education, the obvious nature of virtual space often involves the mode of class conversation (chat, email, lecture, file exchange), media, expertise, familiarity, instruction, interaction, production of deliverables, research materials. These spaces that students and teachers work in also affect learning, and these might include technologically enabled spaces such as notes, PDAs, cell phones, data bases, and Web-based environments, allowing for various levels of interactivity, as well as ease of use, "transparency," and speed, all of which impact communication. A good example of the way virtual space affects online education can be seen in the Rubens and Southard chapter in the next section of this volume. They discuss how students had an easier time with online discussion when it took the form of threaded discussion rather than a chat room or a listserv. While all three technologies offered similar capabilities, they encourage a different sense of virtual space, and one space (the threaded discussion) presented their students with a clearer sense of the virtual space.

Cognitive Space

Finally, cognitive space involves learning styles, personality, gender, prerequisites, aptitude, preparation, power, and shared concepts of education, all of which impact communication. For our purposes, the difference in virtual and cognitive space involves mental processing of concepts as opposed to "mere" representations of space. For example, when students (in either brick-and-mortar or distance settings) are discussing today's reading, they are operating in the cognitive space of critical analysis, exposition, questioning, explaining, and so on, all of which is affected by the sum total of their experiences, their learning, their emotions to date. Depending on the students' individual cognitive traits, this shared cognitive space may be relatively homogenous or highly fractured. We have all experienced the situation where one student either doesn't "get it" when everyone else is ready to move on, or the opposite, where one student is asking questions or using terms that are so advanced (and so different) from the tone of class and the expectations for class discussion that the rest of the class either becomes glassy-eyed or the teacher, recognizing the potential cognitive disruption, either restates the question/observation in more accessible ways or simply defers the discussion to her office hours or until later in the course.

A Classroom Spaces Model

While we have advanced our concept of these three types of space, it is important to realize that we have done so strictly for analytical purposes. In fact, we may take these three components as being present in all situations. Granted, it seems difficult to see the face-to-face classroom as having a virtual component, but that is only because the virtual and the physical are so intertwined that they seem to be the same thing. They are nearly congruous. But not totally. Even in a traditional classroom, virtual space would include using a television to show interview vignettes or using the Internet to research for a project. The television and the computer are part of the physical space, but the television show and the

Internet sites belong to the virtual. And the discussion and mental processing of the television show and website concepts belong to the cognitive. As anyone who has taught in a computer classroom knows, the physical and virtual (and often the cognitive) realms separate when you use a chat program to conduct an online class discussion, even when all the students are in the same physical space. Students and teachers interact differently when using in-class chat. Bump noted that students' Myers-Briggs personality traits seemed to be mediated by the activity of chatting about class readings [3]. Regan observed that gay and lesbian students were more likely to disclose details of their sexual orientation in online settings than in face-to-face ones [4]. And many researchers have made the convincing case that power relations involving race and sex are either reversed or moderated when discussions occur online. And all of these studies involved students using a chat program while they sat in the same physical room together. Our model of space helps account for these differences. While students share the same physical space, the online chat component of the class introduces a major schism, somehow foregrounding the virtual and cognitive in ways that differ greatly from the non-electronic chat classroom. It is suddenly easy to see the physical classroom separate from the virtual classroom.

As a way of looking at a given class, we can map Venn diagrams to show the relative size and importance of these three realms. Locke just finished teaching an online graduate course on a scholarly (rather than practical) topic. Eleven master's students, almost all of whom were practicing technical communicators, comprised the course. In Figures 1 and 2 , P = physical, C = cognitive, and V = virtual, and the relative size of circles is meant to suggest the nature of the shared space of this course.

The smallness of the physical realm is not intended to argue that physical space was not a factor for the 11 students. In fact, on an individual level, it was

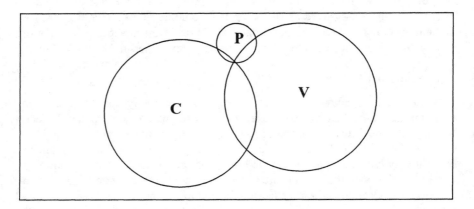

Figure 1. One configuration of a distance course.

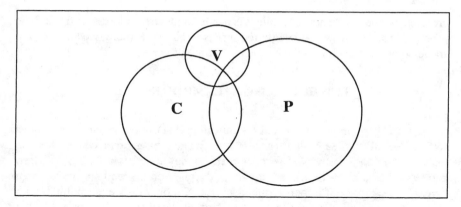

Figure 2. Same course, face-to-face, with a different
configuration of spaces.

very important. One student participated from a time zone six hours different from the rest of the students. Almost all students had to choose which physical space best suited their classroom experience, sometimes choosing to stay at their workplace after work hours in order to take advantage of a faster Internet connection or to avoid children at home, other times racing home from work so they could take advantage of the home setting for class discussion that evening. At the level of the class's shared space(s), the physical site from which students met was relatively unimportant for the syllabus (once we had agreed on a favorable meeting hour), for our assignments, and for evaluation and assessment. But the cognitive and virtual spaces were critical elements of this distance course. These cognitive and virtual spaces turned out to be the spaces in which potential gaps had to be minded, for they had the potential to make or break the course.

Another version of the same course was taught in the same semester, but this one was a face-to-face version with a mixed group of master's and doctoral students in Texas Tech's new English building, and the space map (Figure 2) looks very different. The cognitive gap is smaller because of a more homogenous group, one which is accustomed to theory and scholarship. The virtual component of this course comprises email exchanges, elaborate course syllabi and assignment Web pages, and bulletin board posts for reading responses. The physical component of the course played a much more important role, for the class often broke into small groups for project planning, group revision, and in-class exercises. In other words, the physical cues during interactions and within the classroom space were the predominant space at work.

This book is about online education, and it should be obvious from the preceding section that online courses involve greater distance gaps and fewer physical cues (facial and other visual representations of emotion, etc.), both of which can create gaps in understanding. While it is useful to identify, address, and mind the gaps in physical, virtual, and cognitive spaces in online learning, we also need to spend some time exploring the productive nature of gaps as well.

THE EDUCATIONAL IMPORTANCE
OF GAPS

Why are gaps important in online education? The most obvious answer is self-evident, that students and teachers are separated by gaps in space. This gap makes things like hallway conversation and happy hours impossible. The gap makes visible many of the characteristics of the classroom experience that remain invisible, unthought of in our normal routines. Not only do we not hobnob with each other before and after class, and perhaps at the coffee shop for lunch, but we also have a body-gap. No one has bodies in online education. The gap here lies between physical reality and virtual reality. No one has an immediately distinguishable race or a religion, possibly even a sex, in a online education setting. We are disembodied brains interacting over the course material.

How important are these things to learning? We all have a vague sense that there's something special about having a body at a university. We lug bookbags from class to class, shake hands with classmates, drink coffee during class discussion, cough and sneeze when we have colds, walk up and down stairs to our classrooms and professor's offices, and generally partake of all the physical trappings of pursuing learning. Consider the phenomenon of muscle-memory. You can read a lot of books about hitting a golf ball, but nothing really substitutes for actually hitting one. Is "higher" learning different? Probably so, at least regarding highly physical activities. But when it comes to teaching collaboration, to use one example, how else to do it except to form groups and to collaborate? Even in the most isolated circumstance of collaborative workgroups, every member must take certain physical steps to put themselves in contact with the other members. The physical nature of collaboration is easy to see in the face-to-face classroom, but it is just as easy to picture a student launching NetMeeting or going to the video conference room or dialing the telephone. To be sure, collaboration also requires congruent virtual and cognitive space or else the group would be unable to produce anything.

Is it possible to get rid of gaps? Is it desirable? The answer to both questions is probably no—even with the most sophisticated technology of video, audio, holograms, and the like, students will be separated physically from their class-mates and professors. Their virtual selves may get more sophisticated, of course, and perhaps that may "solve" a lot of the gap problem. As with the example of the London underground, gaps are often necessary for a system to function effectively and efficiently, and it is not always wise for the system to bridge or fill all gaps. Gaps exist in any educational situation. At times, in fact, many gaps should be promoted. Let us explain.

One particular type of gap might be seen as similar to the cognitive dissonance theory as put forth by social psychologist Leon Festinger [5]. This theory, in effect, concerns the relationship among "cognitions" or pieces of knowledge. Much of what we know is the irrelevant bits of cognition or the consonant cumulation of our various cognitions. However, when bits of cognition seem to be in direct opposition, dissonance occurs, and according to Festinger, humans have a basic desire to avoid dissonance, so basic that it rivals our need for food and shelter. When dissonance occurs, an unnatural or unpleasant state that Festinger compares to hunger, the individual experiencing it is motivated to reduce it, which can only be done when the dissonance is examined and the factors causing it identified. It can then be reduced in one of the following ways:

- Rejecting the new cognition: If the new idea is rejected, dissonance disappears;
- Changing cognitions: If two ideas are competing, we can simply change one to make it consistent with the other;
- Adding cognitions: The magnitude of cognitions can be changed by adding one or more consonant cognitions; and
- Altering importance: By examining the cognitions, more or less importance can be attributed to each, allowing the weight to make the dissonance less so [6].

Cognitive dissonance, then, can be a powerful catalyst for eliciting a change in a learner, and thus the wise instructor might do well to create such dissonance in the online education classroom—and we might even go so far as to call this dissonance a gap.

Lev Vygotsky added a social component to the concept of cognition/learning with his explanation of the Zone of Proximal Development, or ZPD, which he defines as

> . . . the distance between the actual level of development as determined by independent problem solving [without guided instruction] and the level of potential development as determined by problem solving under adult guidance or in collaboration with more capable peers [7, p. 86].

In short, it is the difference between what a learner can do on her own and what a learner can do with guidance. By hearing, understanding, and then utilizing the various levels of development of those around her to solve a problem, a student will increase her ability to do so on her own, by imitating the structures, or scaffolding, she has been exposed to; ultimately, she will be able to engage in recursive, reflective metacognition to solve her own problems. (For a more detailed discussion of scaffolding, see Grady and Davis' chapter in this section.) Once again, by creating an e-learning ZPD, complete with peer/instructor interaction as well as a challenging curriculum that requires students to stretch in terms of what they are capable of and expected to do, students are more likely to actually learn. Thus, when an educator purposefully creates a gap in a course—a gap zone where students will construct knowledge collaboratively, that allows them to create new information based on past experience/knowledge—students are more likely to learn.

From these two theories alone, we must note that gaps are important—perhaps even necessary—for learning to take place in any context—including (but not limited to) traditional classrooms and e-learning. And, as we have noted elsewhere in this chapter, gaps occur in both scenarios, but tend to be different (or have different cumulative effect or weight, if you will) in traditional and virtual classrooms. In either situation, however, the gaps must be minded if they are to be useful; too large a gap will result in a rejection of new cognition or the learner not expanding her knowledge base. Too small a gap will result in busywork in which both student and teacher are frustrated because no learning is going on. So how do we as instructors—particularly as instructors of e-learning—decide what kinds of gaps to create in our courses, as well as how to mind those that are pre-existing or that come from the nature of the course itself that might prohibit (or at least inhibit) learning?

ACCOMMODATING AT-RISK STUDENTS AND STUDENTS WITH DIFFERENT LEARNING STYLES

All recommendations must be mindful of the realities of the virtual, cognitive, and physical domains of the course context; otherwise, such recommendations are general maxims and are probably not very helpful. One must also temper these recommendations about virtual, cognitive, and physical with the learning activities desired, the subject matter, the larger institutional context, and the smaller personal contexts that inform such a class. In other words, one approach doesn't fit all.

At-risk students, for example, may require additional attention, special instructions, or interventions. In "Predictors of Performance in the Virtual Classroom," Wang and Newlin note that instructors in e-learning environments can identify "at-risk" students early on through simple data gathering processes, and through this data, alter practices to help these "at-risk" students to succeed from a distance. Aside from general suggestions about distance courses, such as making sure that the content and policies of the course are well-documented on the Web, including both synchronous and asynchronous means of delivery/communication, the authors point out that students who have participated in distance classes previously tend to be more successful; thus, by finding out which students have had previous e-learning experience and which have not, the instructor can use this information to give those without experience more attention. Similarly, students who maintain what the authors call an "internal locus of control"— that is, those who take responsibility for their own success/learning—succeed more so than those with an "external locus of control"—those who feel their success/learning is largely due a matter of chance [8, p. 22]. By determining how confident students are in their own ability to learn, particularly in regard to the course content and the technology employed, instructors have an early predictor of success and they will be better equipped to anticipate and meet the needs of those who are less confident.

During the course, instructors should track communicative activity for each student. Wang and Newlin suggest noting abnormalities or inconsistencies in the following information:

- Number of homepage hits (the number of hits during the first week can be predictive of the final grades in the 16th week);
- Number of forum postings read by each student;
- Number of forum postings written by each student; and
- Frequency and types of remarks in a chat space [8, p. 27].

By engaging in some early information gathering, the instructor can plan the course more strategically. Students who have been identified "at risk" tend to do better when given more attention; therefore, tracking and evaluating specific data early on gives the instructor a better idea who to watch closely, and who might need more information, more interaction, or simply more support. Avery, Civjan, and Johri (in the next section) discuss an experimental method for assessing student interactions.

While accommodating the needs of at-risk students, instructors may also need to consider the needs of all students by casting a wide net, designing an assignment, for example, with all learning styles covered. Why? Because online education time is slower. It is slower because of physical constraints like time zones, 9-to-5 work hours, access to video conferencing rooms. It is slower because of virtual constraints that mediating technologies introduce: turn around time to answer email, turn-taking in chat rooms, and inherent bandwidth limitations. And it is often slower because of cognitive constraints that arise from an often-broader student base for online education courses than for face-to-face ones. Because of this slowness, improvising in online education is like trying to turn the Titanic quickly. But in the space of the brick-and-mortar classroom, there is a great deal of improvisation that takes place that is hardly documentable: eye gestures, a smile from the teacher, a clarification of something in an assignment that all other students can hear. For the face-to-face classroom, one may make one's best effort at an assignment or an explanation and always look forward to time for tweaking in the class when we ask "Are there any questions about the assignment?" The same kind of clarifications may take place in online courses, but they don't approach anything like real time. Students are working, they're checking email twice a day, watching streaming video of the professor once a week, and fast improvisation is simply not possible.

RECOMMENDATIONS

While we have cautioned that one size doesn't fit all, we will, nevertheless, proceed to give you some advice about gaps in online classrooms. As should be apparent from this chapter, we argue that all educational situations involve gaps of one sort or another. For this reason, we point out that none of the advice below is unique to online education; the missing (or different) physical component, the reliance on some kind of virtual component, and the often unknown cognitive component do make some of these recommendations more important. We will note, however, that students who take distance courses generally seem more self-motivated, and can be counted on to take the initiative in many circumstances. Whether this is true across the board or whether it depends on maturity, course material, technology, or a host of other factors we cannot tell. We certainly would argue, in any case, that online education requires students with more motivation.

Preparation

1. **Over-prepare** *everything.* Look out further into the future than you would in a face-to-face classroom because of the slow-motion syndrome discussed earlier. But realize that you will have to drop (or at least modify) about 80% of this over-preparation.

2. **Think globally when you've got students from various time zones, cultures, and technologies.** Be aware in this case that synchronous discussion is more vulnerable and that you may have to shift some of your emphasis to asynchronous discussion. Do not assume that "online education" looks or feels the same to everyone. For example, you may have a new student who is a veteran of video-based online education, but who seems naïve in your class's email and chat modes. Think outside of your own experiences in order to adapt and adjust to different models of online education.

3. **Learn about your students.** Conduct learning style inventories or gather background information from them. Or ask them to post short biographies to the class website. You do this to help you understand the varieties of learning styles and personalities in your class. You do this intuitively in a brick-and-mortar classroom and probably adjust your activities, expectations, and approaches to the course accordingly. For instance, if you have an upper level undergraduate class in the students' major area, you can expect students to know certain things that you can then build on in this course; similarly, if you have a graduate class with all PhD students, you might include more—and expect students to engage in more— theoretical and critical background than if you had the same class with all new MA students. Why forego that opportunity in your online course?

4. **Heed the real world, especially if the virtual world is quite different from the real world.** Becky had a student on the West Coast who was still at work when they met in a chat room at 6:00 P.M. CST. On several occasions, this student had to attend key company meetings. One can either be rigid and kick the

student out or lower her grade—or one can recognize that this is life and that this is the kind of clientele we want in our online courses. In such a world, we may want to redefine curricular concepts like "absence" and "tardy."

5. **Have an explicit backup plan or standard operating procedure (SOP).** In other words, if the video feed is broken at the appointed time, what are the students supposed to do? The next steps should be known to them and ideally should be written down in your course policy statement. Not only should you and your class know about the SOP, but you should also explicitly formulate a plan a, b, and c for each class (see #1, above).

6. **Consider special needs.** Not just the "specialness" that distance brings to your course, but the kinds of things that would fall under the Americans with Disabilities Act or under good Web design. For example, you could produce course materials in several formats—Word, text, pdf, and Web—in order to make it easy for your students who use screen readers (because of sight impairment) to have greater access to your ideas. Or a foreign student may copy your text (if it is copy-able) and translate it in a service like Babelfish in order to discern the granularity of your assignment. Another form of special need involves bandwidth, a luxury that some of your students may not have. Following good Web design principles, you can minimize your use of graphics, signal when a link will cause the student to download a lengthy document or graphic, and generally put the control over the navigation of your course materials into the students' hands.

Communication

1. **Use more than one mode of communication** (email, chat, document sharing, video, audio). Teachers in the brick-and-mortar classroom do this all the time, alternating between writing on the white board, showing something on the overhead projector, lecturing for a while, fostering student discussion. Different modes allow for different learning styles to flourish.

2. **Make the structure and purpose of your course something open to discussion and even amendment.** In other words, consider it legitimate for your students to engage in meta-conversation about the course. Why? In many online education settings, your course materials are available to students, and you cannot possibly shut the door. But even if your course materials are restricted, we argue that online education is, and will continue to be, novel for some time. Its structure and content should be made more explicit and transparent, not only to your fellow instructors and administrators but also to your students. Online education is inherently more vague since it is missing key context, hence containing more opportunities for misunderstandings. Your online students need this context, too—it is not just gossip. The face-to-face students make up stories about why you do what you do—these theories form the background of the context of the institution, gossip if you will. Barring exceptional initiative by your online students, it is unlikely that they will be privy to this gossip-theory talk. It is up to

you to help them "fill in the underlife" of the class. Zachry (at the end of this section) argues that individuals must engage in dialog to come to understanding. Metadiscourses such as these can help students, especially those who are practitioners, to understand the greater educational value of coursework and extend these students' learning goals beyond their immediate what-will-this-information-do-for-me-now expectation.

3. **Set norms for deliverables, and communicate these expectations clearly.** State explicitly if your class will exchange MS Word, rtf, or Acrobat files. You may need to poll your students to see what kind of software and hardware capabilities they have so that you can either adjust the physical requirements of course production or require the students to purchase a common platform for interaction. You might also consider employing different modes for different assignments.

4. **Give more or more frequent assessment and feedback to online students.** Face-to-face students get all sorts of informal feedback about their performance: you nod at them when they say something smart, they hear from other students about how they're doing, and they each get a general felt sense, based on physical reactions of how they are doing and how the course is going. Online students do not have this situation. Even if you give them a brief email a few weeks into the semester about your subjective opinion of their participation, this step will make a world of difference.

Context

1. **Try to provide personal context in order to supplement the missing physical component.** You can do this by having everyone (you included) write a short biography and by uploading a personal picture to a class website. Workgroups can also be given fanciful names in order to foster a sense of unity/belonging. For example, in a recent online class, Locke's students formed groups with names like LockeNess Monsters, Design Divas, and Global High Phive.

2. **You can also try to provide instructional context, explaining what you're doing from a pedagogical or curricular perspective.** Make an overly detailed syllabus. Explain why you've chosen certain readings. Tell your students what you expect them to take away from your class. In short, play with all your cards face up. Indeed, as evidenced by Eaton's survey of online students (in the first section of this volume), students want this kind of openness about assignments and explanation of their purposes.

3. **Be aware of the rhetoric of the medium.** Or, putting it another way, set class norms that are consistent with the medium. Explain how email, chat, documents, and video should look in order to be acceptable if you have standards for how students will be assessed in these media. You might include this information in your policy statement, then repeat it before each assignment. Model behaviors

you would like to elicit as well. And remediate or intervene early because of a) the slow-motion effect in online learning; and b) the permanence of text.

4. **In order to remediate, find out about your students' experience early in the course.** Focus on areas like comfort and experience with online courses, the content of your course, and technology in general. Those who are not comfortable with these things may need extra help. Either take on this responsibility yourself, or, better yet, allow some of the class to work with this student.

ANALYZING GAPS AND SPACE

In thinking about the model of space and gaps presented in this chapter, we might consider how a teacher might make use of this knowledge. Venn diagrams are good for illustrating models not very helpful at formulating strategies for online education courses. What we propose below (Table 1) is to consider space (and gaps) methodically for each course, using something like the following grid. The grid itself is merely a heuristic device designed to help you think about space with more sophistication; the consequences and actions needed from what you observe would strictly be up to you.

First, you jot down everything that seems relevant to your course and the success of all its students. Fill in the "observations" column first and come back to consequences and actions later.

For example, Table 2 illustrates some initial observations made in the first few days of a new online graduate course in technical communication and ethics.

CONCLUSION

While gaps occur both in the face-to-face classroom and the online education classroom, it is important to note that they are not always something to be "fixed"; like the London Underground, well-thought out gaps are necessary for smoothness

Table 1. Grid for Evaluating Spaces and Gaps

Space	Observations	Consequence	Action
Physical			
Cognitive			
Virtual			

Table 2. Evaluation of Spaces and Gaps in an Online Graduate Course

Space	Observations	Consequence	Action
Physical	Ingrid is in Sweden	7-hour lag makes real-time work and scheduling difficult	De-emphasize real-time class participation component and emphasize the reading response
	Paula is in California	Real-time meeting scheduled during her work hours	Ditto
	Lester has carpal tunnel syndrome	He's using voice-recognition software and typing very slowly	Patience in text-production
Cognitive	Half the students are 2nd year PhD, and the other half are brand-new MA	Sophistication varies widely; PhDs may feel like we're going too slow, while the MAs may feel overwhelmed	Separate formal assignments from reading responses and chat.
	Three super-introverts in class	We lose their insight. Low participation marks	Combine the real-time component of class participation with something more reflective, like asynchronous chat discussion
	Fred has never taken an online class before	Fed may be intimidated or uncomfortable	Check on Fred's postings and chat, and write to him if I see an abnormality
Virtual	Half the students know only the Web	Alternative forms of online communication involve a learning curve	Introduce chat, wait 2 weeks, introduce NetMeeting, wait another 2 weeks, then introduce Lotus Notes
	Louise dominates chat sessions	Crowds our student participation and annoys others	Write her an email asking her to tone it down. Perhaps she's unfamiliar with etiquette, in which case, I need to write up an "Online Course Etiquette" page and attach to our syllabus

and uniformity of the train, even if the gaps provide minor inconveniences to the travelers. A good teacher in both face-to-face and online environments will get to know her curriculum and her students, then encourage certain cognitive gaps in creating a sense of cognitive dissonance or a zone of proximal development so that learning might take place. Yet, there are also gaps that hinder learning, and it is those gaps that must be explored and analyzed contextually, then addressed so that they might be minded by both students and instructor.

A gap-enlightened curriculum and pedagogy may choose to foreground gaps, not only in the distance courses but in the face-to-face ones as well. After all, our courses and our experiences are filled with gaps of all sorts, gaps that we cannot hope to fill, even if it were possible. What we can do is provide a context in the learning experience so that gaps are easily minded and adapted to.

And lest we imagine this chapter to be strictly about online education, let us consider the nature of the modern workforce. Virtual spaces are being populated by those traditionally bound to a more familiar physical space, such as teachers and students in academe, but more and more of these virtual spaces are being populated by work teams collaborating both in-house and at a distance. Because these teams are made up of a variety of different people with different goals—for instance, subject matter experts, supervisors, production staff, as well as writers and editors—each with a different cognitive style and cultural background, the ability to communicate effectively in these virtual spaces (as well as the more familiar physical spaces) is imperative. Successful communication depends on how well we understand and navigate these spaces, how well each individual "minds the gap."

REFERENCES

1. S. Charp, Changes to Traditional Teaching, *T.H.E. Journal, 29*:10, May 2002.
2. R. Brooke, Underlife and Writing Instruction, *College Composition and Communication, 38:*2 pp. 141-153, 1987.
3. J. Bump, Radical Changes in Class Discussion Using Networked Computers, *Computers and the Humanities, 24,* pp. 49-65, 1990.
4. A. Regan, "Type Normal Like the Rest of Us": Writing, Power, and Homophobia in the Networked Composition Classroom, *Computers and Composition, 9*:4, pp. 11-23, November 1993.
5. L. Festinger, *A Theory of Cognitive Dissonance,* Stanford University Press, Stanford, California, 1957.
6. H. Stephenson, *Cognitive Dissonance: General Experimental Psychology Cognitive Dissonance Lab,* http://www.ithaca.edu/faculty/stephens/cdback.html, June 1, 2002.
7. L. S. Vygotsky, *Mind in Society: The Development of Higher Psychological Processes,* Harvard University Press, Cambridge, Massachusetts, 1978.
8. A. Y. Wang and M. H. Newlin, Predictors of Performance in the Virtual Classroom: Identifying and Helping At-Risk Cyber-Students, *T.H.E. Journal, 29*:10, pp. 21-28, May 2002.

CHAPTER 8

Enhancing Online Collaboration: Virtual Peer Review in the Writing Classroom*

Lee-Ann Kastman Breuch

Collaborative writing practices have long been endorsed in writing pedagogy. Peer review is one writing activity that reflects collaboration, for it involves the interaction of two or more persons who respond to one another's writing [1-3]. Indeed, as Kenneth Bruffee suggests, peer review—or peer criticism, as he calls it—is an activity in which students collaborate with one another to learn and practice the "normal discourse" of a community. Bruffee contends that collaborative activities are critical to learning in writing classrooms, for they foster the kind of environment that academics value most: discussion among peers about scholarship [1, p. 640]. Beyond the connection between peer review and collaborative learning, however, there is another strand to explore: computer technology. For example, in writing pedagogy, collaborative writing activities like peer review are frequently assigned [4]; in addition, instructors are integrating computer technology more frequently in their classrooms [5]. The combination of these factors—the prevalence of collaborative forms of writing like peer review, along with the rising use of technology in the classroom—creates a unique opportunity to explore virtual forms of peer review.

In this chapter, I explicitly address the act of using computer technology to exchange and respond to one another's writing—an activity I call "virtual peer review." In addition to addressing an important gap between peer review and

---

*The topic of this chapter is much more fully developed in a book titled *Virtual Peer Review: Teaching and Learning about Writing in Online Environments* (SUNY Press, 2004).

141

technology, examining this emerging activity highlights an issue pertinent to students as well as instructors: the transfer of instructional activities from face-to-face to virtual environments. As I explain, peer review is solidly rooted in face-to-face environments, and yet instructors and some scholars have suggested that peer review can simply be transferred to virtual environments without much explanation. I disagree, and I suggest that understanding virtual peer review requires that we recognize the pedagogical assumptions that underlie the activity as well as the fundamental differences of practicing peer review in a virtual environment. My overall argument in this chapter is that virtual peer review shares pedagogical assumptions with traditional peer review, but that its practice differs in terms of time, space, and interaction. To further explain my position, throughout this chapter I address the following questions: 1) What roots does virtual peer review share with peer review in face-to-face classrooms? 2) How well do the practices of face-to-face peer review translate to online environments? 3) How can instructors better prepare students to conduct virtual peer review?

WHAT ROOTS DOES VIRTUAL PEER REVIEW SHARE WITH FACE-TO-FACE PEER REVIEW?

Before discussing what virtual peer review has in common with peer review, it is perhaps most useful to begin with what we know about peer review, such as its definition and the pedagogical assumptions that support it. To begin, peer review can be defined as *responding to one another's writing*. As Anne Ruggles Gere suggests, peer review has been given many names—such as "response groups," "helping circles," and "mutual improvement sessions"—but it essentially can be defined as "writers responding to one another's work" [2; 3, p. 1].

Given this definition, peer review is considered to be an activity that supports the assumption that *writing is a social act*. Kenneth Bruffee has suggested that peer review reflects academic discourse in that colleagues and students converse with one another, share a common vocabulary, and affirm "normal discourse" [1]. As Bruffee and others have argued, the idea that *writing is social* endorses theories of language that affirm social interaction as the origin of thought—specifically theories forwarded by Vygotsky and Bakhtin [2, 3]. However, in relation to social theories of language, most discussions about peer review highlight face-to-face interactions; seldom are *written* interactions highlighted in peer review. For example, scholars such as Anne DiPardo, Sarah Warshauer Freedman, Anne Ruggles Gere, and Karen Spear frequently describe peer review as a speech-based activity, one that occurs in a face-to-face environment in which students talk with one another about writing. As Spear suggests, "the act of talking is a process of discovering, articulating, and clarifying meaning based on the flow of verbal and non-verbal cues the interaction generates" [4, p. 6]. Indeed, while writing may have a role in peer review (especially to record feedback or provide detailed reader response), peer review is ultimately characterized as an exercise in speaking. For instance, noting the inclusion of writing in peer review, Thom Hawkins suggests that "Spoken feedback is the spine of the workshop, the real 'work' of the hour" [6, p. 29]. It is unclear why writing is downplayed in literature about peer review; perhaps scholars felt it necessary to reference talk to affirm the primacy of speech stressed in social theories of language. This point about the privileging of speech communication in peer review is one I return to later in this chapter.

Peer review also supports the assumption that *writing is a process*. Indeed, scholarship on peer review has coincided with discussions about what has since been called the *process paradigm*. Richard Young [7] describes, for example, the move away from "current-traditional" rhetoric that emphasized writing as a product, and toward process approaches such as those described by Janet Emig in *The Composing Process of Twelfth Graders* [8]. Against the backdrop of writing as process, the activity of peer review blends in easily. That is, the very nature of peer review suggests revision because students review one another's writing for the purpose of improving the work in future drafts. In addition, peer review has sometimes been associated with the very aspects of process that other scholars have identified; peer review may be conducted to help students brainstorm ideas for papers (invention), address issues of organization (arrangement), and examine syntax and spelling (editing).

When we consider peer review in virtual environments, some aspects between peer review and virtual peer review are shared. Virtual peer review can be defined as *the activity of exchanging and responding to one another's writing via Internet technology*; no aspect of this activity occurs in a face-to-face environment. This definition is similar to peer review in that the main activity is responding to one another's writing; however, it differs in that virtual peer review involves (indeed, relies on) computer technology and thus relies entirely on written communication. Nevertheless, virtual peer review upholds the same pedagogical assumptions as peer review: writing as a social act and writing as a process.

My suggestion that virtual peer review shares assumptions of writing as a process and social act may not be all that surprising. Indeed, the mantra *pedagogy must drive technology* underscores the importance of placing pedagogical assumptions before any technological applications [5, 9, 10]. (See Cargile Cook's chapter in this volume for a discussion of this concept.) Scholars interested in teaching with technology have acknowledged these concerns, and much scholarship on computer pedagogy reinforces the same pedagogical assumptions as peer review. For instance, several scholars have recognized that one of the great advantages of computer technology is to ease revision and other aspects of the writing process, from invention to arrangement to editing [11, p. 46]. Computers facilitate writing as process, for the tools afforded by software allow for recurrent revision and editing.

In addition, scholars have suggested that networked computers support the assumption that writing is a social act. For example, Thomas Barker and Fred Kemp describe "network theory," in which students can retrieve, comment, and return one another's work through networked computer labs using asynchronous technologies [12]. Several scholars have described various forms of computer conferences, in which students may discuss, either synchronously or asynchronously, their writing assignments with one another [13-15]. Such networking and conferencing has led scholars to make the connection between computers and social construction. As Jeffrey Galin and Joan Latchaw assert in the introduction to *The Dialogic Classroom*, "The computers and writing community generally privileges social construction of knowledge and, by extension, collaborative models of learning" [9, p. 18].

HOW WELL DO THE PRACTICES OF PEER REVIEW TRANSLATE TO VIRTUAL ENVIRONMENTS?

On the surface, it may appear that face-to-face peer review would easily transfer to a virtual environment. Some scholars have suggested much the same, indicating that virtual peer review can simply be done, online, outside of class [16, 17]. However, my answer to the question "How well do the practices translate to virtual environments?" is "Not very well." Despite the common pedagogical (and theoretical) bases that virtual peer review shares with traditional peer review, virtual peer review is fundamentally different in terms of practice. That is, if we associate peer review primarily with speaking, as most scholars seem to do, then we must reconsider our expectation that the activity transfers easily to virtual (written) environments. While the move of peer review from spoken to written environments may appear to be an easy transition, it is not. Because peer review has been predominantly discussed in terms of speech situations, what we know about conducting peer review sessions is grounded in speech behaviors. For example, several scholars have outlined dialogic prompts to aid peer review and related activities [18, 19]. Many of these prompts, taking after the pedagogical assumptions of student-centered learning, support the dialogic techniques of Carl Rogers, which resemble reflective listening and non-directive support. In moving virtual peer review to writing, these speech patterns and behaviors become lost because of the disruptions of time and space that occur in virtual environments. Those teachers and students who are trained in such oral traditions may not know how to proceed. Other scholars have noted discrepancies in face-to-face and online peer review "talk." For example, Beth Hewett discovered that "talk" was much different in virtual spaces than in face-to-face environments. She ultimately affirmed Marshall McLuhan's argument that "medium is the message." She explains: "The [online] talk had different qualities when students used different media, suggesting that medium shapes talk. Oral talk focused contextually on abstract, global idea development, whereas [online] talk focused more on concrete writing tasks and group management" [20, p. 265].

I suggest that even though virtual peer review shares the same pedagogical assumptions as peer review, we must revise our understanding of peer review *practice* to fit virtual environments. Doing so does not reduce the effectiveness of face-to-face peer review (nor does it seek to replace it); rather, it is a matter of understanding differences of the environments and adjusting appropriately to those differences. I find that the easiest way of discussing differences of virtual peer review practice is in terms of the factors of time, space, and interaction. These factors are seldom discussed in literature about peer review. However, the absence of these factors is not surprising since scholars have been most interested in connecting peer review to social theories of language in which speech played a primary role. In considering the move of peer review to virtual environments, suddenly the factors of time, space, and interaction become critical.

Time

In terms of time, the difference of virtual peer review practice can be stated bluntly: traditional peer review occurs immediately while virtual peer review is delayed. This difference requires more explanation regarding the technologies used for virtual peer review, and here I note that virtual peer review, as I am defining it, does not rely on any one particular technology. Rather, virtual peer review can be conducted using synchronous technologies (such as chats and Multi-User Domains or MUDs), asynchronous technologies (such as email), integrated courseware programs (programs that integrate html, word-processing, synchronous and asynchronous technologies), and even specially designed programs that facilitate peer review. One of the beauties of virtual peer review is that there is a degree of technological flexibility in the exercise; it is driven by goals of the writer and reviewer rather than by any particular technology.

That said, however, there are important time differences between asynchronous and synchronous applications of virtual peer review. It could be argued that both forms of technology are delayed, as does Pierre Dillenbourg, who suggests that even synchronous technology has a bit of a delay, ranging from two seconds to up to a minute. He asks "Where is the threshold beyond which one considers communication to be asynchronous?" [21, p. 12]. Considering the slight delay of synchronous technologies, I argue that even synchronous technologies are not quite the same as immediate, face-to-face interaction. Students conducting virtual peer review synchronously, however, can work toward the *semblance* of a live chat, even though contributions to the online dialogue may appear disjointed. Because contributions to synchronous chats are slowed by technology, resulting conversations may appear differently than they would in face-to-face environments. (See Lang's chapter in this volume for more information on synchronous discussions.) One of the benefits, however, of using synchronous chats for virtual peer review is that participants can archive their discussion with peers to better recall the suggestions that were provided. As Eric Crump suggests, "Natural oral fluency, usually ephemeral, is now capturable" [22, p. 183]. In addition, because synchronous chats facilitate fast interaction, they allow students to brainstorm, ask questions, and receive feedback much faster than asynchronous technologies. To use synchronous chats effectively for virtual peer review, it helps if the following guidelines regarding time are implemented: 1) make sure students have already read other students' papers in advance, so that they are ready to discuss one another's work; 2) assign a facilitator within the group to keep the discussion on task; and 3) schedule precise times for synchronous discussions in which all members can participate (either in or out of class).

Asynchronous technologies for virtual peer review, however, demonstrate a much more marked difference from traditional peer review in terms of time, for interaction is *truly* delayed, sometimes by as much as one or two days. That is, virtual peer review conducted asynchronously may frequently involve out-of-class time for students. One of the things asynchronous virtual peer review affords, then, is greater time for reflection on student writing and a chance to respond with fewer constraints. For example, in-class, face-to-face workshops often follow strict time limits, to the point that a student's paper may be excluded from the workshop due to lack of time. Virtual peer review conducted asynchronously eliminates that time problem. An advantage of this increased time is that students may write more complete and thorough responses, as Joseph Walther notes: "With more time for message construction and less stress of ongoing interaction, users may have taken the opportunity for objective self-awareness, reflection, selection and transmission of preferable cues" [23, p. 19]. Because asynchronous technologies allow more time for peer review, responses from reviewers could quite possibly be longer and more detailed (some anecdotal evidence has supported this claim); however, much more research needs to be conducted to determine whether lengthier responses are the result of environment or rather the result of individual writing habits. In addition to the possibility that asynchronous technologies may lead to lengthier responses, the use of asynchronous technologies for virtual peer review may be more convenient for students, since they are able to conduct the activity on their own time instead of a prescribed time. However, while asynchronous technology may somehow seem "easier" because of the elimination of time constraints, students may need reminders to complete their peer reviews on time. For example, a virtual peer reviewer may wait to conduct a peer review the morning of the day a paper is due; naturally, such late feedback would be too late to help the student-author, who perhaps already revised a paper without the help of peer feedback. The openness of time, therefore, can backfire if students are irresponsible. However, asynchronous technology truly puts virtual peer review in the hands of learners. To facilitate asynchronous workshops, instructors can enforce the following guidelines: 1) provide timelines for completion and return of virtual peer review comments to authors; and 2) provide students with prompts or criteria to guide written comments in virtual peer review.

Space

The factor of space, when applied to virtual peer review, can be referred to in terms of "presence." That is, in virtual peer review, participants are often not physically present in front of one another as they would be in face-to-face peer review. Computer-mediated communication scholars have suggested that one consequence of moving online is the lack of non-verbal cues and other forms of feedback that result from a face-to-face environment [24]. Thus, it could be said that moving peer review online means a reduction of the types of feedback students may provide one another—feedback in the form of smiles or frowns, nods of agreement, looks of confusion, sighs, voice intonation, etc. (In their chapter in this volume, Carter and Rickly discuss the absence of physical cues in online learning in further detail.) However, in the absence of physical, verbal, and non-verbal cues, participants can create their own cues using the limits of the virtual space (emoticons are the prime example here). Thus, it is important, as some scholars suggest, that we not think of online environments as devoid of social cues, but rather that there are *fewer* social cues in online environments [23, 24]. Reduced social cues can be a benefit for shyer students who may be reluctant to participate in face-to-face discussions where social cues are more prevalent. Indeed, the reduction of social cues may encourage more equal participation among group members, although such equalization may not always occur [25, p. 4].

Connected to this difference of presence is the issue of interpersonal communication. That is, skeptics of online education suggest that communicating online is less human than face-to-face interaction, and that technology further separates us from our students. For example, in a discussion about online tutoring, Scott Russell compares computers to televisions and suggests that online tutoring (basically, online peer review) dehumanizes the practice of tutoring in writing centers [26]. Such criticisms may not ever disappear, but I find a useful response to such criticisms is to suggest that a range of personal interactions may appear in virtual environments, what Walther has described in terms of "impersonal," "interpersonal," and "hyperpersonal." Impersonal interaction suggests that reduced social cues significantly impair personal connections. Interpersonal interaction refers to the degree to which participants are able to foster relationships in virtual environments; Walther suggests, for example, that interpersonal relationships are entirely possible in virtual environments, but that they may take more time to develop than face-to-face relationships. Hyperpersonal interaction, according to Walther, can be more intense than even face-to-face interaction, and may occur in activities like virtual games or anonymous chats; Walther suggests that hyperpersonal interaction may be even more desirable than face-to-face interactions [23]. As we consider virtual peer review, we need to address the degree to which we expect interpersonal connections to thrive among participants. Considering that there are reduced social cues in virtual environments, it may be useful for instructors to: 1) assign virtual peer review groups that work over longer periods of time (not just for one assignment, but for several); and 2) keep the same group members in the groups over a semester, so that students have the opportunity to get to know one another and work with each other online.

Interaction

Interaction is the final factor that distinguishes virtual from face-to-face peer review, and the previous factors of time and space already allude to the difference of interaction. That is, when moving to virtual environments, interaction occurs through writing instead of through speaking. Scholars have cited a number of advantages of this move, namely that virtual environments encourage students to practice writing [27, 28]. In addition, writing in virtual environments reinforces rhetorical concepts such as audience and purpose because students are often writing to and interacting with their specific group members, rather than an abstract audience of "teacher" or "reader." As they are writing to other group members, they can consider carefully how their peers might respond to their comments and suggestions. In addition, students can archive comments from other students, thus keeping such comments fresh in their mind as they revise their work. In fact, in a qualitative study of four writers, Mark Mabrito found that students conducting peer review online—students who had an archive of suggestions from peers—tended to incorporate their peers' suggestions into final revisions more often than in face-to-face peer review [29]. It is a promising finding, then, that recording peer comments may stimulate recall (it is more difficult to remember exact suggestions from peer reviewers in face-to-face settings). Another interesting finding related to written interactions in peer review is that students may feel more free to offer directive comments for revision suggestions, which is a stark contrast to the non-directive speech patterns encouraged in face-to-face interactions. Mabrito found, for example, that highly apprehensive students offered more directive than indirective comments for revision [29]. Beth Hewett found similar results in an analysis of online peer review "talk." Having students write peer reviews, then, may offer some concrete advantages [20]. Students may have more time to reflect on student work and offer more detailed comments; students may gain practice writing directly to audiences; students may offer more directive and text-focused comments; authors may benefit from archiving comments from virtual peer reviews. Considering the written interaction that virtual peer review affords, instructors may find the following guidelines helpful:

1. Facilitate the organization of group archives for virtual peer review, such as through integrated Web courseware programs;
2. Have students print or save all email peer reviews they receive; and
3. Encourage students to practice detailed, constructive criticism.

Table 1 offers a summary of time, space, and interaction, the benefits afforded by these factors, and classroom guidelines.

HOW CAN INSTRUCTORS BETTER PREPARE STUDENTS FOR VIRTUAL PEER REVIEW?

Because peer review is a common activity in writing courses, instructors may not need to convince students that peer review itself is valuable. However, students may never have conducted virtual peer review as a class assignment, nor may their instructors. Thus, an important starting point for both instructors and students would be to discuss differences of time, space, and interaction that virtual environments foster and to stress that traditional peer review may not be easily transferred to virtual spaces. A helpful exercise might be to ask students to reflect on any previous experiences they have had using synchronous or asynchronous technologies to exchange feedback on documents. In conducting this exercise, instructors may find that students have been informally engaging in virtual peer review on their own time, making use of email and attachment functions. In addition, it may be worthwhile to have students conduct this exercise using synchronous or asynchronous discussion tools in class; such an exercise would encourage students to provide meta-commentary about differences of time, space, and interaction in virtual environments.

After students have discussed differences, a second suggestion instructors can implement is to encourage students to think of virtual peer review in terms of concrete goals. Through this suggestion I mean to deviate from our understanding of a traditional peer review conference, in which students may perceive of goals in terms of exchanging feedback, talking about writing, and completing the activity in a specific time frame. Because the factors of time and space fundamentally change in virtual peer review, it is important for students to become even more specific about the goals they want to accomplish in virtual peer review. Setting goals for virtual peer review is also critical because it may dictate the types of technology that would be used for the activity. For example, I propose the following goals as options for virtual peer review workshops:

1. To brainstorm with readers on ways to improve writing;
2. To provide thorough, detailed reader response on specified criteria; and
3. To provide global perspective on writing and a sense of overall strengths and weaknesses of one's writing.

In articulating these goals, I do not mean to suggest that each virtual peer review workshop should aim to achieve *all* of these goals. On the contrary, I suggest that virtual peer review workshops be arranged to focus on one or two goals at the most. The reason is because certain technologies work better for some goals than others. For example, synchronous technologies work well for encouraging students to brainstorm ideas and receive immediate feedback. However, synchronous

Table 1. Time, Space, and Interaction Description, Benefits, and Classroom Guidelines

Factor	Description	Benefits	Guidelines for Classroom
Time	Synchronous chats~slight delay	• Quick feedback and interaction • Conversation can be captured in print for reference • Convenience of conducting chat over distance	1. Require students to read peer papers before chat. 2. Assign a facilitator of each group who keeps discussion on track. 3. Schedule precise/firm times for chats.
	Asynchronous chats~pronounced delay	• Fewer time constraints for peer review than face-to-face classroom • Greater time for reflection (potential for longer responses) • Convenience for students who prefer to work on their own time	1. Provide timelines for completion and return of virtual peer review. 2. Arrange for email exchange or Web courseware to facilitate asynchronous virtual peer review. 3. Provide prompts or specific criteria to guide asynchronous response.
Space	No shared physical presence of peer review participants; fewer social cues	• Potential increased participation among shyer students • Interpersonal ties strengthen over time	1. Keep same group members within a group. 2. Assign groups to work over long periods of time.
Interaction	Written instead of spoken	• Increased practice with *writing* • Students write comments with specific audiences in mind • Peer comments can be archived • Written peer review comments stimulate greater recall for revision • More directive, detailed comments	1. Organize/track virtual peer review archives through integrated Web courseware programs. 2. Have students keep record of all emails (print and/or save) for instructor review. 3. Encourage students to provide constructive, detailed criticism in written comments.

technologies may not work well for providing detailed reader response, particularly when synchronous chats lead to an overwhelming amount of off-task talk as Jeffrey Sirc and Tom Reynolds discovered [30]. Let me address these goals one by one and address the range of technologies that may accommodate them.

The first goal, brainstorming with readers about ways to improve writing, fits best, I believe, with synchronous technologies. As Beth Hewett found, such activities are closely associated with speaking situations; if instructors and students prefer this faster, interactive dynamic, synchronous technologies would be more effective [20]. In addition, those who would like to encourage community building may prefer synchronous chats. For instance, Sirc and Reynolds found that synchronous chats may not have been as task-focused in peer review sessions, but they found that such chats were "highly significant in terms of negotiating a larger cultural meaning of public stances and identities" [30, p. 67]. That is, these authors found that synchronous chats served the needs of writers in terms of forming community. Furthermore, those who strongly prefer face-to-face environments may find synchronous interactions more to their liking. Writing center scholars, for instance, have begun to embrace synchronous technologies for tutorials. As Eric Crump suggests, synchronous chats present unlimited—yet largely untapped—potential for interacting with students about writing: "For online writing centers, hoping to discover how network computing tools might help them create the realms in which student writers can develop and grow, MUDs are rich with possibilities" [22, p. 190]. Synchronous technologies, then, may be more useful for virtual peer review sessions in which brainstorming, spontaneous feedback, and quick interaction is desirable.

The second goal, providing thorough, detailed reader response, is best suited to asynchronous technologies for asynchronous technologies like email allow readers to take time to read, reflect, and write detailed responses. Further, email allows virtual peer reviewers to insert what Barbara Monroe calls "intertextual comments" in an author's text [31]. Intertextual comments are those that may interrupt an author's text with a reader response or comment. Often intertextual comments are distinguished by a different font or style, such as using **bold face**, ALL CAPS, or a different font altogether. In email messages, virtual peer reviewers can also signal an intertextual comment using a particular symbol, such as through hashmarks (##) or asterisks (**) (see Figure 1).

Lost Valley Community has a couple differences from More's Utopia and the Oneida community. One major difference is its close connection to the outside society. **Can you explain further how More's society was different from this?** The group's non-profit educational center accommodates many children and some adults from several of the nearby cities.

Figure 1. Intertextual comments using symbols.

Besides email, word-processing allows for many options for inserting inter-textual comments. Many word-processing programs allow people to "highlight changes" in a different color of text. This tool also marks deleted words or any changes in spacing (see Figure 2).

For those who do not like to interrupt an author's text, many word-processing programs may have a function called "inserting comments," which allows readers to highlight a relevant passage and write a comment about the passage, which is stored similarly to a footnote. The comment does not appear until a reader puts their mouse over the highlighted passage, and looks much like a 3M "sticky note" (see Figure 3).

Such features, also found in collaborative software, allow groups to tailor their methods of response; but in addition, students can receive their texts and truly get a sense of how readers responded to specific passages. These word-processing tools can then be used in combination with email, for students can attach word documents with their comments to email messages in the form of attachments.

The third goal, providing global perspective on a student's writing in terms of overall strengths and weaknesses, could be accomplished through either synchronous or asynchronous exchanges; however, asynchronous technologies may allow reviewers the opportunity to reflect more fully on their impressions of strengths and weaknesses. Indeed, in a case study I conducted on the use of virtual peer review, several students chose to use asynchronous technologies to provide

---

There are a few likenesses and many differences from group to group, but they share in some common basic tradition, blue-printed by More's Utopia, including a sense of ~~unsatisfaction from~~ dissatisfaction with the outside society, a common view, and some version of a communal aspect of life.

Figure 2. Intertextual comments using tools function.

Utopian Tradition

Throughout human history there [...] people start groups with other peo[...] on aspects of their society that the[...]

Lee-Ann Kastman Breuch:
It would help if you could more fully explain the characteristics of More's Utopia. This would be important to establish a basis of comparison for the other community you describe.

and resemble what is thought of as a utopian society. One of the first blue-prints for a utopian society was created by Thomas More, in his fictional novel Utopia.[1] Other groups, such as

Figure 3. Intertextual comments using "Comments" function.

what Barbara Monroe calls an "end note" [31, p. 22]. An end note is a global comment composed by the reviewer that appears at the end of a text; often, these comments summarize strengths and weaknesses in the text. (Instructors should be quite familiar with this type of comment, for it is often employed in evaluation of students' papers.) Consider the following example in Figure 4 in which a student provided an "end note."

A benefit of asynchronous technologies for this type of commentary is that reviewers may feel more comfortable providing such statements literally from a distance. Mabrito [29] and Hewett [20] both found, for example, that students provided more direct comments when conducting peer review online than in face-to-face situations. In addition, Sirc and Reynolds found that students in synchronous chats were extremely hesitant to offer criticisms to other writers; they concentrated much more effort on "saving face" in synchronous chats [30]. Using asynchronous technologies may encourage virtual peer reviewers to fully articulate criticism.

Preparing students for virtual peer review, then, requires that instructors help set goals for what the virtual peer review workshops are to accomplish. Instructors must also be aware of how specific technologies help or hinder certain goals.

Implications of Virtual Peer Review

While I have suggested here that virtual peer review is a relatively new activity, it is new only in the sense that scholars are beginning to formally recognize it. That is, although virtual peer review may not yet be commonplace in classrooms, I suspect that it is becoming more commonplace in our daily writing activities, as increasing daily volumes of email and word attachments may demonstrate. My efforts here are to draw attention to this activity and to suggest that virtual peer

---

From:	xxx@umn.edu
To:	xxx@umn.edu
Sent:	Sunday, February 27, 2000 3:08 PM
Subject:	Re: paper

Your memo is very well written and obviously researched well. I think you covered all that was required (the questions) and more. This paragraph is a little unclear:

I understand that ultimately, the decision of what to do with the Polecat Bench is not in my hands alone, but I am making the following recommendations if development occurs. The Polecat Bench is located a good distance from the Buffalo Bill Reservoir. Because of this fact, irrigation of the area will involve construction of canals, storage dams, and pumping plants.

What exactly are your recommendations? You may want to present them upfront at the beginning (bulleted list?) and then clarify in the body. Otherwise it looks good.

Figure 4. End note comment.

review offers us an extraordinary opportunity to bridge what we already know about writing and pedagogy with what future technologies may bring. Indeed, virtual peer review has solid roots in an activity that has been documented in past scholarship, but it is unique and it can adopt technologies of the future. As we look toward virtual applications of peer review, the boundaries are limitless. That is, this basic activity of exchanging and responding to writing online has implications for workplace writing and technical communication (document cycling, online editing, collaborative writing); professional publication (anonymous review and draft exchange conducted via email); online writing centers (discussing writing and responding to writing in tutorial sessions); and even writing-across-the-curriculum (implementing virtual peer review as a writing-intensive activity in discipline-specific courses). Formally recognizing virtual peer review, then, is simply the tip of the iceberg. Future research may examine whether or not virtual peer review improves the quality of response or whether or not virtual peer review technologies are widely accessible for students. However, encouraging students to establish concrete goals for virtual peer review, as well as drawing attention toward differences of time, space, and interaction, provide a helpful starting point as we move this activity into virtual environments.

REFERENCES

1. K. Bruffee, Collaboration and the "Conversation of Mankind." *College English, 46*, pp. 635-652, 1984.
2. A. DiPardo and S. W. Freedman, Peer Response Groups in the Writing Classroom: Theoretic Foundations and New Directions, *Review of Educational Research, 58*:2, pp. 119-149, 1988.
3. A. R. Gere, *Writing Groups: History, Theory, and Implications,* Southern Illinois University Press, Carbondale, Illinois, 1987.
4. K. Spear, *Sharing Writing: Peer Response Groups in English Classes,* Boynton/Cook Publishers Heinemann, Portsmouth, New Hampshire, 1988.
5. S. Harrington, R. Rickly, and M. Day (eds.), *The Online Writing Classroom*, Hampton Press, Cresskill, New Jersey, 2000.
6. T. Hawkins, *Group Inquiry Techniques for Teaching Writing*, National Council of Teachers of English, Urbana, Illinois, 1976.
7. R. Young, Paradigms and Problems: Needed Research in Rhetorical Invention, in *Research on Composing: Points of Departure*, C. R. Cooper and L. Odell (eds.), National Council of Teachers of English, Urbana, Illinois, pp. 29-48, 1978.
8. J. Emig, *The Composing Processes of Twelfth Graders,* National Council of Teachers of English, Urbana, Illinois, 1971.
9. J. Galin and J. Latchaw (eds.), *The Dialogic Classroom: Teachers Integrating Computer Technology, Pedagogy, and Research*, National Council of Teachers of English, Urbana, Illinois, 1998.
10. F. Kemp, Surviving in English Departments: The Stealth Computer-Based Writing Program, in *The Online Writing Classroom,* S. Harrington, R. Rickly, and M. Day (eds.), Hampton Press, Cresskill, New Jersey, pp. 267-284, 2000.

11. G. E. Hawisher, P. LeBlanc, C. Moran, and C. L. Selfe, *Computers and the Teaching of Writing in American Higher Education, 1979-1994: A History*, Ablex, Norwood, New Jersey, 1996.
12. T. T. Barker and F. O. Kemp, Network Theory: A Postmodern Pedagogy for the Writing Classroom, in *Computers and Community: Teaching Composition in the Twenty-First Century*, C. Handa (ed.), Boynton/Cook, Portsmouth, New Hampshire, pp. 1-27, 1990.
13. B. A. Bowen, Composition, Collaborations, and Computer-Mediated Conferencing, in *The Online Writing Classroom*, S. Harrington, R. Rickly, and M. Day (eds.), Hampton Press, Cresskill, New Jersey, pp. 129-146, 2000.
14. C. K. Cyganowski, The Computer Classroom and Collaborative Learning: The Impact on Student Writers, in *Computers and Community: Teaching Composition in the Twenty-First Century*, C. Handa (ed.), Boynton/Cook, Portsmouth, New Hamphsire, pp. 68-88, 1990.
15. A. H. Duin and C. Hansen, Reading and Writing on Computer Networks as Social Construction and Social Interaction, in *Literacy and Computers: The Complications of Teaching and Learning with Technology*, C. L. Selfe and S. Hilligoss (eds.), Modern Language Association of America, New York, pp. 89-112, 1994.
16. H. R. Ewald, A Tangled Web of Discourses: On Post-Process Pedagogy and Communicative Interaction, in *Post-Process Theory: Beyond the Writing-Process Paradigm*, T. Kent (ed.), Southern Illinois University Press, Carbondale, Illinois, 1999.
17. M. Palmquist, K. Kiefer, J. Hartvigsen, and B. Goodlew, *Transitions: Teaching Writing in Computer-Supported and Traditional Classrooms*, Ablex, London, 1997.
18. B. L. Clark, *Talking about Writing: A Guide for Tutor and Teacher Conferences*, The University of Michigan Press, Ann Arbor, Michigan, 1985.
19. T. J. Reigstad and D. A. McAndrew, *Training Tutors for Writing Conferences*, National Council of Teachers of English, Urbana, Illinois, 1984.
20. B. L. Hewett, Characteristics of Interactive Oral and Computer-Mediated Peer Group Talk and Its Influence on Revision, *Computers and Composition, 17*:3, pp. 265-288, 2000.
21. P. Dillenbourg, Introduction: What Do You Mean By "Collaborative Learning?" in *Collaborative Learning: Cognitive and Computational Approaches*, P. Dillenbourg (ed.), Pergamon, New York, pp. 1-19, 1999.
22. E. Crump, At Home in the MUD: Writing Centers Learn to Wallow, in *High Wired: On the Design, Use, and Theory of Educational MOOs*, C. Haynes and J. R. Holmevik (eds.), The University of Michigan Press, Ann Arbor, Michigan, pp. 177-191, 1998.
23. J. B. Walther, Computer-Mediated Communication: Impersonal, Interpersonal, and Hyperpersonal Interaction, *Communication Research, 23*:1, pp. 3-43, 1996.
24. M. Lea and R. Spears, Paralanguage and Social Perception in Computer-Mediated Communication, *Journal of Organizational Computing, 2*, pp. 321-341, 1992.
25. Z. Berge and M. Collins (eds.), *Computer Mediated Communication and the Online Classroom*, Hampton Press, Cresskill, New Jersey, 1995.
26. S. Russell, Clients Who Frequent Madam Barnett's Emporium, *The Writing Center Journal, 20*:1, pp. 61-72, 1999.

27. W. Condon, Virtual Space, Real Participation: Dimensions and Dynamics of a Virtual Classroom, in *The Online Writing Classroom*, S. Harrington, R. Rickly, and M. Day (eds.), Hampton Press, Cresskill, New Jersey, pp. 45-62, 2000.

28. M. Harris and M. Pemberton, Online Writing Labs (OWLs): A Taxonomy of Options and Issues, *Computers and Composition, 12*:2, pp. 145-159, 1995.

29. M. Mabrito, Electronic Mail as a Vehicle for Peer Response, *Written Communication, 8*:4, pp. 509-532, 1991.

30. G. Sirc and T. Reynolds, The Face of Collaboration in the Networked Writing Classroom, *Computers and Composition, 7*, pp. 53-70, 1990.

31. B. Monroe, The Look and Feel of the OWL Conference, in *Wiring the Writing Center*, E. Hobsen (ed.), Utah State University Press, Logan, Utah, pp. 3-24, 1998.

CHAPTER 9

Replicating and Extending Dialogic Aspects of the Graduate Seminar in Distance Education

Susan Lang

What defines a useful and beneficial class discussion at the graduate level? The graduate seminar of the late twentieth/early twenty-first century has valued dialog over lecture, student-led presentations over teacher-centered discussions, and incrementally sequenced assignments over the single term project. In teaching graduate courses via online education, one tendency has been to attempt to replicate this model of the graduate seminar and thus to create a multi-voiced interchange of ideas or concepts that transcends the traditional, lecture-based course. However, the online classroom alters our expectations and often challenges our capabilities to respond to what might be very routine in an onsite classroom. Of the issues I considered when planning a course in Web Publishing and Usability for Texas Tech University's MATC program, those dealing with the topic of class discussion seemed in some ways the most thought-provoking in light of the transfer into an online environment. This chapter asks and examines a number of questions about synchronous and asynchronous class discussion, including:

- What are common assumptions, goals, and theories underlying the use of class discussion in an onsite graduate course?
- How do these assumptions, goals, and theories drive our attempts to integrate synchronous class discussion into online graduate courses?
- What kinds of decisions and preparations do instructors need to make in order to conduct successful synchronous class discussions? And what can an instructor do if a particular discussion does not seem to be working?
- What is the future of synchronous discussion in distance courses?

ASSUMPTIONS, GOALS, AND THEORIES OF
CLASS DISCUSSION IN ONSITE COURSE

Let me say at the outset that the topic of class discussion takes on a different spin when considering its role in undergraduate classes. While some of what follows may well apply and work in an upper-division course, students enrolled in lower-level service courses often enter with knowledge levels and motivations that will vary significantly enough to force instructors to implement strategies different from those described here for conducting class discussion. While much discussion of general pedagogical principles has been devoted to those used in undergraduate courses and curriculum, sadly little has been written about graduate education in terms of pedagogy; the majority of debate concerning graduate courses focuses primarily on content rather than pedagogy. Thus, to set some common ground for our examination of class discussion, this first section offers some observations about the nature of class discussion in onsite graduate courses and uses Von Krogh, Ichijo, and Nonaka's discussion of knowledge confirmation and knowledge creation in the workplace as a framework for considering the elements of beneficial class discussion. While their book, *Enabling Knowledge Creation,* presents a single perspective on the role of conversation management and does so from a workplace perspective, it provides us with a way to articulate clearly what for many instructors has remained in the realm of tacit knowledge about conducting class discussions at the graduate level [1].

Currently, there exist two primary modes of graduate instruction—student-led discussion and professorial lecture. That is, classes in many disciplines still take the form of instructor-centered lectures in which professors bestow their knowledge of a given subject upon their students, and discussion serves a perfunctory purpose: to ensure that students have read and gained some elementary understanding of the material. Von Krogh et al. refer to the term "knowledge confirmation" when examining conversations in the workplace, and their definition also rings true for lecture-based graduate courses [1]. Exchanges that have knowledge confirmation as their goal ". . . focus on the present, on facts, on solid reality. The scope and impact of the issues discussed is quite limited. The purpose is mainly to confirm explicit knowledge. Furthermore, the concepts used in the conversation already exist and have been justified" [1, p. 128].

While these types of discussions and classes serve to "confirm and reconfirm established experience" as well as "allow for effective problem solving," they would seem to have a limited use in more contemporary paradigms of graduate education that advocate more participatory, discussion-driven courses in which students often lead discussion for all or a portion of most classes and where value is often placed on the generation and construction of new ideas and concepts. Von Krogh et al. refer to this type of learning as "knowledge creation," which they describe as follows:

There is no sound knowledge base on which expertise can be established if it has not yet been created. In this situation, no solid facts or explicit models are at hand to indicate whether the participant is right or wrong. The purpose is for participants to establish not only new knowledge but a new reality . . . the scope and impact of the issues to be discussed are essentially unlimited at the outset [1, p. 128].

Although some more cynical critics of this essentially constructivist view would say that the transition from a lecture-driven to a participatory-driven class often occurs in order to minimize instructor preparation time before each class and that discussions directed by students frequently, if not inevitably, lead to watered-down or simplistic coverage of the course content, those who advocate a constructivist pedagogical view would argue otherwise. Constructivists would contend that quite a bit of significant student learning occurs during the time when participants pose questions, hear responses both in agreement and contrary to their positions, and negotiate an understanding based on the informed conversations that follow. In the constructivist paradigm, the instructor functions somewhere between mediator and coach, perhaps stepping in to offer clarification of a certain point, arbitrate a heated discussion, or redirect the group if the topic has strayed far from the assigned topic of the day. But to what end? While it is generally a simple task to bring graduate students into a room and get them to offer their opinions on assigned material, enabling learning so that participants wrestle with new information in meaningful ways, articulate their own ideas in a public forum (even as those ideas are just beginning to form), and share in the important process of community knowledge building at the end of the class time is a complex and difficult endeavor.

To understand the extent of the task, consider the four guiding principles for good conversations offered by Von Krogh et al. Effective conversation managers should:

- Encourage active participation;
- Establish conversational etiquette;
- Edit conversations appropriately; and
- Foster innovative language [1].

The first two principles probably sound familiar to any instructor who has ever given "participation grades" to students, as active and appropriate participation forms the basis for those grades. The final two might at first glance seem less familiar—we rarely see ourselves as the verbal (as opposed to written) editors of our students, and more often we find ourselves teaching the language of our field rather than encouraging students to "invent their own." Yet all four of these hold more complexity than first glance might suggest in terms of what they require from a classroom instructor. Before moving on to a discussion of online class discussion, we will briefly consider each in turn.

Encourage Active (and Balanced) Participation

My amendment to the first principle reflects the primary difficulty of working in the physical classroom—achieving balanced participation levels among students without silencing potentially beneficial contributions. Instructors *must* set the procedures for establishing conversational relationships among students. Doing so does not create the "teacher-centered" class that much pedagogical scholarship has maligned; on the contrary, it provides a context in terms of both initial subject matter as well as overt and tacit ritual (in terms of order of speakers, protocol for asking questions, etc.) in which to conduct the dialog. Having set the opening conditions, though, is usually not enough to sustain consistent and active participation of all students; the instructor is always actively managing the conversation in order to assure the greatest opportunities for continued, balanced participation. (In addition to this discussion of managing conversations, see Grady and Davis' chapter in this volume. Their discussion offers another option for structuring synchronous discussions online.)

Establish Conversational Etiquette

"By etiquette, we do not mean politeness above any other form of behavior or old-fashioned good manners," state Von Krogh et al. [1, p. 134] when speaking of establishing productive workplace conversations. Indeed, one has only to lead one or two classes in which all participants are excruciatingly polite in manner yet ineffective in conversation to realize that whether it be workplace or classroom, the culture for discussion must be made clear to all. Of the eight rules of etiquette listed by Von Krogh et al. for use in the workplace, five hold particular value for the graduate seminar:

- **Avoid unnecessary ambiguity:** Both faculty and students use this tactic to disguise when immediate facts or information needed to answer a question are forgotten or otherwise unavailable. Some ambiguity, however, is inevitable when students are working toward explanations of new concepts;
- **Avoid intimidation:** Participants often feel intimidated because of the frequency of one individual's contributions or body language or speech mannerisms that accompany them;
- **Avoid exercising authority:** An instructor, a student, or group of students who concur on a topic can successfully turn the conversation in a specific direction;
- **Avoid premature closure:** Instructors must guard against enabling students to agree on an outcome or concept to the extent that they wish to close down discussion of it; and
- **Help other participants to be brave:** This rule may mean many different things—from convincing the shy student with ideas to share them to enabling a student to admit that she made an error in a previous statement, the instructor has a responsibility to foster a climate in which students can experiment with ideas.

Edit Conversations Appropriately

Class discussions are places where students work to translate tacit knowledge into public discourse. Instructors can facilitate this process by: 1) intervening to assist a participant in clarifying a concept so that the rest of the class can participate in the discussion; and 2) intervening to move a conversation on to another area when participants cannot come to agreement on a particular concept and when lack of agreement prevents the group from moving on to an area which might help illuminate meaning.

Foster Innovative Language

By fostering innovative language, I do not mean that instructors are encouraging students to create new words, new definitions, or a new language. Rather, I mean that instructors are guiding students in the acquisition and use of critical terms and their various denotations and connotations via their active use of such terms in class discussion as they voice and develop ways of speaking about concepts that are new to them. Thus, students learn to integrate the jargon of the field into their growing knowledge base. Of the four principles mentioned here, this final one is most essential to the individual student's development in graduate seminars. The first three principles establish a context for conversation, but this last item ensures that students will be capable of carrying on the conversations of the field once they leave that classroom environment. For this reason alone, it behooves instructors moving graduate courses into the distance environment to consider how best to incorporate activities that can offer the benefits of this experience.

INTEGRATING SYNCHRONOUS CLASS DISCUSSION IN ONLINE COURSES

Given the complexity of conducting discussions in face-to-face settings, one would imagine that transferring this environment to a dedicated online course would have received considerable attention. Such does not seem to be the case. While considerable attention has been paid to the role of technology in teaching and practicing technical communication, little or no sustained discussion concerning synchronous discussion and distance education has emerged. We take for granted the importance of making our onsite classes learner- or student-centered, and in the face-to-face environment, that generally means having students engage in active discussion. Ironically, however, one of the primary advantages pointed to by a number of authors when it comes to online courses is the notion that students *do not* need synchronous conversation as a regular part of their online or distance courses, or that such conversations are ancillary to other pedagogical tools. For example, Leonard's account of the development of the distance learning graduate program at Mercer University specifically points out that the university-wide commitment made to asynchronous communication technologies occurred out of a desire to free students from the constraints of time and location. Although Leonard maintains that "a sense of community among students and the teachers is vital to the learning process," such a rapport will come out of collaborative work and "quarterly face-to-face meetings, as well as through high tech electronic means" [2, p. 399]. Additionally, in Stuart Selber's *Computers and Technical Communication: Pedagogical and Programmatic Perspectives*, the primary foci in Part II, which deals with pedagogical frameworks, is the use and design of Web spaces for classes and the role of electronic collaboration in existing courses [3]. Duin and Archee confine their discussion of social construction and interaction among course participants to the context of the course web. For example, they note that instructors "should still consider the social interaction perspective as highly relevant," but doing so would seem to require no more than listening to feedback on the website and providing interactive forms and chat rooms, thus "encouraging learners to submit their responses to the information and discuss their ideas with others" [4, p. 161]. Perhaps this perspective grows out of the research they recount in their 1996 article, "Collaboration via Email and Internet Relay Chat: Understanding Time and Technology," in which they relate the experiences of students who attempted to use both synchronous and asynchronous methods to complete course assignments. Duin and Archee found that although the IRC enabled students "to construct a somewhat more open context" for discussion, they often became frustrated with the slow speed of the chat rooms and resorted to sending email, which allowed for more rapid conversation [4, pp. 409-410].

In some ways, then, the conversational element seems ancillary to the solitary learner in a remote locale. Both Burnett and Clark, as well as Allen and Wickliff, focus on aspects of developing electronic collaboration using various applications; while Burnett and Clark's examination of "synchronicity, fixity, durability, and multiplicity" [5, p. 178] in the context of collaborative tools has a potential application in the analysis of class discussion, their work focuses on an environment for conversation where the conversation is but a means to an end in the form of a specific project. Similarly, Allen and Wickliff examine the potential of electronic collaboration as a component of a larger course [6]. Finally, Mehlenbacher's discussion of online environment design ultimately focuses more on the role of technology in faculty development and promotion than on any particular technique for teaching [7]. Again, my point in revisiting these texts is to underscore the fact that they contain no focused or sustained discussion of synchronous activities approximating class discussion.

More recently, of the authors published in the Winter 1999 edition of *Technical Communication Quarterly*, several provide valuable information about student/student and student/instructor interaction but give the majority of their attention to asynchronous rather than synchronous discussion. David Gillette advises online instructors to construct "lecture halls, workshop space, and a student lounge," but focuses on the use of asynchronous tools such as Web boards in order to promote student interaction [8, pp. 28-29]. Similarly, while Schneider and Germann state that "the use of 'chat' and conferencing is becoming an increasingly important part of the [authors' online technical communication] courses," they propose a stronger case for the use of asynchronous communication. They find asynchronous communication "perhaps more useful, because students can browse messages from the instructor and other students, research and plan responses, and enter the replies when ready instead of having to react immediately during a synchronous chat...the convenience of asynchronous communication makes it the preferred method of communicating" [9, p. 45]. Finally, when considering the translation of onsite tasks into the online environment, Thrush and Young also list asynchronous activities such as listservs, discussion groups, and email as viable options [10, p. 52].

While asynchronous activities are a significant and important component in graduate-level distance courses in that they do provide opportunities for students to reflect on the assigned readings and projects, as well as respond to others' comments, these activities cannot completely substitute for synchronous discussion if we articulate as one of the goals of graduate instruction the student's move from entry-level practitioner to professional. That is to say, while asynchronous discussion may enable wider participation by all students in a conversation and provide those participants with time to reflect and craft their contributions, synchronous discussion requires students to "think on their feet" as they respond to ideas or problems which more closely mimic many workplace situations where employees do not have the leisure of time to reflect on various courses of action prior to making a decision. As any instructor who has tried to explain a complex concept via a series of emails to a student knows, such processes often lose their contextual immediacy when spread over a day or two (or more) of asynchronous comment and response. Additionally, if we assume that our students need continued exposure to a range of technological artifacts, we are shortchanging our students if we do not give them ample practice in the immediacy of electronic synchronous communication whether it be through MOOs, videoconferencing, or some other available method of communication; while our institutions' technologies may not precisely mimic those that our students will encounter in the workplace, they provide a somewhat comparable electronic, synchronous experience in articulating, interpreting, and responding to others. In planning our distance courses, we should be aware that by offering asynchronous activities that respond to a perceived need for convenience for our students, we are neglecting other aspects of their graduate education. Finally, as instructors, having the opportunity to translate classroom discussion into electronic, synchronous environments allows us to examine carefully the assumptions each of us hold regarding the nature and the goals of classroom discussion. In the next section, I will examine some of those assumptions in the context of a particular graduate seminar in our technical communication program.

DECISIONS AND PREPARATION FOR CONDUCTING
SYNCHRONOUS ONLINE DISCUSSIONS

Synchronous discussion is an integral part of Texas Tech's English Department's online Master's degree in Technical Communication (MATC). The program overview states that

> ... students "meet" via the Internet rather than in classrooms at the university. Graduate distance learning courses are taught as organized courses on the semester schedule. Students are expected to meet course deadlines assigned by the instructor and to participate in a one-hour synchronous class discussion from 6–7 P.M. on one designated weekday during the semester. A graduate level course requires a commitment of approximately ten hours per week for participating in group online activities, for reading, and for working on course projects [11].

To facilitate synchronous discussion, courses are capped at 15 students, the same as for our onsite graduate courses. Because of the shorter length of the summer term, courses taught during that time actually meet two nights a week for a total of approximately 20 meetings. Texas Tech's courses use a virtual educational environment known as a MOO (Multiple User Dimension/Dungeon, Object-Oriented). Although some might assume that a MOO has some connection to some of the famous Texas longhorn cattle, such is not the case. As Haynes and Holmevik note, "The history of educational MOOs is essentially a story about adaptation and reconception of gaming technology for professional and educational use" [12, p. 2]. MOOs are descendants of MUDs, virtual environments for multi-player adventure games, which were in turn adapted to the online environment from such inspirations as TSR's *Dungeons and Dragons*. Like the Internet Relay Chat (IRC) described by Duin and Archee [4], MUDs and MOOs began as text-only environments. However, while the IRC is organized as a seemingly infinite series of chats, or channels, in which participants can gather to discuss topics of mutual interest, MOOs present users with virtual spaces—such as caves, dungeons, and, with the advent of Amy Bruckman's MediaMOO, the media lab at M.I.T. Unlike chat rooms, however, MOO users can actually contribute to the building of their environments by designing and programming new spaces and objects to interact with. For example, instructors may decide to create a primary classroom, a series of small conference rooms, and a series of recording devices that can capture and display transcripts of class conversation, rather than simply use a single chat room. They can also textually decorate and customize their spaces. Holmevik and Haynes write that "textual expression has always been what makes MOO distinctively and qualitatively the most powerful real-time electronic environment for educational and professional purposes" [12, p. 325]. However, the TTU English Department MOO, built with enCore (an open source application) and located at http://moo.engl.ttu.edu:7000 (see Figure 1), integrates the text-based MOO with a graphical Web browser and can be accessed via either a text-based or

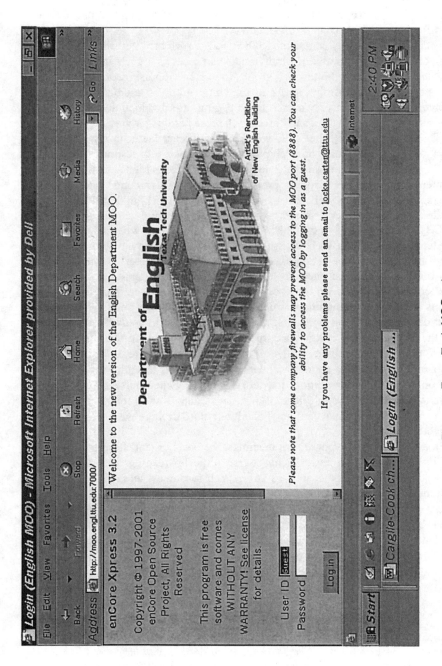

Figure 1. Texas Tech MOO entry screen.

graphical client. (For further discussion of open source applications, see Faber and Johnson-Eilola's chapter in Section 4.)

Students and faculty access the MOO using a Web browser; this interface can support a variety of activities. Individuals can meet as a class in a single room on the MOO, break out into small groups in separate rooms, record conversations for storage on a transcript, speak to the entire group or a single person (such conversations, known as whispering or paging, are not included on the MOO transcripts), and post URLs and PowerPoint presentations for viewing by the class.

These capabilities of the MOO were one significant factor in my planning for my Summer 2001 course on Web publishing and usability testing. Other factors that came into play included the levels of student experience with the course content and with the graduate program itself (some students were new MA students, others were well into their MATC coursework, and still others were students in our doctoral program in Technical Communication and Rhetoric [TCR]). Finally, I had to establish my course objectives—what did I want these students to learn about Web publishing and usability, and how would this learning environment influence the success or failure of the course? Summer courses work at an accelerated pace, so it was essential that the first class meeting set the tone for the course in terms of synchronous online interaction as well as in terms of laying out assignment structures, reading sequence, and the other normal first day matters. Prior to the first meeting, I had been in contact with a number of the students to confirm class meeting location, start times, and the like. Also, the course had overenrolled with both students onsite at TTU as well as distance students; as a result, I suddenly found myself teaching two sections of the online course. In addition, I would be teaching the course from a location other than Lubbock, so in effect all of these students would function as distance students in this course, even though about one-third of them were from our onsite doctoral program.[1]

In addition to the synchronous meetings, the basic organization for the course included four written assignments/course projects; reading assignments from two primary textbooks as well as some Web resources; and, for each reading assignment, a reading response of 500 words posted to WebBoard, a message board software which supports multiple threaded discussions, several hours prior to the beginning of each class meeting. Class meetings, then, were a place in which students would be expected to discuss and pose questions about aspects of the reading assignments, including WebBoard responses from their colleagues, talk about their approaches to upcoming projects, and discover through conversation

---

[1] The trend of having an instructor, as well as students, work from a distance may well become a valuable component of distance education. Although I was the first instructor in Tech's MATC program to teach from a distance, two courses in Spring 2003 had similar situations. Patricia Goubil-Gambrell instructed the "Teaching Technical and Professional Writing" course from Austin, TX, while Fred Kemp taught "Rhetorical Analysis of Texts" from Lubbock and Raleigh, NC.

innovative ways of synthesizing and articulating concepts related to course content. While the bulk of students' course grades would be determined by their work on course projects and asynchronous responses to the reading assignments, attendance and active participation at MOO sessions would make the difference in borderline grades.

Ultimately, preparing for the synchronous MOO discussions required that I recognize and address upfront some of the potentially complicating factors of conducting discussion online. One primary difference between MOO discussions and face-to-face classroom interaction that instructors must prepare for lies in the fact that everyone in the class can type responses at once and post these rather rapidly. Thus, for the instructor and student alike, it can be difficult to participate as a writer, reader/interpreter, and facilitator simultaneously. To alleviate this tension, I planned to begin each class as a writer with prepared remarks before moving into what I saw as the inevitable and necessary role of reader/interpreter of student comments and questions. In order to do this, given the large amount of material that would serve as the subject of conversation, it was essential that dialog in each meeting begin with some structure—in this case, I chose to use 2–4 discussion questions drawn from the readings and student responses to those assignments—since, with 10-12 people in each course, keeping up with the conversation could become difficult. Furthermore, I would compose a few (less than five) prepared observations about the topic of the class meeting that I would post as needed throughout the hour. These generally were less than 300 words but served to either jumpstart conversation or give students something to read and react to if they found themselves floundering for any reason.

While the above might well also be part of my preparation for an onsite seminar, I'd spend a few minutes completing some additional tasks on class meeting days. Most preparations were focused on two areas—ensuring that the MOO technology was set up properly to accommodate an enthusiastic, wide-ranging discussion and composing notes on the topics of discussion that could be used as the basis of some of my responses to students in the MOO. Having ready responses to common questions enables me to focus my efforts on composing on the fly to unanticipated queries or questions that grow out of the immediate discussion context. Unlike in an onsite class, I'd usually check my classroom earlier in the day to make sure that the MOO was operational and that the recorder that logged transcripts was ready to go for the first class (see Figure 2).

At about 10 minutes before the top of the hour, I'd login to our classroom in order to answer any brief questions and chat with early arrivals. Simultaneously, I kept my email running in the background so that if any students were having trouble with their connection, they could contact me and we would try to resolve the problem. Armed with these prepared remarks, I would begin class—always within a minute of the designated start time—by posting the discussion questions for the evening; with two sections scheduled at 4:00 and 6:00 P.M. CDT, the

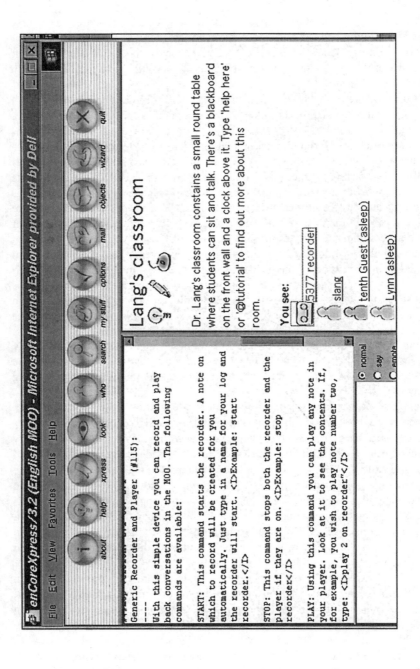

Figure 2. Instructions for using MOO recorder.

first class needed to run on time in order to provide my eyes, fingers, and brain with a short break before the second class.

Once the questions were posted in the classroom, there would be a short lull while students began responding. Within a minute or so, first responses would appear onscreen, and the conversation would begin. For the remainder of class, I would multi-task, participating in the conversation, monitoring student participation, responding to private queries (backchannelling),[2] and managing multiple threads of the discussion, if appropriate, all the while keeping an eye on the clock to ensure that all essential topics were addressed. I'll return to the topic of instructor participation in a moment. First, a brief explanation of the other tasks is in order. To monitor student participation, I would frequently scan the portion of the screen which listed participants and the time that had elapsed since they had been active contributors to the conversation. If an individual had been silent for more than 4–5 minutes, I would page them, that is, send them a private message within the MOO to see if they were 1) confused by portions of the discussion; or 2) distracted by something in their immediate physical environment. Doing so was a tactful reminder to them that they needed to engage in the public conversation.

I would send the same message if a student was shown as active but had no contributions to the public discussion appearing onscreen; this meant that the student was engaged in some sort of backchannelling activity—a private conversation which would not appear on the MOO transcript. While these conversations can be valuable to the participants for purposes of clarifying or confirming information, prolonged backchannelling can also siphon off participants from the main public discussion, thereby limiting their ability to engage with the others in meaningful discussion of the material. Backchannelling is not actively disruptive to discussion and may well serve useful purposes if students want to try out a question to the instructor or another student before posing it to the entire group or if an instructor wants to suggest to a student that she raise a particular point from her reading response without putting the student on the spot. However, instructors need to monitor backchanneling as best they can and encourage students to share ideas with the entire group as much as possible.

Another essential task performed by the online instructor is providing synthesis and an organizational framework for the multiple threads of discussion that almost always arise. Since everyone can speak at once in the MOO, it is possible to have

---

[2] Cogdill et al. define the virtual backchannel as "a private and unofficial channel of communication used for a wide variety of communications that cannot or should not be made in public: private discussions with friends; tangential or completely off-topic exchanges; assistance with rhetorical strategies, the meeting software, or group etiquette; phatic exchanges, and so on." In "Backchannel: Whispering in Digital Conversation," they define five categories of backchannel discourse: process-oriented, content-oriented, participation-enabling, tangential, and independent backchannel discourse. In MOO discussions, participants use two commands to initiate these private conversations: whisper, which allows private discussions with others in the same room, and page, which enables conversations with people in different parts of the MOO [13].

several strands evolving at once. It is the instructor's task to monitor these and respond to them in order to draw connections whenever possible and keep students from feeling overwhelmed by the amount of information exchanged. In addition to offering a synthesis, I would frequently, as the semester continued, find ways to connect conversations to upcoming assignments. While this seems a small detail, it was one about which students voiced their appreciation after the course ended.

The final task involved keeping a close eye on the clock at all times. I quickly realized that the pace of discussion was both faster and slower online than in a face-to-face classroom, and that in order to cover all scheduled topics, I would need to enforce a time limit on various parts of the class conversation.

Time—in terms of limits and download times—became even more crucial when we entered the final stages of the course. In keeping with a more participatory pedagogy, I had assigned all students the task of giving a 10–15 minute presentation on the website that they had chosen to construct/redesign. The students could incorporate visuals by using PowerPoint slides that could be uploaded to a Web directory and displayed in the MOO. I provided students with directions for uploading presentations and displaying them in the MOO and suggested that students use the classroom to rehearse the timing of the uploading of slides and scripts prior to giving the presentations during class. Most of these presentations could be considered successful; students constructed generally useful slides, created a script that they chunked and posted in the MOO in coordination with the visuals, and kept reasonably within the time limit. However, the occasional glitch did occur. The most common problems were caused by students using uncompressed image files[3] in PowerPoint slides or failing to crop images to show only the elements under discussion, which led to extended download times for class members with slower connections.

One more unique difficulty occurred after a student began his presentation. After discussing the first few slides, the student fell silent. I quickly sent him an email message to see if his connection to the MOO had gone down—no response. After 3–4 minutes, we decided to continue with the next scheduled presentation. The student did not reappear during that hour. Later that evening, I received an email from the student explaining that a line of thunderstorms had moved through and knocked out the electricity and phone lines. While equipment failure is hardly unusual in an onsite class, the inability of the student to communicate the nature of the problem should remind instructors of the continual need to step back and assess events from a variety of contexts, some clearly less familiar than

---

[3] While a comprehensive discussion of image files is beyond the scope of this chapter, instructors should know that some image file formats (JPEG, TIFF) can be compressed and thus create smaller, though lesser quality images, while others, most notably BMP, the standard Windows image format, remain uncompressed and can take up a lot of disk space. For example, the image used in Figure 2 is 25.3KB, download time 7 seconds over a 56.6K modem when saved as a JPEG file, 338KB, download time of 92 seconds over a 56.6K modem, when saved as a BMP file.

others. The lesson learned from this event—check the regional or national weather forecast prior to class and remind students that they may be called on to present at anytime on their scheduled day.

While the range of activities described in the preceding pages may seem overwhelming to some readers, rest assured that during the actual meeting time of the class, instructors are primarily involved in a single task, that of facilitating discussion among participants. While this does mean that one must read and respond quickly to the conversation, an instructor must also accomplish this same task during an onsite course. Instructors must also consider ways in which online synchronous discussion does pose challenges to the process of wrestling with concepts in complex and useful ways. I will conclude this section by enumerating some of the most challenging issues to that important goal of the class discussion.

To do so, let's return to the dynamics of the MOO conversation. Participants can simultaneously be engaged in both talking to the entire group in conscious response to other utterances and in privately broaching new topics to one or two individuals in a private discussion that often ends up moving the dialog of the entire class in a different direction. Knowing that two members of the class are speaking in a private aside while the public conversation continues, the rest of the group continues to talk, not knowing precisely who is actively, synchronously listening and who will sample the public discourse at random moments and interject a comment based on what is immediately visible on her screen. Those looking for a philosophy of language to underpin such activities should turn to Bakhtin's work on dialog, carnival, and heteroglossia. MOO transcripts give us a partial record of these speech acts, in which Bakhtin describes how "subjective experience perishes in the objective fact of the enunciated word utterance, and the enunciated work is subjectified in the act of responsive understanding in order to generate, sooner or later, a counter statement" [14, p. 57]. Add variations in connection speed to the ever-present interpretive questions posed by language and the anticipated counterstatements can appear at unanticipated times.

This matter of linguistic representation takes on greater significance in an arena where tacit signals to confirm understanding or at least an interpretation of an utterance are largely absent in recognizable form. Figure 3 helps illustrate the point that much of what transpires in the MOO becomes "*a verbal performance in print*" (14, p. 58, italics in original) and instructors and students alike must develop ways to react and respond to this performance that allow the reciprocation of understanding without the violation of new expectations of the participants. For example, in an onsite class when an individual contributes a non sequitur, the class may stumble for a moment as all process this unusual bit of information but recovers and continues as someone else moves the group on with another comment. Attention shifts to the latest verbal communication, and the ill-fitting comment is quickly forgotten. In the MOO, the expectation is there that someone can address the utterance; it remains a part of the transcript and may even be repeated in order to evoke a response. Reviewing the transcript at a later date

Figure 3. Portion of a MOO transcript.

reveals the tangents that would otherwise fade because of time constraints or because participants simply had no time (as often happens in a face-to-face discussion) to react, interpret, or respond. However, being able to rediscover the non sequiturs after class, perhaps several weeks or months later, may serve a valuable purpose in that it enables students and instructors to reevaluate the conversation, generate new ideas, see different connections, or reach alternate conclusions. Thus, the recording of these tangents supplies a level of enrichment that is often lost in an onsite class. At its busiest moments, the MOO classroom seems carnivalesque in the Bakhtinian sense, what with its ability via freewheeling discourse to subvert the orderly nature of even the most spirited onsite class discussions. Those used to the serious, "academic" nature of the onsite discussion may find the shorter utterances, the shorthand, the use of the "emote" feature (e.g., "Susan scratches her head in disbelief"), and the informal tone of many exchanges disrespectful, regardless of how well such tactics enable the free flow of voices.

Finally, readers should recall that a key criterion to implementing successful constructivist, or knowledge-creation, pedagogies is the ability to enable any class discussions to function as open genres; closure is forestalled, and meaning in an ultimate sense remains just out of reach. While Von Krogh's four principles of conversation management—actively encouraging participants, establishing conversational etiquette, editing of conversations, and fostering of innovative language—apply equally in both settings, instructors may find an urgent sense of need, borne out of previous experience, to pin down conclusions and interpretations, given the lack of a physical speaker. Perhaps the inability of participants to see each other in the current text-based MOO conversations exacerbates this need. However, it is far more productive for instructor and students to get accustomed to the notion of the open-ended speculation that can only foster more grappling with concepts and ideas.

THE FUTURE OF SYNCHRONOUS CLASS DISCUSSION IN ONLINE COURSES

Synchronous discussion has a future in distance graduate education; however, further exploration is necessary to determine how and when to integrate such activities into the graduate seminar. Thus, we should actively pursue research in synchronous discussion as it applies to graduate education in technical communication. Projects conducted in the short term might include detailed rhetorical analysis of MOO-based classes using Cogdill et al.'s taxonomy of backchannel discourse alongside of an examination of the public discourse [13]. More detailed (comparative) student evaluations of the MOO as primary classroom space should be developed in order to compare perceived advantages and disadvantages of the technology with actual conversational and course outcomes. As students and instructors alike obtain access to faster (56k and above) Internet connections, integrated video/audio/text conferencing/chat applications such as

Microsoft NetMeeting and Netscape Conference will provide another option for class meetings; research will be needed to establish what role(s) such applications will have in graduate courses.

Planning and conducting a distance course where successful synchronous online discussion occurs is a demanding task, albeit no more taxing than managing a successful onsite seminar. In the final analysis, the measure of success of these discussions is in how well the participants can transcend whatever representational and interpretive obstacles they experience in this initially unfamiliar environment. Despite whatever trepidation each of us has about teaching online courses (and some of us eagerly approach this task), it is foolish to expect that we will not be asked to take a leading role in online education initiatives. As technical communicators, we should relish the challenge of teaching and re-mediating our courses into these other environments to advance our own professional development as well as that of our students.

REFERENCES

1. G. Von Krogh, K. Ichijo, and I. Nonaka, *Enabling Knowledge Creation: How to Unlock the Mystery of Tacit Knowledge and Release the Power of Innovation,* Oxford University Press, New York, 2000.
2. D. C. Leonard, The Web, the Millennium, and the Digital Evolution of Distance Education, *Technical Communication Quarterly,* 8:1, pp. 9-20, 1999.
3. S. Selber (ed.), *Computers and Technical Communication: Pedagogical and Programmatic Perspectives,* Ablex, Greenwich, Connecticut, 1997.
4. H. Duin and R. Archee, Distance Learning via the World Wide Web: Information, Engagement, and Community, in *Computers and Technical Communication: Pedagogical and Programmatic Perspectives,* S. Selber (ed.), Ablex, Greenwich, Connecticut, pp. 149-170, 1997.
5. R. E. Burnett and D. Clark, Shaping Technologies: The Complexity of Electronic Collaborative Interaction, in *Computers and Technical Communication: Pedagogical and Programmatic Perspectives,* S. Selber (ed.), Ablex, Greenwich, Connecticut, pp. 171-200, 1997.
6. N. Allen and G. A. Wickliff, Learning Up Close and at a Distance, in *Computers and Technical Communication: Pedagogical and Programmatic Perspectives,* Stuart Selber (ed.), Ablex, Greenwich, Connecticut, pp. 201-218, 1997.
7. B. Mehlenbacher, Technologies and Tensions: Designing Online Environments for Teaching Technical Communication, in *Computers and Technical Communication: Pedagogical and Programmatic Perspectives,* S. Selber (ed.), Ablex, Greenwich, Connecticut, pp. 219-238, 1997.
8. D. Gillette, Pedagogy, Architecture, and the Virtual Classroom, *Technical Communication Quarterly, 8:*1, pp. 21-36, Winter 1999.
9. S. P. Schneider and C. G. Germann, Technical Communication on the Web: A Profile of Learners and Learning Environments, *Technical Communication Quarterly, 8:*1, pp. 37-48, Winter 1999.

10. E. A. Thrush and N. E. Young, Hither, Thither, and Yon: Process in Putting Courses on the Web, *Technical Communication Quarterly, 8:*1, pp. 49-59, Winter 1999.
11. MATC Program Description, Texas Tech University, http://english.ttu.edu/tc/DL/default.htm.
12. C. Haynes and J. R. Holmevik, From the Faraway Nearby, in *High Wired: On the Design, Use and Theory of Educational MOOs,* C. Haynes and J. R. Holmevik (eds.), The University of Michigan Press, Ann Arbor, pp. 1-14, 1998..
13. S. Cogdill, J. Kilborn, T. L. Fanderclai, and M. G. Williams, Backchannel: Whispering in Digital Conversation, in *Proceedings of the Hawaii International Conference on System Sciences,* January 3-6, 2001, Maui, Hawaii. http://stcloudstate.edu/~kilbornj/backchannel.html, October 21, 2002.
14. M. M. Bakhtin, *The Bakhtin Reader: Selected Writings of Bakhtin, Medvedev, Voloshinov,* P. Morris (ed.), Edward Arnold Press, London, 1994.

CHAPTER 10

Paralogy and Online Pedagogy

Mark Zachry

Engaging graduate students in a professional communication online course can be a tricky proposition. In almost all cases, such students are drawn to such courses because they are working professionals who need to take a course (or program of courses) to improve their workplace credentials. Their motivation for being in the classroom is, consequently, very pragmatic. This pragmatism extends also to their reception of course materials. Specifically, to the extent that they are motivated to learn new ideas and practices, they are keenly interested in ideas and practices that have immediate or near-term implications for the work they do as professionals. Likewise, because the students are predominantly working professionals, they are drawn to take their classes online because such classes afford at least the potential to be flexible in terms of schedule and location. That is, students need a course that more or less offers the benefits of a traditional correspondence course, albeit in virtual space as opposed to packets of printed materials mailed back and forth. If instructors are not cautious about how they design their courses, they may, in fact, find these conditions (and the related student assumptions) so powerful that they will dictate not only how learning will take place but even the very content of what is taught.

In this chapter, I will discuss a somewhat under-explored dimension of professional communication studies that moves online learning beyond what students typically expect from the experience. Specifically, I will discuss connections between the paralogic nature of human communication and online pedagogy in professional communication. As I will suggest, I am not proposing a new topic that would occupy its own course in a curriculum. Instead, I address how the virtual spaces, the assignments, and even the underlying logic of online graduate courses can be designed to give students a new, and certainly more nuanced, understanding of human communication and its connections with the professional work in which they are already engaged. That is, I will address how online classes can be designed to provide a learning experience that exceeds the mastering of practices that can be codified. I will begin by talking in more detail about these students and online graduate studies in professional communication.

THE STUDENTS LURKING BEHIND

In my discussion, I will use a graduate-level course in an online master's program at Utah State University to illustrate my argument. This fully online course was offered in the spring 2002 semester in a strictly online master's program that enrolls students from across the United States and around the world. The subject of the course itself, however, is not of primary importance to the discussion that follows. More important is the identity of the students in this program.

The multiple geographic locations (e.g., Bermuda, Israel, Japan, and Canada) from which students come to this master's program are complemented by a diverse range of social identity positions (ethnicity, religion, gender, age, world view, etc.) and by notably different places in their careers (ranging from newly graduated, entry-level communicators to seasoned, management-level specialists). Some are very much academic-minded, planning to begin work on a PhD after completing the master's program, and some are resistant to learning anything that cannot be immediately applied at work next week. A shared characteristic for these students, however, is that they are "practicing professional communicators employed in non-academic workplaces or working independently as writing consultants." Taken from the program's mission statement, this description of a typical student informs instructors and students alike about the ground upon which class discussion and instruction will likely take place. That is, when students apply to and then begin the program, they do so by occupying the subject position of a practicing professional communicator whose work is non-academic. In a real sense then, students in the program have two identities, both of which are key in the discussion that follows. First, each has a complex identity that includes multiple social positions (e.g., supervisor at work, mother of two, and caretaker for elderly parent). Second, they have a simplified, assigned identity—a practicing professional communicator—that more or less defines how they might choose to (inter)act with others in the program. Such split identities, what Carter and Rickly might call "gaps," are indeed a fundamental part of social interaction and it should not be surprising that they exist in the virtual space of an online class. In this chapter, I explore how acknowledgment or neglect of this split has direct pedagogical implications for learners in online classrooms.

SO, WHAT ARE STUDENTS LEARNING WHEN THEY LEARN TO WRITE IN THIS CLASS?

In this course, 19 students studied a specialized topic in the field, usability studies and human factors. The assignments they completed included complex primary research and a variety of formal texts. This chapter focuses not on the specialized content of the course but rather on how the class constructed knowledge about that topic through writing in the virtual space of an online classroom. The specialized knowledge the students gained in this class included learning a new way of gathering primary information about the uses of texts and technologies and learning ways of representing that information via written texts to accomplish desired results. In other words, they learned ways of acting (methods) in the world of professional writing and ways of expressing information (genre moves and conventional habits) to help them act more like others in similar circumstances. Learning this is not an insignificant thing; it requires knowledge of widely recognized theories, methodologies, and experiences by those who preceded them in this field of professional activity. It also requires students to internalize and demonstrate protocols for acting in ways that will make them credible to others.

In contrast to the things that students are learning in such a class, there are things that they may assume they will learn that, in fact, they *will not*. They may assume, for example, that through such a class they will be exposed to or be able to discover some sort of procedure or scheme for acting that—once mastered and followed closely—will ensure their success as a communicator. In other words, students begin such a class with an implicit assumption that they will acquire special knowledge (e.g., ways of categorizing events or ideas in the world, maps of reality, or truths about their own identity or that of their audience[s]) that can make their work as professional communicators fail-proof.

The assumption that such special knowledge exists—that there are formulas that in some magical way will guarantee a communicator's success—is misguided. For even when communicative interaction is limited to a certain arena (e.g., usability testing) where rules of thumb, tricks of the trade, and even accepted methodologies can be known, nothing can be known that will ensure success in terms of the communicator's goals. That is, regardless of the students' apparent—and even genuine—mastery of analytical heuristics, textual moves, and digital tools, the communication the students engage in may fail in any given instance.

PARALOGIC HERMENEUTICS REVISITED

The underlying reason why knowledge of usability testing (or any other codifiable way of acting as a professional communicator) cannot offer guaranteed success in communication is accounted for by the paralogic nature of human communication. Human communication is paralogical rather than logical because in any given example of communicative interaction, a superfluity of potential understandings is only temporarily and locally arrested when the participants involved in the communication "come to terms" over meaning so that they can interact. In other words, human communication is paralogic in the sense that meaning is not established by rules of logic, but by a sort of parallel but ultimately faulty system that closely resembles logic. The paralogic nature of human communication has been actively discussed for many years now, though this discussion has influenced writing instruction in only a sporadic and limited way. Those exploring connections between paralogy and writing instruction typically cite the influence of Lyotard, who provocatively explored paralogy in conjunction with the postmodern collapse of metanarratives for legitimating knowledge [1]. Lyotard's work has proven generative for a handful of scholars in composition theory [2-4] and, to a lesser extent, professional communication [5]. On a larger scale, Kent [6] offers a general theory of rhetoric based on the paralogic nature of human communication and Taylor [7] uses paralogy as a framework for theorizing complexity in the cultural "dynamics of information." In general, however, those who approach the study of human communication within a paralogic framework share a set of common ideas.

First, they insist that communication always occurs in the presence of an "other" via communicative interaction. That is to say, meaning does not reside "in" texts [8]. Although this point may seem rather obvious, it is not exactly what most people implicitly assume. Specifically, in many theories of communication (particularly in writing theory), the communicator is assumed to be communicating in the act of forming sentences, paragraphs, texts, etc. Consequently, the act of writing becomes synonymous with communicating. Such encoding in symbolic forms, however, is something that happens prior to communicating from a paralogic perspective. Until another intelligence has engaged the communicator in the give-and-take of constructing meaning, communication has not occurred.

Second, because words have no inherent and necessary connection to reality, communicative interaction is the *only* way ideas can be validated. Contrary to the assumption that skilled communication (oral or textual) somehow offers facts about the world, the paralogist works from the relatively radical perspective that words (and indeed all symbolic forms, including such things as numbers) have no correspondence to reality apart from the connections that are locally and temporarily established when two or more intelligences are engaged with each other.

Third, meaning is never predictably constrained because communicative interaction is always defined by ongoing interpretive acts. Much of what people think about effective communication is assumed to be reducible to sets of rules, collections of guidelines, or codifiable strategies. In contrast, paralogists contend that *nothing* is codifiable about communication in the sense that any given rule, guideline, or strategy—regardless of its complexity—cannot offer a fail-proof way for moving ideas from one mind to another. This recognition that communication cannot be reduced to anything codifiable is counterintuitive because most people have worked out a type of folk—or even systematic—knowledge about what has worked for them or others in the past (perhaps multiple times) and have become convinced that such ways of communicating must correspond to how communication works. However, to make this assumption, people must conveniently ignore or otherwise explain away all instances in which that way of communicating fails to yield the expected results. In other words, every single failure of a rule, guideline, or strategy should underscore a fundamental characteristic of human communication: communication cannot ultimately be reduced to something knowable prior to the interaction of people. Furthermore, communication is never a simple event. The reason that a rule, guideline, or strategy is not sufficient to ensure communication is because communication occurs dynamically in an interplay of intelligences. Words are introduced and consumed, meanings are assigned, new words are exchanged, meanings are remade to accommodate this exchange, and the process continues on as long as the communicators are engaged with each other. Communication, therefore, is never static.

A DIFFICULT THING TO SEE

In terms of both the theory and practice of professional communication, the paralogic nature of human communication is a difficult thing for students to see. In general, participants in the field of professional communication aspire to discovering and perfecting codifiable practices. Specifically, practitioners in the field who are interested in accomplishing their work tasks reasonably look for ways of improving the results of their work, which often translates into finding ways to make communication: 1) more predictable in terms of effecting specific results; 2) more efficient in terms of how many transactions have to take place for recipients to understand or otherwise be able to act on the information presented; and 3) more easily constructed in terms of the learnable tools (e.g., software applications and transmission technologies) that seem to carry much of the burden of communication.

An inherent assumption, then, by many in the field (or those who aspire to be in the field) is that there are things about communication that can be known and perfected in practice. For example, they may point to expertise in genres, writing and design conventions, or technologies in professional communication as things that, once known, will make them effective communicators. Such an assumption is reasonable because such knowledge most often does, in fact, translate into creating more effective, efficient, or easily constructed texts. And, in turn, these texts most often speed up the processes of communicative interaction, which translates into the communicator being perceived as being a proficient communicator.

While such knowledge often speeds up the processes of communication, however, it should not be confused with knowledge about some transcendent truth about human communication. An aptitude for trafficking in the genres, conventions, and technologies of professional communication—regardless of the degree to which this aptitude is perfected—guarantees nothing about communication [see also 9]. This is an almost impossible thing for students to see and, in terms of accomplishing specific and limited goals at work, it may not be of paramount importance. However, it is knowledge that is worthy of a graduate student who has already more or less figured out how to work the knowable genres, conventions, and technologies of professional communication. In other words, it is a knowledge that is worth acquiring for a working professional communicator who is pursuing a deeper understanding of what is at stake and what is happening when she exercises that which is knowable about the field, and yet communication does not proceed predictably.

(UP)SETTING CONVENTIONS FOR THE COMPLACENT PROFESSIONAL

In a graduate course populated by students who already work as professional communicators, a great deal of knowledge about what "works" in the profession is already present. In such instances, asking "What is the something new that a professional writer can know after a course like this?" takes on new significance. Such a class stands in contrast, for example, with those classes where students do not already have workplace experiences on which to build. In those classes, learning can and should largely be focused on genres, conventions, and technologies commonly used in the profession. Such focused learning, however, does not satisfactorily address the question above for the online graduate course in usability testing and human factors being presented in this chapter.

Part of what is "new" in such a class may indeed fall into the general categories of genre, convention, and technology. For example, students in such a class may reasonably expect to learn new ways of gathering information that are recognized in the field. They may also expect to learn new ways of representing information in text so that they may be credible when communicating with others about the subject matter. Such knowledge is essential if the class (and, by extension, the program in which it is offered) will have any perceived value for potential students over time. However, a more fundamental question is, shouldn't they also learn how incredibly limited this knowledge is—that it has no transcendent value and is always exceeded by, eclipsed by, the communicative interaction of which it is only a trace?

A LITERACY THAT EXCEEDS THE CONVENTIONAL TEXT

Professional communication students in a class such as that being discussed here have little difficulty becoming literate in new composing conventions and genres. It hardly challenges them as learners to make such moves given the fact that they are already succeeding in their use of closely related knowledge. Learning a literacy that exceeds the codifiable, however, is not something that is immediately valued by such students. Despite this, becoming literate about the paralogic nature of human communication is something that may serve such students in that it requires them to recognize the ultimate unpredictability and instability of the communicative acts in which they are engaged. That is, it presses them to always operate as informed communicators who cannot ultimately depend on conventions and genres to achieve their ends. It causes them to recognize the limitations of text in social interactions, and, more importantly, provides them with a language for being conversant about such limitations with others.

With this new literacy—something very much like the "communitarian literacy" Davis [4] describes—students are able to move beyond the relatively simplistic idea that communication successes may be ascribed to the skilled execution of some knowable procedure. And, likewise, that when the communication in which they participate fails, it was not necessarily because they did not know or execute a procedure that would have guaranteed success. Instead, they recognize that communication is not a codifiable, logical system that they can somehow gain special knowledge of and then perfect. This recognition then enables them to treat genres, conventions, and technologies for what they are—useful shortcuts for moving forward the processes of communicative interaction. Such knowledge is not likely to sell them any new contracts as a consultant, but it may give them new insights into their assessment of a problem they will address as professional communicators. It may, for example, help students to understand why their communication sometimes fails even when they have followed the best practices (e.g., audience analysis, conventional design, meticulous editing, iterative usability testing) they have learned—and even mastered—in their different courses.

SO, HOW IS THIS ACHIEVED IN ONLINE PEDAGOGY?

Despite the potential value of this knowledge for students, learning (whether in an online environment or in a face-to-face setting) about the paralogic nature of human communication is not something that can or should be the explicit focus of readings and assignments in most classes in a professional communication program. Indeed, that is not necessary for students to develop a deep understanding of its implications for their work. This is particularly the case in online classes given the opportunities such classes afford for learning something seldom emphasized in face-to-face professional communication classes.

In part, this opportunity springs from a limitation of online classes: presence is constituted only via textual (re)presentations. That is to say, students and instructors alike do not exist in online classes apart from their symbolic contributions in virtual space. People are in class and participating to the extent that they are engaged in communicative interaction. The implications for course design are serious given the variety of ways that students might be asked to learn in an online class [10], ranging from very autonomous and self-directed activities to highly interactive, digitized exchanges (see also [11]). When courses are designed so that students are positioned as nearly autonomous learners, they may, in fact, acquire a great deal of information, but they are able to learn almost nothing new about communicative interaction because the give and take of such interaction is reduced to its most simplistic form (e.g., a student reads static text, negotiates a way to integrate that information with what she already knows, and selectively repeats portions of that information when prompted by some static form such as an online quiz). In contrast, when a class is structured to be highly interactive—that is, students are required to interact not only with static texts, but also with the instructors, classmates, and even with people external to the class— a great deal can be learned about communicative interaction. And, ideally, this learning is exercised as students are demonstrating recently acquired knowledge of specialized information, theory, and methodologies.

Structuring a class so that students are exposed to and required to probe new areas of communicative interaction is especially appropriate in a graduate professional communication program because it readily gives students an opportunity to experience and then reflect on the paralogic dimensions of human communication. Creating such a structure, however, is no small task for the instructor because it requires the class to support two kinds of learning that are not exactly parallel. That is, students must be afforded the opportunity to

- Acquire knowledge of content material (i.e., specialized information, prevailing theories, conventional practices, and recognized methodologies); and
- Negotiate the meanings and implications of this knowledge.

If the assignments in such a graduate program are limited only to exercises in genre work, for example, the unpredictable liveliness of communicative interaction becomes almost completely masked in nearly generic presences. That is, the class assignment simply reinforces an overly simplified understanding of what it means to be a professional communicator working in the area of usability testing by asking the student to create a test plan like the test plan in the textbook. Though such an activity does have some merit, terminating the learning experience there hardly seems worthy of credit in a graduate course populated by working professional communicators. To enrich student understanding of the paralogic dimensions of test plans and the multiple other genre work associated with usability testing (or any other specialized area of professional communication for that matter), instruction in an online class may be more productively designed to maximize the opportunities for interactivity. Specifically, students may be required to engage in extensive, informal textual expressions—unbound by genre and conventions—about knowledge being created in the class. For example, students may be required to constitute themselves as an active voice in an asynchronous weekly discussion forum within the class site (see Figure 1 for an example of how this activity may be facilitated in an online class).

Assignment: Becoming a Presence in the Weekly Discussion Forums

Every week, you are responsible for posting a minimum of five substantive messages to the "discussion forum" for that week. Your messages should be posted on at least two different days during the week to encourage conversation between class participants.

For those weeks that have assigned readings:

- One of your posts should be a thoughtful response to the assigned readings that demonstrates a genuine engagement with the text(s).

- At least one of your posts should be a well-reasoned response to the observations of another classmate.

- Your remaining posts may repeat one of the options above or they may include (1) an attempt to synthesize competing ideas presented in readings from previous weeks, (2) an extension of the ideas presented in one of the readings, (3) a theory for reconciling competing definitions of terms, (4) a continuation of a response message posted by another class participant, (5) a representation of a new set of ideas you are exploring through outside readings, (6) a concept map or other type of graphical representation of the relationship(s) between ideas being examined in class, or (7) an example that seems to contradict conventional procedures or understandings in the field.

Your combined posts for a week should be 1000+ words. You should focus more attention on presenting valuable ideas for yourself and your colleagues in these posts than on crafting pristine prose.

Figure 1. A class assignment to encourage students to become active participants in an on-going conversation about the class and knowledge about the professional skills they are acquiring.

Adding such a requirement to the class ensures that some of the things that happen in the virtual classroom will appear less than productive to those who think learning activities should focus exclusively on practicing definable skills. These fully textualized happenings will include unproductive speculation, open contesting of widely accepted ideas, mis-starts in new lines of inquiry, and misguided conclusions. All of this is part of what happens when the unsystematic processes of negotiating knowledge is exposed. For all of these happenings, however, there is a counter-balance that is much more productive in terms of student learning than merely requiring students to engage in pre-defined patterns of genre work. This counter-balance is located in the required communicative interaction of the class, wherein all ideas are explored outside the framework of formulaic responses.

CLEARING SPACE FOR
COMMUNICATIVE INTERACTION

Designing technological spaces to support the communicative interaction of all potential participants is, of course, not a concern exclusive to instructors (see, for example, [12]). However, because students in an online class are basically unsure of how to (inter)act in the space of a online classroom until prompted, it is necessary for an instructor who wants to advance learning about the paralogic dimensions of human communication to foster such learning through interactive spaces and course assignments. The irony of having to create such spaces to accommodate genuine communicative interaction and then connecting these spaces to required coursework is obvious. However, online classes that do not do so almost always anemically evolve into nothing more than spaces for electronic file exchanges. In other words, it appears to be a rarity for communicative interaction to spontaneously emerge in an online class, which at this juncture in online education should be reason enough for instructors to realize that they will have to take the lead in designing supportive classroom spaces and assignments that foster paralogic interaction, as is the goal of the "Becoming a Presence in the Weekly Discussion Forums" assignment (see Figure 1).

In keeping with this observation, communicative interaction in the usability studies and human factors class being discussed in this chapter was supported with a variety of spaces and through specific assignments. An entire 25% of each student's grade was tied to participation in open-ended communicative interaction in the class, and the weight that this type of activity would carry (along with the rationale for doing so) was clearly presented to students. Periodic responses from the instructor to all students who participated in the discussion forums were provided as the entire class was engaged in its communicative interactions. However, such participation was not graded in a traditional sense: that is, all students who met the frequency and volume requirements for this activity earned full credit for doing so. The syllabus informed students about the proportion of their grade that would be tied to the largely open-ended engagement with others about course concepts and materials. Communication between the instructor and students filled in additional important information about the role of communicative interaction in the class. First, the instructor posted bulletin board correspondence with students (see Figure 2 for an example), explaining to students how *presence* in the class was constituted only through their regular textual contributions to a collective conversation. This seemingly univocal correspondence with students was then answerable in that everyone was invited to converse about textual presence and its benefits for mutual learning—as well as its burdens, as some students were quick to point out. Although the requirement for students to be textually present in the class was not something that could be negotiated away, the ways of achieving such textual presence were negotiable, as I will discuss later.

Participating in Weekly Discussions

Online classes like this depend upon everyone being willing to state their ideas publicly and respond thoughtfully to the ideas of others. In other words, we must all commit ourselves to work cooperatively—to share our nascent ideas with one another and to thoughtfully consider what others have to say about a topic.

As a class participant, you should anticipate posting a minimum of five messages to our weekly discussion forums. Class readings will provide a wealth of material to which you might respond in your weekly postings. In addition, current resources in usability studies and human factors are far more extensive than those included in the formal activities for this class. As a graduate student, you should take the initiative to develop your own sub-areas of interest, and to bring information, ideas, and resources into the class discussion.

Publishing pristine prose in our weekly discussion forums is not really important at all. What is important? The most valuable contributions you can make to our weekly discussion forums include drawing provocative connections between class discussions and your experiences with users, communications practices, and technologies in the world, identifying valuable resources to supplement those in class, responding to classmates' questions, forming new ideas based on class materials, and asking smart questions.

Figure 2. Bulletin board posting provided for students during the first week of class and archived for retrieval later in the semester.

To engage in voluminous and robust communicative interaction in an online classroom, participants work best in virtual spaces that support multiple types of interaction, some of which have been described by Lang and Breuch in their chapters in this volume. In this class, at different times in the semester, students could select from and engage others in spaces that included live chat rooms, discussion forums threaded to a range of topics, file sharing with commenting functions, and broadcast and private email exchanges—each of which complemented different communication objectives and values [13].

Prior to negotiating how these spaces would be used, students were provided with general guidelines about the kinds of things that would define textual presence in the online class. These guidelines were supplemented with additional ideas so that by the time the conversation was fully begun, participants knew that in addition to the formal genre assignments they would be completing, they would also be routinely engaged in textual exchanges, such as those described in Figure 1 as well as others, including arguments with claims made by others in the field who had published their work on the Internet and comments on draft work that would eventually evolve into the genre-based assignments in class.

No one in class—including the instructor—was exempted from participation with others in this communicative interaction. In fact, the primary mode for the instructor in such exchanges was as a regular participant in the conversation. When students for any reason wanted to engage the instructor as the instructor (e.g., course designer, assignment grader, etc.), they were prompted to frame their exchange as invoking the instructor function, typically beginning their correspondence with "As the instructor. . . ." Unless they did so, all participants in the class were jostling with ideas and ways of becoming community-oriented constructors of unorthodox or undocumented knowledge about the topic at hand.

At certain junctures, specific types of interaction were emphasized in formal assignments. For example, in workshop weeks prior to a genre assignment being due, a response to the draft work of other students was one of the required forms of participation. Over the semester, however, the dominant mode of textual presence preferred by students was engagement with one another so that even when they were trying out a new idea, it was typically framed with text that connected it with the prior posting(s) of another person in the online class.

Nothing about this class arrangement of space or assignments is offered as being the one best way to teach online. Rather, this brief overview of a class is offered as one way in which communicative interaction was fostered in an online classroom. Such communicative interaction was an important supplementary learning experience for the students in the class because it underscored in various ways the paralogic nature of human communication—even in professional activities such as those associated with usability studies and human factors that may initially appear to be rigidly defined by methods, accumulated knowledge, and set genre practices. That is, students did not emerge from this class experience with a sense that succeeding in a sub-area of professional communication was merely a matter of mimicking codifiable forms of writing behavior. Instead, they learned that much of what might be done in the area and *all* of how it could be communicated relied on an ongoing and local negotiation of ideas with others. Upon experiencing that, a general realization emerged in classroom conversation and coursework that nothing about communication is guaranteed prior to engagement with others regardless of the degree to which the participants have mastered conventions, genres, or other documented practices.

CONCLUSION

When instructors are considering what advanced professional communication students might learn in a graduate class, they can do more than offer knowledge of conventional practices, commonly shared theories, and genre moves. Such knowledge of practices, theories, and moves should not be neglected—indeed, it may be the initial attraction of the course for nearly every student. However, students need something beyond that which can be known through the acquisition of codifiable knowledge. This something more that students need is experiential knowledge of the paralogic nature of human communication. Gaining this knowledge will serve students well in that it will shatter a general human tendency to have faith in formulaic exchanges and it will develop their adeptness at negotiating understanding in communication. This deeper understanding of human communication will help students to abandon the assumption that effective communication is simply a matter of getting an assertion right [3] through perfectible textual forms. It will help them acquire a more sophisticated approach to becoming engaged professional communicators who can understand and explain why communication in any given instance may fail, and the alternative forms of engagement through communicative interaction that may be called for.

An online classroom is a particularly productive forum for engaging students in this type of learning because it supports (and even calls for) types of engagement that are fundamental to highly textualized communicative interaction. If, in addition to standard knowledge acquisition of theories and genres practices, class participants are required to engage in less well-defined communicative interaction about the course's subject matter, they will have the opportunity to develop a paralogic sensibility that will likely prove more nuanced than if they learned only codifiable knowledge of the subject at hand. Specifically, an online class offers the possibility for participants to engage in forms of learning wherein the imperfect nature of human communication about the world is evident. Students experience the ultimate instability of language for fixing meanings as they use conversation to triangulate and attempt to understand one another. They discover that "truths" expressed through symbolic forms are always refutable because there is an excess of meaning in such symbolic forms and nothing exists outside such forms that can be used to communicate with another person. And, finally, they learn that communication is always completely a dynamic, communitarian activity.

REFERENCES

1. J. Lyotard, *The Postmodern Condition: A Report on Knowledge*, University of Minnesota Press, Minneapolis, Minnesota, 1984.
2. L. Faigley, *Fragments of Rationality: Postmodernity and the Subject of Composition*, University of Pittsburgh Press, Pittsburgh, Pennsylvania, 1992.
3. G. A. Olson, Toward a Post-Process Composition: Abandoning the Rhetoric of Assertion, *Post-Process Theory: Beyond the Writing Process Paradigm*, T. Kent (ed.), Southern Illinois University Press, Carbondale, Illinois, pp. 7-15, 1999.
4. D. D. Davis, Finitude's Clamor; Or, Notes Toward a Communitarian Literacy, *CCC*, *53*:1, pp. 119-145, 2001.
5. N. Blyler, Research in Professional Communication: A Post-Process Perspective, in *Post-Process Theory: Beyond the Writing Process Paradigm*, T. Kent (ed.), Southern Illinois University Press, Carbondale, Illinois, pp. 65-79, 1999.
6. T. Kent, *Paralogic Rhetoric: A Theory of Communicative Interaction*, Bucknell University Press, Lewisburg, Pennsylvania, 1993.

7. M. C. Taylor, *The Moment of Complexity: Emerging Network Culture*, University of Chicago Press, Chicago, Illinois, 2002.

8. B. Mirel, "Applied Constructivism" for User Documentation: Alternatives to Conventional Task Orientation, *Journal of Business and Technical Communication, 12*:1, pp. 7-49, 1998.

9. C. Spinuzzi and M. Zachry, Genre Ecologies: An Open-System Approach to Understanding and Constructing Documentation, *Journal of Computer Documentation, 24*:3, pp. 169-181, 2000.

10. K. Cargile Cook, Layered Literacies: A Theoretical Frame for Technical Communication Pedagogy, *Technical Communication Quarterly, 11*:1, pp. 5-29, 2002.

11. W. K. Horton, *Designing Web-Based Training*, John Wiley & Sons, New York, 2000.

12. C. Spinuzzi, Documentation, Participatory Citizenship, and the Web: The Potential of Open Systems, *Proceedings of the Twentieth Annual International Conference of Computer Documentation*, ACM, New York, pp. 194-199, 2002.

13. M. Zachry, The Ecology of an Online Education in Professional Communication, *Technology & Teamwork: Proceedings of the Eighteenth Annual International Conference of Computer Documentation*, ACM, New York, pp. 433-442, 2000.

SECTION 3

How Should We Monitor and Assess the Quality of Online Courses and Programs?

CHAPTER 11

Students' Technological Difficulties in Using Web-Based Learning Environments

Philip Rubens and Sherry Southard

In order to provide quality education for the changing needs of students in technical and professional communication, faculty continually have to re-conceptualize what constitutes a classroom and what characterizes our roles as effective teachers, as we seek to employ emerging electronic technologies. To explore these issues, we focus on the technological difficulties students encounter when learning in a Web-based environment that includes using websites for course content, email to interact and send attachments, instant messaging, and listservs or threaded discussions. How do students with varying experiences in using these types of computer technology learn to complete the tasks required by their courses successfully? How do faculty prevent them from becoming so frustrated with the technology that they give up or transfer that frustration to the course content, creating a barrier to their learning?

When considering these questions, one finds a paucity of supporting literature that provides even the semblance of an answer to these questions about student technological difficulties. Easier to find are discussions of other subjects such as administrative concerns in planning and implementing distance education as well as pedagogical and technological considerations when designing Web-based environments. Thus, the locus of concern focuses on necessary infrastructure, appropriate software and emerging technologies, and cost considerations, neglecting the difficulties students may encounter or assuming that the only students who will succeed in online courses have either the requisite computing experience or the self-motivation to learn the skills they need quickly.

At East Carolina University, we found ourselves faced with this lack of guidance and the reality of online students encountering technological problems.

These problems were occurring in the courses associated with our two online post-baccalaureate programs—a Certificate in Professional Communication and an MA in English, Technical and Professional Communication. In these courses, our target audiences include the following:

- Traditional full-time students and persons working full-time;
- Students physically near campus and ones distant from campus; and
- Persons seeking degrees as well as professionals (such as MBAs) completing some of our courses as part of their degree programs and life-long learners interested in courses for professional development.

As we planned our program, we had spent a considerable amount of time and effort implementing new technologies to support our students' information needs. We had assumed that our students would need our help to understand the technology while they interacted in useful educational experiences through the technology. While implementing our plans, we discovered that the so-called "digital divide" may be poorly defined. In our experience, both digitally impoverished and digitally elite users exhibited strikingly similar behaviors when they encountered technological difficulties interacting with the course website. Consequently, we embarked on our study to identify the techno-logical difficulties students were having and to resolve these problems through experimentation with other delivery technologies and website designs. This chapter is the story of our evolving efforts to create a course website that all students, whether technologically impoverished or elite, could easily access and use.

TECHNOLOGY PLANNING ASSUMPTIONS

Our initial attempts at employing emerging information technologies to support training and learning usually proceeded, at least in the earliest stages, without formal evaluation, although as time passed and our evaluation became more specific, we relied on a variety of sources to develop our assessment methodology [1-8]. At first, we assumed that a majority of our students would be accessing curricular materials from home using modems and that they would employ basic technologies. Our Web-based curricula, therefore, were designed for the lowest common denominator in terms of computer systems and computing knowledge, in order for all students to be able to learn core content successfully [9, 10]. Our future plans involved incorporating supplemental resources created, for example, using PowerPoint and streaming video. For students having appropriate sound cards and head sets with microphones, we planned to conference in real time (synchronous communication) using instant messaging.

We created our curricular websites and employed freeware or shareware (software that can be downloaded for free or nominal cost) for students to complete the course work, rather than using courseware programs (course management systems such as Blackboard or WebCT). (In their chapter in Section 4, Faber and Johnson-Eilola also discuss open source courseware as a viable option for course delivery.) Our home pages, accessed using a browser, had pale yellow backgrounds because research indicates that color reduces eyestrain. We used headings in cool colors, such as blue for "course title" headings, teal for all other headings, and a combination of light orange, pure white, and five percent gray for navigation bars. Each page also provided a "placement" line of live links as a redundant placement cue. All of our Web-based courses have these same design features to enable students to know when they are on pages we have created and when they have accessed a site outside of the curricula that we have developed. Figure 1 illustrates the format of our syllabi.

Home pages in all our courses resembled traditional print syllabi as much as webpages can resemble pieces of paper. By creating this similarity between print and Web-based documents, we hoped to solve some of the difficulties students encounter in adapting to virtual environments.

The syllabi, of course, provided traditional syllabus information, such as class procedures, grading scale, and submission policies for projects. In addition, from the syllabus on the course home page, students could determine weekly readings and due dates for projects. When necessary, they could access off-campus websites to supplement textbook content or acquire content if a textbook was not

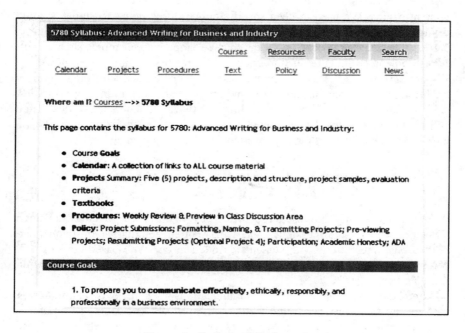

Figure 1. Online syllabi format.

used. They could also access descriptions and samples of projects. Finally, from the home page's navigation bar, they could access weekly updates and discussion sites.

We created distribution lists for classes and groups within classes using our email system, and we encouraged and enabled students to use instant messaging for communication with faculty and collaborative group members. The distribution lists allowed us to convey procedural information to all students in a class, rather than through individual emails to each student. These distribution lists, unlike listservs, were not intended for discussion and did not archive information distributed. Instant messaging services such as AOL Instant Messenger (AIM) and ICQ served as chat rooms primarily for communication between two persons or among very small groups.

To assist students with using these technologies, we provided various training opportunities. For example, when possible, students attended an initial class meeting in a computer lab, during which they "walked through" the technology. We found that our initiating interaction was especially valuable for students with little prior experience, a factor that often heightens their anxiety. If appropriate, we telephoned students and talked them through the technology. We relied on the "portability" of this training to introduce students to the use of two additional and very important communication technologies for their success: instant messaging, the basic tool for online tutoring and office hours, and the threaded discussion, the location where the bulk of interactions about course content occurs. We tried to keep specific online office hours so students could easily contact us using instant messaging as we encouraged them to. Similarly, we led practice discussions based on course readings about topics such as collaboration and defining terms important to a course (e.g., editing and ethics).

Despite our best efforts in designing these educational sites, selecting seemingly appropriate communication software, and providing novel training opportunities, students still reported difficulties with two types of technology: discussion software and browsers, the technologies used for knowledge-making activities as opposed to the ones used for organizational and management activities.

RESOLVING STUDENT TECHNOLOGY PROBLEMS

To help us identify and assess the difficulties we observed, we collected email messages, threaded discussions, and hand-written summaries of phone and face-to-face interactions with students enrolled in our Web-based courses. We focused on information related to learning and using supporting communication technologies.

After analyzing our students' communications with us over a number of courses and semesters, we found that slightly over 60% of course communication occurred in the first three weeks of a course. Forty-two percent of those communications reported information; 58% requested information. That probably should come as no surprise for two reasons. First, students have a considerable number of start-up interactions to report: instant messaging address, biography transmittal, and discussion area identification. Further, it is the most likely time for them to resolve problems they have encountered in either using the technology or understanding the course content.

After this initial flurry of activity, most interaction is limited to class projects and usually occurs slightly before a project due date. These results have led us to restructure course content so that the first few weeks are spent teaching students the technology; in fact, often the first week's readings and tasks include only "learning the technology" content, without any subject matter content. For example, instead of teaching students to use email, then saving files in a specific format, and finally using email to send attachments, we teach students all three tasks together by having them prepare short biographies in the first class to save as "rich text format" (rtf) files and send to the instructor as email attachments. Students also learn to access a fact sheet template saved as an rtf file on the website, save that file to their local disk or hard drive, fill in the requested information, save the file again in the specified rtf format, and transmit it as an email attachment. (Note that rtf files are ASCII files, files that avoid compatibility problems existing among various versions of Word, for example.) Completing these tasks allows us to determine if students can find specific information on the website, retrieve that information, and manipulate it by using a word processor and email client.

In addition to implementing more specific technology training, we began to experiment with other technologies and website designs to resolve discussion software and browser problems students were experiencing.

Using Discussion Software

Participating in online discussions obviously differs from participating in traditional classroom settings. Online discussions require critical thinking by students to synthesize and express ideas about discussion topics as well as their manipulating the technology. Responses, in addition, are presented in written form, not oral. Some students may find written expression more difficult and anxiety-producing than oral expression, and those who can type quickly may be advantaged. To respond to these reported difficulties with discussion software, we experimented over a period of time with various types of communication software for sharing ideas and insights about course content: chat rooms, listservs, and threaded discussions.

Chat Rooms

We initially used chat rooms allowing students to type in responses for real-time discussions, but we found them unsatisfactory for students in our classes whose work, school, and family responsibilities made synchronous meetings, even in a virtual environment, difficult to attend. In our assessment of communications, for example, about 42% of the "reporting" communications during the start-up weeks for class discussions (usually weeks 3 or 4) cited "attendance" difficulties as a reason for non-participation. Interestingly, the immediacy of the chat room presents its own difficulties. Students report that they felt compelled to respond quickly to postings. This lack of "contemplative" time often resulted in "trivial" posting such as "I agree with that point." Further, keeping a discussion "on task" was often impossible; chats sometimes became little more than gossip sessions. Our assessment of synchronous chat rooms, in contrast to the experiences of others in this volume, suggested that we needed to experiment with other discussion software applications.

Listservs

To alleviate the difficulties introduced by the synchronous communication of the chat room, we turned to the asynchronous capabilities of the listserv. Listservs (a mailing list server such as the one used by ATTW members for sharing ideas and resources) typically function by posting submissions to each group member's individual email account and archiving postings on the listserv website. Thus, group members have the leisure to consider the content other members have offered to advance the discussion. Although this method of interacting asynchronously seems to provide a useful interaction style, the listserv caused students a variety of difficulties:

- They found it difficult to join the list even when invited to join, so they entered the class discussions being frustrated and ready to give up on any technology.
- Because the listserv sent postings as email to class members whenever comments were posted, students were overwhelmed by the abundance of email they received.
- They found listserv email could become confused with class email having other purposes even when they were directed to delete listserv email.
- Participation in discussions could be completed in two ways, both equally cumbersome: 1) they could read listserv postings sent as email, normally mixed with other academic and personal email, then respond by sending their response in an email to the listserv; or 2) they could access the archived discussion postings from the listserv website, return to their email program, and send their response as an email to the listserv.
- Because the listserv archived the postings according to the date posted and without imposing any hierarchy according to subject matter, students using the archived postings as their means of participating in discussions found the discussions somewhat fragmented. The same was true if they used the email versions sent to them.

Threaded Discussion

To resolve the confusion introduced by the listserv, we tried another asynchronous approach: the threaded discussion. Threaded discussions allow group members to access a specific site where discussions are stored hierarchically. (Some discussion software provides a specific site where all discussion activities occur, but posts responses according to date posted without allowing for any hierarchy, similar in this way to listserv archives.) This last method seems to support students with limited technological experience quite possibly because it offers them a specific location where all of their discussion activities occur:

- To "join" a threaded discussion website, students go directly to the threaded discussion website using a link on the course syllabus.
- Responses and postings are archived only on the website without an email version being sent to students. Students participate in discussions by deliberately going to the threaded discussion website. This control keeps them from being overwhelmed by frequent emails.
- Students respond and participate in discussions by using a form on the discussion website without accessing their email. Moreover, they can easily respond whenever they want to while reading other postings.
- Because responses/postings are organized hierarchically according to the discussion topic and its responding postings, discussions do not suffer from fragmentation. If used correctly, the threaded organizational approach creates a meaningful visual and verbal outline.
- Color-coding for active and visited links enables students to return to the discussion site and determine quickly which responses they have not yet read.

The student responses to differences among these three discussion tools suggest that they found it difficult to participate and to stay "on-task" in chat rooms; listservs overwhelmed them with information; and threaded discussions offered both easy access and interaction unavailable in the other two options.

Using Browsers

Although one might argue that discussion software may require one to learn an atypical interaction style regardless of the choice of supporting technology, one would expect, reasonably we think, that the use of a browser to access course content ought to be a fairly routine capability in this day and age. However, in investigating the problems that students reported in dealing with browser commands, we categorized typical browser commands into four major categories: movement, directives, configuration, and wizards.

Movement includes those activities that involve some type of transit action: icons control many of these actions. For example, forward, back, stop, and scroll all use icons to represent specific actions. Movement also includes links. We place links in this category because they take users in some direction. However, in our own investigation we found that users had considerable difficulty identifying links because they can occur in so many different forms. Although links typically appear as blue underlined text, to some users that variation seems to be far too subtle. Another link variation, image maps (graphics that provide the ability to link to other locations), proves even more difficult because no single element of an image map signals its special purpose. Only the subtle change in the cursor from the arrow to hand image signals the individual links on the map. The subtle change only occurs if users move the cursor across the designated parts of the image map and requires users to understand the meaning of the change from arrow to hand image. This difficulty was particularly surprising because of the widespread and typical use of links. In fact, we had our best success when we used some variation of "Click Here for . . . ," a method generally eschewed in the design literature [9, p. 66; 10, p. 125].

Directives require users to complete an entry field to complete an action. Typing in an address for a URL, selecting a search term, opening or saving a file, all require users to enter a unique set of characters in a specific and easily identifiable location. A reasonable expectation on the users' part is that their entry will permit the program to perform a task, such as move, open, or save.

Configuration commands, in contrast, can be seen as either guided or decision-based. The former includes such commands as "page set-up" and "print" in which users must select from a range of available interactions; the latter includes toolbars for such items as selecting text size and encoding features. Usually decision-based configuration requires fewer selections, often only one. All of these configuration panels present users with a mixture of tabs, pull downs, and check boxes.

The last category, wizards, requires users to make decisions along prescribed paths while interacting with either pull downs or check boxes to perform a specific action. Unlike configuration commands, this latter group forces users to respond to all panels presented by the wizard.

Commands and Their Locations

It is little wonder that users find these activities somewhat illogical and/or ambiguous. For example, when we consider what ought to be a relatively simple "find" command, we discover users may, in fact, encounter five or more unique "find" commands in any single browser or its surrounding screen. They might encounter "find" under the "edit" command for finding a specific term on a page; they might use an icon on the standard button bar to search the Web; they might use a similar search command under "history" to recreate activities they performed in the past; or, finally, they might encounter a search facility incorporated into a single page or a complete website.

An educated, and admittedly logical, guess on a designer's part might be that typical users should be able to differentiate among the kinds of "finds" cited above or the various scrolling functions. However, our experience suggests otherwise. "Find," for example, seemed incredibly perplexing. Users, regardless of their supposed expertise, simply could not determine the exact object of their searches—website, webpage, specific database, etc. The net result of such simple difficulties seems to be a rejection of subsequent uses of the "find" command and the concomitant frustration attached to that decision. Users' rejection of such a basic and useful function may create other rejection behaviors on their part. These resulting behaviors could have a considerable impact on the success of any web site, regardless of how carefully it has been designed.

Similarly, users may find as many as four different kinds of scrolling possibilities in a browser. A window, for instance, may scroll both horizontally and vertically; it may have internal frames with both horizontal and vertical scrolls; a secondary browser window might appear with similar scrolling possibilities. Scrolls may also be found in favorite or bookmark windows, address fields, and the like. To confound interactions even further, some platforms allow scrolling using a scroll wheel on a mouse.

In a similar fashion, users exhibit difficulty using submit buttons and links. One semester we tried to have students submit the fact sheets mentioned above by completing an online form. Typically, students would submit nothing or two to three copies of the form. We learned from a corporate counterpart that, at one company, corporate users, for instance, often failed to submit a lengthy form they completed online. Admittedly, the "submit" button was the last item on the page, but adding a second submit button to the top of the page had no impact on this behavior. Adding an organizing note that said "Please complete all four parts of the form" followed by numbered headings for the four parts, including part four that contained ONLY the submit button, DID solve the problem, although we believe another aspect of this particular problem may be that submit actions typically provide users with no feedback about the progress or success of their choices. Our students either didn't understand that they were to use the submit button or, because nothing happened after "submitting," they hit the submit button several times to ensure sending the form.

Online students also seem to have more difficulties using links. One feature of our curricular websites is the availability of samples of previous student submissions for projects. Simply listing them after a heading—Sample Student Submissions—results in few hits on those samples, as well as a student outcry about the lack of samples! By using "Click here for an example of Project 1," "Click here for another example of Project 1," "Click here for yet another example of Project 1," we were able to resolve this problem. However, given the appearance of similar difficulties in both groups (students and corporate users), we believe our own expectations, as Web designers, needed to be re-examined, rather than the behaviors of our audience.

Browser Usability

Obviously, this study of access behaviors, particularly accessing curricular content, represents only a beginning. We have classified many functions into specific categories but those remain arguable, and our hope is that they will be examined critically. For now, we suggest that faculty as Web designers take a four-part approach to improve the usability of their pages based on our evaluation.

1. **Identify browser characteristics and use them where appropriate**. One aspect of Web design that seems to have eluded designers is that a fair amount of functionality is already built into browsers; that is, browsers already have techniques that need no further support from a webpage. Failure to use these existing techniques, or incorporating competing techniques into curricular webpage design, can only confuse students as users. For example, we found that asking students to use the "back button," rather than incorporating a return function on the webpage, produced better success in navigating the site.

2. **Catalog the kinds of activities, tasks, or actions you want users to be able to perform**. Just as we created four operations to account for the kinds of activities that we saw students trying to undertake, we suggest that designers create similar catalogs. The major advantage derived from this activity will be a better understanding of the kinds of real tasks faculty expect students to perform and the features faculty believe both the browser and their own Web design will provide to support students' needs. Obviously, our categories of operations are arguable; we encourage that argumentation.

3. **Associate specific techniques with an identifiable operation/command**. Once designers have created a catalog of operations, the next step is to map the operations/commands catalog against the available, or typical, browser capabilities or techniques for implementing these operations/commands. These techniques are typically implemented through icons, data entry, or paths (either guided or decision-based). These paths may be implemented through pull-down menus, tabs, or check boxes, or a combination of these three methods. The rationale for associating techniques with operations or commands is that it can provide a matrix of expected interactions that have the potential for helping students complete their tasks successfully. In Table 1, for instance, we offer one possible matrix for unraveling the kinds of difficulties we were able to identify. These difficulties were categorized by both commands and techniques for implementing these commands.

Notice that in this matrix, both configuration and wizards tend to use similar techniques to implement commands. Interestingly, neither of these two categories was problematic for either our students or users in the corporate environment studied. The remaining two categories—movement and directives—accounted for the majority of the confusing behaviors we found. Notice also that the level of commonality found in configuration and wizards seems to be lacking in these last two categories. For example, movement can be accomplished by entering text

Table 1. Commands and Techniques Matrix

Techniques	Commands			
	Movement	Directives	Configuration	Wizards
Iconic	B, O, P	P	B, O	B, O
Entry	B	B, O, P	B, O	B, O
Paths				
Pull-Downs	B, P	B, O, P	B, O	B, O
Tabs	P	B, O, P	B, O	B, O
Check Boxes			B, O	B, O

Legend: B = Browser-based; O = Operating System-based; P = webpage- or website-based.

at the browser level, but not on the page. In contrast, a directive may be invoked in the browser, the operating system, or the page to accomplish such tasks as finding search terms and saving or opening files. It seems to be precisely this ambiguity in the use of specific techniques that gives students the most trouble.

4. **And finally, test, test, evaluate, evaluate.** When we discovered the kinds of difficulties outlined above, we found it necessary to return again and again not only to our design, but also to an evaluation of the underlying techniques and technologies we had expected would help students. We were often baffled by the disjunction between our expectations and their performance. Initially, we assumed that the problems were in our design; we did not consider that the difficulty might have been introduced by conflicting techniques found between our webpages and the browser's basic functionality.

Unlike a word processor or accounting program, which produces a text that can exist as an archival document independent of any computing support, a webpage or website relies on a browser to be usable. Despite our best efforts to create useful designs for our users, the most confounding variable seems to have been our over-reliance on programming skills to create what we believed would be useful page designs and interactions. We neglected to account for the possible confusions that could arise from interactions between the techniques used on the webpage itself and those offered by typical browsers. We suspect this oversight influences many of the difficulties one finds with the usability of many webpages and websites.

CONCLUSION

Our explorations of the literature and our data analysis suggest ways to help students with the technological difficulties they face when learning in Web-based environments. Our research suggests that faculty should structure course content so that activities during the first few weeks of the course engage students with the basic technology that they will use for the entire course. These activities include procedural activities like communicating electronically with each other and the instructor as well as informational activities like generating ideas and content.

Recently, because at the graduate level almost all courses are now distributed as Web-based curricula, teaching students the basic technology is being addressed as a program matter as well as a course one. As soon as students are admitted, they are asked to complete start-up activities on a program website. We assume that in the near future teaching the needed technology skills will involve mainly the ones used for knowledge-making, not procedural activities. Students' learning about browser techniques is especially important in reducing students' frustration with browsers as they access course content and complete tasks required. Faculty, in turn, can facilitate this learning by designing curricular websites that build on the functionality already built into browsers.

As more and more knowledge-based activities move to asynchronous, Web-based venues, we need to keep in mind the promise and power of the best techniques and technologies that can be employed for making such ventures successful. We also need to consider that relative computer sophistication does not adequately explain all of the reported successes and failures of Web-based designs. Armed with that knowledge, faculty, curriculum planners, and Web information designers can use tales, such as the one we report here, to help them move toward "best" practices. To do so, they must be willing to explore, probe, and test, test, test to create practices that DO support student learning; they must also be willing to face the many, many failures that will frustrate their fondest dreams of success.

REFERENCES

1. J. Harris and G. Jones, Descriptive Study of Telementoring Among Students, Subject Matter Experts, and Teachers: Message Flow and Function Patterns, *Journal of Research on Computing in Education, 32*:1, pp. 36-54, Fall 1999.
2. Y. Katz, The Comparative Suitability of Three ICT Distance Learning Methodologies for College Level Instruction, *Educational Media International, 37*:1, pp. 25-30; March 2000.
3. B. Mehlenbacher, C. R. Miller, D. Covington, and J. S. Larsen, Active and Interactive Learning Online: A Comparison of Web-Based and Conventional Writing Classes, *IEEE Transactions on Professional Communication, 43*:2, pp. 166-184, June 2000.
4. B. Rubens, Designing Websites for the Intranet, *Proceedings of International Professional Communication Conference,* pp. 267-274, 1999.
5. B. Rubens, Reactions of Computer Savvy Users to Information on the Intranet, *Proceedings of IPCC/SIGDOC: Technology and Teamwork,* pp. 191-196, 2000.
6. P. Rubens and S. Southard, Using New Technologies for Communication and Learning, *Proceedings of IPCC/SIGDOC: Technology and Teamwork,* pp. 185-189, 2000.

7. P. Rubens and S. Southard, What Do We Really Know About Audience and Online Information? *Proceedings of IPCC: Communication Dimensions,* pp. 13-18, 2001.

8. S. Southard and P. Rubens, Students' Technological Difficulties in Using Web-Based Learning Environments, *Proceedings of Society for Technical Communication Annual Conference,* pp. 82-86, 2001.

9. J. Nielsen, *Designing Web Usability: The Practice of Simplicity,* New Rider Publications, Inc., Indianapolis, Indiana, 1999.

10. J. Price, *Hot Text: Web Writing That Works,* New Riders Publications, Inc., Indianapolis, Indiana, 2002.

CHAPTER 12

Activity Theory and the Online Technical Communication Course: Assessing Quality in Undergraduate Online Instruction

Kristin Walker

When I first began teaching technical communication online, I was surprised by how different it was from teaching in a face-to-face classroom. Of course, I assumed that the teaching process would be very different, but I didn't fully realize the complexities of changing my commenting strategies using the Track Changes function in Word, storing and then trying to locate various student drafts on my zip disk, and dealing with the different hierarchy and architecture of information that was presented through the course's online interface. Even more complex, though, were observing and participating as my undergraduate students adjusted to this online atmosphere; many students were not only first-generation and/or non-traditional college students but were taking courses online for the first time. Their difficulties in understanding my assignments (assignments that *seemed* to be clear in a face-to-face course, where the students could ask me questions and I could respond), technological adjustments required to submit assignments, and the frequent coaxing from me to participate in class discussions—all of these things highlighted the need for me to reflect on my online teaching processes and on ways online teaching was different from teaching face to face.

In this chapter I will discuss some of the unexpected situations I have encountered while teaching technical communication online to undergraduate students who come from diverse backgrounds and bring varying skill levels to the class, and I will discuss what I have done to improve the quality of my courses and address the needs of these students. My reflections on these issues are informed by a number of researchers' work on activity theory [1-11]. It is beyond the scope of this chapter to attempt an adequate overview of activity theory, but the assumptions and approaches I have encountered while reading about it have led me to realize that, even more than traditional classrooms, online course environments need to be seen as "activity systems." That is to say, we need to be aware of the online class as a place where many different factors—some of them technological, others cultural—are in play simultaneously and changing all the time as a result of their interactions. Since this evolving web of classroom dynamics can thwart a teacher's well-intended plans, I have learned to watch for certain factors, to try to anticipate their possible influences on the class, and to adapt the tools of the class accordingly. In this chapter I will discuss ways I have assessed three vital components of my online courses—instruction, peer interaction, and researching.

ASSESSING ONLINE COURSE INSTRUCTION

Tool Use

Assessing course instruction from the perspective of activity theory means examining all the tools involved in (socially) constructing and producing knowledge and looking particularly at the social interactions involved in the processes of creating, communicating, discovering, and discussing knowledge [2]. The following types of interactions might be assessed in a course: students' relationship to the course interface (such as navigation and usability issues); students' facility with technological tools (such as tools for uploading drafts for peer review, the application of graphic tools in document creation); the ways certain words (introduced during online chats or discussions) become tools that link to certain abstract concepts during the semester; and the frequency of student participation in online discussion tools in comparison to student satisfaction with the course. These interactions are also "situated" in that they occur in relation to particular activities, such as the relationship between reading and absorbing knowledge from the course textbook and then applying that knowledge through responding to online discussion questions. The interactions have to be analyzed within the context of the activity going on and the relation of that activity to the participants [6]. Two incidents from my online teaching experiences demonstrate how tool use can be examined considering the context of the activity and the participants' relationship to that activity. These incidents also illustrate problems that occurred in my course and point to options for resolving these problems.

During the semester, I received several email messages from students indicating that they had some difficulty adjusting to the use of the course's technology. They wrote:

- "The only question I have so far is how do I send you a direct email without having to go through the discussion section to do that."

- "Sorry, I only hit send and not attach file. Ha, I didn't even notice Attach File until you brought it to my attention."
- "I had technical trouble with the analysis. When I sent the piece to you, for some reason, my separate paragraphs all smushed into one giant paragraph. And no matter what I did, it wouldn't let me attach my web site for the document I used. I'm still trying to get used to an online class."

Some of these problems and comments are inevitable, given the fact that technology does advance rapidly, and online course software is advancing as well. These characteristics necessarily affect the design of the course instruction. However, some of these comments indicated cultural differences, differences that demonstrate students' discomfort not only with technology in general but also with the fact that they are entering a new educational environment which requires use of an unfamiliar technological medium, the course's interface. Awareness of this discomfort helped me to reconsider how I would require my students to use tools in future classes and how I might better instruct students in these tools' uses.

Similarly, another incident helped me to discover that my own assumptions about students and their abilities to use technology tools were sometimes misguided. For example, in a discussion post, I wrote: "Each week, a unit will be released that contains assignments. Readiness tests are due the Sunday following their release. Other written assignments will have other due dates, like the technical document analysis, which is due February 4th." I made this comment in an attempt to clarify dates for submitting assignments. My comment resulted from extreme confusion that seemed to be occurring about when assignments were due. After some reflection, I concluded that the confusion must be because the due dates were published in different places. First, there was a "Schedule at a Glance" that I developed so that students could see the "big picture" for the course; all of the assignment deadlines were in one place. Second, there was a calendar that contained all assignment due dates. Finally, whenever I released an assignment, the deadline for that assignment was included on the assignment sheet. Throughout the semester, however, no matter how clear I thought I had been, the students kept emailing each other on the discussion board, asking when various assignments were due.

My point in mentioning this difficulty is not to present a concrete solution to the problem but to suggest that a reason for the confusion might be the use of different tools within a course's activity system, tools that are technologically based and relate to different cultural-historical educational expectations. Usually, for a face-to-face course, a paper syllabus would be handed out, or students could download the syllabus from online. While students in this class could have downloaded the syllabus easily, many apparently didn't. When one student complained on the discussion board about not being able to keep up with the assignments, another student replied, "I downloaded the schedule and highlight assignments I have yet to complete and cross off the ones I have already completed."

Even though this recommendation sounded like an obvious one, the student who received this message had not been able to keep track of the assignment deadlines and needed this kind of assistance, assistance I did not think to offer because I wasn't a student in that particular class and frankly was hearkening back too much to the "old" tradition of the printed syllabus and how to use it. In addition, the role of teacher changes in such a complex learning environment as the online course; students become teachers of themselves and of the teacher as well. In the example above, another student had to suggest ways that the assignments could be remembered and kept track of, while I had not thought of such an "obvious" strategy, having assumed that students would want to download their syllabus to resemble more clearly the physical syllabus tool they must have grown accustomed to in their face-to-face classes.

Course Activity

Assessing online course activity could involve a process as simple as evaluating when students need access to new course material, based on when and where they interact with the course. For example, it might be difficult for an instructor to know when or where students are accessing the material, especially when a course is asynchronous. Such was the case in my first online courses. While many of my online students in Professional Communication I (a junior-level, undergraduate class often populated by Engineering, English, Professional Communication, and Journalism majors and minors) were taking courses physically on the campus where I teach, other students worked full time and had difficulty completing coursework during the week. After identifying student problems accessing course materials and assessing students' needs, I changed the release of new units from Mondays to Fridays to help working students focus their study time on the weekends so they wouldn't feel behind in class discussions or assignments. While it may not always be possible to correlate course content with *where* students access online courses, considering the physical course environment is important for possible course improvement. For example, if a teacher knows that students are routinely accessing an online course from a computer lab or library, rather than from a personal home computer, the teacher might be able to question how that more public environment might affect the comprehension of course material, especially as opposed to a more traditional classroom environment. As another example, Lang, in her chapter in this volume, describes how she assessed her teaching methods and adjusted her online graduate class procedures after a thunderstorm episode disrupted a student's access to her synchronous class. Activity theory reminds us to consider not only the material learned but also the physical environment surrounding it, leading instructors to assess how such factors in the physical environment as the room itself, the computer hardware, and the people in the room interact with the required course activities. While most courses do require some type of homework outside physical classrooms, online courses may rely almost exclusively on that kind of independent learning, which should lead instructors to think carefully about the ways that various physical learning environments affect the material presented.

Community Participation

Community participation, as Lave and Wenger stress [6], is essential for "cultures of practice"—patterns of behavior and communicative activity that are expected by a community—to develop, and community in an online course can be difficult to develop and evaluate. One thing that makes the online classroom so ripe for research, questioning, and development now is that the participants in this environment can be so different: some may be proficient in general values that might transfer across online educational communities, while others are being exposed to these concepts for the first time. For example, the online technical writing course that I teach serves mainly students in the Tennessee area, students in a specific population targeted because they are not usually able to attend classes on a college/university campus because of work, family, or physical restrictions. In addition, because many of these students have been away from a school environment for a while and may not be exposed to emerging technologies in the workplace, the students are often not technologically savvy. These students do not bring the same cultural educational history to the course as students from my institution who have progressed through the sequence of freshman English (Introduction to Composition and Writing about Literature), which requires the use of interactive computer software when composing, discussing, and providing feedback on others' papers.

Examples of how these differences in student preparation appear in our online courses are in students' responses to online discussion questions and their formulation, in students' responses to instructions given at the beginning of the semester that specify requirements for responses, and in response patterns that develop over the course of the semester. Within the community context, textbook content might be discussed without any connection to students' personal experience, or students with experience in the workplace might be encouraged to connect course principles with workplace contexts. While the culture of practice is something the teacher can implement and nurture, it is also something that grows and develops over time as the course evolves as an activity system so that the dynamics of students interacting with the material over subsequent semesters could feasibly produce different cultures of practice.

To assess the culture of practice that is in effect in any given course, a teacher might look at students' online discussion responses, individual public emails to peers regarding paper drafts, grades on reading quizzes, questions about assignments, references the student may have made to difficulties accessing the course or using the technology, and even assessments of written/visual assignments. Such assessments can then be compared to similar evaluations of other students.

Students can participate in the evaluation process itself, perhaps by dialoging with the teacher about the information gathering process. While this process sounds complicated and time consuming, instructors can choose which elements to assess, thereby allowing for flexibility, based on course goals and the design of the course. Such analyses of community participation can reveal much about students' preparation for the course and the causes for teaching and learning obstacles online students and their instructors sometimes encounter. They can also point to solutions to these obstacles.

Cultural Histories

The traditions of teaching culminate in a cultural history for us as teachers, and this history can sometimes conflict with new strategies for online teaching. While many of us did not receive formal information about actual teaching strategies for traditional courses during graduate or professional training, nevertheless, over the time we have been teaching, we have developed certain tools that we believe are useful for teaching our courses. This teaching knowledge and history to some degree have become tacit. We might use peer groups for class discussion and for providing feedback on writing; we have developed certain commenting strategies and patterns on the printed page for drafts that are handed to us to grade or given to us spontaneously in the hallway for some input before the next class; we correlate our use of printed texts with the course discussion in certain ways; we have integrated technology in various ways through website construction, analysis, and publication. These strategies and others have become part of our cultural teaching history.

When faced with a new teaching environment, such as online instruction, however, the old cultural-historical information and practices may not be as effective. For example, commenting strategies may become altered through the technology of inserting comments in drafts, as well as physically writing on other drafts that are received through snail (postal) mail. As we encounter such changes, many of us realize that the old forms of teaching that may have worked in the past may not work as well in an online environment. Regardless of the seemingly permanent features of some of our teaching strategies, we need to consider how these strategies might need to evolve to meet the needs of a new, online activity system, one that is changing so rapidly that even new changes need to be constantly re-evaluated to ensure that appropriate pedagogical goals are being met. The cultural tools we have been using in face-to-face classes may not be effective in a new online medium; we and our students will be using new tools, connecting these tools with our "old" educational culture in some ways, but diverging into the process of making new cultural meaning as well. (For a detailed example of this process, see Breuch's chapter in this book, which explores the cultural history of peer review and its evolution in online teaching and learning.)

The cultural histories students bring with them to the online classroom can also affect the success or failure of an online course activity. Because my traditional onsite technical communication course includes instruction in oral and written communication, I wanted to include an oral component in my online course, even though students could not meet physically to give their presentations. (My online course is part of a degree program that requires asynchronous learning, with no face-to-face contact, to provide equal opportunity for all students taking the course.) To meet this requirement, online students conducted research on a technical subject and then presented that information to a general audience (me) using videotaping. My ideal goal, then, was for students to focus on assimilating the technical knowledge they had gained and then translate that knowledge for a more general audience (a common task technical communicators have to accomplish in the workplace).

However, when I asked students how the creation process was going, I received many comments about the taping process: the lighting was difficult to adjust; the sound wouldn't pick up; they were alone and had to get up and turn off the video recorder by themselves, and that caused a distraction for the audience, in the students' minds. Although I had not provided students with an example of a videotaped oral presentation, the students already had envisioned in their minds what the final product should look like, even though, on the evaluation sheet that students used to prepare their presentations, little mention was made by me about actual requirements for the videotaping process. While students in a face-to-face class have much difficulty with this assignment anyway since it involves speaking in front of a group, the online students had greater difficulty since they were dealing with technology they found difficult to control. The ways I evaluated their presentations changed, then, based on the different tools the students were using, their degree of familiarity with them, and my inexperience with anticipating what difficulties students might encounter so that I could prepare students more effectively to deal with them in the future. The new tools the students were using affected the activity of giving the oral presentations to such an unexpected degree that I had to alter my own expectations of what was required.

ASSESSING PEER INTERACTION

For the purpose of discussion here, I'd like to narrow the concept of peer interaction into three types: one-on-one peer collaboration about paper drafts, required responses to formal discussion questions, and meta-comments about the course made on the discussion board. To illustrate these concepts, I'll draw from my own online teaching experiences, describing instances where peer interactions did not occur as I had hoped and explaining how I examined and sometimes resolved these problems.

One-on-One Peer Collaboration

In my online courses, students are required to work together on three paper drafts, and in the first iterations of the class I allowed students to make independent choices about how to share drafts and make comments on them. Some students chose to post their papers to the online discussion board where anyone in the class could read the papers and respond to them. Over the course of the semester, other students felt more comfortable singling out someone whom they knew would respond to their request, and then that person responded to all three papers. The selection of a peer to review the paper at this point became the students' responsibility, and, rather than choosing a peer reviewer because of an area of expertise or skill in commenting, the choice of a peer became based on the simple criterion of who would respond to the request. This less-than-ideal feedback selection strategy resulted from a lack of community participation among some class members, an absence which Lave and Wenger argue inhibits learning [6].

At the same time, the online environment did not seem to change the *types* of comments I observed students giving to each other; they remained localized. For example, in a procedural writing piece on how to cook an egg, a peer responded, "I think you should say that you need to spray the pan with cooking spray before it's heated. It's not clear from your original draft that that should be the case." No other suggestions were given. Although I had provided the students with some more global prompts in the form of guiding revision questions to mediate this activity, they did not seem to produce the kind of global feedback, in addition to "fine-tuning" revision suggestions, that I was hoping to see. In my role as instructor, I resisted intruding too much into students' collaborative processes, and, as a result, students may not have had the guiding direction they needed as they collaborated in this unfamiliar environment.

The format in which the commenting took place varied from brief comments on the drafts themselves (using the Track Changes feature) to comments sent through email alone, but as the semester progressed, an interesting phenomenon occurred: the activity of commenting ceased altogether, even though it was a required part of the course. By the end of the semester, I received comments such as, "I tried to receive peer feedback but never received a response," and "I posted my paper three times to the discussion board but never heard back from anyone."

Given these two collaboration problems, I assessed the tools students were using to collaborate as well as the comments they made. I also examined when collaboration began to fail and tried to understand why this problem had occurred. From these observations, I concluded that students either weren't receiving valuable help and so quit giving it themselves or perhaps they did not see the activity as valuable. Similar lapses in activity, not only in discussion-board environments but also in other cases, caused me to question why the activity stopped and what might be revealed about the purpose of that part of the course within the context of course goals. Considering the interaction between the tools, the participants, and the activity itself provided me with insights that allowed me to improve the course in future iterations.

Required Prompts and Metacomments

Because the online learning environment requires the use of several tools (assessing the computer interface in order to absorb information, working with the interface to produce and deliver information, and communicating with the course instructor and peers throughout the process to accomplish these tasks), metacomments made about the course itself (relating to content as well as the technology) can be revealing ways for assessing how the activity system of the course is working as a whole, although the constraints of the course do not always allow for improvements. For example, in my course I required that students participate in discussion questions for each weekly unit. There were usually about five to ten questions or prompts that students were required to answer. A broad example might ask students to "discuss ways that rhetoric applies to technical communication," or "describe how *ethos* might be portrayed on a website." The students responded to my questions, and I was pleased with how the students seemed to be interacting with the textbook, my questions, and the technology to produce the "results" I was looking for. I wanted to be able to assess them accurately to determine whether they were absorbing the material, and ultimately to determine what their class participation grades would be. From my perspective, I assumed the students were reading each other's postings and were responding thoughtfully, considering these different perspectives; I assumed that they were participating in the activities I had deemed culturally significant for our course.

I was surprised one day to read that one of my students thought the questions were "boring." To her, the writing they elicited was canned, formulaic, and not enlightening. To her, the writing should have been "entertaining." Another student responded by saying that she thought the purpose of the discussion questions was for me (the instructor) to assess the ways students were assimilating the information, and that was indeed what I was hoping to accomplish. However, in response to the student's need for "entertaining" questions (and in response to several similar comments from other students), I began trying to make the questions more personal, thinking that personal stories would elicit more lively feedback. Even though the questions invited a more personal point of view, the students did not seem to accept the invitation but instead stayed true to the formulaic response I had originally requested. At one point, a student mentioned that if there were more time, then more entertaining responses could be formulated but that, in her case, she was simply trying to do what was necessary to complete the course; she did not have time to enhance her comments.

In this example, the tool of the discussion questions, as well as the genre used to respond to them, became the focus of meta-comments about how the discussions should be characterized. Because students felt free to voice their comments, I encouraged a change that could have taken place in this aspect of the course's activity of participation; the change would still have allowed me to accomplish my purposes, and the students perhaps would have been more motivated to read the others' responses. However, within the limited space of this course's experience, it wasn't readily clear whether such a change would have accomplished anything different in the responses. This example reminds us that, although individuals' responses can be studied, responded to, and incorporated into the course context/content, we may not have the power to effect change. In this case, time and perhaps lack of motivation seem to be factors that overpowered the desires of a few students and myself to enact change. At the very least, though, I have some indication that the next time I teach the course, I could start out with a different focus for the discussion questions, with possibly more positive results.

ASSESSING ONLINE STUDENT RESEARCH

Many online courses require students to conduct research online, and courses often include external links to provide students with supplementary information. While it's not possible to control or even assess what students choose to view outside the course, it is possible to evaluate how that outside information affects the course's content (through discussions, for example) or ways the information appears in students' papers. One assignment I gave students was to study Karen Schriver's document design principles for integrating text and graphics (redundant, complementary, supplementary, stage setting, and juxtapositional) [12], apply them to a website, and then comment on ways those principles did or did not apply to a particular website. This assignment was complicated by the fact that websites are designed differently from hard copy texts, and the principles applied differently, as well, to different genres. A website designed for guests to respond to a wedding invitation online may or may not have a stage-setting graphic, for example. Difficulties for me arose because even though the students all had received the same assignment, they did not apply it in the same way. In a face-to-face classroom, students could use class discussion about the assignment to calibrate their own work, but in an online environment where the students were often too "busy" or felt too isolated from one another to interact through discussion, there were many different interpretations of the assignment. A common misinterpretation was that the principles of integrating text and graphics simply had to be mentioned in the analysis, without supporting details being presented from the sites. I wanted to see details to convince me that the students had accurately assessed the information, so I emphasized analysis in comments I made to the students.

My intention in creating the assignment was setting forth some rules to be followed within the activity system of the course (and within the assignment, in particular), and when those norms were not met by all of the students, I felt the need to enforce them. In addition, the students' misunderstanding also informed me that I may not have been as clear as I should have been in designing the assignment and that more specificity was required, either in my assignment or in the way I discussed it, in order for students to succeed. Because I had taught this online course in face-to-face form many times, my tendency in designing the course was to put the same research assignments online, not really knowing how the different learning/teaching environment would affect those assignments designed for a different teaching medium. The students' reactions helped me to learn what changes I needed to make to ensure the course was more effective and accessible for the students so that we could all participate.

Outside research may not be just in online form. Many students taking online courses also work full-time, and documents they use for assignments may directly relate to their field of work, where various versions of hard copy documents exist: a brochure detailing wireless application protocols, instructions for straightening curly hair, an information sheet for veterinarians about specialty dog foods. Here, students can attempt to connect an activity system they may be more familiar with (work) with a system they are just entering and may not feel as comfortable with. The topic of the course I taught, technical communication, lent itself very well to the integration of this type of material, and the students also supported the integration of the material when it was discussed on the discussion board. During the final project for the course, a document revision, some students from similar fields would critique each other's projects. Most people chose to revise a document they had had to use or produce at work, such as a website for teaching literature, an instruction sheet for developing a pre-school educational program for children, or documents on housing qualifications for Habitat for Humanity. While somewhat obvious, the topic of my course, taught in an academic environment, encouraged interaction with other related activity systems that students felt comfortable with. Since unfamiliar learning environments can cause students to seek material and practices that are more familiar to them and since online learning environments provide many opportunities to integrate outside material, a beneficial assessment question might be to ask what elements of a course might relate to outside fields that students could tie in to the current academic activity system.

CONCLUSION

Each semester that an online course is taught, the students will change, the material might change to some degree, and the technological tools are likely to change as well. When analyzing the dynamics of courses and reflecting on how we can make them better, activity theory encourages us to view the entire context and all activities involved in it and to discover solutions and new questions appropriate to our local situations. In a time when education is being revolutionized through developing technology and is constantly changing, this approach is essential to help us understand the ramifications of the changes we are initiating and encountering. It is essential, if teacher training is to include not just technological instruction but also training in overall course assessment, design, and effective theoretical foundations, to encourage both teachers and students to keep reflecting upon technological literacy.

REFERENCES

1. D. Russell, Rethinking Genre in School and Society, *Written Communication, 14*:4, pp. 504-554, 1997.
2. D. Russell, Looking Beyond the Interface: Activity Theory and Distributed Learning, in *Distributed Learning: Social and Cultural Approaches to Practice*, M. Lea and K. Nicoll (eds.), Routledge/Falmer, London, pp. 64-82, 2002.
3. M. Cole, *Cultural Psychology*, Harvard University Press, Cambridge, Massachusetts, 1996.
4. W. Morgan, A. Russell, and M. Ryan, Informed Opportunism, in *Distributed Learning: Social and Cultural Approaches to Practice*, M. Lea and K. Nicoll (eds.), Routledge/Falmer, London, pp. 38-55, 2002.
5. Y. Engestrom, Activity Theory and Individual and Social Transformation, in *Perspectives on Activity Theory*, Y. Engestrom, R. Miettinen, and R. Punamaki (eds.), Cambridge University Press, New York, pp. 19-38, 1999.
6. J. Lave and E. Wenger, *Situated Learning: Legitimate Peripheral Participation*, Cambridge University Press, New York, 1993.
7. M. Cole and Y. Engestrom, A Cultural-Historical Approach to Distributed Cognition, in *Distributed Cognitions: Psychological and Educational Considerations*, G. Salomon (ed.), Cambridge University Press, New York, pp. 1-46, 1993.
8. M. Cole, Y. Engestrom, and O. Vasquez (eds.), *Mind, Culture, and Activity*, Cambridge University Press, New York, 1997.
9. O. Tikhomirov, The Theory of Activity Changed by Information Technology, in *Perspectives on Activity Theory*, Y. Engestrom, R. Miettinen, and R. Punamaki (eds.), Cambridge University Press, New York, pp. 347-359, 1999.
10. D. Winsor, Genre and Activity Systems, *Written Communication, 16*:2, pp. 200-224, 1999.
11. Y. Engestrom, *Learning by Expanding: An Activity Theoretical Approach to Developmental Research,* Orienta-Konsultit Oy, Helsinki, 1987.
12. K. Schriver, *Dynamics in Document Design*, John Wiley and Sons, New York, 1997.

CHAPTER 13

An Assignment Too Far: Reflecting Critically on Internships in an Online Master's Program

Keith Grant-Davie

This chapter is about an attempt to adapt a traditional internship assignment to make it more meaningful to students in Utah State's online master's program in Technical Writing who already have practical experience, an attempt that was eventually abandoned—or at least temporarily shelved—due to logistical constraints. Our intent was to increase the intellectual rigor, relevance, and quality of the assignment, but we ran into the simple reality that faculty time is limited. The story of the rise and fall of this internship assignment will serve perhaps as a reminder that expansionary zeal must be sustained by available resources. In the end, one can only do so much.

This story of expansion followed by retraction is also about the value of engaging in praxis—critical reflection on practices, with a view to improving those practices. We wanted to teach our students to engage in praxis for their internship projects, taking a scholarly, inquiring approach to the communicative practices of their workplace, and we engaged in praxis ourselves as we revamped the internship assignment, refined it through email dialogues with students who were attempting the assignment, and eventually decided to remove it from the curriculum until a time when we are better equipped to support it. Continual praxis—the kind of critical, theory-driven or theory-forming reflection that leads to revisions and improvement in curriculum and pedagogy—is essential to the assessment and improvement of instructional quality in any program. However, I think the habit of praxis is particularly important in online programs, since the field of online education is still in its pioneering stage, developing the theory that will guide and rationalize its practices. This chapter illustrates the kind of praxis that can take place whenever a program develops a new assignment or revises an existing one. The chapter also shows the value of email dialogues with students, not only as an important instructional tool in an online program, but as an important textual archive that can help teachers and program administrators engage in critical reflection.

Let me back up now and explain the context in which all of the above occurred, before recounting the story in more detail. Utah State University's English Department began a pilot project offering online seminars to master's students in the Technical Writing program in Summer 1997. The project continued through the following academic year, during which time we proposed a fully online curriculum aimed primarily at working professional writers whose location and career commitments would have kept them from coming to campus as traditional, full-time students. This proposal was approved, and the online master's program in Technical Writing was officially launched in the Fall of 1998, coinciding with Utah State's switch from the quarter system to semesters.

Prior to these changes, the program had had fewer than a dozen students who commuted to the Logan campus from the surrounding Cache Valley area and from the Wasatch Front, which lies within two hours' drive of Logan and contains most of Utah's population. In the first three years after moving online, the program grew to about 40 students participating from points all over North America and as far away as Israel, Okinawa, and Bermuda. Students in the online program complete the degree through a 33-credit, non-thesis plan, earning all their credits from coursework. This plan allows them to complete the degree at a distance, without having to come to campus for a thesis defense. Most of our on-campus students, by contrast, opt for thesis plans that include an on-campus defense. Since a master's degree with a thesis requires only 30 credits, and since 3-6 of those credits are earned by working on the thesis, our online students end up taking two or three more graduate seminars than their thesis-writing counterparts on campus. The only classes in this program currently taught on campus are a few summer workshops, so we seldom meet our master's students in person. Although a few live nearby and visit us from time to time, we interact with most of them only by email, by asynchronous discussion on the Web, and occasionally by phone.

Before the switch to semesters and the new curriculum, the program had included a traditional internship requirement defined in much the same way as our undergraduate internship. Traditionally, internships are periods of supervised practical training intended to increase a student's experience, typically supplementing academic or theoretical learning acquired from books and the classroom with knowledge gained through apprenticeship in an environment where students have a chance to apply their academic knowledge to fully contextualized problems. At the end of traditional internships, interns are usually asked to report what they did and what they learned. The internship report, therefore, tends to be an egocentric document, focusing on the student and his or her personal education, often narrating the neophyte's process of initiation into a workplace, rather than attempting to advance the field's knowledge.

For our new population of online graduate students, most of whom were already experienced professional communicators, a traditional internship of the kind I have sketched above seemed pointless. To make internships valuable for our online students, we redefined them as supervised workplace research projects in which students aimed to advance knowledge in their field through primary research. We wanted our students to engage in praxis—to reflect on some of the practices in their workplace and to approach them with the critical eye of a researcher. These projects might be better described as scholarly fieldwork, but we retained the internship course number and title partly for administrative convenience. Gaining approval to change course numbers and titles, and then making sure the changes appear in the next printed catalogs, can be a troublesome process. We also retained the internship title partly for flexibility. For the few students in the program who were not already employed as professional communicators, the assignment would also be a traditional, experience-gaining kind of internship. Below is our first attempt, in the Fall of 1998, to describe the internship as an onsite research project. These sentences appeared as a thumbnail description of the internship assignment that appeared in the curriculum summary on our program website: "Students will analyze a work environment where they are employed. Selecting a focused topic, students will research theory and practice as it relates to that topic and to the work environment. Students will write a paper and will present their findings orally or in an online discussion with faculty" [1]. This description introduced the idea of the internship as an occasion not just to gain personal experience through completion of a new project but to see the project in a broader context and to advance the profession's knowledge about the topic through primary research. In the more detailed instructions that we released to students at about the same time, we defined the internship further:

> Typically, the internship takes the form of a small, focused case study that addresses some specific, rationalized research questions. Students should develop these questions in consultation with a member of the technical writing graduate faculty and the Director of Graduate Studies in English. The study may be descriptive, aiming to provide the field with information about workplace writing practices, or it may be evaluative, testing the practical applications of a particular theory, or it may combine descriptive and evaluative aims.
>
> Research activities for the internship could include interviewing technical writers in the workplace, observing negotiations at meetings, tracking document production cycles, analyzing the text of documents, or researching corporate archives. The written report that concludes the internship may take the form of an article prepared for a specific technical writing journal. However, the research is not limited to such activities and there are no strict guidelines on the format for the internship report. Rather, the design of the study should reflect the student's knowledge and interests and the needs of the workplace practices in the light of technical writing theory. A good internship should serve both the student and the workplace.

The wording in these directions was broad and speculative. Students were offered multiple options, freed from strict guidelines, and invited to propose still more alternative forms for the internship report. At this point we (the technical writing faculty who had developed the new curriculum) had not yet seen any internship proposals from our remote students, and the concept of a research internship was not yet fully developed in our own minds. We had a general sense of what we were looking for, but we felt our requirements might be met successfully by a range of quite different kinds of projects, not all of which we could anticipate. We were anxious to avoid wording the assignment in a way that might limit that range, so the assignment description became a rather broad "call for proposals."

On the other hand, although the first sentence of the assignment opened with a hedging word ("Typically, . . ."), that sentence contained a phrase we felt was essential to the assignment: "some specific, rationalized research questions." Somewhat naively, perhaps, we assumed students would understand what we meant by that phrase. However, in the spring semester of 2000, when the first wave of students in the new, online program began writing internship proposals in response to our original directions, it became clear that the phrase did not mean as much to our students as it did to us. We began to realize that we would need to provide more explicit instructions and guidelines and to spend more time *teaching* our students how to formulate and rationalize good research questions. Although the new internship requirement had been developed by the whole technical writing faculty, at this point the job of supervising the internships still fell on me, in my dual capacity as program advisor and Director of Graduate Studies in English, as it had when we followed the traditional, less demanding model of internships.

In the first internship proposals I received, most students described what they planned to do for their project, but they showed little grasp of the difference between a workplace *writing* project and the kind of workplace *research* project we were hoping to see. They were proposing to engage in familiar workplace *practices*, and it was at this point that I realized they would need help understanding how to engage in *praxis*—how to apply some of the theory and practices they were learning in their courses to a practical problem in their workplace, then reflect on that application and consider how the experience might suggest ways to refine theory or to develop alternative practices. As Carolyn Miller explains, praxis provides "a locus for questioning, for criticism, for distinguishing good practice from bad" [1, p. 23]. Praxis involves migrating frequently between application and reflection, between doing and pondering the way things are done. Practice, which provides an opportunity to apply and test theory, becomes praxis when it is followed by reflection, leading to the revision of existing theory or the development of new theory, from which, in turn, the best new practices can be inferred and tested.

In teaching our students to understand and engage in praxis, we too were engaging in praxis, reflecting on both the details and underlying concepts and motives of our pedagogy and exploring ways to improve them. One thing we realized in the course of this process was that praxis is a kind of intellectual activity that may come more readily to academics than to students immersed in non-academic workplaces, particularly if they have been out of a university environment for a number of years and if their work does not usually allow much time for critical reflection and generalization. The distance between us and our students is often not just physical but also conceptual. We are faculty members who work in the same building on a state university campus. They, for the most part, are professional communicators working full-time jobs in a variety of contexts, each of which can have a different influence on their interpretation of what we tell them.

Many of our students have been out of school for a good many years, and as online students they remain immersed in their own workplace cultures and do not have the experience of being initiated into the academic workplace culture of our department. Academic initiation can and does occur in online seminars, but our on-campus students experience a fuller immersion in the academic culture, not only through their formal interactions with faculty and other students in face-to-face classes but also through the informal contacts that can occur in the rest of the working day—particularly if they belong to a cohort of students who share the same office space and are all learning to be graduate instructors. Our on-campus students need clear, explicit communication about program requirements too, but their physical presence around the department may make it easier for them to understand, clarify, or confirm what is expected of them. Our online students, on the other hand, have to grasp our requests and assignments from within quite different cultural settings, where a different set of values and priorities may govern their daily activities. They can confer with fellow students by email but probably not in person. In other words, we found it was not enough simply to *ask* students to engage in praxis. Our working students needed help learning how to observe their work and think about it from a critical perspective, how to discover and shape good research questions, and how to construct an effective research project. For example, in May 2000, a student working as a hospital administrator was planning to write an Information Management Strategic Plan for his hospital. In his proposal, perhaps cued by the suggested research activities we had listed in the assignment directions, he described the research component of his internship in terms of the following activities:

- Interviewing Information Systems staff [about] existing and anticipated use of computers at XYZ Hospital;
- Attending strategic planning meetings;
- Managing strategic plan document to assure timely delivery and quality content; and
- Researching future of information in the health care setting.

In an email response to his proposal, I tried to explain the difference between research *activities* and research *questions*—between methods of gathering information (such as he had proposed) and questions that motivate the research and give it exigence—questions that were missing from his proposal. I asked:

- How might you use the project to learn more about some aspect of strategic plan writing, or about some part of the communication process involved in the project?
- Do you expect the project to pose some particular problems or challenges?
- Could you use theory to consider possible solutions to those problems and discuss the solutions you end up choosing?

My aim here was not to suggest specific research questions that would drive his project, but rather to ask him the kinds of questions that would lead him to develop his own, project-specific research questions. Metaphorically, I wanted to give him the rod and casting technique rather than the fish itself.

My email conversation with this student was typical of several that I had during the spring and summer of 2000. As I responded to successive internship proposal drafts that gradually became better approximations of research proposals, each of my responses better approximated the guidelines that we needed to offer students for writing their proposals. I and the colleagues with whom I was discussing the assignment were learning as much from our students as they were from us. I think this improvement can be seen in an email exchange I had later that summer with a student who had been working alone for several months as chief developer of a data-driven website for his employer. He wanted to use the project for his internship but was unsure how to connect it with our original internship requirements that were still posted on the program website. He wrote: "It seems that I don't fit the situation described in your course description, such as 'interviewing other technical writers' . . . I understand that the course can take an evaluative or descriptive approach, but I am not sure what that means." To which, I replied:

> Research projects are always driven by "problems," by which I mean they are driven by a need to know something or to fix something. For the internship project, we need you to identify a problem. For example, what are the issues involved in developing a very large, data-driven website? What are the challenges? How is the task different from other, similar projects? What are the unique problems it requires you to solve? The final report for your internship might say, 1) here was the task I faced and these were the challenges it presented me, 2) this is what others have said about similar tasks, 3) these were the possible solutions I considered or attempted, 4) here's how I made my solution work, and 5) this is what I learned about data-driven websites from the whole experience.

In suggesting a possible structure for this student's report, I was aware that I risked appearing to prescribe the organization he should follow, but I felt I needed to offer him at least a general model of the kind of approach he might take, in hopes that he would meet us half way and be able to customize it to his project. A month later, the student emailed me again:

> I would like to do a case study of the project I am working on: Customer Support Web Site. Based on my situation and the criteria you spelled out, the project would consist of two parts: 1) a "primer-like" discussion of data-driven web sites and how to develop them, and 2) a description of my project (lessons learned, my methodology, the tools I used, e.g., Coldfusion) and the reasons for my decisions. In my literature search I noticed that there has been practically no discussion of this topic in STC's journal, *Technical Communication*.

In this overview I saw the promise of a publishable article, and in my reply, I encouraged him to go ahead with the project. Since he had begun his literature search, I decided to suggest the kinds of questions that might drive that part of his internship proposal. Students unfamiliar with academic research projects may need help not only grasping the concept of research questions but also seeing the exigence for a review of literature. Here is how I tried to model that exigence:

> I don't know how widely you searched for relevant publications, but when I read the Literature Review section of your internship proposal I'll be looking for answers to questions like these: "What has been written about data-driven website technology and its applications?" "Who's been doing the R & D in that area and what have been the recent developments?" Also, "How has customer support traditionally been accomplished? What are the available methods, and what is the current thinking about how it should best be done? How has the World Wide Web been used for customer support?"

There is a fine line between teaching students how to be researchers and giving them so much direction that we end up appropriating their projects and solving their problems for them. With this student, I came close to that line, but I think we ended up meeting more or less at the line. In the introduction to the final report on his internship project, intended for submission to *Technical Communication*, the student wrote the following passage, which I think illustrates the kind of praxis we hope to see from students in our program, and which goes beyond the generic questions I had offered him. The student establishes a problem, poses a research question, and explains how he has addressed it. In doing so, he indicates the broader significance of this particular project in his workplace for the field of technical communication:

> As the demand for data-driven Web sites increases, Web developers and technical communicators face many challenges they never encountered when developing static Web sites. The added complexity of integrating database technology with the Web has forced Web developers to look for more effective development methodologies and strategies. To do this, we need to ask one question: "How can we integrate a database to the Web to produce a site that has a single, consistent, user-friendly presentation?" To answer this

question, I draw upon my own experience as well as the research literature of others. I analyze the technological issues that developers have confronted and the solutions they developed to solve them. First, I provide a brief historical overview of UVW, the company. I then explain the background of the project. I use an extended case study of a printer manufacturer as a basis of the article.

The article will discuss the strategies that have been successfully used to launch a site. The article also makes the case that establishing some fundamentals of user-centered methodology, proper database design principles, and the best Web development tools is vital to developing a useful, dynamic web site. It is hoped that the article will not only help other technical communicators tackle similar projects, but it [will] also help them consider the many issues involved in data-driven Web development.

By the end of Summer 2000 I had exchanged the same kind of email correspondence with about half a dozen students who were enrolled in internship credits, and it was clear to me that we needed a much fuller, more explicit description of the requirement. In corresponding with individual students, I had been rehearsing this description, and my next step was to print out all these email exchanges. Printing and reviewing this email archive reminded me of the steps that were involved in the process of reflection and discovery, making the process much easier than if I had had to remember what had been said in the same number of face-to-face conversations with students. I could print the emails, lay them side by side, look for common themes both in students' questions and my responses, then highlight the passages that I felt clarified our expectations for the internship, and finally use this annotated archive as notes when I drafted the expanded internship description.

During the Fall 2000 semester I circulated the newly revised, expanded internship description among my colleagues on the Technical Writing Committee, we discussed them at meetings, and I incorporated their suggestions—notably, to add subsections on budget, employer support, and non-disclosure agreements in a section on Procedures. The resulting document was then posted on our program website.

Reflecting the crux of students' difficulties with the original guidelines, this version devoted considerable space to a discussion of the problem and significance of the research project and to an explanation of the purpose of the literature review. Under the heading Procedures, several questions helped students think about the subsections in which they would describe their methods of research and analysis and the place of publication for their final report.

In addition to elaborating the written instructions for the internship project posted on the program website, we also decided to share the responsibility for coaching internship projects, in the same way that supervision of thesis projects is shared in the department's other graduate programs. Instead of just one faculty member overseeing all the internships, each student would now have a Supervisory Committee of three faculty members, with most of the responsibility for supervising the internship falling on the committee chair. However, committee chairs soon found that teaching students how to conduct credible workplace research was a very time-consuming process, for two main reasons. First, students were immersed in a non-academic culture and had no background in research methods, so the learning curve was steep; and second, training individual students to conduct primary research was a very inefficient way to teach, particularly when the main medium of instruction was email, supplemented by occasional phone calls.

One answer to this problem was to develop a course in the kind of primary research methods that our students might find useful to interrogate the practices of their workplaces. Students in the course would be introduced to a range of methods and by the end of the semester would also develop a proposal for their research internship, which would then be conducted as an independent study project in a subsequent semester. At the time of writing this chapter, our department has such a course planned as part of a new PhD program in the Theory and Practice of Professional Communication, scheduled to begin in Fall 2005. The research methods course will serve both PhD and MS students, and teaching assignments will be rearranged to allow us to offer the course once a year. However, in 2002 we did not have the faculty resources to add the research methods class to our annual course rotation. Without that course as a prerequisite to the internship, we did not feel we could continue to assign the internship as we had defined it, so in Spring 2002 we reluctantly decided to remove the internship from the curriculum until such time as the research methods course could be taught.

What, then, have we learned from our experience with the internship assignment in our master's program? The specific lesson is that an internship can be given greater relevance to students who are already situated in non-academic workplaces by giving it a research purpose, but that achieving this purpose depends on students having a foundation of scholarly knowledge that is better taught to a group of students in a seminar than to individual students. I can also think of two more general lessons we have learned from our experience: first, that increasing the academic rigor of an assignment may be laudable but is not always practical if it overburdens faculty already stretched by teaching online; and second, that it is critically important for online programs in these still-early days of online education to engage in praxis—a continuous cycle of application, reexamination, improvement, and reapplication—in order to cope with the inevitable mistakes and dead-end passages that characterize the exploration and development of online instruction.

REFERENCE

1. C. R. Miller, What's Practical about Technical Writing?" in *Technical Writing: Theory and Practice,* B. E. Fearing and W. Keats Sparrow (eds.), MLA, New York, pp. 14-24, 1989.

CHAPTER 14

Online Course and Instructor Evaluations

Kelli Cargile Cook and Keith Grant-Davie

Evaluation of courses and instructors has become a fixture of most onsite, traditional college courses. At semester's end, students typically complete a standardized institutional evaluation form that asks them to evaluate how well the course was designed, taught, and assessed by their instructor. Most forms ask students to report opinions about their instructor's knowledge and teaching abilities. In recent years, many institutions have moved these standardized forms to an online environment for easy student access and data collection and analysis. Along with this move has come the online report of student satisfaction with both the course and instructor performance. Using these online reports, students can learn how other students have felt about their learning in a course or from a particular instructor. Informing other students, however, is just one purpose of course and instructor evaluation; instructors use these evaluations to improve future iterations of their courses, and tenure and promotion committees and administrators consider student evaluations when making personnel decisions about instructors. Because of their varied uses, most administrators, instructors, and students acknowledge the value of course evaluations, and they have become a common, if not always popular, component in courses.

As courses have moved online, however, administrators and instructors have questioned how to evaluate online courses and instruction. Who should evaluate online classes, how should those evaluators be prepared for that task, and how should the evaluations be conducted to ensure accuracy and confidentiality? Should course evaluation forms given to students in onsite classes be used for online classes? To what extent can criteria be transferred or adapted from assessment instruments developed for onsite classes, and to what extent do we need to develop new criteria to address the distinctive features of online instruction, such as threaded discussions or real-time chat? In other words, do the old questions we continue to ask about course design and instructor effectiveness all still apply, and are they sufficient? How can the assessment tools we use for online classes reflect differences between online and onsite instruction and yet participate in the existing system of standardized instructional assessment already in place at our institutions? Are supplementary assessment tools for online classes the answer? Answering these questions has, thus far, been primarily a local concern at institutions offering online education because research studies in online course and instructor evaluation have focused on benchmarks for online instruction, not standards for measuring quality. While these benchmarks are useful for articulating what activities should occur within an online course, they rarely, if ever, distinguish between the excellent and the mediocre performance of these activities.

This chapter will not try to answer all these questions; its purpose is to raise and examine them and to identify the variety of data sources (students, peers and administrators, and instructors themselves) that can be used to gather information for evaluating online instructional effectiveness. We will also suggest that while information about online instruction is abundant because completed online courses serve as archives or testaments to instruction, the practice and process of evaluating online instruction reliably and validly is in its infancy. Complicating this problem are the facts that few standardized student-rating forms exist specifically for online courses, and that very little research has been conducted to examine peer and administrator evaluation or instructor self-report of online instruction. At our chapter's conclusion, we suggest areas for future research, focusing on issues of adequacy and excellence in online instruction and its evaluation.

WHAT ARE THE COMPONENTS OF EFFECTIVE ONLINE INSTRUCTION?

As we have seen in previous chapters of this book, online instructional practices commonly emerge from onsite or traditional instructional practices that are modified to suit the peculiarities and idiosyncrasies of the online learning environment. Similarly, online course and instructor evaluations have taken standards from the traditional classroom as their basis for developing instructional standards. Among the organizations working to establish guidelines for evaluating online instruction, the Western Interstate Commission for Higher Education (WICHE) noted this similarity in its 1999 *Best Practices for Electronically Offered Degree and Certificate Programs:* "The *Best Practices*. . . are not new evaluative criteria. Rather they explicate how the well-established essentials of institutional quality found in regional accreditation standards are applicable to the emergent forms of learning; much of the detail of their content would find application in any learning environment" [1, p. 1]. Likewise, reports such as *Quality On the Line: Benchmarks for Success in Internet-Based Distance*

Education and *Quality Assurance for Whom? Providers and Consumers in Today's Distributed Learning Environment* address the many components of online program evaluation, including online course and instructor evaluations, and discuss both similarities and differences between online and onsite evaluations [2, 3]. Although these reports examine evaluation of online distance education broadly, elements within each of the reports point to key measures or components of effective course and instructor evaluations. Six key measures of quality online instruction addressed in all three reports can be summarized as follows:

1. Before enrolling in an online course, students should receive information about course expectations, about required study skills and personal motivation for success, and about minimal technology requirements.
2. Online courses should have clearly articulated expectations or goals appropriate to the degree or certificate to which the courses apply.
3. Given these expectations, students should be able to focus their time on completing well-defined assignments that directly relate to goal achievement.
4. To complete assignments, students should engage in a variety of learning activities, including interactions with their instructor and other students in the course.
5. When assignments are completed, students should receive timely feedback from their instructors.
6. Through these interactions with their instructor and others, students should feel themselves a part of an academic community that includes student support services, such as library research facilities and technological support.

These guidelines or benchmarks are not so different from popularly cited measures of effective traditional or onsite education, such as the seven principles developed by Chickering and Gamson, who note that effective teaching at the collegiate level:

1. Encourages contact between students and faculty;
2. Develops reciprocity and cooperation among students;
3. Encourages active learning;
4. Gives prompt feedback;
5. Emphasizes time on task;
6. Communicates high expectations; and
7. Respects diverse talents and ways of learning [4, par. 4].

In many ways, these seven principles are applicable to the online learning environment, yet a few significant differences are noteworthy. For example, online learning requires a different kind of student discipline than onsite learning where instructors may provide less scaffolding (see Grady and Davis in this volume) and more time-constricted activities. Additionally, online courses require that students possess access to technology to receive course information and, at least, a modicum of technological literacy (see Rubens and Southard for more on students' technological difficulties). Students need to be aware of these requirements prior to enrolling in the course because, without this knowledge, they may be unable to attend even the first class.

In addition to forewarning students about course and technology requirements in a clear and timely manner, online instructors may need to provide more detailed assignment descriptions and explanations of assessment practices than they might in a traditional classroom, where these descriptions and explanations are often provided in oral presentations and handouts. (Grant-Davie and Walker each discuss the importance of detailed assignment descriptions and assessment explanations in further detail in their chapters in this volume.) Online students lack the oral cues and opportunity for questions found in onsite teaching environments, so they need to be able to find clear written explanations of assignments and evaluation practices, and to find written answers to their own and other students' questions. Without these kinds of written communications of expectations, students will be less likely to complete assignments successfully and, therefore, encounter more difficulty in meeting course objectives or goals. Finally, instructors need to discuss their feedback policy and procedures with students working at a distance. Sometimes this discussion may entail acknowledging email receipt of an assignment with a tentative return date while, at other times, this discussion may be more technologically based, such as explaining how students can use technology to view the instructor's comments on a returned assignment. Whatever form it takes, effective instruction in the online classroom requires instructors not only to think about practices that have worked in onsite classrooms but also to take into account differences in practice necessitated by the online learning/teaching environment. (For a more specific, detailed discussion of how the seven principles of effective teaching can be applied to online learning, see Graham et al. [5].)

WHO SHOULD EVALUATE ONLINE INSTRUCTORS AND INSTRUCTION?

Given these components of effective online instruction, this section of the chapter discusses several potential evaluators of online instruction and instructors: students taking online courses; the instructor's peers, administrators, and outside experts; and instructors themselves. Describing the importance of using multiple sources of data such as these, Cashin argues: "Writers about faculty evaluation are almost universal in recommending the use of multiple sources of data. No single source of data, including student rating data, provides sufficient information to make a valid judgment about teaching effectiveness" [6, p. 1]. Similarly, one might argue that incorporating information from multiple data sources (whether they be students, peers, administrators, outside experts, or instructors themselves) is as important in determining the effectiveness of online teaching as it is in traditional, onsite teaching. This section examines the contributions different evaluators can make, explores the kinds of evaluations that are possible, explains how these evaluations can be made, and suggests how they may be used to improve online education.

Student Evaluations

Ratings of students' perceptions about and satisfaction with online instruction can be an important indicator of the instructor and course quality. In traditional classrooms, such ratings have been used to provide instructors with both formative and summative feedback about the course and its delivery. Instructors who ask students for formative feedback typically do so during the course to shape course activities and requirements more precisely to meet student needs and expectations; consequently, instructors are most commonly the only users or readers of formative feedback. Students offer summative feedback at the course's end or after graduation. Summative feedback, which responds to the course's overall or final outcomes, is not only used by instructors for course improvement but also may be used by administrators to make personnel and programmatic decisions.

Preparing Quality Questions

Whether the evaluation is formative or summative, students can respond to a variety of teaching quality questions. For best results, these questions should correlate with the benchmarks for quality online instruction and request information from students that will assist instructors in better meeting these benchmarks. Addressing these benchmarks may mean that an institution's standardized forms for traditional, onsite instruction are not directly applicable to online instruction; new questions will mostly likely be needed to supplement and address online-specific issues. As Birnbaum notes: "While the bulk of questions used for traditional and distance education settings should remain the same, a separate section that asks specifically about distance education delivery may yield valuable information about distance education delivery that was not even considered in the initial planning phases of the course of program" [7, p. 138]. Whether the instructor decides to add a separate section or simply incorporate online-specific wording into evaluative questions, evaluations should probably request the following kinds of feedback from online students:

1. How well were students informed about course objectives and activities, technology requirements, and other online learning requirements *prior* to the course's beginning? (This kind of information might be provided in course catalogs or brochures, on program websites, or through pre-semester email messages sent directly to enrolled students.)
2. Was the course's organization and structure (scaffolding) apparent to the student from the beginning of the course, and was it easy to follow through the course's duration?

3. What types of online interactions did the student have with the instructor and with other students? (Answer prompts might be added here, such as email, telephone conversations or voice mail, threaded discussions, chat room conversations, etc.)

4. Through these interactions, were students able to develop a rapport with the instructor and other students? (Stated more specifically, in what kinds of community-building activities did students participate, did they have a sense that the instructor was fully involved with the class and cared about students' learning, and how much did other students contribute to the learning experience? These kinds of questions are important to ask because a sense of community and rapport between students and instructor in online classes is established largely through online interaction, without the assistance of such other signals as body language, tone of voice, and being physically present together in the same room during class meetings.)

5. How effectively did the instructor manage the online discussion forum? (For example, did the instructor stimulate student discussion without dominating it? Were students provided the right amount of time and virtual space to discuss topics?)

6. In what kinds of learning activities (reading, discussion, homework, collaborative assignments, etc.) did online students participate? Did the instructor make effective use of the available technological features of the course to facilitate these learning activities?

7. How clearly did the instructor articulate course goals, facilitate learning activities, and explain and use communication channels?

8. How challenging was the course and its workload?

9. How accessible was the instructor? How promptly did students receive feedback from the instructor about questions, assignments, or examinations, and how clearly was the instructor's feedback communicated to students?

10. How usable was the course's technology and its technology interfaces?

11. How well did the course meet students' expectations and needs?

12. What were the strengths of the course, and in what areas could it be improved?

Questions like these, whether open-ended or revised to a closed form for more standardized responses, are the kinds of questions that target the effectiveness and quality of instruction in online courses. They can be used for both formative and summative feedback, and answers to them can help instructors to shape their courses more effectively to meet students' needs and expectations for the course. (For another excellent, finely-grained list of questions to which students might be asked to respond about their online learning experiences, see Twigg [3].) The questions listed above are reflected in the course evaluation form that we have been sending out to students in our online master's program in Technical

Writing. Like the form used campus-wide at Utah State for onsite courses, this form includes a blend of closed and open-ended questions. The closed questions list features of the course and ask students to rate their value on a scale, or they offer value statements about the course and ask students to rate their agreement with those statements. The closed questions give us some grounds for comparison between students' responses, while the open-ended questions—particularly the final question that asks students to identify strengths and areas for improvement in the course—give students more freedom to express their opinions about the course and to describe their experience in it. The open-ended questions can serve to confirm or explicate the evaluations suggested by the closed questions.

What have we learned from the evaluation forms our graduate students have returned to us in the last two years? Our online students appear to value well-organized syllabi and discussion forums, with clearly explained assignments and expectations for students. They value instructors who participate regularly in class discussions, posting mini-lectures on the course material and substantive responses to student work—not just brief, general expressions of praise and encouragement. They expect instructors to respond to student work promptly, and they appreciate instructors who let the class know when they will be away and unable to respond to students' questions for a while. Students with some experience in online classes expect instructors to exploit the strengths and features of the online medium and feel short-changed if, for example, an instructor substitutes email dialogue for a discussion board and creates a relatively impoverished online class environment. Although there are always one or two students who express a preference for a course that makes few demands on their time, allows them to take much of the responsibility for teaching themselves, and does not force them to meet weekly participation quotas, the course evaluations returned by our students have indicated a general feeling that instructors need to compensate for the physical remoteness of themselves and their students by creating a rich, responsive online environment where there are no long, unexplained silences. Online students who have felt neglected by the instructor in a course tend to express their criticisms strongly.

Getting Feedback from Students

How to deliver the questions to students and how to receive their responses are the next set of challenges once questions have been prepared. A variety of methods exist for gathering evaluative information; choosing between these methods depends on the type and purpose of the evaluations as well as the importance of student confidentiality in the evaluation process.

Formative evaluations. When instructors are interested in formative feedback to improve their course during its delivery and confidentiality is not highly important, then direct contact with students is a simple and effective way to gather information. Using technologies such as email, threaded discussion boards, and chat rooms can provide venues for formative evaluation questions. As Walker's chapter in this book illustrates, if an instructor is wondering whether online discussions might be richer with more structured prompts from her, she might ask whether students prefer an open discussion or a list of specific questions to which they must respond. If students are uncertain what they would prefer, then she can demonstrate the different methods over the next two discussion periods and request student preferences following these experiments. Using this kind of direct demonstration and feedback, instructors can more clearly evaluate which type of discussion prompt works best with her particular students in a given semester and decide which is the most appropriate course of action for the rest of the course. In this type of formative evaluation scenario, student confidentiality is not as important as individual feedback and preferences. Questions about usability of the website's contents and technological framework are also easily addressed through this kind of formative questioning and decision-making. In these cases, instructors may simply ask questions that seem relevant to the teaching/learning situation without much concern about standardized form or method.

Summative evaluations. Summative evaluation processes, however, are often more formal and standardized because they are typically used by administrators to help make personnel decisions, such as those concerning tenure and promotion status. Evaluative questions, therefore, need to be asked in such a way that data from all students can easily and quickly be gathered, analyzed, and presented to administration or personnel committees. For this reason, summative evaluation rating scales usually take one of three forms: omnibus forms (a fixed set of questions), goal-based forms (students rate their learning or the course based on stated course goals), or cafeteria system forms (questions are derived from a bank of standardized forms) [8, p. 175]. According to the literature on course evaluation, using more standardized forms such as these results in higher reliability and validity among student ratings and provides what some instructors and administrators believe to be a sounder basis for personnel decision-making. Research in traditional classroom summative evaluation has shown that student ratings are reliable; that is, student ratings typically show relative agreement among students in classes and prove stable over time [9, p. 79]. Student ratings, however, are less likely to be valid; that is, they do not always directly measure teaching effectiveness. Nevertheless, student ratings are recognized as one of several important sources of information about effective teaching. For this reason, most institutions prefer standardized forms, which have been tested for reliability and for validity, rather than informal questions developed by individual instructors. Finally, because instructors and administrators want students to give their honest opinions about the instruction they have received, summative evaluations are most frequently confidential. Issues of confidentiality are important because research in onsite summative evaluation has shown that "students who identify themselves in ratings are expected to be far more generous, especially if the forms are returned to the instructor before final grades" and that "identification is probably only crucial if students think their grades may be affected or if they have to explain the reasons for their ratings of the teacher" [9, p. 77]. Currently, little to no research exists about the effects of confidentiality in online courses or about reliability and validity of online summative evaluations. So, as is often the case with online learning, instructors and administrators are basing their decisions about summative evaluation on research from traditional classroom settings.

Because of the confidentiality issue, therefore, summative evaluations require more controlled delivery to students and more controlled receipt from students. To address this challenge, some institutions have moved course and instructor evaluation forms online. A number of online options exist, including email exchange and use of Web-based forms. Some instructors send out summative evaluation forms to students via email and request that students complete the forms and return them to a department administrator, who then removes identifying information and sends the data to the instructor. Although using email technology is a simple way to send and receive student evaluations, it has clear disadvantages, including possible lack of confidentiality and its time-consuming nature (not only for students but also for administrators who must remove student information and for instructors who must analyze data individually). Because of the drawbacks of email exchange, Web-based forms are recognized as a less time-intensive means of gathering data and a means that more clearly protects student confidentiality. To use a Web-based form, students log on to a password-protected website and then complete the standardized form online. Responses are reported to the instructor or a program administrator without direct connection to specific students, and they may even, like onsite evaluations, be reported to the instructor as aggregates.

Peer, Outside Expert, and Administrator Evaluations

In addition to student information, peers, outside experts, and administrators can effectively review components of effective online instruction. For example, reviewers can examine and evaluate course components such as teaching materials, syllabi, interactions between students and the instructors and among students, and the instructor's incorporation and use of technology in the online course. Although such evaluations can be used for formative evaluation purposes, most outside reviewer evaluation is summative and used for making personnel decisions.

Reviewers can evaluate course materials, including the instructor's choice and sequencing of reading materials, course activities, and individual and collaborative assignments. They can also look at the instructor's responses to student questions and feedback on student interactions. In a discussion of peers' traditional evaluation of onsite courses, Hoyt and Pallett note: "Observers are expected to rate such factors as knowledge of the subject, enthusiasm, sensitivity to class level of knowledge, preparation and organization, and clarity of presentation" [10, p. 2]. Reviewers of online instruction can provide similar kinds of evaluations, but online courses may raise additional assessment issues. For instance, reviewers have the opportunity to comment on the instructor's success in managing online discussion, whether it be real-time chat or asynchronous discussion. While discussion in online classrooms has a counterpart in onsite discussion, the dynamics of the different media are not the same. For instance, in an onsite classroom, an instructor can influence discussion among students without saying anything, simply by being physically present and attentive, but an online instructor has little presence in the virtual classroom unless he or she actually participates in the discussion. Managing an online discussion may, therefore, need to be a more discursive process than managing an onsite conversation.

To give another example, in an onsite classroom, a student can effectively participate in only one discussion topic at a time. Even if the class breaks into small groups, each student is likely to be engaged in only one topic at a time. In a threaded online discussion, on the other hand, topics can remain open indefinitely and the instructor may need to decide which topics to declare closed (to keep student attention from becoming too scattered and thinly stretched), and which topics to invite students to continue discussing in a new discussion group (in order to keep the main board from becoming too cluttered and cumbersome to download). Assessing how well an instructor has displayed these kinds of discussion management techniques that are unique to certain online media is an added challenge to reviewers of online classes.

Reviewers of online instruction also need to come to terms with the fact that they can evaluate online courses more comprehensively than onsite reviewers. In almost all instances (voice mails, telephone conversations, and perhaps emails excepted), online interactions between an online instructor and the students in the course are archived within the course environment itself. The syllabi are present and available through a hypertext link, and the instructor's discussion of the syllabi is present in a threaded discussion area or an archived chat or MOO log. Assignment descriptions are archived in the courseware, as are the instructor's responses to assignments or clarifications of them. Conversations from the first day of class to the last are archived within the technology files of the course, and peer or outside experts have the opportunity to sample from all the course's elements. Given this abundance of course information, reviewers are able to examine one or all of the course meetings through these archived records rather than depending on only one or a few class visits to gather the gist of an instructor's effectiveness with his or her students. In sum, the entire course is available for evaluation in all its richness and complexity.

The challenge that arises from this richness and complexity is in determining what to view or read from the class archives. Online reviewers may be overwhelmed by the wealth of information available to them. For this reason, it is important for peer and outside expert evaluators to develop some plan for assessing the course's effectiveness before going into the course archives and, if possible, discussing this plan with the instructor. In this way, instructors can assist the outside reviewers in finding the information they need to make an evaluation of the course, and they can direct reviewers to instances for which they would like some formative feedback. With this guidance, reviewers can then enter the website with some sense of direction, find what they need to evaluate the course, and gather evidence for documentation of teaching excellence or deficits. With such information and guidance, reviewers, whether they are peers, outside experts, or administrators, will be better able to report on the effectiveness of the instructor's online learning environment.

To illustrate how peers or administrators can review an online course, we excerpt below a few sentences from a peer observation letter written by Dr. Christine Hult, professor and associate head of the English Department at Utah State University. The letter reports her observations of an online graduate course. She writes:

- I read through the course syllabus and description of assignments and found them to be extremely well planned out and suitable for graduate-level work. The syllabus was presented with hyperlinked text with clearly organized, detailed information. . . .

- By reading through the archived discussion, I was able to see that [the professor] has complete command of the material, and [the professor's] skill in setting up the discussions was clearly evident. . . . For each discussion, [the professor] used appropriate prompts and questions to lead . . . students into materials. . . . Both the assignments and the discussions made lasting impressions on the students: "Since our discussions of legal and ethical issues, I have been seeing more and more implications for this type of [work]. . . . I now have a better understanding of copyright law, intellectual property, and trademarks. I see their application in most everything."

- Through . . . frequent posts online, it was apparent that [the professor] established a comfortable rapport with students that was maintained throughout the sites. Students were obviously engaged and actively learning through the entire process [11].

Dr. Hult's comments demonstrate how peers and administrators can review a course website/archive. In her comments, she addresses teaching materials, the instructor's command of subject matter, and course organization—all teaching components that apply to both onsite and online instructor. Yet, her comments also address components more specifically related to online instruction—the instructor's use of hyperlinks within course materials, electronic discussion forum management, and the instructor's classroom "presence" and rapport with students who work from a distance. Her references to the course syllabus, to the description of assignments, and to specific student comments indicate that she understood how to read the course archive, how to identify relevant data for her observation, and how to interpret such data to evaluate teaching effectiveness. It is important to note here that, unlike many administrators, Dr. Hult already had considerable experience as an online instructor herself. That experience gave her reference points against which to evaluate what she saw in this instructor's class and a better sense of the significance of what she found in the course archive.

Instructor Self-Reports

A final means of gathering information about an online course's effectiveness is through an instructor's self-analysis and report of the course and its outcomes. Instructors can provide both descriptive and reflective accounts of their courses. For example, an instructor's report, whether descriptive or evaluative, can assist outside reviewers of a course in identifying course and instructor strengths and weaknesses. Such reports, according to Hoyt and Pallett, can discuss "course objectives; readings, assignments, and other learning activities, the creation of instructional materials or learning opportunities; procedures for appraising student achievement; results of, and course modifications based on, classroom research and other faculty efforts directed to improving instructional skills" [10, p. 2]. Specifically, in online instruction, discussions might also include instructor notes about how to conduct discussions (what prompts worked and why, what happened when discussions were open rather than led by prompts, what kinds of interventions worked when student discussions moved off-task), and how to use technology more effectively. Questions related to effective technology use include when to use asynchronous versus synchronous discussions; how and where to post information for easy student access—as weekly notices on website front page, as discussion posts, as calendar posts, or as a combination of several of these placements; and how to disseminate specific information to students and how to receive information back from students (email vs. threaded discussions vs. online chats/MOOs; filesharing vs. email attachments vs. FTP).

Another source of information an instructor can draw upon is the record of student interaction within the website. For example, instructors can often determine and record how often students are checking into the courseware site or course website, how long they are spending in specific areas, and which parts of the course or website are most frequently visited and which parts are not. This kind of data can help an instructor to streamline course information and to make decisions about what to include and what to exclude in a course website. As Walker describes in her chapter in this volume, formative feedback can also help instructors to determine student preference for instructional delivery methods. If students access the course calendar, for example, more frequently than a bulletin board, then instructors can modify their postings to make better use of students' preferred method of information delivery.

Finally, instructors can write reflective report entries that discuss how well students met instructors' expectations and why. Referring to information gleaned from more descriptive analyses of the course at its end, instructors may be able to determine where students had difficulty accomplishing a course's goals and make adjustments to support student learning more effectively.

Reading reflective reports such as these can help administrators and other outside reviewers to understand the dynamics of the course and instructors' attempts to modify and improve these dynamics as the course unfolded. Such reports are also particularly important from the instructor's point of view if the instructor is more experienced with online instruction than the administrators who are charged with evaluating and reporting on the instructor's performance. A well-written report can allow the instructor to have a say in defining what counts as excellence in online instruction by establishing criteria and presenting a rationale for what the instructor has done. It can draw administrators' attention to particular parts of the course that might otherwise be overlooked in the rich archive, and it may help administrators avoid misinterpreting what they see. In this way, information written into instructor self-reports can be useful not only for formative evaluation purposes (assisting an instructor in revising future iterations of the course) but also for summative evaluation purposes related to personnel decisions. These reports work well when conducted at the course's end, but they can be used during course instruction as well. Because of the fluidity of the online course environment, instructor reflection can result in modification of the course during the semester for more optimal instruction opportunities.

CONCLUSIONS AND SUGGESTIONS FOR FUTURE RESEARCH

We opened this chapter with a list of questions that we feel represent the challenges faced by administrators and educators as they look for ways to measure the quality of online instruction. In brief, we asked how we can assess the distinct and still evolving characteristics of online instruction yet also integrate online assessment with the institution's existing criteria, instruments, and practices developed for onsite instruction. There is a pressing need to meet both those goals without delay. As we develop online courses and programs using media that are still relatively new, we need to know how well they are working, for both formative and summative purposes. We need a basis for revising and improving what we do in online classes, and without assessment instruments, procedures, and criteria that administrators can accept and understand, tenure-line faculty with significant online teaching assignments are in danger of being assessed only on their onsite teaching.

Many of the traditional assessment criteria seem to apply as much to online instruction as to onsite, e.g., clarity of course objectives, relevance of assignments to course goals, appropriateness of readings, opportunity for students to make comments or express opinions, and the instructor's level of preparation and helpfulness in responding to student questions. Furthermore, it seems relatively simple to arrange peers' and administrators' access to online classes and to solve the logistical problems of distributing course evaluation forms to remote students and gathering the completed forms in again. However, while many traditional assessment standards and practices readily apply to online classes, some modifications seem necessary. For instance, we need to look at the impact of the online medium on the class—a whole area of assessment not addressed in the campus-wide course evaluation form distributed to students at Utah State University. How effectively were the various online media used in the course? Were they an asset or an obstacle to the functioning of the class as a community? How well was the instructor able to overcome the physical remoteness of class members? These are not questions we would think to ask students or peers about an onsite class.

In addition to issues of space—the fact that students and teacher may never meet in the same physical location—online classes also raise issues of time that are different from those in onsite classes. "Instructor's use of class time" is a classic measure of the onsite classroom, but it takes on a new significance in an online class based on asynchronous discussion, perhaps blended with sessions of real-time chat. The dynamics of a discussion conducted orally, in a room, for between one and three hours, are different from those of a discussion conducted in writing, with contributions made and read over a period of perhaps several weeks by people who may never have seen each other. Do we yet know what "good use of class time" means in such a class? Students are in a position to describe the experience of online classes and to express their satisfaction or dissatisfaction with it, but do peers and administrators know enough to recognize skillful, effective management of an online discussion, whether asynchronous or synchronous? Could they distinguish it from less effective management of the class and offer suggestions for improvement? Or is it enough simply to record that online discussion occurred and that the instructor participated?

In asking these questions, we recognize that we are making a distinction noted by Twigg—a distinction between *adequate* practices and *best* practices, between the merely acceptable and the excellent [3, p. 7]. To what extent do we want to pursue that distinction which offers the goal of quality but tends toward a prescriptive set of features? We share the concern of participants in that symposium who rejected several proposed benchmarks of quality. For example, they believed that collaboration amongst students and recognition of different learning styles were proven measures of good instruction, but they chose not to include them as components that ought to be found in every class, recognizing that an online class could be excellent without necessarily involving students in collaboration or catering to different learning styles. The dilemma, then, is whether to specify the characteristics of excellence and run the risk of institutionalizing a narrow definition of quality in online education, or whether to accommodate a diversity of teaching methods and styles with broader, looser criteria, but in so doing settle for measuring only minimal, common standards. Of course, this dilemma is not peculiar to online instruction. Onsite assessment has faced the same dilemma and has generally settled for measuring only adequacy, in the form of a set of commonly accepted standards that can be applied to a wide variety of classes. Whether online assessment will settle for the same compromise or whether the attempt to measure what is different about online instruction will lead us to apply standards of excellence rather than adequacy remains to be seen.

Whichever path online educators choose, it is clear that more research in online course and instructor evaluations is due. The opportunities for evaluation of online courses are abundant, as are the kinds of data that can be gathered about online instruction (see, for example, Avery et al.'s next chapter describing an application that can map the patterns in online discussions, thereby providing data that might be useful for assessment). But, like so many aspects of online instruction, research in the effectiveness of these evaluations is only beginning and, for the most part, current evaluation practice relies upon research conducted in the traditional onsite classroom. For these reasons, we see future research opportunities in a variety of areas, including studies leading to standardized online course and instructor evaluation forms, studies examining the benchmarks of effective online teaching, and studies considering questions about technology, its accessibility and use. As we look forward to these studies and others like them, however, we anticipate that our learning will eventually come full circle—what we learn about evaluation of courses and instructors in online classrooms will shed new light on its predecessor, the traditional onsite classroom, improving how well instructors teach and how well students learn, whatever the learning environment.

REFERENCES

1. Western Cooperative for Educational Telecommunications, *Best Practices For Electronically Offered Degrees and Certificate Programs*, http://www.wcet.info/Accrediting%20-%20Best%20Practices.pdf, April 3, 2002.
2. The Institute for Higher Education Policy, *Quality on the Line: Benchmarks for Success in Internet-Based Distance Education*, NEA, Washington, D.C., April 2000.
3. C. A. Twigg, *Quality Assurance for Whom? Providers and Consumers in Today's Distributed Learning Environment*, Center for Academic Transformation, Troy, New York, 2001.
4. A. W. Chickering and Z. F. Gamson, *Seven Principles of Good Practice in Undergraduate Education*, www.hcc.hawaii.edu/intranet/committees/FacDevCom/guidebk/teachtip/7princip.htm, November 6, 2002.

5. C. Graham, K. Cagiltay, B. Lim, J. Craner, and T. M. Duffy, Seven Principles of Effective Teaching: A Practical Lens for Evaluating Online Courses, *Technology Source,* http://ts.mivu.org/default.asp?Show=article&id=839&action=print, 2001.

6. W. E. Cashin, Student Ratings of Teaching: A Summary of the Research, *IDEA Paper No. 20,* Center for Faculty Evaluation and Development, Kansas State University Continuing Education, September 1988.

7. B. W. Birnbaum, *Foundations and Practices in the Use of Distance Education* (Volume 66), Mellen Studies in Education, Edwin Mellen Press, Lewiston, New York, 2001.

8. L. A. Braskamp and J. C. Ory, *Assessing Faculty Work: Enhancing Individual and Institutional Performance,* Jossey-Bass, San Franscisco,1994.

9. J. A. Centra, *Reflective Faculty Evaluation: Enhancing Teaching and Determining Faculty Effectiveness,* Jossey-Bass, San Francisco, 1993.

10. D. P. Hoyt and W. H. Pallett, Appraising Teaching Effectiveness: Beyond Student Ratings, *IDEA Paper No. 36,* Center for Faculty Evaluation and Development, Kansas State University Continuing Education, November 1999.

11. C. Hult, unpublished document, 2002.

CHAPTER 15

Assessing Student Interaction in the Global Classroom Project: Visualizing Communication and Collaboration Patterns Using Online Transcripts

Cassie Avery, Jason Civjan,
and Aditya Johri

Current technology allows for assessment techniques that are relevant and unique to the online collaborative learning environment. This chapter addresses the need for assessment tools that are integrated into real-time, computer-mediated learning environments. It details the development process and outcomes of VisOC (Visualizations of Online Communication), a digital assessment tool that was created specifically to allow visual analysis of student communication and learning outcomes in an online environment. VisOC's goal is to provide educators with a versatile automated process for building interactive graphical representations that compare aspects of student profiles with performance patterns and analyze these aspects' role in contributing to the overall learning goals of the classroom. These representations can assist in better understanding the effectiveness of educational strategies that employ Computer-Mediated Communication (CMC).

This chapter also provides an overview of the foundations of classroom analysis, details the role that new technology can play in online course assessment, and discusses the possible ramifications of improved assessment technology in educational environments. It describes the VisOC assessment tool and its operation, illustrates the tool's utility, and explains the project developers' initial findings. Throughout the chapter, the authors try to abstract useful, general knowledge for building assessment tools for the contemporary online educational environment.

EVOLUTION OF ASSESSMENT MODELS

The evolution of educational system assessment has always been influenced by the technology and tools available to an educator as well as the changing focus of educational theory, which has developed from a behaviorist to a cognitive, and, most recently, to a situated approach. In any assessment of a behaviorist educational system, where close study of students' and instructors' actions is paramount to understanding the system, analysts originally had to physically sit in the classroom and take handwritten transcripts of each student's behaviors in order to carry out rigorous assessment. Strict methods were employed to limit inherent corruption of gathered data. Tape recorders and then video cameras were introduced to record transcripts more effectively and accurately. As theoretical trends shifted to a more cognitive approach to education, new assessment tools (pre- and post-course testing, interviews, focus groups, and surveys) were created and directed at students to ascertain if the learning goals established by instructors and institutions were being met within a classroom [1, p. 1516].

As trends in education are beginning to transcend the physical classroom and focus on the rich interactions allowed by the digital classroom environment, *situated* models of cognition place increasing importance on how activity, context, culture, and especially the tools students use affect their ability to assimilate knowledge in a social setting. The *situated* model maintains that "thinking is situated in a particular context of intentions, social partners and tools" [2, p. 20]. The classroom or the class environment, as used in this chapter, refers to the situated model of cognition, where all interactions between "social partners" (instructors and students) and with "tools" (the computer environment and other media, such as books) that are influences in the classroom system are taken into consideration as essential to the whole [3]. The classroom system is seen as a specific situated environment that has stated "intentions" or educational goals. Any assessment of such a system is aimed at defining how well the situated classroom system works to reach its particular goals.

In CMC, the computer itself is a part of the situated classroom context that influences how students think and learn. It offers an extended library of information and resources that can be adapted easily to fit the specific context of the learner. The interactions change from face-to-face, real-time, social interactions to faceless, asynchronous conversations which revolve around the community, the social networks, and their specific "rules of behavior" [4]. All of these factors of CMC, which have no meaning when separated from an online classroom context, rely on interactions within the entire system for worth. Much like situated analysis of the physical classroom, context must be retained in order to maintain relevancy in the assessment of a CMC environment.

DIFFICULTIES IN ONLINE COURSE ASSESSMENT

Informal assessment is an important way that instructors measure the progress of a course and ascertain if their instructional goals are being met. As Airasian points out, informal assessment practices in a traditional classroom setting "occupy more of a teacher's time and arguably have a greater impact on instruction and pupil learning than do the formal measurement procedures" [5, p. 15].

In a traditional classroom setting, the avenues for informal assessment from physical indications are numerous. Students ask questions, take part in spontaneous discussions, and offer timely suggestions. Instructors can walk among students as they work in order to determine whether they understand course material. They can use visual and auditory signals to gauge how students are reacting to assignments or progressing in their group work by observing facial expressions, chatter levels, and the proximity of students to one another.

In an online classroom, if it can be called a classroom, these cues are absent. There are fewer sensory indications to help form impressions about participant personality or enthusiasm for contributing to a constructive discussion. The lack of sensory cues makes it more difficult for instructors to get a reliable impression of what is happening in their classes. Often those who wish to quickly comprehend the dynamics of a particular online discussion have to depend on subjective assessments of discussion posts or on simplistic measurements such as total number of posts or word count of messages to try to judge whether students are participating often and exhaustively. These measurements say little about the relevance of individual messages to group conversations and say nothing about the role the messages' content plays in contributing to the overall quality of an educational dialogue. The lack of sensory feedback also fails to give students a sense of what is going on around them. Information about other students can help in forming groups, facilitating teamwork, and increasing overall interest and participation levels in a course; yet, most online courseware provides minimal support for such signals.

Even with face-to-face group contact, it can be difficult to create formulas that make explicit appropriate factors for encouraging effective teamwork and learning. In an online classroom, many additional factors complicate the equation: lack of rapid sensory feedback, the often asynchronous nature of communication, the speed at which archived messages grow and become unmanageable, and fewer opportunities for group members to get to know and trust each other in informal settings. Most importantly, an online classroom generally lacks tools that can effectively allow for meaningful, relevant, moored-to-context assessment of the learning system.

ASSESSMENT TO CREATE EFFECTIVE
EDUCATIONAL ENVIRONMENTS

Many of the online classroom's difficulties can also translate into advantages over traditional classroom formats [6]. Due to asynchronous communication, students have more time to compose thoughtful responses to the questions instructors and other students pose, and students can contribute to course discussions as they form ideas and feel prepared to share them. The informal setting of communication can allow for all to feel on equal ground, free of the political dynamics of the physical classroom. With enormous breadth of space for all members of the class to be active participants in conversations, everyone is invited to contribute rather than having to compete for attention in a single room during a specified time. However, proper organization and implementation of the online course, with its supporting technologies, is necessary to make sure that these advantages are realized.

Integration of digital assessment tools into the online educational environment can help instructors take advantage of the differences inherent in online classroom environments. The National Academy of Sciences, in its report "Knowing What Students Know: The Science and Design of Educational Assessment," discusses and reviews opportunities for advancing educational assessment using information technologies. The authors of the report propose that technology's role in assessment "should be based on modern knowledge of cognition and its measurement, should be integrated with curriculum and instruction, and should inform as well as improve student achievement" [7, p. 261]. This integration of assessment tools into "curriculum and instruction" is now possible in online educational environments. Stiggins suggests that student achievement is hindered when educators rely solely on prescribed tests administered at lengthy intervals. "[T]hese . . . tests are incapable of providing teachers with the moment-to-moment and day-to-day information about student achievement that they need to make crucial instructional decisions. Teachers must rely on classroom assessment to do this" [8, p. 15].

A system of assessment must be able to assess dynamically, in real-time, and to react to unpredictable changes in student attitudes and behaviors. Instructors should have technology available to help dynamically assess the current educational situation and to provide essential data for determining the best direction in which the class should evolve in order to achieve and maintain system goals.

DEFINITION AND PURPOSE OF ASSESSMENT

One important distinction that must be made is that assessment of a classroom system is not simply an evaluation of the system. While evaluation would presume that one is only inspecting the system to determine its value, assessment is examining the role each component of the system plays in making the system succeed in relation to its defined goals [9]. In assessment, scrupulous attention must be paid to the details of the system, and improvements must be suggested for future redesigns in order to strengthen the ability of each component of the system to fulfill its assigned or chosen role [10]. Tools for classroom assessment must evolve to effectively accommodate the redefinition of system goals and to target reactions to significant system adjustments, while taking advantage of the most appropriate technologies available.

The highly contextualized nature of a classroom system and the goals defined for each specific educational situation must be understood in order to determine the relevancy of any sort of assessment [11]. Each classroom must be assessed using the definitions and terminology that are specifically relevant to that particular classroom, and no assumption of relevancy, based in the context of a different classroom, can be levied. For assessment to be valuable, it must be carried out in a manner that is relevant to the instructor and to the students who take part in the system under scrutiny.

Digital technology like VisOC provides the opportunity to assess not just learning but the processes that most effectively allow it to take place. For this reason, VisOC does not focus exclusively on the learning of specific subject matter but on the social processes that are essential if learning is to occur. These processes include student and instructor interactions that lead to communication and collaboration as a means of producing higher-order thinking skills [12, 13]. The tool looks for indications that students are internalizing knowledge and revising their mental frameworks to accommodate learned material though negotiation of meaning and co-construction of knowledge [14]. These indications of higher-order thinking skills can be traced by analyzing transcripts of online discussions.

APPROACHES TO TRANSCRIPT ANALYSIS

Archives of synchronous and asynchronous CMC are valuable resources, containing both explicit and implicit knowledge about interactions among participants of online discussions (as is evidenced in the heavy reliance on synchronous and asynchronous transcripts as examples throughout much of this book). These archives are often largely untapped information resources because the sheer volume of textual information they contain is daunting to analyze. In addition, these information sources are often only accessible in multiple short and discrete chunks that are time-consuming to access chronologically.

However, it is possible to create reproducible and reliable means by which to carry out analysis of electronic transcripts using the very tools that create them—digital technologies. Using digital technologies, researchers have employed several methods to analyze online communication with the assistance of computational algorithms: log-file analysis, content analysis, social network analysis, and information visualization.

Log-File Analysis

Log-file analysis employs statistics that can be easily gathered by a computer in order to track how users are accessing an online environment. Interpreted properly, log-file analysis can provide base statistics that indicate use levels and flag unusual activity, but log-file analysis is a poor indicator of user motivation. Top user lists, for example, do not distinguish students who read messages without contributing to the discussion from active participants and do not indicate whether the messages that users posted were thoughtfully composed or of value to others [15]. Figure 1 depicts an example of a top user list that ranks users according to simple statistics. A top user list tracks students who have logged on to or viewed content in the system the highest number of times, but such lists can be misleading when students log onto the system multiple times to reread messages or due to faulty connections. They are poor indicators of user activity beyond noting how often students have viewed some amount of content in the online environment.

Content Analysis

Content analysis involves examining what is said during learning interactions. It endeavors to provide an objective methodology for analyzing quantitative data related to learning interactions. The main goal of content analysis is "to formulate an understanding of the representation of knowledge used in cognitive performances" and to recognize how understanding changes as people learn [16, p. 271]. Using content analysis, researchers can identify occurrences of words

Rank	User	Log-ons
1.	lurker	512
2.	highspeeduser	432
3.	superrefresher	412
4.	rereader	345
5.	activeparticipant	98

Figure 1. Top user list.

or concepts as they appear within a set of transcripts and then make inferences about how and why they are used by examining surrounding statements.

Many researchers have examined online transcripts with content analysis and have recommended further content distinctions based on the roles messages play in contributing to collaborative learning. Bakardjieva makes an important distinction between two dimensions of online discourse, the cognitive and the interactive dimension, noting the difference between restatement of knowledge and negotiation of understanding among members of the group [17]. Pena-Shaff et al. use coding categories to distinguish between types of participation in dialog [18]. They make distinctions based on whether messages are monologue, independent statements, or interactive, explicit or implicit references to other messages. Newman, Johnson, and Cochrane offer a case study of content analysis and give examples of language used in transcripts from both onsite and online class transcripts that constitute evidence of higher-order thinking skills being developed through social interaction [19].

Although content analysis provides adequate constructs for examining collaborative learning while taking into account participant motivations, it is time consuming to conduct and raises issues regarding objectivity, reliability, replicability, and systematic coherence [20, pp. 6-8].

Social Network Analysis

Social network analysis is the visual and mathematical analysis of complex group exchanges where users are represented as nodes and instances of communication as paths between the nodes. This method examines communication flow within groups as they use computers. Social network analysis is carried out by asking questions that help isolate which students are communicating with one another and then plotting those interactions to visually represent social connections among subgroups of varying sizes. In exploring social networks, one can find clues into the building of communities in a network and identify where breakdowns and constraints in communication occur [4]. Social network analysis involves plotting members of groups as nodes in a web with lines between nodes representing instances of communication. Figure 2 depicts a basic social network in which a single person (Jim) is pivotal in keeping communication flowing between more peripheral members of the group.

Information Visualization

Information visualization helps users better examine data by accumulating individual elements into an aggregate framework that maps related data to a physical representation. The process translates information into visual representations that support analysis and decision-making. Such visualizations provide an overview of data from which users make abstractions as well as conduct closer inspections to get details about individual elements.

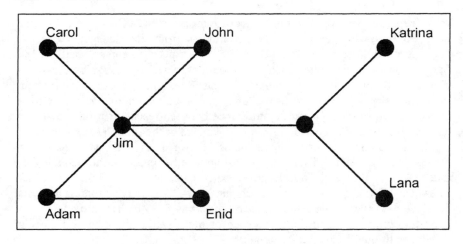

Figure 2. Diagram of a simple social network.

Many researchers have looked at visualizations of online data using transcript analysis. Chat circles, an abstract graphical interface for synchronous conversation, portray large group conversations as conversational clusters [22]. Theme River visualizes online discussions as rivers flowing through time with changes in width depicting changes in thematic strength [23]. An advantage of information visualization is that it is responsive to constant data influxes that depict system changes over varying periods of time.

Figure 3 portrays a visualization of the same raw information shown in the table in Figure 1. The number of logons made by each user is represented by the size of each user's respective circle. The overlap of circles correlates to the number of simultaneous logons made by the users. In a digital environment, the visualization depicted by the figure might respond to system changes by showing the circles growing as logons accumulate and by allowing a user to interact with the system to compare different sets of students by choosing which circles are represented. Contemporary technology offers the opportunity to find new methods of automating the time-intensive process of transcript analysis and to view the information contained in these records in novel formats.

The Need for More Efficient and Expressive Tools for Transcript Analysis in Educational Context

A tool providing dynamic overviews of the information contained in posts and drawing attention to points of interest as defined by instructors can significantly increase the effectiveness of online instruction. It can also add new dimensions to interactions among instructors and students. Such a tool should examine the

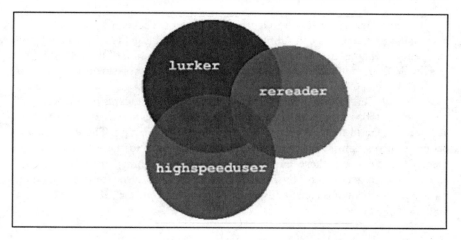

Figure 3. Information visualization of student logons.

patterns of interaction that facilitate productive online discussions and allow the architects of online environments to gauge each environment's effectiveness at facilitating enthusiastic exploration and cooperative discussion.

At present, there are numerous software tools that can aid in transcript analysis (Nudist, Atlasti, HyperRESEARCH, and other qualitative software tools), but none of them has an advanced visualization component, which dynamically mines transcripts and offers visualizations relevant to the educator. Although researchers have developed social visualization tools (Babble, The Loom Project, Netscan), none of these tools has been developed specifically for educational settings to reveal effective communication and collaboration patterns among students and instructors [15, 21, 22]. Also, none of these tools is adaptable to the specific context of the environment being assessed. The efforts behind VisOC's creation seek to address this need by employing theories of graphic design, Human Computer Interaction, and educational models in order to bring new perspective to the rich collection of intellectual exchanges that online transcripts provide. The development ground for VisOC was the Global Classroom Project, a series of online courses that exemplifies the changing face of educational environments.

A CASE STUDY:
THE GLOBAL CLASSROOM PROJECT

The Global Classroom Project (GCP) is a distance-learning environment that provides students from Russia and the United States a chance to engage in cross-cultural digital communication. The project's courses are co-taught by

Dr. TyAnna Herrington of the Georgia Institute of Technology and Dr. Yuri Tretyakov of the European University at St. Petersburg (see Herrington and Tretyakov's chapter in the next section for further discussion of the GCP).

The GCP provides an ideal development case for an assessment tool such as VisOC. It is a CMC-based classroom that can significantly benefit from an analysis tool. Textual conversations involve a number of students over a period of two years. A thorough record of individual student profiles serves as an interesting accompaniment to the vast archives of textual communication. These communication archives consist of transcripts that contain clues to the effectiveness of the GCP system, but these transcripts have not been mined for relevant data and are too large to mine by hand effectively. There is no efficient method by which to isolate the constraints in the collaboration of the GCP network and begin to adjust them.

Tool Built to Address Needs of Case

VisOC's visualizations provide an "at-a-glance" perspective, from which instructors can observe where tension points might be developing and then zoom in for details of conversations in order to better understand how learning is progressing. During the perception process, humans do not see individual, low-level elements but rather sense complete packages that "combine disparate sensory elements to form the high-order entities called 'objects' or 'groups'" [1, p. 102]. VisOC presents information as visualizations that allow users to easily discern patterns. These patterns may help users confirm knowledge or hypotheses by revealing trends, relationships, anomalies, and structure in the data.

In the GCP, student cognition is situated. Students apply knowledge to create group projects and grapple with communication issues while working together rather than simply reading about potential communication issues and commenting on them. VisOC, as a tool of analysis, is situated in the environment and can be integrated into the class format to allow ease of use for instructors. The tool not only visualizes interactions but assists in generating interactions by showing both instructor and students the social processes that are taking place.

The Design of the Tool

Because there are several types of qualitative research software available that help researchers code or markup data, VisOC explores how to represent coded data visually in a meaningful way, rather than focusing on the coding process.

VisOC looks at GCP postings for affective indications of "agreement" and "disagreement" because these tags can be used as indicators of tension points in the dialog, potentially revealing patterns that might allow researchers to more clearly understand how students reach consensus and overcome misunderstandings during the collaboration process in a CMC environment. The tool searches for patterns that might allow GCP instructors to better isolate the instructional methods that assist students in collaboration.

Transcripts were selected based on the structure of GCP classes. During the semester, students work in small mixed groups composed of Russian and American graduate and undergraduate students. Each group has their own set of conferences in which to discuss their projects.

The prototype for VisOC examines a single conversational thread titled "Proposal Discussion" that was present for all GCP groups because the thread begins with the same parallel instructions from Herrington and Tretyakov. The professors instructed students to choose a topic for analysis and then to begin creating a group proposal that would explain how the students planned to create a Web-based project that would explore their chosen topic appropriately. During the period the thread covered, students were likely to have many conflicts as they tried to argue the merits of their ideas for a group project and come to accord on a project that appealed to all members of the group.

The Process

VisOC uses a combination of an interactive browser-based visualization interface, server-side scripting, and a database in order to build graphics from text messages that contain the number of agreements that took place at specific time periods and compares them based on the characteristics of individual students. In addition to searching for explicit markup of agreement and disagreement which were inserted into messages in a form similar to html tags, scripts flag instances of words and language constructs that might point to additional instances of tension points such as occurrences of the words "but" or "of course." The scripts then compare data about individual messages with external data relating to student profiles. Through this process, text transcripts are rendered as visualizations. Visualizations are rendered using calculations created from the variables of tag prevalence and student profile statistics. Figure 4 illustrates VisOC's visualization process.

Functionality of the Prototype

VisOC allows researchers four views from which to make different types of comparisons and carry out assessment. These comparisons look at combinations of factors, ranging from instructor input to individual student backgrounds to chance interactions that may later be replicated to enhance the effectiveness of the online educational experience. Instructors may integrate their findings to improve the online course in future implementations, as well as use the information gathered to provide for real-time problem solving and assessment throughout the course of a class.

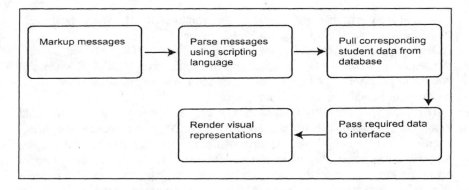

Figure 4. The data retrieval and visualization process.

Overall Class Structure

Full class overview allows instructors to see how the structure of the course has influenced the behavior of the entire class at different intervals of time. Instructors can also gauge external factors with this comparison. This mode was designed to facilitate "at-a-glance" analysis of complex information, where the user would pinpoint general areas of interest and then probe for more detailed information.

Figure 5 illustrates this view, which offers users a graph of the total daily sum of agreements and disagreements over the entire course timeframe. It uses an underlying grid to represent real classroom deadlines and other benchmarks that are contextual anchors in which to orient the visualization. Cones above the x-axis represent total daily agreements and cones below the x-axis represent total daily disagreements. Dots represent days, which are labeled with dates.

Comparison by Group

Comparison by group allows instructors to look for effective or ineffective group interactions among sets of collaborators by drawing attention to differences in tension points that indicate where particular sets of circumstances may discourage or disrupt a group from moving forward or encourage and strengthen the sharing of ideas.

The group factors relevant to the GCP that VisOC analyzes include in-class subgroup performance, country of residence, educational concentration or major, and education level. Comparison by subgroup is designed to indicate which research topics or combinations of students working together produce better results more smoothly and quickly than others. Comparison by country

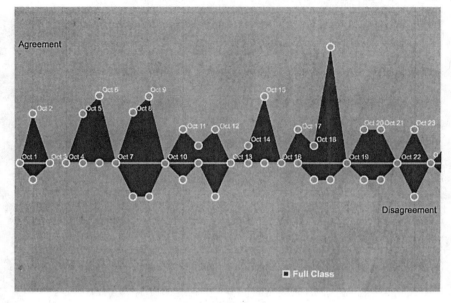

Figure 5. The overall class view.

reveals areas where cultural differences may affect the contributions of class members. Comparisons by major and education level allow educators to reveal how differing educational backgrounds and maturity levels may influence collaboration.

Figure 6 illustrates group comparison. When users choose to display agreements and disagreements by country they see two overlaid graphs, one representing all U.S. students and one representing all Russian students. These graphs can be pulled apart and moved to change the level of detail displayed over time. Users can quickly compare the graphs to answer specific questions about group interactions.

*Topic Threads and Media Exchange as
Communication Patterns*

The thread and media exchange view illustrates which students are agreeing and disagreeing with one another and gives a visualization of the flow of the conversation throughout the bulletin board. It is designed to reveal the communication patterns of individual students, as well as the social networks that are formed among students, and, furthermore, among groups.

This view provides visualizations of exchanges between individuals and groups along a selected thread of communication. In addition to being able to follow

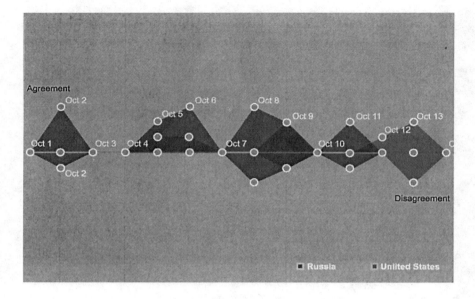

Figure 6. Group comparison view.

threads, VisOC considers that instructors may also want to trace media flow because, as Haythornthwaite explains, "The way in which resources flow in a learning network has an important impact on each individual's exposure into information, as well as their sense of belonging to a community" [4].

Exploring individual student communication patterns can allow for dynamic assessment of social interactions as they occur among individuals. By cross-referencing these with a database of student profiles, the opportunity exists to pinpoint individual students' effects on the system. Figure 7 shows how VisOC incorporates influences from social network analysis. Users access the screen in Figure 7 by toggling a button on any of the previous screens, retaining the already selected comparisons of group, country, educational level, or educational concentration. The darkest lines on this screen represent lines of communication initiation and response among individual students across a single communication thread. Dots represent individual messages that contain agreements or disagreements. Squares represent messages that do not specifically address comments contributed by other students. The thickness of an individual student line correlates to a student's total involvement in the particular thread being viewed. The thicker the student's line, the more central the role the student plays in a particular thread, while the thinner lines represent more peripheral contributors.

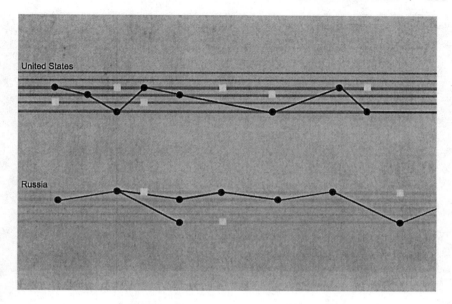

Figure 7. Thread view.

Individual Message Analysis

Users zoom into areas to funnel down to increasingly detailed views of individual messages (Figure 8). As Figure 8 shows, when users have dragged a comparison graph sufficiently downwards, they can see details of the messages written on a particular day. When a user rolls over a circle, it expands for easier readability. The circles represent individual messages and include the name of the author and the number of agreements or disagreements that took place that day. As users zoom in, they expose more information on a particular message and on the individual who posted the message. The finest level of granularity displays the marked-up text of a message with "agreement" and "disagreement" phrases and relevant keywords highlighted in different colors in the body of the message. Individual message analysis allows instructors to see what concepts were introduced by particular students and what words they used in the context of discussion initiation and response.

Implications of Implementing this Technology

At present, the prototype works with information from a course conference that is no longer active. Transcripts have been replicated to stabilize data and prevent coding from interfering with the proprietary bulletin board system that the GCP uses. However, VisOC would be most useful if it could be integrated

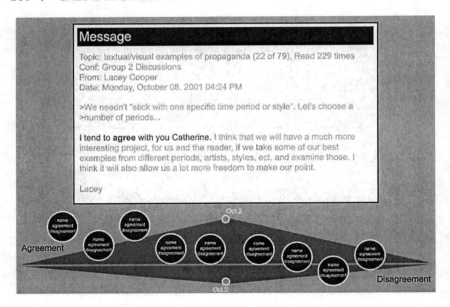

Figure 8. Individual message view.

into the daily activities of the online classroom, abstracting in real time the collaborative processes that students undertake and providing participants and instructors with sensory mappings that contextualize how groups are progressing in relation to course goals and in comparison to one another. In order to assimilate the system into the larger, day-to-day workings of courses, the boundaries of the project need to be expanded. To reduce the need for instructor involvement in coding transcripts and to make VisOC easier to integrate into real-time courses, VisOC may evolve toward two additional approaches to document markup. Both student characterizations of their own statements and intelligent algorithms to pinpoint methods of communications may help identify tension points in communication more effectively and easily [24, 26]. How these approaches might affect students' willingness to interact with the system and their understanding of the course requires further user testing, but the implementation of the tool will necessarily affect the online classroom environment.

Since the system mines online transcripts for instructor-defined keywords, this question naturally arises: Should students be informed of what these keywords are and be encouraged to use them? Making students aware of the specific words that the instructor and assessment tool are looking for and exactly what the working definitions of these words are in the particular context of the class would make it easier for VisOC to identify meaningful data.

There may be additional benefits to this approach. Giving students the keywords used by VisOC could improve the clarity and efficiency of online discussions. A common vocabulary eradicates ambiguity. If students know that the word "wonderful" is defined as "full agreement" by VisOC, regardless of whether they agree with the definition or not, then when a student uses "wonderful" in communication with other students, all students will clearly understand that the author of the message has no reservations about following through on a particular idea.

On the other hand, if there is no common vocabulary, then students' intention in using specific terminology becomes much more uncertain. However, common and sometimes highly valuable language patterns, such as positive-reinforcement and sarcasm for the sake of humor and tension release, are preserved. Furthermore, the spontaneity and freedom that are afforded by online discussions become stilted when students are confined to expressing themselves using a predetermined vocabulary. The mere suggestion that students use certain words or that they cultivate an awareness of how their language affects class patterns would drastically alter student behavior and limit their experimentation with language.

Problems also arise when one imagines using VisOC for purposes that were not originally intended. VisOC specifically addresses the assessment of an online classroom system in achieving preset educational goals and meeting the needs of students from divergent backgrounds. However, the data gathered and processed by this tool suggest uses beyond analysis of group interaction. For example, instructors might be tempted to use affective data to assess students' performance and to determine if their interaction has been beneficial to the course.

While participation is routinely considered a percentage of the grade in an onsite classroom setting, using overall impressions of participation that are collected and mediated by a machine is not as reliable as instructor impressions, nor can an application like VisOC completely account for quality or richness of thought. This weakness is further complicated by the abstracted nature of online communication, in which messages sent in the heat of discussion are archived for atemporal retrieval. When these documents are read later, it can be difficult to fully understand what factors may have influenced an author, such as supplementary in-person or email communication among students and with the instructor. These types of communication are not monitored by VisOC, but instructors can better understand and make speculations about them. To alleviate its weaknesses, a tool such as VisOC is most useful when combined with other emerging methods of assessment such as portfolio assessment, which requires students to display their learned and negotiated knowledge with projects that demonstrate what they have learned as a result of their collaboration.

In any educational setting, students know that they are expected to meet certain standards of performance and social behavior. VisOC makes some of these rules and their effects more explicit, but the online classroom is little different in this respect from the onsite classroom where the physical presence of the instructor also has an obvious effect in curbing student behavior. Social negotiation difficulties and potential over-reliance on the system are inherent in the medium and need to be understood and responded to by the instructor when developing and implementing assessment methods.

CONCLUSION

While online courses utilizing text-based information transmission have proven to be a successful means of fostering collaborative interactions that lead to higher-order thinking skills such as knowledge negotiation and construction, methods for organizing and understanding these exchanges are often time-consuming to conduct or have limited utility. Combining information visualization and situated perspectives on cognition to create tools for examining these interactions has the potential to allow instructors to better and more easily assess collaborative processes in a goal-driven, online environment.

VisOC is only the beginning. The next step is to develop standards for coordinating the design of assessment tools with the design of tools that support learning in specific classroom contexts so that the two types of tools work together in real time to analyze and visualize online communication, assess the effectiveness of the educational context in supporting communication, pinpoint where breakdowns in communication occur, and succinctly suggest to the instructor the best possible course of action to remedy these breakdowns. Integration of assessment tools in educational systems is the basis of designing flexible classroom environments where appropriate intervention can be carried out to instantaneously maximize the efficiency of communication and help the system to achieve its goals. Such environments are the future of modern classroom systems.

REFERENCES

1. G. Salvendy, *Handbook of Human Factors and Ergonomics* (2nd Edition), Wiley and Sons, New York, pp. 102, 1451-1468, 1514-1567, 1997.
2. J. G. Greeno, A. Collins, and L. B. Resnick, Cognition and Learning, *Handbook of Educational Psychology*, D. C. Berliner and R. C. Calfee (eds.), Macmillan, New York, Chapter 2, pp. 15-46, 1996.
3. K. Krejins and P. Kirschner, The Social Affordance of Computer-Supported Collaborative Learning Environments, *ASEE/IEEE Frontiers in Education Conference*, 2001.
4. C. Haythornthwaite, Building Social Networks Via Computer Networks: Creating and Sustaining Distributed Learning Communities, in *Building Virtual Communities: Learning and Change in Cyberspace,* A. Renninger and W. Shumar (eds.), Cambridge University Press, Cambridge, United Kingdom, 2002, http://alexia.lis.uiuc.edu/~haythorn/hay_bvc.html.
5. P. W. Airasian, Perspectives on Measurement Instruction, *Educational Measurement: Issues and Practice*, pp. 10, 13-19, 23, 1991.

6. L. Sproull and S. Kiesler, *Connections: New Ways of Working the Networked Organization*, MIT Press, Cambridge, Massachusetts, 1991.
7. Knowing What Students Know: The Science and Design of Educational Assessment, Committee on the Foundations of Assessment, *Board on Testing and Assessment*, J. W. Pellegrino, N. Chudowsky, and R. Glaser (eds.), Center for Education, National Research Council, NAP Press, Washington, D.C., 2001.
8. R. J. Stiggins, *Assessment Crisis: The Absence of Assessment FOR Learning*, Phi Delta Kappa. 2002, http://www.pdkintl.org/kappan/k0206sti.htm.
9. T. C. Reeves, Alternative Assessment Approaches for Online Learning Environments in Higher Education, *Journal of Educational Computing Research, 23*:1, pp. 101-111, 2000.
10. P. E. Parker, P. D. Fleming, S. Beyerlein, D. Apple, and K. Krumsieg, Differentiating Assessment from Evaluation as Continuous Improvement Tools, 31, *ASEE/IEEE FIE*.
11. L. Darling-Hammond and J. Snyder, Authentic Assessment of Teaching, Context, *Teacher and Teacher Education, 16*, pp. 523-545, 2000.
12. J. S. Brown, A. Collins, and P. Duguid, Situated Cognition and the Culture of Learning, *Educational Researcher, 18*, pp. 32-42, 1989.
13. L. Vygotsky, *Mind in Society: The Development of Higher Psychological Processes*, Harvard University Press, Cambridge, Massachusetts, 1978.
14. C. McLoughlin and J. Luca, Cognitive Engagement and Higher Order Thinking Through Computer Conferencing: We Know Why But Do We Know How? *Flexible Futures in Tertiary Teaching, Proceedings of the 9th Annual Teaching Learning Forum*, A. Herrmann and M. M. Kulski (eds.), Curtin University of Technology, Perth, pp. 2-4, February 2000, http://cea.curtin.edu.au/tlf/tlf2000/mcloughlin.html.
15. M. Smith, Tools for Navigating Large Social Cyberspaces, *Communications of the ACM*, ACM Press, New York, 2002.
16. M. Chi, Quantifying Qualitative Analysis of Verbal Data: A Practical Guide, *The Journal of the Learning Sciences, 6*:3, pp. 27-315, 1997.
17. M. Bakardjieva, Collaborative Meaning-Making in Computer Conferences: A Sociocultural Perspective, *Proceedings of EdMedia'98*, T. Ottmann and I. Tomek (eds.), AACE, Charlottesville, Virginia, pp. 93-98, 1998.
18. J. Pena-Shaff, W. Martin, and G. Gay, An Epistemological Framework for Analyzing Student Interactions in Computer-Mediated Communication Environments, *Journal of Interactive Learning Research, 12*, pp. 41-68, 2001.
19. G. Newman, C. Johnson, and C. Cochrane, A Content Analysis Method to Measure Critical Thinking in Face-to-Face and Computer Supported Group Learning, *Interpersonal Computing and Technology, 3*:2, pp. 56-77, http://www.helsinki.fi/scienc/optek/1995/newman.txt.
20. L. Rourke., T. Anderson, and W. Archer, Methodical Issues in the Content Analysis of Computer Conference Transcripts, *International Journal of Artificial Intelligence in Education, 12*, pp. 8-22, 2001, http://cbl.leeds.ac.uk/ijaied/abstracts/Vol_12/rourke.html.
21. T. Erickson, D. N. Smith, W. A. Kellogg, M. Laff, J. T. Richards, and E. Bradner, Socially Translucent Systems: Social Proxies, Persistent Conversation, and the Design of "Babble," in *Human Factors in Computing Systems: The Proceedings of CHI '99*, ACM Press, New York, 1999.

22. J. Donath, *A Semantic Approach to Visualizing Online Conversations, Communications of the ACM,* ACM Press, New York, 2002.
23. S. Havre, B. Hetzler, and L. Nowell, ThemeRiver: Visualizing Theme Changes Over Time, *Proceedings of IEEE Symposium on Information Visualization, InfoVis 2000,* pp. 115-123, 2000.
24. K. Kreijins, P. Kirschner, and W. Jochems, The Sociability of Computer-Supported Learning Environments, *Educational Technology and Society, 5*:1. 2002.
25. T. Duffy, B. Dueber, and C. Hawley, Critical Thinking in a Distributed Environment: A Pedagogical Base for the Design of Conferencing Systems, *Electronic Collaborators: Learner-Centered Technologies for Literacy, Apprenticeship, and Discourse,* C. Bonk and K. King (eds.), Lawrence Erlbaum Associates, Inc., Mahwah, New Jersey, pp. 51-78, 1998.
26. B. Krulwich and C. Burkey, The InfoFinder Agent: Learning User Interests Through Heuristic Phrase Extraction, *IEEE Intelligent Systems Journal (Expert), 12*:5, pp. 22-27, 1997.

SECTION 4

How is Online Education Challenging Our Assumptions?

CHAPTER 16

The Global Classroom Project: Troublemaking and Troubleshooting

TyAnna Herrington and Yuri Tretyakov

As an associate professor at the Georgia Institute of Technology in Atlanta, Georgia, and a director of the language departments at the Russian Academy of Sciences and the European University at St. Petersburg, we have been collaboratively teaching a distance learning course since Spring 2000. At this writing, we are in our seventh successful semester of the course, taught on both graduate and undergraduate levels to students at the Georgia Institute of Technology (Georgia Tech) and the European University at St. Petersburg. To our knowledge, our project, The Global Classroom Project (GCP), is the only distance learning course that has been jointly developed from its inception and truly reflects the academic and cultural interests of the United States and Russia. It is completely interactive in nature and is not dependent on canned "course in a box" materials such as CD-ROMs or video lectures. Project partners are equal in their access to information and their right to express and criticize ideas, which excludes the element of one-sided "missionary" instruction typical of many global distance-learning courses. The project provides experiential learning environments in which students in Russia and the United States truly collaborate in class discussion and analysis of issues in cross-cultural and digital communication and produce creative digital artifacts that reflect synthetic knowledge acquired in their analyses. Our work with the GCP at times seems to create more questions about cross-cultural, digital communication than it answers, but we have found that the unanswered questions continue to drive us and our students and challenge us to persevere. We provide this chapter as a way to share what we have learned from our experiences, to put forth a series of unanswered questions to which others may respond, and to encourage others to participate in similar projects whether those projects reach across the globe, nations, cities, or even individual campuses.

We include two distinct sections within this chapter. The first is a description of the project, its inception, its development, and each of the broad elements that it encompasses. These fall under the general heading "Global Classroom Project Description." In the second section, "Chaos, Contextual Functionality, Technical Communication, and the Global Classroom Project," we explore the revelations that working with the project provided for our own understanding of elements of technical communication as a field and suggest an approach both to teaching and researching technical communication that includes the chaotic realm of "contextual functionality."

PART 1: GLOBAL CLASSROOM PROJECT DESCRIPTION

Grassroots Development and Support

The contact between the School of Literature, Communication, and Culture at Georgia Tech and the St. Petersburg Department of Foreign Languages, Russian Academy of Sciences, was first established shortly before 1990, when Kenneth Knoespel and Yuri Tretyakov, chairs of their respective departments, began an exchange program between the two institutions. At the same time at Texas Tech, after participating in Fred Kemp's Interclass, the first online project to link graduate students to share class discussion across national boundaries, TyAnna Herrington began testing computer-based pedagogy, theory, and online technology in technical communication and composition courses to pursue a working framework of what was then only an idea for the GCP. Simultaneously, the European University, a new private graduate university, was developing in St. Petersburg. Knoespel and Tretyakov's association during its development helped to lead to the European University's optimal choice for Global Classroom collaboration.

Recognizing that the budding project began at a grassroots level is essential to understanding its nature and its development. Many international or inter-institutional projects begin with a cooperation agreement signed by heads of two institutions and then slowly wither for lack of enthusiasts willing to work along lines directed by others; cooperation between Georgia Tech and the Russian Academy of Sciences, however, depended from day one primarily on the enthusiasm and goodwill of a growing number of people who became involved in it. This ensured a broad "popular" foundation for the ongoing work and eventually made the project credible enough to qualify for institutional support.

In 1997, Herrington started employment at Georgia Tech and began working closely with Knoespel, by that time dean of the college, to find ways to expand the exchange program that he and Tretyakov had developed. By 1999, the European University's Rector (President) Firsov supported Herrington's Fulbright grant to teach a full-fledged course in technical communication for Russian students and faculty at the European University and allowed Herrington and Tretyakov to begin planning the GCP and testing the European University's technology.

Soon thereafter Tretyakov worked with Herrington to pilot the first class in Spring 2000, and they have continued to teach the course every semester since. In Fall 2003, they were joined in collaboration by the Blekinge Institute of Technology's Swedish students, who were guided by their instructors in Sweden, Jane Mattison, Gösta Viberg, and Sheila Feld-Manis. (Although the addition of the Swedish students has been a huge benefit to the GCP and expands the interesting issues of our project analysis, this article focuses on the collaboration between Russians and Americans because this relationship motivated the project inception.)

The GCP and Cross-Cultural Technical Communication

The overall intent of the GCP is to study technical communication in practical application, and specifically, to develop effective cross-cultural, digital communication in subject-specific areas such as history, sociology, and political science. The assignments are centered on student collaboration. Students jointly develop print and digital products based on analyses of a content-specific topic.

The quality of the students' work depends on their ability to determine the most effective means to communicate accurately, clearly, and effectively in the form of resumes, proposals, analytical reports, and creative digital projects. The GCP is supported by World Wide Web (Web) conferencing software to enable what would be impossible without it; as such, digital communication is used to focus on class goals rather than the technology itself. The Russian and American students meet face to face in their home country locales but also meet in integrated classes online to read common materials, discuss the issues in them, and collaborate on their analytical projects.

The student makeup of the course continues to be an interesting mixture, though it changes from course to course. Georgia Tech graduate and undergraduate students come from across a broad range of majors in mostly technical fields; most of them take the course to fulfill a requirement in technical communication. The graduate students are typically enrolled in the Information Design and Technology and Human Computer Interface programs. The European University graduate students take the course to develop their English language and other communication abilities; their subject area interests are in humanities fields, including political science, sociology, ethnology, economics, art, and history.

The disparate mixture of student characteristics goes far beyond their choice of majors. The cultural differences in the Russian and American students' background knowledges are very significant. In comparison to the American students' limited understanding of Russian culture and education, Russian students appear to be better informed about American culture in general and the educational/research system in particular. But since the language of communication is English, they find themselves at a disadvantage—not so much with respect to the general ability to express themselves but with the ability to express themselves in a way that would be regarded as "correct" by their American counterparts. Thus, the Russian students require specific instruction concerning the modality of their messages, ways of making suggestions, expressing agreement/disagreement, satisfaction/dissatisfaction, and other affective signals, while the Americans need to be made aware of cultural differences as expressed in speech. For example, American students would need to understand that cultural patterns in Russia support straightforward comment and criticism of shared work so that they would not be offended by straightforward replies to their discussion contributions.

Yet another aspect of cultural diversity is that students from each nationality, the Americans especially, are multicultural in themselves, which effectively turns the problem of communication between two cultures into the problem of interaction among multiple cultures. This mixture provides the students with a clear notion of cultural awareness and becomes an extremely important part of instruction. We supplement instruction with research in a case study methodology and ask students to analyze cases on intercultural communication failures described in technical communication literature (see [1]). We encourage students to study cases to help prepare them to be aware of and to resolve problems arising in their own communication practices. In this way, we are able to combine two bases of pedagogical effort in case study: to interject theory and praxis [2] and to ask students to work through and apply theory within their interactive class experiences.

The odd mixture of students has actually led us to find further benefits of the project. In addition to our intended creation of a multicultural mix, the fortuitous combination of students from disparate majors has led us to concentrate on methods for supporting a multidisciplinary student community as well as an international community. In the case of our current class, for example, the students studying subject-area topics in humanities provide their expertise on content-area material and research methods while students working with multimedia issues or computing concentrate most of their efforts on digital product development that reflects research findings. Students work jointly on each aspect of their projects, but those with greater skill or knowledge in one area over the other take leadership roles in dealing with that material. In the following sections, we delineate some of the more pragmatic aspects of the course, focusing on pedagogical issues and online learning issues, especially those connected to technological constraints and opportunities.

Pedagogical Issues and the GCP

Egalitarianism and Mutual Instruction

When we started developing the GCP, our purposes were driven by our academic experiences in linguistics, technical communication, rhetorical theory, and pedagogy. Early on, the project goals were based on the needs of our two universities, educational structures, and courses—one in English language education and communication, the other in technical communication. The project was intended as an experiment in cross-cultural, digital communication to provide a forum for experiential learning and a basis for communication research and analysis. Central to the themes of early pedagogy were the ideas that eliminating instructor control over a class would allow students to take responsibility for their work, to make writing and content choices of their own, and to allow for a more egalitarian setting, giving students the room to convey and support their own ideas, safe from epistemological or political agendas of their instructors. This concept was particularly appealing to us as this project brings together not only students from different political and epistemological backgrounds but also professors with historically different academic and pedagogical experiences. Employing a pedagogy based in egalitarianism allows us to mesh our theoretical backgrounds which, although both in communication-based areas, are different to a considerable degree, as are our native languages.

To ensure that course development and progress reflect the needs of everyone involved and to teach a truly shared class environment, we follow a plan that we call "mutual instruction." We try to reflect the joint nature of instruction in every aspect of the course. We provide one set of class assignments for all students regardless of country affiliation, and the assignments are attributed to both instructors by including both our names. We date the material following both the Russian pattern of day, month, and year and the American of month, day, and year. Ideally the course would be conducted both in English and Russian to further a pedagogy supporting truly balanced collaboration, but at present we use English. There are several reasons for this decision: the Russian students participating in the project are taking the course in part to pursue their requirement in English language study; American students rarely have even a beginning facility with Russian, which holds true with our students; and Cyrillic encoding is not yet sophisticated enough to allow consistent and accurate transmission of Cyrillic characters.

When teaching the course, we discuss each step we take in grading students, assigning work, encouraging them, or chiding them before taking action so that we ensure that all the various needs noted above are met. Also, because the course is a form of "mutual instruction," students pursue their own learning that goes beyond what we could provide in a static course of rote teaching, so in this way, they are also mutual participants in class instruction. This process is often difficult and always time-consuming, but we feel that it provides an important basis for class interaction.

Course Activities and Collaboration

Within this egalitarian pedagogical environment, students pursue a different topic area based in communication study each semester. The pilot course allowed students to read common articles and discuss them, but they engaged in their separate analyses of communication issues. Since the pilot course, students have been preparing joint analytical work for all project undertakings ranging from the second semester's comparison of visual and verbal rhetorical representations in Russian and American postcard sites on the Web to the Fall 2002 semester's examination of different media and their effects on our culturally based perceptions of acts of terrorism. Georgia Tech graduate students in Human Computer Interface and Information Design Technology also participate in "Project Studio" work in which they focus both collaborative and independent energy on special research projects that further support the Global Classroom Project. In addition, two graduate students have written graduate theses based directly on the Global Classroom Project. Working within and through these projects, students develop expertise in cross-cultural communication and collaboration. In fact, for many first-year European University graduate students, the projects provide their first experiences in online learning and collaboration. Central to its success, it is collaboration in its many forms—among faculty members, among faculty members and students, and among students themselves—that allows the Global Classroom Project to operate.

Experiential Learning

Another essential pedagogical decision behind the GCP is our use of experiential learning in all courses. The nature of intercultural and digital interaction is complex and affected by differing contexts from semester to semester, often week to week, and sometimes even day to day. For this reason, we decided that the best way to start the course would be to plunge the students into an environment where they would be naturally motivated to communicate with one another. Communication in the GCP arises from this need. If students communicate with each other at all, they do so by overcoming difficulties in cross-cultural, digital communication. They may be driven by the need to complete assignments, but the actual communication that allows them to complete the assignments themselves, by necessity, is real. All students use a common language that is more difficult for Russian students who are learning English as their second language, and, by necessity, they negotiate the more difficult tasks of moderating tone, colloquial expressions, and writing styles, both to communicate with each other and to complete differing types of assignments for class. The result is that language study at times becomes a central focus for both Russian and American students, just as communication as a content focus is always a central aspect of study for all students.

Online Learning and Technology Choices

Although online learning and technology are central to the GCP and the project would not exist without them, the online component of the course falls to the background of our thinking and seems to be less important than the interaction itself. Certainly, issues of online teaching directly affect the GCP in a number of specific ways: American students have greater access to technology and are more proficient with its use than are the Russian students, giving the Americans greater power in class. We spend more time working with technological problems both in and out of the classroom setting than we would if our course were on land instead of in cyberspace. We adjust assignment depth to accommodate potential problems with technology, time, language, and cultural differences. Most important of all, of course, is that the online component makes the course possible. The expense of travel and face-to-face interaction among Russian and American students is extreme, and sharing class space with whole groups of students from one culture or another is near impossible.

But, as we also noted previously, the online component of the project not only makes possible what would not be possible without it, but it also provides additional benefits that make the time and expense worth it. The online component creates a more egalitarian setting for cross-cultural interaction, which is particularly important for us since our pedagogical, theoretical, and political backgrounds are so different. The online component provides a means for students to experience collaborative interaction both through digital media and across temporal incompatibilities. We expect that this experience will be invaluable to students who will be a part of a world in which much of the global interaction in business, politics, government, and education will follow this pattern. At a time when global interaction is more important than ever, students' opportunity to experience online interaction may be more valuable than ever.

Nevertheless, an undertaking like the GCP that spans landmass, language, technological access, and national and institutional cultures requires creative planning and creates special challenges in each of these areas, challenges which are created and sometimes resolved through technological choices.

Temporal Challenges

One of the first challenges we faced was to arrange the course to accommodate the different semester schedules at the European University and Georgia Tech. Georgia Tech classes begin and end two weeks earlier than those at the European University. This difference in semester schedule has given us time to concentrate on individual course goals during the time the students are not able to join together but has required clear planning to ensure that the two groups of students mesh into one class as soon as and for as long as possible. An additional difficulty is that the classes are not only scheduled on different days of the week, but also the eight-hour time difference between the Russian and American locations makes it important to develop strategies to ensure that classes are actually "attended" by all the students with regularity. This means that we have had to plan class assignments sometimes four days ahead of our institution's scheduled class times to provide assignments for all students at the same time. It also means that students must develop habits of logging into class on a very regular basis and must keep up with what may seem like a difficult thinking pattern at first, to make the course flow. For example, the American students must log in and post materials to class by Mondays and Fridays in order to participate in discussions with the Russian students who meet class (when they have access to computers) on Tuesdays and Saturdays. The American students would ordinarily meet classes on Mondays and Wednesdays instead.

Access, Maintenance, and Bandwidth Challenges

Our choice of technology had to be well considered to optimize our ability to create one online class from two separate groups of students and to ensure that the technology would function well for both groups of students, would be possible on a very limited budget, and would allow us the option of building the course into the future. In addition, all this had to be accomplished with technology that would also support our ideological and pedagogical goals. To accomplish these goals, we employ WebBoard, a Web-based communication software that allows graphic as well as textual interchange over distance. To date, we have found that WebBoard allows the most accessible and efficient connection. It can be accessed from anywhere in the world by anyone with a Web-based connection to the Internet. There are no licensing fees in addition to the price of the software, so it remains usable by any number of participants who wish to access it. It can be maintained simply at one location, avoiding the problems inherent in using multiple software programs located on many servers and on multiple hardware platforms and operating systems. In addition, WebBoard allows multiple asynchronous and synchronous discussions to occur simultaneously. Within these discussions, any materials that can be loaded to the Web can also be loaded into discussion postings. Students sometimes add links to websites they find helpful, to graphic images, and to sound or video files. An image or sound may also be imbedded within a post itself to help facilitate discussion of its characteristics or significance. Furthermore, since bandwidth can sometimes be a consideration, we also chose WebBoard because it does not require a high bandwidth connection. We have found that when we limit our posts to no more than three long paragraphs and make sure that we create new conferences for every discussion, students on both sides of the world are able to access their assignments and discussion materials with efficiency. In addition to WebBoard, both students and instructors use email for one-to-one and small group discussions for collaborative project development. WebBoard is a public forum, just like a classroom, and is not always optimal for working out details for student group project development or instructors' discussions on lesson plans and students' work evaluations. For these reasons, email is a good supplement to what is already provided in online class space.

Given the various project activities, collaborative development, maintenance, and troubleshooting that result from the pedagogical and technological choices we have made in the GCP, there are frequently so many differing aspects of the project to maintain and troubleshoot at any given time that we often feel that we are dog paddling in a deep pool of chaos, confusion, and disarray. But we have learned over the semesters that we have been teaching the project that the chaos we experience reflects communication issues that embody the important social aspects of technical communication as a practice as well as a field of study. Part 2 of this chapter is our attempt to understand and explain why "chaos" cannot be excised from experiential teaching, to argue that the chaotic aspects of communication are central to a "definition" of the field of technical communication, and to ask that researchers continue attempts to study communication within its own framework of chaos.

PART 2: CHAOS, CONTEXTUAL FUNCTIONALITY, TECHNICAL COMMUNICATION, AND THE GLOBAL CLASSROOM PROJECT

Confusion, Chaos, and Disarray

This section situates the GCP in the study of technical communication. As a result, it explores the nature of technical communication as an entity of its own. Rather than attempting to create a new theory of technical communication or to claim a theory as its foundation, we are exploring, through our own experiment with the GCP, a way to understand technical communication processes and our own version of online technical communication pedagogy in action. Specifically, this section describes and explains the confusion, chaos, and disarray in what technical communication, as an entity, is. It also examines how the GCP reflects and embodies these aspects of technical communication. Because the words "confusion," "chaos," and "disarray" have negative connotations, we certainly do not declare these as project goals, but they are natural states accompanying any kind of communication that involves diverse groups of participants whose contributions are valued, such as those in cross-cultural, digital communication. Our project goal, therefore, is to understand the sources of and potential solutions to the chaos that occurs in communication in order to lessen it.

While it may not be completely impossible to eliminate chaos and confusion in teaching and in transmitting information from one culture to another, methods that impose order to eliminate chaos and transfer information in a way that privileges order over student participation imply a dictatorial imposition of ideas and thinking processes. Participants who are required to implement an instructor's agenda would produce mimicry and rote repetition of authoritarian concepts rather than their own projects shaped by actual communication and collaborative negotiation of ideas. As instructors, we motivate members of collaborative teams to communicate with each other, to share responsibility and control over communication content and processes, rather than mimic processes or create products we have outlined for them. Collaboration that encompasses ideas from opposing viewpoints may not be efficient, but it can lead to a richer, deeper, more fully developed product [3]. Because efficient collaboration is difficult to develop when crossing cultural, technological, temporal, and linguistic boundaries, confusion and chaos are natural results. The chaos may be uncomfortable, but it is real and it is necessary (in the sense of both "unavoidable" and "beneficial") when struggling to reach cooperative goals.

The same kind of complexity embodied in our collaborative microcosm in the GCP exists in technical communication as a field of practice and body of scholarly work. Technical communication study constitutes work across a vast range of philosophical foci—research methods, participant-subjects, and communication forums, including both the workplace and classroom. Both the complexity and richness of ideas, methods, and experience make technical communication study difficult to categorize and understand. At the CPTSC Plenary Session in October 2002, questions arose regarding whether technical communication is a field, a discipline, or some other entity. In addition to our reluctant support of the chaos that embodies cross-cultural, digital communication, we also argue that the complexity of technical communication that makes it difficult to categorize is necessary both for technical communication and for teaching a course like the GCP.

Theory in Practice

In the first stages of the course, we made decisions about project goals, organization, technology, and pedagogy based on separate knowledge bases developed from experiences in our different and distinct fields of research and our differing pedagogical and institutional experiences in the Russian and U.S. systems. The overwhelming amount of time and effort it took to initiate the project was enough to keep us from working together to hammer out a negotiated basis of strictly scholarly research from which to build applied theory to practice. In afterthought, we believe that it might, in fact, have been counterproductive to develop a narrowly categorized theoretical basis because the time consumption and difficulty in finding the negotiated space between our two systems, backgrounds, and educational structures might have kept us from beginning the project at all. We had to jump in, unafraid to encounter problems that could result from meshing our different administrative structures, content

backgrounds, educational systems, language bases, and technological and pedagogical backgrounds. In a sense, we had to embrace the impending chaos that
would inevitably come from mixing two cultures and use the luxury we enjoy in
academic work to further our knowledge by learning from mistakes.

The GCP itself has been a catalyst to teach us a means to examine communication in practice, technically and otherwise. The very nature of the course is
theory in practice, so we continue to examine theory in multiple iterations as we
try to adjust and improve the project's functionality. The result has been to
realize the value of lore [4, pp. 21-30], the practical, experiential knowledge
that can only be developed by participating in actions and activities that cannot
be approximated through other forms of research. We do not mean to imply that
empirical research should be replaced by lore. In fact, we find the knowledge
produced from empirical research helpful as a basis to critically examine communication from theoretical viewpoints and to provide a foundation for student
communication practice within the classroom forum. However, the goal of the
GCP has not been to study research in the field or to be a practical application
of this research. Rather, its goal has been to provide new experiences of the
intricacies of joining cultures in online, cross-cultural collaboration.

We have found that providing an experiential setting where both our students
and we can practice our respective pedagogies has led to a form of internal
understanding of what is involved in this realm of communication, despite the
accompanying and necessary chaos. We cannot know what each new semester
may bring in the way of student makeup, interests, or world political, economic,
and cultural problems; nor can we apply research done, necessarily, in static
realms of study to develop methods for online, cross-cultural communication.

We have begun to learn from the GCP that the choices we made in creating it
and now evaluating it both come from and lead us back to the question, "What is
technical communication?" The GCP both illustrates and reflects concerns in
technical communication that could be addressed from programmatic, academic
theoretical, pedagogical, and pragmatic industry perspectives. The best and worst
thing about the GCP is that it has forced us to incorporate all the seeming binary
oppositions in the technical communication field: teaching/research, academy/
industry, practice/theory. The very nature of the project brings all these things
together, making it difficult to manage, understand, evaluate, and assess. So to
assess the GCP, we must first begin with a critical assessment of technical
communication, then attempt to understand the project in its relation to technical
communication.

The Interdisciplinarity of Technical Communication

Technical communication is soundly interdisciplinary and, in fact, it might be
said that technical communication is not a discipline in itself because it encompasses the issues addressed in other disciplines as well as being encompassed by

them. Researchers in technical communication study issues based in sociology, technology study, linguistics, psychology, philosophy, ethics, law, digital media, rhetoric, communication technology, graphics, and visual rhetoric, among many others. Researchers base their research and instructors base their teaching in cognitive study, social constructionism, and ideological constructivism, among other ideologies and research approaches. Studies in technical communication are empirical (quantitative and qualitative), textual, and ethnographic. Each researcher's approach to technical communication study is centered in a theoretical basis, sometimes like those of others in technical communication, but more often than not, in that which is independent. We study policy and politics, economics, ethics, power, access, law, multiculturalism, internationalism, and feminist and other theories. We also study multiple forms of communication, document and activity-based, such as computer-mediated communication, collaboration, and oral presentation, and genre categories including technical reports, memos, email, and letters. Therefore, it is very difficult to find a unifying theory of technical communication, which is necessary for its classification as a discipline, in the mix of the various perspectives and approaches. We cover the map both in subject matter and theory.

In an even broader sense, across the study of technical communication itself, our field's relatively newly appointed administrators have developed differing technical communication programs, accompanied by varying designs, that reflect differences in definitions of technical communication as well as the influences of widely varying source departments from which administrator's technical communication programs have grown. Our informal and brief survey of technical communication shows that it is taught in departments across a broad spectrum, including Engineering, Medicine, Communication, English, Mass Communication, Language, Literature and Culture, Communication Planning and Information Design, Multimedia, Texts and Technology, Computing, and Human Computer Interface, among others. Not only does the influence of the fields in these varying departments affect instructors' choice of research and pedagogy, but the administrative support for course content, technology access, space provision, and tenure processes mediates the kind of research and teaching that is done under the umbrella of "technical communication."

Contextual Functionality

Given this interdisciplinarity, it is no wonder that questions still arise: Is technical communication a discipline? What makes it a field? Is there a basis to unify it? It could be said that technical communication is unified in its focus on communication in specific contexts, but this is also the case for areas of study such as linguistics, journalistic media study, and literature, for example. To distinguish technical communication as a specific field within the general area of communication, it may be productive to turn to the functional-stylistic approach

[5], based on consideration of the interplay of function and form in the process of communication. From this vantage point, technical communication may be viewed as a type of communication aimed at efficient and effective exchange of information in professional areas (unlike, for example, fictional communication, whose purpose is often reduced to entertainment). To accomplish a functional goal, technical communication employs specific forms, or genres, from memos to resumes to multimedia presentations to articles to constitutions, each possessing specific structural, logical, and linguistic characteristics [6].

What sets technical communication study apart from other kinds of communication study begins with its additional focus on functional communication. The combination of context and function creates a specific view—contextual functionality. Because technical communication embraces a wide variety of contextual areas in a variety of functional genres, communicators' goals, also an aspect of function, can differ from context to context. Potentially almost any number of generic and situational permutations can exist, changed by only one factor within the blend of contextual elements. For example, even though both student and workplace communicators write memos, their functional goals are different: students write to achieve a grade and workplace communicators write to meet workplace goals and receive a paycheck. In this case, the genre is the same and the context elements that drive the writing may even be the same, but the functional goals are different, affecting writer motivations and any number of other factors. In each scenario, technical communication requires an awareness of contextual functionality. There is little surprise that when the two elements, context and function, come together in particular communication scenarios, they create a mass of complexity unprecedented in other areas of academic study. In fact, it may be this very mixture of elements that makes technical communication a significant and unique discipline. Technical communication is predominately practical, thus it is, of necessity, an applied discipline. But academics in the field also attempt to understand it on theoretical levels. "The theory/practice binary is . . . the defining act of technical communication" [7, p. 414]. Technical communication actually envelops practical aspects of communicative interaction, which are studied in well-developed fields such as psychology, linguistics, ethics, technology, and other fields of influence that we have embraced in our own technical communication study. Thus, research in technical communication expresses itself as interdisciplinary and therefore cannot, at least in its present state, be founded on a single, however broad, fundamental theory.

We find that teaching within the experiential setting of the GCP provides a marriage of theory and practice and has led us to surmise that experiential learning may be the only way to address all of the elements noted above in context. In this learning forum, students can understand function in context and begin to understand the complexity of online communication across cultural boundaries. The experiential learning setting allows the complex mix of elements in the technical communication field to be reflected in content and process within intercultural, digital communication. We create the context each semester: students must develop new collaborative assignments with international partners who have different cultural and educational backgrounds, different scholarly goals, and different levels of technological experience. They must communicate only by way of technology at their disposal, through email and WebBoard conferencing software. They know each other only through photographs and their shared correspondence. Each semester, teaching circumstances change: we have a different set of students; they confront new problems and find new ways of solving them; we face new teaching questions and look for new answers to them. Applied technical communication, by its nature, must be adaptive to operate effectively. We believe that the nature of changing contexts within the GCP helps to make our students aware of the complexity of the processes of communication and teaches them how to deal with at least some of its elements in action. In our attempt to provide students with a unique experience in international, digital collaboration, the project has in turn provided us with a microcosmic view of communication processes that reflects the contextually functional nature of technical communication while it also embodies contextual functionality that is the basis of its existence. In this way, the development of the GCP reflects the development of technical communication in general.

We have found technical communication alive in the interstices of context and function, the contextual functionality that calls for multiple areas of research, teaching, program development, and various assessment projects that come together to reify technical communication as an entity. All of this complexity creates a seeming confusion that may actually be an indicator for success in accurately reflecting the core content of the field. As Zachry has noted in his discussion of paralogy, real-life communication is messy and is not containable. Snowflake-like, it cannot be characterized in the same way more than once, and thus it cannot be controlled from communication instance to communication instance. We can control context to the extent that, as researchers, we can describe and characterize it and, as instructors, we can create and control its parameters. But technical communication is also functional. To some extent, we can control the function of communication by defining its goals. But when context and function combine, all the elements that technical communication addresses come into play at once. Technical communication—communication in general—is affected by and affects multiple layers of life.

In the GCP, these multiple layers cannot be isolated for more effective, linearly examined teaching and study; they must be experienced as they occur, in the messy mix of multiple elements that change from instant to instant, that differ based on the mix of one set of personalities and another, and that are affected by external factors that could never be predicted, accounted for, and treated in a pristine course plan. This fusion of theory, practice, and human interaction is what experiential learning entails. Our own experiences have helped us begin to see the complexity that embraces and defines the technical communication field itself. An awareness that contextual functionality is at the base of technical communication also helps us to explain what may feel like confusion, chaos, and disarray in the GCP, and what seems similar in technical communication studies when we try to categorize our research or when we teach many of our technical communication classes.

In some cases, scholars in our field have declared failure or engaged in harsh self-criticism when trying to create real-life learning forums for our students [8, 9]. But understanding that chaos and disarray are elements of real communication that lead students to authentic learning can help ease the burden of teaching without total control of the classroom setting. Computer-based teaching has always called for instructors to give up authoritarian control of the classroom and embrace the chaos that often comes with online teaching. Our GCP experience has taught us that this ability to adjust to chaos becomes even more necessary when teaching experiential courses across cultural and temporal boundaries. And we believe that providing a forum in which students can also learn to adjust to the chaos of cross-cultural, digital communication well help them better handle difficult communication situations in the future. The students' experience with complex layers of context and function mirrors the complexity of theoretical inquiry in the field that leads us to examine issues in multiple content areas.

As professors operating within the GCP, we are beginning to understand and embrace the premise that communication elements studied outside their context and function cannot be studied accurately because accuracy demands that communication occur in context. The nature of the communication changes if it exists outside its original synthetic context and functions in ways other than intended within the specific context from which it arises. Similarly, the study of technical communication is a conglomeration of all aspects of contextual functionality and needs a unification of all the elements of contextual functionality to make it distinct from other fields. It is not possible to examine communication cleanly and still maintain accuracy, and it is not possible to isolate it in writing or in formulas. Technical communication only lives within a functional framework, so it can only be studied as a live practicing animal and it can only be learned if a student participates within it as a piece of that live, practicing, functional animal. This is why technical communication cannot be taught by rote, cannot be taught as a system, and cannot be taught as a cleanly packaged structure. The context of technical communication changes instance by instance, and that affects its function, so students can only learn how to adapt to it. The only way to learn to adapt to it is by experiencing it.

The GCP has been our own experiential learning forum. It has taught us that both technical communication research and teaching require a mixture of all communication elements that imply chaos, confusion, and disarray and that we have to readjust our thinking to determine what is failure and what is not as well as what is good research and what is not. The need to leave room for chaos and unanswered questions is inherent in technical communication teaching and research because it is in this space that new discoveries can be made and that individuals can experiment with communication styles that work for them and make them their own. In addition, each context of writing/teaching/researching requires a different set of elements that butt against each other in different ways every time; thus, researchers must examine and re-examine them and students must experience and re-experience them in their various mixtures.

Researching technical communication and participating in an experiential technical communication class can be like shaking a kaleidoscope: the elements are the same but, when shaken, they interact in different ways, creating a new picture. The field as a whole is embracing multiplicity in technical communication study, and teaching is beginning to do the same. This may be an indication that the field of technical communication is "growing up" and really is becoming a discipline with a unique set of characteristics. This set of characteristics reflects the multiplicity that is embraced in all its aspects, which are acquired from but also required of contextual functionality. Our goal has been to accept the challenge of teaching function in context by providing means for students to experience ways to produce functional communication in context.

Effective functional technical communication is not located in one place, genre, class, or program. It is dispersed. It gains its power as a field not in theoretical isolation (which is why you cannot pinpoint an answer to the question, What is the theory of technical communication?). Rather, it comprises multiple kinds of thinking brought together by the common thread of functionality. It is possible to define and/or describe the context of a class, workplace setting, or other communication setting, and it is possible to isolate functional goals. But to research and test the actual communication that occurs and to teach students authentic communication practices of applied experience, both context and functionality are required. This is why technical communication research and teaching cannot focus on one area of literature or one example of discipline. Although embracing this kind of complexity is difficult, it allows freedom to develop a project like the GCP anywhere, under any technical communication or other program focus. We continue to try to meet that goal as long as we feel that both our students and we are continuing to learn through the process of the challenge. The process, by its nature, can be chaotic and confusing, but our students come away with an understanding of the intangible aspects of communication that cannot always be explained through theory or hard research. They also maintain their own voices, their cultural motivations and goals, and their own authority to make choices that best fit needs within their respective cultures.

REFERENCES

1. D. S. Bosley, *Global Contexts, Case Study in International Technical Communication,* Allyn and Bacon, Boston, 2001.

2. J. Corbett, From Dialog to Praxis: Crossing Cultural Borders in Business and Technical Communication, *Technical Communication Quarterly*, 5:4, pp. 411-424, Fall 1996.
3. M. M. Lay and W. M. Karis, *Collaborative Writing in Industry: Investigations in Theory and Practice*, Baywood, Amityville, New York, 1991.
4. S. North, *The Making of Knowledge in Composition: Portrait of an Emerging Field*, Boynton Cook, Portsmouth, 1987.
5. M. N. Kozhina, *O Rechevoi Sistemnosti Nauchnogo Stilia Sravnitel'no s Nekotorymi Drugimi* [On Systematic Discourse Characteristics of the Scientific Style Compared to Several Others]. Permski Gosudarstvennyi Universitet, Perm', 1972.
6. M. S. Chaikovskaya, *Vzaimodeistviye Stilei Nauchnoi I Khudozhestvennoi Literatury* [Stylistic Interplay of Scientific and Fictional Discourse] Vyshaya Shkola, Moscow, 1990.
7. J. Johnson-Eilola and S. A. Selber, Sketching a Framework for Graduate Education in Technical Communication, *Technical Communication Quarterly*, 10:4, pp. 403-437, Fall 2001.
8. N. Allen and G. Wickliff, Learning Up Close and at a Distance, in *Computers and Technical Communication: Pedagogical and Programmatic Perspectives*, S. A. Selber (ed.), Ablex, Greeenwich, Connecticut, pp. 201-218, 1997.
9. C. Spinuzzi, Pseudotransactionality, Activity Theory, and Professional Writing Instruction, *Technical Communication Quarterly*, 5:3, pp. 295-307, Summer 1996.

CHAPTER 17

Knowledge Politics: Open Sourcing Education

Brenton Faber and Johndan Johnson-Eilola

Online education is big business. The education and training industry represents 10% of the United States' economy [1], and throughout the 1990s ambitious companies turned proprietary online education into one of the fastest growing industry groups. The Apollo Group Inc., which operates the University of Phoenix, is one of the most successful for-profit education companies of the 1990s. They provide accredited university education programs for adults in 36 states, British Columbia (Canada), and Puerto Rico. Through its online division, The University of Phoenix Online, the company offers courses worldwide. The Apollo Group went public in 1995 and its stock has risen steadily to a high of 57.54 on April 17, 2002. In 2001 it reported a total net income of $107.8 million on revenues of $769.5 million. On May 14, 2002, the company was added to the S&P 500 index of stocks, formalizing the new role for-profit education plays in the North American economy.[1]

There is a growing list of for-profit education companies that provide accredited higher education programs. In addition to the University of Phoenix, other significant companies include DeVry Inc., Education Management Corporation, ITT Educational Services, Learning Tree International, and Strayer Education. DeVry offers technical and business education on 19 campuses in Canada and the United States, operates the Keller Graduate School of Management in 40 locations across the United States, offers CPA preparation courses for accountants in 300 locations, and owns the Denver Technological College. DeVry's 2001 sales were reported at $567 million, up 12.2% from 2000. Net income for the company was reported to be $57 million. Education Management Corporation

---

[1] Corporate and Financial Data gathered from *Washington Post* online.

offers certifications, associate degrees, and bachelor's degrees in culinary arts, graphic design, photography, and website administration (2001 net income $29 M). ITT Educational Services is owned by a group of nine investment firms and provides technical education on 70 campuses in 28 states. The company offers programs in information technology and a master's program in project management. ITT's revenues grew 18.2% from 2000-2001, its 2001 net income was $33 million. The Learning Tree (2001 net income $25 million) provides high technology education to working professionals worldwide. Finally, Strayer Education (2001 net income $22 million) operates Strayer University with 14 campuses in the Washington, DC area, focusing largely on working adults. The company also operates Educational Loan Processing, which finances student loans.

These success stories from the world of for-profit higher education contrast sharply with examples of education companies that did not make it. Fairfax, VA-based Computer Learning Centers, which provided computer training at 17 institutes and reported 1997 net revenues of $64 million, filed for Chapter 11 bankruptcy in January 2001. SmartForce, which offers Internet-based technology and business courses, saw its stock price fall from a high of 41.22 to 7.426 (April 22, 2002). In 2001 SmartForce reported an annual income of $3 million after a 2000 loss of $28.66 million.

What do these stories of corporate gain and loss have to do with online education? Why should technical communicators be concerned about a growing market for proprietary educational services? In this chapter we argue that with the growth of the proprietary for-profit education market, one's choice of educational media and the economics and political decisions involved in choosing to release that media have become significant issues worthy of discussion and debate. This is because the ways online educational texts are designed and made available has considerable impact on who may have access to knowledge and who will benefit from that knowledge. These decisions, what we are calling the *knowledge politics* of online education, are not entirely new to educational discussions. However, in this chapter we will argue that the democratizing possibilities of online education are at risk of being eroded by the expanding proprietary interests of the knowledge economy. Whereas online education has the potential for the large scale dissemination, sharing, and creation of new knowledge, commercial interests see in this same media opportunities for profits that are based on withholding access to knowledge, limiting users' choices for software and computer systems, gate-keeping, and restricting who may participate in the knowledge economy.

Our argument is as follows. First, we review the transition from commodity-based capitalism to knowledge-based capitalism, noting the consequences that knowledge-as-capital has for educators, researchers, and others who have been working in knowledge environments. Second, we discuss the relationship between knowledge-as-capital and online education, course building, and dissemination.

Third, we offer an alternative to proprietary online education by discussing open source software and the open source development process.

Our goals in this chapter are twofold: First, we want to join with those scholars who have raised concerns with the impact of proprietary knowledge on university research, knowledge creation, and dissemination. Second, we want to offer a viable, alternative method for publishing academic courseware that enables broad dissemination and ease of use. Although technical communicators are not regularly taught to view software choices, distribution methods, or product availability as political choices, we hope that online educators will become critically aware of the ways their material is used and the interests this material serves.

UNDERSTANDING KNOWLEDGE CAPITALISM: FROM COMMODITIES TO INFORMATION

Whereas labor and physical ability were key factors for successful commodity production, knowledge, know-how, and innovation have been characterized as crucial resources for information-based organizations [2-5; 6, pp. 18-19]. Knowledge and innovation are key to work sites as equipment and work processes become more complex and as technological changes occur more often and transform work more significantly. A commonality across modern organizations is a new emphasis on efficiency and rational management which has led to what Gee, Hull, and Lankshear have called the "new work order" or "fast capitalism," by which they refer to a hyper-competitive, global market for goods and services. They note that in the new capitalist environment, knowledge is crucial because it is knowledge that enables companies to "innovate, design, efficiently produce, market, and transform products" [7, p. 28]. More importantly, this knowledge turns products from simple commodities into symbols of "identity and lifestyle" through competitive differentiation and customer-specific tailoring. A key result of this heightened awareness of and desire for innovation, product customization, management efficiencies, and workplace rationalizations has been the commodification and subsequent marketing of knowledge as both a product and a service. In other words, as knowledge is increasingly valued for its ability to transform commodities and commodity production, knowledge itself has become a commodity–able to be priced, marketed, and added to existing products and services.

This concept of knowledge-as-commodity further pushes existing notions of knowledge management [8] and instructional design concepts of knowledge transfer or exchange [6]. For example, knowledge management and knowledge transfer concern the appropriate and effective learning, implementation, storage, and use of relevant (and irrelevant) information. As Wick notes, knowledge management can be viewed as knowledge extraction, analysis, synthesis, and development; knowledge capture, storage, and dissemination; and knowledge databases, software infrastructures, and applications. However, knowledge-as-commodity evokes a much different orientation. As a commodity, knowledge principally becomes a device for revenue generation valued through the economic forces of supply and demand and by one's ability to leverage, withhold, or restrict knowledge. Thus, a stock analyst's research provides investment insight for the firm's traders; a consulting firm's change-management strategy enables their clients to restructure their manufacturing processes; a chemical company's research and development produces a lucrative new cosmetic. Although the ways in which this kind of knowledge are leveraged into financial investment, advice and strategy, and commercial product are not new, the profit model does introduce a new orientation to the role of knowledge production in universities, and it points to the potential for new fiscal relationships between the knowledge produced by university faculty, those who require or use that knowledge, and those who provide or deliver that knowledge.

Sheila Slaughter and Larry Leslie describe these new fiscal relationships available to university faculty as "academic capitalism." They note that in the world of knowledge creation and innovation, "high-technology knowledge is particularly valuable because it lends itself to being patented and copyrighted" [9, p. 140]. High-technology knowledge enables university researchers to enter markets and quasi-markets not only with new products but also with the ability to educate people in how to use and leverage technology. In fact, as numerous for-profit education providers have discovered, the relative lack of overhead for education services often translates into higher profit margins since there are fewer fixed product-related costs such as manufacturing, inventory, or transportation associated with these services. In addition, as Slaughter and Leslie describe, researchers can leverage up-front development costs through research grants provided by corporate, foundation, university, or public sources. This money comes to universities in the form of research grants and is usually subject to overhead funding. As a result, the researcher and the funding agency work in a similar fashion as an entrepreneur and a venture capitalist. However, the research context differs from the entrepreneurial one in that researchers have significant facilities, labs, and equipment available to them, a talented, eager, and inexpensive student labor pool, and a university salary to fall back on.

Universities have long been in the game of leveraging research into successful technology transfer arrangements, co-agreements with corporations funding research, and patent certifications. But more recently, these same schools have pushed to become involved in the distance education market, competing directly with the University of Phoenix, DeVry, ITT, and other for-profit education companies. A difficulty here comes when the university's motives for going online are not to further the university's educational mission but to turn teaching into a new profit center, alongside research overhead, grant writing, and technology transfer initiatives. We recognize the perhaps necessary tension between a university's educational mission and its financial obligations, which are often imposed from the outside. However, once teaching becomes re-conceptualized as a profit center, it loses its value as an enabler of community learning. Instead, teaching becomes subject to the same market forces as other retail and service industries. Teaching can then be measured as a profit driver or loss maker. Student-teacher ratios can reflect university-wide investments in curriculum and instructional support. Successful departments (those that attract more students) can argue for disproportionately more funding, and university curriculum can be driven by expense ratios. For example, most current for-profit distance education companies specialize in business courses, since these are inexpensive to offer yet draw a large enough demand to create an economy of scale. In addition, the curriculum can be standardized and easily replicated without incurring high instructional development fees or overhead. More expensive, resource intensive programs such as science or engineering degrees are vastly under-represented in the for-profit education market.

As a field, we might need to step back here and ask ourselves what our educational goals really are. Although many in academia perpetuate an Ivory Tower image that appears to remove us from the dirty concerns of finances, on a day-to-day level we understand that the generation of surplus value is required for our continued existence: with very few exceptions, our salaries and infrastructure needs are supported by some combination of state funding, tuition dollars, research funding, or other capitalist forms of finance. We are not attempting in this chapter to remove ourselves from the capitalist sphere. We are not suggesting that we research and teach for free. Instead, we are advocating a sustainable ecology, one that allows both profit and healthy community development. The Open Source model we describe later in this article represents an attempt to reframe our notions about the location of value within education so that we can see both its commodity and noncommodity forms (both of which are necessary to education). In other words, we want to affirm that commodified knowledge represents little in the way of value outside an economy of scale that most of us (either as individuals or institutions) do not have access to. The mere transport of pieces of information or cookie cutter frameworks from institution to learning individual is of little value on a case-by-case basis. This is not to say that commodified information has no value, but that it cannot alone sustain a community.

Most of us are interested, even if we have not articulated it yet, in a model that places value on the interpersonal relations among teacher, students, and commodified information. In other words, it is not merely the mass of data present in online courses; it is a teacher's ability to connect up the various bits of commodified information in ways appropriate to different individual students; it is the student's ability to understand those connections and to extend them, in consultation with teacher and other students, in useful and critical ways; it is, in the end, the community's ability to continually reinvent and extend itself. Commodified information is often a necessary condition of education, but it's not a sufficient condition.

In a sense, decisions that educators have made about the use of specific types of media in education can be associated with the development of education as a commodity. The rise of print literacy and mass printed information, on one hand, enabled a revolution in education because educational resources were now easier to produce and disseminate. At the same time, the use of print materials tends to place value on a decontextualized, commodified artifact rather than on the ongoing interaction among teachers, students, and context. Increases in standardization, in the size of markets for advanced education, and in online educational tools have succeeded, in many cases, in locating the value of education within the acquisition of decontextualized bits of information. In other words, education in this model has become a commodified product rather than a contextualized process, a textbook that tries to replace a living classroom and teachers.

From another perspective, we should also remind ourselves that extracting profit from commodity exchange is a complex and risky business, despite the fevered claims of many (now extinct) Internet startup companies. Commodities require a delicate and often unpredictable balance between very large markets and low profit margins. In the rush to jump into the for-profit market for online education, many universities have overlooked basic market factors such as competition, product investment, marketing, and customer relations. Instead, distance education gets characterized superficially as a license to print money. As the successes of the Apollo Group and other for-profit providers have shown, there are good fiscal reasons for being involved in the online, for-profit educational market. At the same time, for every Apollo Group and Sylvan Learning Systems, there is a Wade Cook Financial Corporation (2001 loss of 7.3 million) and a Computer Learning Centers. In between these companies are numerous small and large companies with stock values ranging from $1.29 (Prosoft Training), $1.30 (Edison Schools), and $3.05 (Franklin Covey), to $35.26 (Apollo Group), $40.47 (Education Management Corporation), and $49.33 (ITT). As Nicole Rivard has noted, distance education is costly and, in most cases, it does not provide academic universities with significant revenues apart from equally significant investments. In fact, Rivard argues that the least successful ventures have been for-profit spin-offs managed by universities seeking high-profit returns [10]. However, for us, the point is somewhat different. In this world, despite the relative success or failure of one's distance education spin-off or education enterprise, distance education has functioned to commodify education as a market, and, as a consequence, the measure of good instructional design, courseware, and pedagogy becomes revenue generation and profit.

KNOWLEDGE-AS-CAPITAL AND ONLINE EDUCATION: COURSE BUILDING AND DISSEMINATION

As we noted above, an important implication of academic capitalism concerns the product of education, by which we mean the knowledge produced by students, by faculty, and by communities of learners. Inevitably, this discussion rests on certain assumptions about universities. First, we are assuming that universities exist to create and disseminate knowledge. Second, we also assume that in order for universities to create and disseminate knowledge, they must allow and enable their members to research, publish, and freely exchange information, products, and knowledges. While these may appear to be relatively innocuous assumptions, they are antagonistic to the mission of academic capitalism and the market-based ideology of for-profit education. In this section, we will discuss the issues academic capitalism brings to course building and knowledge dissemination in university contexts.

In his *Postmodern Condition,* Lyotard argues that future societies will come to view knowledge as a scattered, pragmatic collection of particles rather than as a unified, conscious whole [11, p. 72]. This scattering of particles will lead to what Lyotard called a "heterogeneity of elements," which will represent a patchwork of knowledges with only local meanings and relevances. At the same time, decision makers will manage these scattered particles in ways that predict a rational whole evidenced only through the application of specific proprietary systems. Geoff Sauer has described this as a move toward "the proliferation of fields" and the simultaneous "commodification of knowledge" [12, p. 215] by citing the simultaneous growth of the information industry and the expanding strictures of intellectual property rights employed by publishers, media industries, and public policy makers. He writes that "knowledge distribution has become increasingly motivated by the logic of commodity trading and market demand" [12, p. 215]. Sauer notes that since 1962, the maximum duration of a copyright has been changed 11 times and extended from 59 years to 95 years (or 70 years past the author's death). Publishing and proprietary interests in academic knowledge have not remained a fixed enterprise but have regularly changed to increasingly restrict access and uphold proprietary rights. As Sauer notes, the results of these changes can readily be seen in pricing structures that push forms of knowledge out of reach and interest for general consumers and in financial contracts that alienate writers, musicians, and artists but produce large revenues for publishers and record companies [12, p. 223].

The key issue here is that university faculty turn their research over to third parties who profit by restricting access to knowledge. Even though the creation of this knowledge was subsidized by taxpayers (in the form of government grants or direct university payments), students (in the form of tuition), or other public groups (in the form of grants, tax-free policies, and other donations), these same groups are cut off from this knowledge or must pay again to access it. Worse, when these groups are deeded access to this knowledge, it is only partial access since the mechanics of the publishing software or the online courseware are not accessible to the general public. This means that users cannot adapt their courses for local or changing needs, fix problems, or even use the software itself as a learning text. For example, clients may purchase online courses in C++ computer programming, but they may not access the C++ code used to create the courseware they are using. Although they may be learning the tools of courseware authoring, they are prohibited from modifying or adapting the very course they purchased.

One consequence of the dramatic increase in the value of information over the last few decades has been a move toward licensing over copyright in terms of information markets. With copyright, buyers possess a number of key rights. For example, fair use doctrine provides protection for critical discussions of copyrighted works and spontaneous educational duplication. In addition, first sale provisions allow people who have purchased copyrighted documents the right to, in turn, allow others to use the document they've purchased or to sell that concrete product to another user. First sale rights, for example, allow libraries to purchase one copy of a book and allow patrons to view that book.

In addition to the extensions of copyright duration discussed above, the increasing tendency to enforce licensing (rather than copyright) puts users on terrain that removes freedoms constitutionally enforced by copyright. For example, "End User License Agreements" (EULAs, the screens full of legalese information all of us routinely click "I agree" to when we're installing software) now have legally binding status as contract in several U.S. states. Despite our assumption that such agreements are mundane, in several cases corporations have used users' assent to enforce restrictions on the use of that software. In one case, Microsoft's threatened legal action convinced an online magazine publisher to remove a comparative software review of several database servers [13]. The argument? The licensing agreement the reviewer assented to prohibited explicitly the use of the software in comparative reviews. In other words, the end user license agreement removed key free speech rights that would have been protected under the provisions of copyright. But because EULAs are often held to be binding contracts, users often sign away such rights in order to use the software. The status of license agreements as binding contracts may increasingly restrict the uses of other forms of information: corporations could prevent users from using their education to develop additional educational products (e.g., students who have previously used online textbooks to improve their writing skills might be prevented from developing competing online textbooks if they subsequently take a job as writing teachers) or from criticizing the product they've purchased.

UNDERSTANDING OPEN SOURCE SOFTWARE: AN ALTERNATIVE TO PROPRIETARY COURSEWARE

Of course, there is nothing inherently wrong with courseware or with technologically-driven pedagogy. Whereas there is a cultural bias to see new technology as necessarily preferable, we are suspicious when the rationale behind the adoption, use, and wide-scale implementation of courseware violates the primary mission of the university: to create and freely disseminate knowledge. In this section, we will provide a definition of Open Source Software (OSS) and articulate our rationale for using OSS in our own course development.

OSS has received increased attention in recent years [14] with the technological success of projects like the Linux operating system, the Apache Web server, the Perl programming language, and the release of Netscape's source code for Mozilla (an open source Web-browser). Open source products and business models (Red Hat Linux, Zope, VA Linux, for example) have even been reported widely in the business press [15-18] though a good deal of this attention has been paid to the competition between OSS and proprietary software [19-21]. OSS means that the source code for a software program is freely distributed so that other people may modify, adapt, and then freely redistribute it again. It is common in OSS communities to talk about how a software "evolves," which refers to the way users modify programs, fix bugs, add new components, or build additional features. Once a piece of software is released as "open source," it becomes a community product able to be used and improved by a community of users.

A software program's source code is the foundational language that creates the software. Restricting access to source codes has been the primary way in which software developers are rewarded for their innovations and how software companies control product development and distribution. For example, when customers purchase proprietary software, they are only purchasing the ability to use that software. Customers are unable to modify or fix the software at a source code level since the code is restricted from viewing. However, open source software inverts this practice by freely distributing the source code to users, competitors, and other developers. This means that a different set of intellectual property rights, patents, and copyrights apply to the software and the process of software development.

The Open Source Initiative (OSI) is a non-profit corporation that manages and promotes the Open Source Definition and certifies software to be "open source" through its "Certified Open Source Software certification mark and program" [22]. The definition of "Open Source" has nine features. We include them here in summary form but encourage readers to view the definition in full at the following location, *Open Source Definition* (http://www.opensource.org/docs/definition.html):

1. **Free redistribution.** OSS licenses cannot restrict people from selling or giving away the software. This applies to pieces of the software that may be bundled within other programs.
2. **Source code.** However, any redistribution of the software must include the source code so that others may freely adapt, change, and potentially redistribute ("evolve") the software.

3. **Derived works.** The license must allow users to modify the software and create their own derivatives. These modifications and derivatives must be allowed to be redistributed under the same terms as the original software.

4. **Integrity of the author's source code.** Original authors may restrict others from distributing their original code if the license allows others to use "patch files" with the source code to modify the software. But the license must allow users to distribute any software that is built from the modified source code. In these cases, the license can require that subsequent versions be named differently from the original. This requirement enables software to carry the original code, which allows users to know whose software they are using. In addition, it allows authors to remain identified with a specific code which they may have created. The license may restrict the source code from being distributed in modified form only if the license allows the distribution of "patch files" with the source code for the purpose of modifying the program at build time. The license must explicitly permit distribution of software built from modified source code. The license may require derived works to carry a different name or version number from the original.

5. **No discrimination against persons or groups.** The license must not discriminate against any person or group of persons.

6. **No discrimination against fields of endeavor.** The license cannot forbid certain groups or fields from using the software. In the words of the original definition, "The license must not restrict anyone from making use of the program in a specific field of endeavor. For example, it may not restrict the program from being used in a business, or from being used for genetic research" [22]. This requirement was included to avoid cases where authors would ban commercial uses of their software.

7. **Distribution of license.** The license applies to everyone to whom the program is redistributed. This means that people cannot use nondisclosure agreements to stop distribution of the software.

8. **License must not be specific to a product.** The license applies to the software even if it is included within other larger software. This means that if people use the software within proprietary programs, the open source software must be distributed with the source code freely available.

9. **The license must not restrict other software.** At the same time, simply because a programmer has used some open source software in creating a product, this does not mean that the entire product must be open source. This allows programmers to use open source software but ultimately decide if all of their program will be open source. However, as noted above, if a programmer does use some open source software in creating another program, the code must remain open source.

The underlying rationale behind OSS is the creation or evolution of better software. The OSI writes, "[w]hen programmers can read, redistribute, and modify the source code for a piece of software, the software evolves. People improve it, people adapt it, people fix bugs. And this can happen at a speed that, if one is used to the slow pace of conventional software development, seems astonishing" [22]. Proponents of OSS claim that OSS is technologically superior to proprietary software because the software has been tested, de-bugged, and used by a much wider development community. Proponents also claim that because the OSS code is shipped with the software, users can make the software more secure, more adaptable to local conditions and needs, and more dynamic (quickly changed, debugged) than they can with proprietary systems. Generalizing beyond the technological merits of their work, OSS proponents also argue that by freely distributing the source code with their software, OSS organizations serve public, scientific, and educational purposes since users can explore the software at a programmer's level and use the code for their own education, testing, and research.

The implications of OSS for intellectual property rights, copyright practices, and research and development (innovation) have been debated in both popular and academic contexts. Craig Mundie, Microsoft's chief software strategist, has argued that OSS turns a company's intellectual property into a public good, "and thereby destroys innovation" [23]. However, in response to Mundie's speech, Linus Torvalds, creator of the Linux operating system, argued that "pretty much all of modern science and technology is founded on very similar ideals to open source" [23]. More recently, the Open Source Institute published dueling letters between Microsoft Peru General Manager Señor Juan Alberto González and Peruvian Congressman Edgar Villanueva Nuñez regarding a Peruvian Government Bill requiring all government software to be open source [24]. The academic literature has suggested that the long-term consequence of OSS and the OSS model for corporate innovation is still unknown since few longitudinal studies of OSS development and organizational practices exist. The studies that do exist of OSS development have largely focused on three issues: motivation to innovate and work on OSS projects, the OSS development process itself, and how developers manage complexity in OSS organizations.

These studies have suggested that OSS developers are motivated to produce OSS because of the way the process builds technologically superior software, generates collective wealth (e.g. Red Hat), and provides social benefits in the forms of altruism, reputation, ideology, and enjoyment [25-28]. Discussions of coordination in OSS projects have led to conflicting interpretations of the process. Whereas some scholars have stressed the use of highly structured governance models [26] and strong leadership, which includes vision and delegation [28], others reported parallel development by loosely organized participants [27] and a lack of team work and project sharing in the development phase, but extensive peer review and modification after publication [29]. Others report that OSS projects are able to create an effective balance between trust and control [30]. Lastly, other theoretical models have suggested that the OSS community functions as a "gift economy" that has translated gift-giving practices into digital spaces [31].

Lastly, when examining how OSS developers manage the complexity of the software development process, several theories suggest that OSS developers are "biased towards action rather than coordination" acting first and discussing or coordinating later [29, p. 334]. This bias creates a culture in which hidden experiments and failed results are common, accepted, and anticipated before results are distributed and then modified. Since most OSS communication is asynchronous, participants often take extra time to reflect on and revise messages to ensure accuracy and plausible reasoning. This process helps to create an iterative and cooperative process in which design involves the active partici-pation of developers, users, and designers [29, 32]. To some extent, the existence of common methodologies for developing software such as The Rational Unified Process and Extreme Programming, can account for complexity management [33].

CRATEWARE:
OPEN SOURCE COMMUNICATIONS PEDAGOGY

In this chapter, we have identified key issues relating to the commodification of online learning, and we have discussed how OSS in general provides a mechanism for resisting some of these market forces without resorting to a non-technological or anti-technological position. In an understandably paradoxical way, we are interested in using appropriate methods and materials without automatically rejecting or preferring one method over another. In this final section, we elaborate the early development of Crateware, an OSS course building system that we have developed. By adopting an OSS framework, we are attempting to develop online courses that are less subject to capitalist forces but still enable us to use and experiment with current and developing technologies. Crateware represents an attempt to develop educational resources that lie somewhere between textbook information and complete, turnkey online courses. As we discussed earlier, our value as teachers often lies primarily in our ability to orchestrate the use of relatively decontextualized and fragmented bits of information by students within concrete learning communities. We take, for example, general textbook materials on generalized skills (teamwork, screen design, textual style, etc.), then develop specific assignments that ask our real students (face-to-face or online) to draw on those resources in order to address some specific issue.

When developing our own online courseware (Crateware, www.crateware.org), we were drawn to an OSS model for four reasons. First, and primarily, we wanted to build courseware that could be widely implemented, could be adapted to local needs and interests, and could be easily evolved as users found new ideas, applications, or lessons they wanted to integrate with the courseware. The OSS is free both to develop and to use. This means that students do not pay for textbooks, and faculty and instructors do not have to pay to use the course creation materials.

Unlike recent open courseware initiatives, such as the recent campaign by MIT to publish course materials online, our vision for Crateware seeks input from users who may create their own version of courses and then share that version with the user community. This approach also differentiates Crateware from the course management system recently released in source code by the for-profit Jones University [34]. Jones University officials announced that they would release the source code for an existing proprietary course building software. However, as Olsen reported, the software was not the most recent version and it was not going to be supported. Crateware is designed to build a user community in which faculty work together to co-develop and support classroom materials. This means that Crateware is a community resource and product. In addition, by freely providing Crateware we are providing an inexpensive, yet high-end, technological alternative for teachers. The high cost of many online products is detrimental to widespread adoption. Our goal here is to provide an Internet resource for those classes that may not be able to afford proprietary online resources.

Second, we wanted to build an integrated online learning environment. This means that we wanted to build courseware that supported learning through its content and its architecture. By remaining open to community evolution, Crateware supports learning and student projects in all of the fields that help to build online education: computer science, instructional design, technical communications, graphic design, information architecture. By making the Crateware code freely available, we enable students to use the site as a reference and as a site to publish their own projects. This is accomplished by involving users as potential developers in the courseware evolution cycle. Unlike proprietary courseware, with Crateware users (teachers, students) can be involved in updating material, creating new material, and then integrating this material into successive versions of the courseware.

Third, we wanted to be able to focus on creating innovative and useful courseware without the restrictions imposed by the for-profit educational marketplace. Unlike existing courseware, Crateware is dynamic and evolving as it responds to the needs of its users. Quality is maintained by an editorial board of peer reviewers. Since we are not marketing Crateware as a commercial resource, we are able to pursue interests and directions that may be too specialized or unique for a general audience.

Fourth, we wanted to create an online learning site that could become a focus for both teaching and research. As part of the site, we have integrated essays, such as this one, that constitute open source scholarship in our field. We have also published technical papers and have created links to online forums for scholarly publishing. Here, we will publish articles about Crateware, studies conducted using Crateware resources, and other materials involving Crateware.

THE FUTURE OF CRATEWARE

Crateware was envisioned as a way for us to develop and use online courseware without our having to participate in the for-profit educational market. As such, we see Crateware to be as much a political as an educational choice. However, in the merging worlds of online education, for-profit education, and proprietary media, the practical distinctions between concepts like education, scholarship, politics, and economics are quickly blurring. Currently, Crateware is a project-in-development as we work with new users, continue to develop and evolve the site, and create new resources for our own courses. Ironically, despite our desire to escape the market, we still realize that the actual success of Crateware as a community resource will depend on community acceptance, user buy-in, ease of use, and quality of materials—market forces that influence any kind of online courseware.

In this chapter, we have positioned Open Source Software as an alternative to for-profit, market-based educational software. We argued that for-profit educational companies risk transforming teaching into a profit center rather than a central component of community learning. In addition, we argued that a central component of for-profit education is the proprietary restriction of knowledge even though many users have already paid for this knowledge. Thus, the proprietary withholding of information, from the content of courses to the source code that creates the online software, violates the fundamental mission of the university: the creation and free dissemination of knowledge. OSS enables users to freely use and learn from university-based knowledge resources. OSS also creates a community of users who evolve the courseware for their own local needs and teaching resources. We look to OSS as an alternative to traditional proprietary methods of publishing and disseminating courseware. We are not advocating OSS as the only option available for courseware but simply as one method among many. After all, OSS is really about choices, opportunities, and alternatives. As such, it is potentially more aligned with the free market than we may have first assumed.

REFERENCES

1. E. Wyatt, Investors Are Seeing Profits in Nation's Demand for Education, *New York Times,* November 4, 1999,
   http://www.nytimes.com/library/national/110499private-business-edu.html.
2. P. Drucker, *Post-Capitalist Society,* Butterworth-Heinemann, Oxford, 1993.
3. P. Drucker, Management's New Paradigms, *Forbes, 5,* pp. 152-177, October 1998.
4. R. Reich, *The Work of Nations,* Vintage, New York, 1991.
5. R. Reich, *The Future of Success,* Alfred A. Knopf, New York, 2001.
6. C. Reigeluth, What Is Instructional-Design Theory and How is It Changing? *Instructional-Design Theories and Models: A New Paradigm of Instructional Theory Volume II,* C. Reigeluth (ed.), Lawrence Erlbaum, Mahwah, New Jersey, pp. 5-29, 1999.

7. J. Gee, G. Hull, and C. Lankshear, *The New Work Order,* Allen & Unwin, Sydney, 1996.
8. C. Wick, Knowledge Management and Leadership Opportunities for Technical Communicators, *Technical Communications, 47*:4, pp. 515-529, 2000.
9. S. Slaughter and L. Leslie, Professors Going Pro: The Commercialization of Teaching, Research, and Service, in *Campus Inc.: Corporate Power in the Ivory Tower,* G. White (ed.), Prometheus Books, Amherst, New York, pp. 140-156, 2000.
10. N. Rivard, The Cost of Going the Distance, *Matrix,* pp. 25-28, September 2001.
11. J. F. Lyotard, *The Postmodern Condition: A Report on Knowledge,* G. Bennington and B. Massumi (trans.), University of Minnesota Press, Minneapolis, 1979.
12. G. Sauer, Community, Courseware, and Intellectual Property Law, in *Online Communities: E-Commerce, Online Education, and Non-Profit Online Activities,* C. Werry and M. Mowbray (eds.), Pearson, New York, pp. 215-238, 2001.
13. E. Foster, Is It OK For Microsoft and Others to Forbid Disclosure of Benchmark Results? *InfoWorld,* http://www.infoworld.com/articles/op/xml/01/04/16/010416opfoster.xml.
14. E. Raymond, *The Cathedral and the Bazaar: Musings on Linux and Open Source by an Accidental Revolutionary,* O'Reilly, Sebastopol, California, 1999.
15. S. Ante, Big Blue's Big Bet on Free Software; It's Pouring Cash into an All Out Effort to Promote Linux, *Business Week, 3761,* p. 78, December 10, 2001.
16. J. Biggs, New Uses Help Introduce Linux Operating System to Non Geeks, *New York Times,* p. G.6, November 29, 2001.
17. L. Lessig, *Code and Other Laws of Cyberspace,* Basic Books, New York, 1999.
18. L. Lessig, *The Future of Ideas: The Fate of the Commons in a Connected World,* Random House, New York, 2001.
19. L. Gomes, Linux Campaign is an Uphill Battle for Microsoft Corp., *Wall Street Journal,* p. B.10, June 14, 2001.
20. L. Flynn, Despite Microsoft's Best Efforts to Kill It, The Free Software Movement Shows No Sign of Quietly Rolling Over and Dying, *New York Times,* p. C.4, June 4, 2001.
21. G. Moody, Online: Free Software Survives Downturn: Bill Gates Beware: Open Source Is Flourishing Even if the Companies are Not, *The Guardian,* p. 1, January 10, 2002.
22. *The Open Source Initiative,* 2003, www.opensource.org.
23. Business: An Open and Shut Case, *Economist, 359*:8221, p. 67, May 12, 2001.
24. Peruvian Congressman Refutes Microsoft's "Fear, Uncertainty and Doubt" (F.U.D.) Concerning Free and Open Source Software, *The Open Source Initiative,* May 24, 2002, http://www.opensource.org/docs/peru_and_ms.php.
25. S. Weber, The Political Economy of Open Source Software, *The Berkeley Roundtable on International Economy,* 2000, http://brie.berkeley.edu/~briewww/pubs/pubs/wp/wp140.pdf.
26. M. Markus, B. Manville, and C. Agres, What Makes a Virtual Organization Work? *MIT Sloan Management Review, 42*:1, pp. 13-26, 2000.
27. J. Feller and B. Fitzgerald, A Framework Analysis of the Open Source Software Development Paradigm, *Proceedings of the 21st International Conference on Information Systems,* Association for Information Systems, Atlanta, Georgia, pp. 58-69, 2000.

28. J. Lerner and J. Tirole, The Open Source Movement: Key Research Questions, *European Economic Review, 45,* pp. 819-826, 2001.

29. Y. Yamauchi, M. Yokazawa, T. Shinohara, and T. Ishida, Collaboration with Lean Media: How Open-Source Software Succeeds, *Proceedings from ACM Conference on Computer Supported Cooperative Work,* ACM Press, New York, pp. 329-338, 2000.

30. M. Gallivan, Striking a Balance between Trust and Control in a Virtual Organization: A Content Analysis of Open Source Software Case Studies, *Information Systems Journal, 11*:4, pp. 1-28, 2001.

31. M. Bergquist and J. Ljungberg, The Power of Gifts: Organizing Social Relationships in Open Source Communities, *Information Systems Journal, 11*:4, pp. 305-320, 2001.

32. S. Bodker, C. Nielsen, and M. G. Petersen, Creativity, Cooperation, and Interactive Design, *ACM Conference Proceedings on Designing Interactive Systems: Processes, Practices, Methods, and Techniques,* ACM Press, New York, pp. 252-261, 2000.

33. E. Berglund and M. Priestley, Open Source Documentation: In Search of User-Driven, Just-in-Time Writing, *Proceedings of the 19th Annual International Conference on Systems Documentation: Communicating in the New Millennium,* S. Tilley (ed.), ACM Press, New York, pp. 132-141, 2001.

34. F. Olsen, Jones Knowledge Will Give Away Its Course-Management Software, *Chronicle of Higher Education,* August 30, 2002, http://chronicle.com/free/2002/08/2002083001t.htm.

CHAPTER 18

Extreme Pedagogies: When Technical Communication Vaults Institutional Barriers

Billie J. Wahlstrom and Linda S. Clemens

As a discipline, technical communication is no stranger to technology. Communication technologies have been at the center of the technical communication production curriculum since its beginning. Technical communication has also been a leader in focusing the lenses of research and theory on technology and its uses [1, 2] as well as helping students hone their critical skills on technology issues such as intellectual property, globalization, and technological literacy [3]. Since the mid-1990s, technical communication programs have used communication technologies to vault classroom walls. Courses no longer are confined solely to classrooms where professors and students gather together at predetermined times and study technical communication issues until the clock tells them it's time to stop.

Most technical communication programs have used technology to some extent to lower the barriers of time and space for students by providing a mixture of courses. Some classes meet face-to-face on campus and have course materials and methods of interacting available online. Other courses use a hybrid or low-residency model in which students are on campus for a few class meetings and then complete the remainder of their interactions with faculty and other students using a variety of technologies. In the last decade, we've also developed "distance" or no-residency courses and a few complete programs in which students complete all of their work for the class using communication technologies, never meeting face-to-face in a traditional classroom.

Before the beginning of the 21st century, then, technical communication as a discipline used technologies to serve learners on campus, at remote campuses, and online. Collectively, we offered courses and programs to cohorts of students at their workplaces. We've offered traditional and noncredit courses on campus during regular school hours and terms and in summer and off-hour workshops. And most recently, we've been reaching out to place-bound students in other cities, states, and nations by offering courses and degree programs online and through interactive television, as we did decades ago with paper and pencil correspondence courses.

All this effort is just swell, and we should feel good about it, but at the same time, we must realize that this level of piecemeal effort isn't good enough to meet the needs of our students or the needs of our discipline to use technology strategically in its own best interest or in the best interest of democratic society. We have yet to vault several key barriers, and the failure is not in a lack of technologies but in the way our discipline thinks of itself and permits itself to be constrained by tradition. Instead of being leaders, in a fundamental way within the academy, we're stuck as a discipline, and in essay after essay and at conference after conference, even our most innovative thinkers are left rehashing the same problems and pointing out ways to unstick ourselves. For example, Brenton Faber and Johndan Johnson-Eilola muse on some of our discipline's failures in a recent essay—our failure to produce leaders of the sort needed in an information age [4, p. 141]; our failure to establish workplace and academe relationships that allow us to "position technical communicators . . . as knowledge workers" within their organizations [4, p. 142]; our failure to overcome our disciplinary fragmentation [4, p. 144]. Even our doctoral students play variations on the same themes in their dissertations that the discipline has provided them, such as the difficulty technical communicators have in establishing what value they add to an organization [5].

Even a cursory examination of some of our most successful and long-lived programs points to our failure to think outside the academic box of certificate, minor, degree, advanced degree, credit courses, and a few summer institutes. We graduate students and then for the most part we ignore them. We do put alumni on our advisory boards and rely on them to provide internships and give guest lectures. Once in a while we give them a collegiate distinguished alumnus award, but we do not systematically or seriously provide our graduates with ongoing, continuing education. We ask doctors, car mechanics, and teachers to come back to their institutions and get updated on a regular basis if they wish to retain their edge and their certifications, but we don't do this for technical communicators. Neither do we recruit systematically the best and the brightest from high schools, offering advanced placement and post secondary option classes to gifted students who combine communication skills and technology sense.

Many reasons exist for our unwillingness to move beyond traditional academic structures. Technical communication programs have often had such a struggle to establish their legitimacy that they don't want to do anything to call it into question. Other reasons are programmatic or result from unresolved philosophical positions. We don't want to think about lifelong learning and continuing professional education as a discipline because we've never been able to resolve tensions between the workplace and the academy or within our own departments between those who focus on rhetorical theory and those who study practice. We (as a discipline, not as individuals who often consult in industry) seem unconvinced that we have anything to offer (beyond a workshop here or there) once we have launched our students and provided them with what we call a professional framework that blends theory and practice, skills and critical thinking. Or worse than that, we don't want to jeopardize a hard-won academic standing by providing something that smacks of training.

Disciplinarily, our niche has grown comfy. We have degrees, journals, conferences, textbooks, dissertations, and tenure. We understand our tensions and divide up our curricula so that the interests of each group in our departments are represented in a "competency area." We've reached an institutional balance between those who want rhetorical theory and those who want usability testing. We prepare future technical communication faculty the same way we've always prepared them, and that centers on teaching in traditional classrooms and computer labs. Departmentally, we can point to our excellent placement records and the steady influx of students to our programs. These successes, after all, are what convince deans to allocate money for equipment, travel, and new positions.

Why then are we surprised, if indeed we are, that so many corporate universities have developed to meet the needs of practicing professionals? Why are we not surprised that books looking at technical communicators in the future [6] still include chapters on the importance of forming or redefining or revitalizing collaborations between business and industry? Something is really wrong here if we haven't been able to work out this relationship after so many decades of writing about it in our technical communication books and journals, talking about models for doing it at our conferences, and creating a slew of councils, advisory boards, and centers. It really is time for some major changes.

RETHINKING TECHNICAL COMMUNICATION IN THE CONTEXT OF "TECHNOLOGY FOR LIFE"

Technical communication as a discipline needs to think more boldly than we've been doing. In the age of reality TV and extreme sports, we may need to incorporate some extreme views into thoughts of the future. Maybe our problem is more fundamental than modeling new partnerships between business and academe. Maybe there's something more productive to do than argue about which our curriculum should have more of—rhetorical theory or practical design. Maybe we should stop beating the dead horse of value added. Maybe we can get over our arrogance about not wanting to work with students once they are part of the "workforce" and in need of some additional "training."

This is the ideal decade in which we can think bigger thoughts about our profession. Universities are considering their intellectual futures [7]. Libraries are wondering what their "digital" destinies should be. Land-grant institutions are reconsidering their missions and wondering how to transform the Morrell Act into a living commitment to Public Engagement, and major foundations are helping them do so. Study after study has shown that universities have to change how they are financed and the ways they meet students' needs; and we are seeing those changes happen [8]. A driving force of change is what the "adult public wants from higher education" [7]. The public wants access to education on its terms, not ours. According to International Data Corp, e-learning will overtake classroom-based instruction as the primary method of instruction by 2004. Now, 70% of American universities have at least one course online, and by 2005 that number is expected to grow to 90% [9]. The dotcom bust of the late 1990s and spectacular educational e-learning failures such as those involving the University of Michigan's portal and Columbia's for-profit arm haven't slowed down these fundamental alterations in education underway. *The Chronicle of Higher Education* documented this change in its examination, "Phoenix Rises," of the University of Phoenix Online where enrollment has gone from 4,700 students in 1997 to 49,400 students in 2002 and 25 degree programs are offered in 16 fields and taught by 7,000 faculty, of whom 95% are part time [10].

Our discipline as a whole needs to reexamine its relationship with our students in the context of the extensive communication technologies being deployed in educational institutions. What change of perspective can we get, for instance, if we stop thinking exclusively about traditional degrees, "graduation rates," and getting students launched successfully in four to five years? What if we think about our relationships with technical communication students and practitioners as lifelong, as 40 years (and longer) of productive interactions? What if we try to understand, as we're trying at the University of Minnesota, what it means for a learning institution to make a "technology for life" commitment to our students?

Technology for life means that, at the very least, a learning institution is committed to providing access to its intellectual assets over the long haul. Students keep their email and their authentication identity after graduation (and without having to join the alumni association), so that they have access to university resources for their entire lives. On the cynical side, one might think universities are developing a cradle to endowment strategy for their students—recruiting them in high school or earlier and then keeping them engaged with the university until they draw up their wills, and selling them a few sweatshirts and homecoming football tickets in the interim. On the not-so-cynical side, what if universities actually believe that technology for life affirms their commitment to lifelong learning, critical thinking, and civic engagement? A university's motivation aside, technical communication departments can shape such opportunities to work out lifelong learning relationships with their students.

Okay, then. Let's think about how a "technology for life" concept could help us vault institutional barriers. How do we create a lifelong relationship with technical communication and what could it look like? First of all, let's throw out our concept of calendar—the legacy of agricultural times that necessitated a school year of eight or nine months so the summer time could be allocated to work in the fields. Secondly, let's throw out our concept of "class schedule"—the legacy of an industrial world where parts were uniform, assembly lines employed workers and not robots, and classes met for 50 minutes on MWF or more minutes on T/TH because that's how schedules worked. Let's think about a different world where there are many opportunities for learning.

If we really rethought our programs in the context of a lifelong relationship with our students supported by the learning technologies we have and the ones that are coming, what could we do? First of all, we would be a lot more flexible. Secondly, we could think much more broadly about whom we want to reach, how often, and with what purpose. Lastly, we could throw out some of the restrictive notions we have about curriculum because in an ongoing relationship with learners, we wouldn't have to squeeze everything into a single rigid format. What is the state of current knowledge that might equip us to make significant change?

WHAT WE ALREADY KNOW ABOUT TECHNICAL COMMUNICATION AND TECHNOLOGY-ENHANCED LEARNING

When technical communication departments first thought about moving some of their courses online or relying heavily on learning technologies, resistance developed among some faculty. Scholars and teachers questioned whether it was possible to teach technical writing at a distance, for example. Today we know that the answer is, clearly, that we can. After offering an advanced course in technical writing as a course that met only occasionally in a face-to-face format and the rest of the time online, Tebeaux concluded in 1995 that "students can learn a rhetorical approach to the development of technical documents without a traditional classroom setting" [11, p. 378]. In Tebeaux's course, students attended an initial class meeting in a classroom on campus, and they came to campus to take a final exam; they completed all other course work via the Web. Comparing grades earned in this low-residency or hybrid class with those of a traditional face-to-face technical communication courses she taught, Tebeaux found that students in the two types of courses earned comparable grades. Tebeaux's experience adds to the large body of research establishing that students can learn with comparable success in technology-mediated environments.

Technical communication faculty have learned that they can teach well and experience satisfaction with their and their students' performance in a technology-mediated environment. As technical communication instructors move from one type of class to another, they have to make adjustments in how they teach and in sequencing their assignments. Tebeaux has emphasized, for example, that the design of assignments and course materials must reflect clarity and careful planning and the course should incorporate multimedia. Tebeaux also indicated that the instructor should "operate[s] more like a facilitator who strives to help the student" [11, p. 382] than like a traditional classroom teacher. This means that students focus more on the course materials than on the teacher. Our own experiences teaching classes online have convinced us that teaching can be done well in both face-to-face and online classrooms, but that each setting calls for different skills.

We have continued to refine the first attempts of technical communication programs to vault the barriers of traditional classrooms; both research and teaching experiences have established a critical foundation. In Tebeaux's class, offered nearly a decade ago, course materials consisted of a textbook, a course pack of supplemental materials, and information posted online. In her article, Tebeaux does not address interaction in the course, and she comments that "distance versions of technical writing courses may preclude collaboration" [11, p. 386].

Subsequently, three scholars [12] studied another foundational element of teaching technical communication courses in technology-enhanced settings: the role of virtual learning communities. In each of four different traditional courses, students used Web-based tools to collaborate, complete projects, and participate in discussions among themselves and with guests. The students interacted and used technology to complete tasks, but they did not form lasting communities. Their conversations focused on completing their projects and on technical issues, and conversations ended at the end of the term. The authors believed we are creating learning communities that were "not quite good enough" [12, p. 183] and asked how we might "design to promote robust interactions and not just efficient access to information . . . to create a community that is defined by interest and a determined length of time. . . . [and] model the concept of community in our classes that will allow our students to focus both on tasks and social interactions" [12, p. 183]. They noted that the technologies allow instructors to create a sense of place but not yet to "create a community of scholars with the power to transform the individual the way we have been able to do with face-to-face communication" [12, p. 187].

Today, in a far more technologically complex environment that provides wireless connections, PDAs and pocket computers with more memory than our older desktops, portal technology that integrates personal data (address, social security number, transcripts, class schedule) with course content, enterprise systems (registration, bookstore, financial aid, advising), and with greatly improved multimedia and online library resources, many of the last decade's logistical problems in academia have disappeared or diminished. When technical communication classes are taught online now, instructors have assignment shuttles that permit students to upload their work—regardless of how it was created—into student galleries so that everyone can see and critique it. They have "e-reserves" provided by the library that allow students immediate access to, and the ability to print, readings. They have wireless connections that allow students to access full text articles from the library and lectures they want to review while they sit in public spaces before and after class. They have instant messaging so students and faculty can interact in real time and asynchronous messaging that lets them interact when they have time. They have streaming audio and video to accommodate guest speakers and supply materials for review and enrichment. They have authentication systems that allow faculty to see their advisees' records and allow students to access library and museum digital holdings. They have e-portfolios that allow students to carry their best work from high school AP classes, through their undergraduate days, and into grad school.

Technical communication instructors also have had time to develop bodies of theory and research to direct and evaluate our efforts. For example, researchers in our field have examined issues of instructional design for technical communication courses delivered entirely over the Web. From that research emerge suggestions that we use cognitive flexibility theory to inform our design of course homepages, dramaturgical theory to promote engagement—"emotional involvement on the part of the learner" [13, p. 157]—social construction theory to design course sites that encourage learners to "practice the discourse of the larger technical communication community" [13, p. 161], and social interaction theory to promote dialog among learners within a Web-based course.

From other researchers in our discipline, we have learned that course design, especially if learners in online courses are adults, should feature reciprocity, experience-based learning, an emphasis on personal application, individualized and self-directed learning experiences, and integration of learning and living [14, p. 44]. In addition, courses should incorporate materials and information available on the Web, examine and evaluate the Web itself as a communication medium, and ensure that assignments require interaction [15].

Our research examines the experiences faculty have had using new technologies and documents the strengths and weaknesses of these experiences. For example, one faculty member who built and taught an online course discovered that he spent great amounts of time building the course, and more time "dealing . . . with technical issues . . . than actually teaching" [16, p. 22]. Gilette indicates that, when teaching online, an instructor steps into "the multi-faceted, continually shifting roles of architect, building administrator, departmental secretary, postal worker, custodian, security officer, grounds keeper, equipment purchasing officer, maintenance supervisor, and overall technical ombudsman" [16, p. 25]. Unpublished conversations among technical communication faculty who teach online focus on whether to use course management applications such as Blackboard and WebCT, and whether to use html and other coding to build course websites or to use course-creation software; the conclusion seems to be that a single right answer does not exist. O'Sullivan suggests that "course-in-a-box software may offer opportunities or constraints to the teaching endeavor" [17, p. 62].

At the University of Minnesota, our technology-enhanced courses include those linking students at multiple sites via interactive television (ITV). As a consequence, technical communication faculty are studying multiple issues related to teaching via ITV, some related to logistics and others to how technological artifacts affect teaching and learning. Having taught many courses via ITV, one of us (Clemens) considers how to form small groups efficiently for intra- and inter-site discussions; help students look past the television screens to see people; help students learn to use technology to collaborate across distance and prepare panel presentations with speakers at several sites; and work with the sites, each with a different academic culture, so they form a unified class rather than a set of four separate sites with unconnected people. She examines how to coach students across a distance who already are reluctant to ask onsite instructors for assistance, and how to help students learn that a conversation and office hours by telephone or online are just as useful as face-to-face conversations and office hours. ITV faculty face challenges of becoming comfortable with the technology, and of managing such logistics as transmitting handouts for timely duplication and arranging for examination proctors at distant sites.

Although some technical communication faculty believe ITV to be an ineffective medium for conducting experiential- and discovery-oriented courses that are built on student involvement, other faculty focus on discovering how to devise courses and teaching strategies that exploit the medium. Racine and Dilworth examined strategies for teaching the first day of an ITV class, arguing that that day "often sets an indelible tone for the duration of the course" [18, p. 351]. In their research they explored the "physical and mental spaces constructed by ITV and the expectations created by the presence of such technological artifacts as television screens, microphones, and lighting banks" [18, p. 351]. These researchers concluded that "ITV offers both instructors and students new opportunities to understand communication and media and to develop skills that are clearly marketable as we face ever-expanding ways to communicate at a distance" [18, p. 369].

Scholars in our field also examine technology-enhanced learning as a cultural change, especially the "system of learning, ideas, and patterns of thought " [19, p. 367] involved in designing, developing, and implementing a no-residency course. Duin believes that "technical communication teachers, scholars, and administrators [need] to view distance education as a cultural change and study our efforts through a cultural lens" [19, p. 367], commenting that "the Internet is much more than just another educational tool" [19, p. 386]. She argues that "the Internet allows for a renewed commitment to the land grant mission" [19, p. 387].

Beyond our discipline, scholars study methods for designing and developing technology-enhanced courses. Those with experience designing and teaching such courses recognize the overwhelming amount of time required to develop and maintain their courses while also teaching online. Generally we are finding that we must alter our single-source approach to developing courses [20, p. 11], in which the professor as sole practitioner designs a course, gathers all of the content, devises all of the examples and assignments, produces all of the media, locates all of the outside experts who will contribute to the course information and activities, and manages all of the resources of a course, creates and participates in all of the interaction opportunities—while also remaining responsive to student concerns and questions, usually expressed within volumes of email to which students expect prompt responses. Increasingly we realize the value of the course team model of development, in which as many as 20 people, all specialists, collaborate to develop technology-enhanced courses. The team includes academics who provide content expertise, as well as instructional designers, editors, graphic artists, audio and video producers, and others [20, 21]. The course team model usually develops course materials that are "much more complete and effective" [21, p. 106], and teams usually emphasize the use of several media rather than just one.

Scholars also study characteristics of effective technology-enhanced courses. They advocate such instructional design elements as "asynchronicity . . . , group support . . . , [opportunities for] reflection . . . , control . . . , interactivity . . . , intensive reading and writing" [22, p. 37], and indicate that learners value online conversations with students and faculty as well as "flexibility of time and location . . . , interesting content . . . , an enhanced learning environment . . . good or excellent tutor performance" [22, p. 39]. Course designers should include provisions for establishing community [23, 24] and for purposeful interaction [25]. In addition, we who teach technology-enhanced courses must consider learning objectives, the desired role of the technology in the learning situation, development time, budget, and student motivation [26] when selecting from the range of technologies. Useful and practical resources on how to build community by conducting effective online groups abound (see, for example, [27, p. 147]).

Scholars study the work of "groundbreakers"—the institutions that have moved beyond merely putting a course online—and of "the new pacesetters," the institutions that use new approaches to technology-enhanced learning. Such institutions offer "students a buffet of learning opportunities that can be customized to their learning needs" [20, p. 11]. Some of these institutions are comprehensively redesigning approaches to online courses and report higher student achievement as well as important cost savings.

All of this research, as well as that presented in hundreds of other publications and at hundreds of conferences, has been a necessary part of initiating the move from conducting technical communication courses in traditional face-to-face classroom settings at universities to incorporating technology into our course designs. We have the tools and the knowledge to make certain that we can teach courses effectively even if students never see their instructors or classmates and that students can communicate and collaborate at a distance. Continued work is needed on how technology affects the establishment of communities and how we must modify our approaches to instructional design and course development as technology becomes an increasingly important component of our work. To do justice to teaching in our discipline, we must continue to research the implications, advantages, and disadvantages of technology-enhanced education, but we are well on our way to doing a good job with the new tools at our disposal. None of this should be intimidating because we need only look at what our colleagues in the health sciences around the country have done successfully (and confirmed with research) to see what is possible [28].

The problem is that these competencies alone aren't enough to get us where we really need to be.

VAULTING INSTITUTIONAL WALLS

Making real change in a discipline means doing more than improving what we already do well or changing it by simply adding new technologies. To vault institutional walls means that technical communication programs, faculty, and students must make more than changes in how we teach the classes in our traditional programs.

New Roles for Professional Associations

First of all, we must forge different relationships with our professional organizations. It's time for technical communication organizations to plow new ground, to follow the path provided by other associations, and to take an active role in shaping the national agenda on issues of importance to us. Consider how the Modern Language Association (MLA), National Council of Teachers of English (NCTE), and Conference on College Composition and Communication (CCCC) have played activist roles in shaping their disciplines by issuing white papers, setting national goals for the profession, and setting standards. For decades, these organizations have taken a position on a range of issues including students' right to their own language, standards for inclusive language, the need for diversity in the profession and in the student body, and the size of writing classes. The agenda of each of these national organizations, shaped and carried by its membership, has changed the disciplines with which they are connected. Our national associations must take the same kind of leadership. Some of the changes these organizations might call for are detailed below.

National Standards of Technology Literacy

Nationally, our profession should set standards for technological literacy for our graduates and hold all programs accountable for meeting those standards. These same standards should also shape, in part, the content of the continuing professional education we provide to all of our alumni and to the community at large. Increasingly, members of industry expect our graduates to be able to communicate effectively using a variety of technologies and to work within groups distributed across the United States or even the world. One of the students in the technical communication partnership program involving the University of Minnesota Twin Cities (UMTC) and University of Minnesota Crookston, campuses that are 300 miles apart, completed her degree by taking courses online and via ITV; the company that hired her indicated that one factor influencing their hiring decision was her experience using technology to work and collaborate successfully at a distance; she gained that experience taking courses via ITV and the Web—courses incorporating assignments that challenged students to exploit the technology to communicate across time and distance. As part of her work responsibilities as a technical communicator, this graduate now participates regularly in videoconferences and online meetings.

Moreover, standards of technological literacy should shape our training of the next generation of the professorate and be reflected in the new position descriptions we circulate. Already, technical communication programs that make use of communication technologies to reduce place or time barriers require faculty trained to thrive in these environments and who will be able to make compelling arguments for their teaching at tenure.

Such faculty will be equipped to prepare students for the kinds of work they are already being called upon to do. Shortly after the September 11, 2001 terrorist attacks on the United States, an article appeared in the *St. Paul Pioneer Press* [29] focusing on the increasing use of video conferencing for business meetings. Quoted in the article, Steve Dale, spokesperson for Minneapolis-based U.S. Bancorp, indicated that this company had been using video conferencing for executive meetings for years—primarily for efficiency. He explained, "You don't have to put everyone on a plane to have a meeting. Every time we're going to have a meeting, we look at the situation to see if it warrants someone being there. Or is it something we should be using video conferencing for?" [29, p. C-1]. At The St. Paul Companies, nearly all of the 10,000 employees participate in video conferences from their desktop computers; the company also conducts video conferences that link participants in conference rooms at multiple sites. A spokesperson for ADC Telecommunications commented "we're likely to see increased use of video conferencing because of travel concerns. And we're making sure that what travel we do is really necessary" [29, p. C-1].

Faculty who have been incorporating technology and teaching at a distance constantly learn more about issues to consider, practices to avoid, problems to prevent, approaches to use, and ways to exploit the technology in order to help students. Where are the courses to prepare future technical communication faculty to teach in all of the new settings, including distance, demanded by the public and made possible by technology? In the United States, the technical communication programs primarily charged with preparing future faculty are those that include a PhD component. Interviews in 1999 of faculty and department heads of the seven technical communication programs offering the PhD revealed that only one program planned to offer a formal distance pedagogy program of courses and practical experiences for graduate students to complete before teaching distance courses [30]. In 2003, that pedagogy program does not yet exist.

Partnerships in Higher Education

In Minnesota, the state legislature has mandated that the two largest state systems of higher education—University of Minnesota (UM) and Minnesota State Colleges and Universities (MnSCU)—each consisting of multiple coordinate campuses and institutions throughout the state, must seek opportunities to collaborate and partner in order to make resources available to greater numbers of state residents and to reduce duplication of programs and resources. In 1998, UM President Mark Yudof and MnSCU Chancellor Morris Anderson signed the Partnership Agreement for Public Higher Education; at that time 60 collaborative programs were in place. By 2001, nearly 170 formal academic collaborations and partnerships had been implemented or were in development [31]; a year later there were nearly 200. Other states and higher education systems also explore and implement collaboration and partnership programs [32]. The field of technical communication presents many opportunities for participating in such programs; we must examine, therefore, how we might use technology in our technical communication programs to vault a range of barriers—between faculty within our technical communication departments, between departments in our universities, between universities, and between academic systems in our states and country.

If we are unable to create partnerships within our states, our legislatures will do it for us, so great is the pressure from citizens to have higher education play a more responsive role in workplace training and lifelong learning. In Minnesota, for example, the Legislature passed a bill in 1997 (House File No. 273) that created a virtual university of the state and provided ongoing funding for that entity as well as a "joint powers" structure to govern it. This entity has since become ISEEK (The Internet System for Education and Employment Knowledge, www.iseek.org), and it brings together 200 educational institutions from across the state to create a gateway for citizens to access learning, employment, and career opportunities. In 2002, the ISEEK site received more than 3,000,000 hits a month as it provided educational and workforce information for the people of the state. Funding for ISEEK comes from line items provided to the University of Minnesota, MnSCU, and the Department of Children, Families, and Learning (K-12) by the legislature. The mission of ISEEK is, in part, as the website indicates, to provide that lifelong learning and e-learning opportunities are developed and that comprehensive, current, and accurate content that enables people to make smart choices about their education and careers is available.

In 2002, the partnership including the public higher education institutions in Minnesota, ISEEK, public K-12 education, and state government launched an effort to develop a statewide digital plan, *Statewide Digital Learning: A Plan Supporting Minnesota's Lifelong Learning Opportunities*. Such plans exist in other states and typically look at both infrastructure and content. They provide the opportunity for our discipline to develop standards and integrated programs on a statewide and regional level.

Portals, digital asset management tools, learning content management systems, course management systems, and robust digital infrastructures mark most major educational institutions. And these tools are allowing us to reinvent education. Current educational information and opportunities are available all the time and are updated weekly and, in many cases, daily. Universities are developing "news" channels for learners, college by college and major by major, so students can have access to news about their education—what assignments are due? What new books are available? How has the syllabus been modified? Who's available to collaborate with? Daily (and often hourly) updates to the news channels provide students and faculty with everything from information about the newest library acquisition in their field to reminders of quizzes and notification of noncredit as well as credit offerings.

These services are here now, but how is technical communication as a discipline using them? Where's the *TechCommNews* that aggregates information from all our programs and that we can put on every technical communication student's and alumnus's personal portal page? Where are our lifelong learning efforts? Where are our position papers as a discipline describing the importance of lifelong learning in the field of technical communication? Where are the national standards for such education? And finally, where is the national leadership working to establish regional and national consortia to guarantee coverage for all learners and to set the bar for high standards? Many of these efforts are too big for a single department to do alone. National organizations must give leadership.

Serving the Public Good

If technical communication as a discipline were to vault its institutional boundaries, it would think broadly of the learner's needs as well as the needs of the United States and international community for trained communicators to facilitate robust discourse on the issues of importance to us today. Where are the consortia of programs in a region working out their plans for continuing education? Where are our professional consortia developing workplace training? Any of us with access to the Internet can take a class on Flash programming for free as one of us did from Barnes and Noble in 2002. But where can any of us get an update on what technical communicators need to know about genomics or nanotechnology, for example, that will increase our knowledge base and help our company's bottom line? Adult learners can take a class on Web development online at 50 different sites, but where are the consortia of technical communication programs providing research updates on issues we, as a discipline and as a profession, believe critical?

We might, as a discipline, decide, for example, that practicing professionals need to be updated on issues of readability on small screens. This is critical and potentially lifesaving information message designers need to know. More and more academic health services are deploying wireless technologies and providing medical students with PDAs to download information. Already thousands of applications exist in the public domain for the health professions to download into such devices. Issues of resolution on small screens means that all information on the Web may not be automatically suitable for the PDA. Does this matter? It may well matter if documents are designed to include x-rays, and the resolution on a small screen makes viewing critical details impossible. What if a tumor were part of the detail missing on a lower-resolution screen? One of us (Wahlstrom) teaches the class in message design required of all MS students in our program. Prior to Spring 2002, students didn't explore the issue of designing for small screens. Where is the regional or national (or even local) structure for bringing this issue, and others, systematically to alumni?

Many other examples like this one exist where providing continuing education to practicing technical communicators could save lives. Consider, for example, the safety issues involved in the accelerating number of "info cars" on the road. These automobiles are equipped with GPS, Internet connections, wireless phones, DVD players, gaming equipment, and other voice activated systems. We all have our examples of bad decisions drivers have made while using cell phones, and research is being done on how human attention spans are affected by listening to email while driving, for example. Where will technical communicators get information to use as they design message systems about how incoming messages—displayed on the windshield or read aloud to drivers—will affect attention and ability to drive safely? Creating new knowledge and translating that knowledge into practice is the task of universities. Yet, if we cannot convey that new knowledge to those who need it, we cannot consider ourselves successful.

Where are the K12-university partnerships in a region developing Advanced Placement (AP) and Post-secondary Enrollment Option (PSEO) opportunities for students so that we can engage them in the critical thinking about technology, science, and communication that will prepare them for our program and their roles as citizens? Where is technical communication in civic engagement efforts? Where is our presence in enrichment? We can find out online how to read baseball statistics, but where are our pro bono efforts to increase functional literacy? If many citizens can't understand how to read medication labels or bus schedules or understand the scheduling of childhood immunizations, where are the technical communication organizations and flagship programs using their knowledge and technology to address these issues?

MOBILIZING FOR EXTREME PEDAGOGY

We are succeeding at vaulting the classroom walls—using technology to enhance our teaching and our students' learning as we increase access to education, improve the quality of our teaching and of our uses of technology, and enhance the efficiency with which we incorporate technology into teaching and learning [33]. Classes no longer have to occur within a physical room with students and professor present at the same specified times. Students no longer have to be in the same room to plan, create, rehearse, and deliver a panel presentation followed by audience discussion, and audience members no longer need to be in the room with presenters to engage in a robust conversation with panel members. Teachers no longer have to collect assignments directly from students, who no longer have to prepare the assignments on paper. Teachers no longer have to prepare photocopies of handouts and wait until a class meets to distribute the handouts to students. Students no longer have to track down a faculty member during defined office hours and then wait in the hall in order to speak with the faculty member and ask questions or obtain supplemental information. Learners no longer have to rely exclusively on quickly outdated textbooks and library resources, or local subject-matter experts, to conduct research and study issues. Technology helps us solve problems and enhance education.

We have learned that, in well-designed online courses, students participate and interact—and they value the extensive interaction available regardless of time of day or day of the week [19]. We have learned that we can design courses to meet preferred learning styles and do not need to counsel certain students to avoid online courses [20]. We accept that we can teach technical communication effectively via technology [11]. In short, we have a strong foundation on which to build our experiences and expertise in using technology to enhance the functions of teaching and learning.

It's time to vault greater barriers. Our profession and our work assume that we connect with audiences—as technical communicators, we design and create messages that solve problems for our audiences. As educators, we must vault institutional walls and begin using technology to solve problems for the citizens of our communities, states, and other countries by helping them access the resources of our institutions. We must join with those in industry who struggle with approaches to such issues as localization, single sourcing, reduced travel, understaffing, unrealistic deadlines, reduced budgets, and other realities—via technology we can help those in industry conduct research and work within these environments, and we can help prepare technical communicators to apply theory and use their knowledge and skills to be leaders as industry continues to change. We must consider the implications of technology, and the needs of our graduates as well as of all citizens for technology literacy. We must think of future technical communication faculty and their need to prepare for teaching and conducting research in environments mediated by technology. We must think of opportunities for relationships with such previously ignored groups as: high school students; high school teachers; medical professionals who must communicate with laypeople; senior citizens who are vibrant, healthy, and energetic and have no interest in retiring at age 65—or even 70, 80, or 90 years of age; and even women in

Afghanistan and other nations (including our own) who have been marginalized for so many years and in so many ways.

We must stop thinking of technology and saying "it doesn't work as well as face-to-face." Instead, we must: consider the situations in which technology enhances what we do well already; consider what we can do differently in order to use the potential of technology; identify what we'd like to do that technology can enable; acknowledge what we must do because technology is here. We need to get past any petty competitive impulses that may linger between programs. There is enough work for us all if we tackle lifelong learning and technology for life initiatives seriously. And we need to revitalize and empower our professional organizations to take on the big issues, after we have extensive, national, and focused conversations about exactly what those are today.

REFERENCES

1. R. Johnson, *User-Centered Technology: A Rhetorical Theory for Computers and Other Mundane Artifacts*, SUNY University Press, Albany, 1998.
2. B. Longo, *Spurious Coin: A History of Science, Management, and Technical Writing*, SUNY University Press, Albany, 2000.
3. L. Gurak, *Cyberliteracy: Navigating the Internet with Awareness*, Yale University Press, New Haven, Connecticut, 2001.
4. B. Faber and J. Johnson-Eilola, Migrations: Strategic Thinking about the Future(s) of Technical Communication, in *Reshaping Technical Communication: New Directions and Challenges for the 21st Century,* B. Mirel and R. Spilka (eds.), Lawrence Erlbaum, Mahwah, New Jersey, pp. 135-148, 2002.
5. D. Norton, *The Strategic Technical Communicator: A Critical Action Inquiry of Information Architecture,* unpublished dissertation, University of Minnesota, 2001.
6. B. Mirel and R. Spilka (eds.), *Reshaping Technical Communication: New Directions and Challenges for the 21st Century,* Lawrence Erlbaum, Mahwah, New Jersey, 2002.
7. D. E. Hanna and Associates, *Higher Education in an Era of Digital Competition: Choices and Challenges,* Atwood Publishing, Madison, Wisconsin, 2000.
8. D. A. Dillman, J. A. Christenson, P. Salant, and P. W. Warner, *What the Public Wants from Higher Education: Workforce Implications for a 1995 National Survey*, Washington State University, Pullman, Washington, 1995.
9. S. Charp, Changes to Traditional Teaching, *T.H.E. Journal, 29*:10, pp. 10, 12, 2002.
10. F. Olsen, Phoenix Rises: The University's Online Program Attracts Students, Profits, and Praise, *Chronicle of Higher Education,* p. A29, November 1, 2002.
11. E. Tebeaux, Technical Writing by Distance: Refocusing the Pedagogy of Technical Communication, *Technical Communication Quarterly, 4,* pp. 365-393, 1995.
12. L. A. Jorn, A. H. Duin, and B. J. Wahlstrom, Designing and Managing Virtual Learning Communities, *IEEE Transactions on Professional Communication, 39,* pp. 183-191, 1996.

13. A. H. Duin and R. Archee, Distance Learning Via the World Wide Web: Information, Engagement, and Community, in *Computers and Technical Communication: Pedagogical and Programmatic Perspectives,* S. A. Selber (ed.), Ablex, Greenwich, Connecticut, pp. 149-169, 1997.

14. S. P. Schneider and C. G. Germann, Technical Communication on the Web: A Profile of Learners and Learning Environments, *Technical Communication Quarterly, 8,* pp. 37-48, 1999.

15. E. A. Thrush and N. E. Young, Hither, Thither, and Yon: Process in Putting Courses on the Web, *Technical Communication Quarterly, 8,* pp. 49-59, 1999.

16. D. Gilette, Pedagogy, Architecture, and the Virtual Classroom, *Technical Communication Quarterly, 8,* pp. 21-36, 1999.

17. M. F. O'Sullivan, Worlds Within Which We Teach: Issues for Designing World Wide Web Course Material, *Technical Communication Quarterly, 8,* pp. 61-72, 1999.

18. S. J. Racine and D. Dilworth, Using Interactive Television to Teach Professional Communicators, *Journal of Business and Technical Communication, 14,* pp. 348-371, 2000.

19. A. H. Duin, The Culture of Distance Education: Implementing an Online Graduate Level Course in Audience Analysis, *Technical Communication Quarterly, 7,* pp. 365-388, 1998.

20. C. A. Twigg, *Innovations in Online Learning: Moving Beyond No Significant Difference,* The Pew Learning and Technology Program, Rensselaer Polytechnic Institute, 2001.

21. M. G. Moore and G. Kearsley, *Distance Education: A Systems View,* Wadsworth, Belmont, California, 1996.

22. D. V. Eastmond, Adult Learners and Internet-Based Distance Education, in *Adult Learning and the Internet,* B. Cahoon (ed.), Jossey-Bass, San Francisco, pp. 33-41, 1998.

23. C. Dede, *Emerging Technologies and Distributed Learning,* 1996. http://www.virtual.gmu.edu/SS_research/cdpapers/ajdepdf.htm, May 28, 2002.

24. L. Harasim, S. R. Hiltz, L. Teles, and M. Turoff, *Learning Networks: A Field Guide to Teaching and Learning Online,* Massachusetts Institute of Technology, Cambridge, Massachusetts, 1995.

25. E. D. Wagner, Interactivity: From Agents to Outcomes, in *Teaching and Learning at a Distance: What It Takes to Effectively Design, Deliver, and Evaluate Programs,* T. E. Cyrs (ed.), Jossey-Bass, San Francisco, pp. 19-26, 1997.

26. L. R. Porter, *Creating the Virtual Classroom: Distance Learning with the Internet,* Wiley and Sons, Inc., New York, 1997.

27. D. E. Hanna, M. Glowacki-Dudka, and S. Conceição-Runlee, *147 Practical Tips for Teaching Online Groups,* Atwood, Madison, Wisconsin, 2000.

28. M. G. Moore and J. T. Savrock, *Distance Education in the Health Sciences,* Penn State University Press, University Park, Pennsylvania, 2001.

29. M. J. Moylan, Face-to-Face Screen/Video Conferencing Had Been Climbing as Companies Cut Travel Costs. Last Week's Attacks are Bound to Increase Use of the Tool, *St. Paul Pioneer Press,* p. C-1, September 19, 2001.

30. L. Clemens, *Preparing Technical Communication PhD Students to Teach at a Distance: Guidelines and Principles,* unpublished thesis, University of Minnesota, 1999.

31. *Survey of Collaborative Efforts,* unpublished manuscript, Minnesota State Colleges and Universities and University of Minnesota, 2001.

32. CEOs for Cities & Initiative for a Competitive Inner City, *Leveraging Colleges and Universities for Urban Economic Revitalization: An Action Agenda,* 2002. http://www.ceosforcities.org, May 28, 2002.

33. B. J. Wahlstrom, Presentation to the University of Minnesota Board of Regents, September 7, 2002.

Contributors

CASSIE AVERY is a graphic designer and technical writer for a Web and wireless development company in Atlanta, Georgia. Her expertise encompasses a broad spectrum of digital technologies and crosses disciplinary lines, allowing her to design and develop interactive media that are uniquely suited to her clients' needs. She focuses on providing her clients with distinctive solutions that increase productivity and collaboration online while streamlining business processes. She graduated from The Georgia Institute of Technology with a Masters of Science in Information Design and Technology, after obtaining her undergraduate degree in English with an emphasis in Technical Writing from the University of Central Florida.

LEE-ANN KASTMAN BREUCH, Ph.D., is an Assistant Professor in the Department of Rhetoric at the University of Minnesota. Her work addresses writing theory and pedagogy in the areas of composition, technical communication, computer pedagogy, online writing centers, and writing-across-the-curriculum. She also has interests in usability design and evaluation. Her work has appeared in journals such as *Journal of Advanced Composition, Technical Communication, Technical Communication Quarterly, Journal of Business and Technical Communication, Language and Learning Across the Disciplines, Writing Lab Newsletter,* and *Computers and Composition.*

LOCKE CARTER, an Assistant Professor at Texas Tech University, is the director of graduate studies in technical communication and rhetoric and the director of the User Research Lab, where he works with students in conducting usability testing and research. He teaches undergraduate and graduate courses in rhetoric, argumentation, hypertext theory, and technical communication. His publications include Market Matters: Applied Rhetoric Studies and Free Market Competition, a special issue of the journal *Technical Communication* on single sourcing, and articles in *Computers and Composition* and various IEEE and ACM conference proceedings related to his work on argumentation in hypertext.

JASON CIVJAN studied Industrial Design as an Undergraduate and, in 2002, received his masters in Human-Computer Interaction from The Georgia Institute of Technology, where he researched leveraging new technology/media for education purposes. Currently, Jason resides in the Atlanta area, working as Production Coordinator for GlobalDoc, Inc., a New Media translation company.

In his free time, Jason serves as co-founder and Artistic Director for Bent Frequency, a non-profit Art/new Music ensemble dedicated to bringing contemporary, culturally significant music to Atlanta, exploring ways to engage the audience in fully immersive events rather than in the passive context of the concert hall.

LINDA S. CLEMENS coordinates instructional design and educational development for technology-enhanced learning (TEL) initiatives from the Office of the Vice Provost for Distributed Education and TEL at the University of Minnesota (UM). This work supports the teaching mission of the University by helping faculty, staff, and students work effectively with instructional technology. She has taught extensively via interactive television and the Web as well as in traditional classrooms. Linda also is completing her Ph.D. in the UM Department of Rhetoric. Before coming to the University, she was an instructional designer, medical writer, and editor, working with pharmaceutical and medical device companies.

NANCY W. COPPOLA is Associate Professor in the Humanities Department at New Jersey Institute of Technology. As Director of the Master of Science in Professional and Technical Communication, she teaches all of her graduate courses online. Dr. Coppola's research in online pedagogy has received grants from Alfred P. Sloan Foundation and the Department of Defense, won an STC excellence award, and been published in technical communication and information systems journals. In addition, she researches and writes about communicating technology transfer, and environmental rhetoric (with William Karis, eds., *Technical Communication, Deliberative Rhetoric, and Environmental Discourse: Connections and Directions,* Ablex Publishing, 2000).

MARJORIE T. DAVIS is professor and founding chair, Technical Communication Department, School of Engineering, Mercer University. She led the development of the BS and MS degrees. Mercer's BS degree is featured in Keene, *Education in Scientific and Technical Communication: Academic Programs That Work* (STC, 1997). Active in Society for Technical Communication, she received the Jay R. Gould Award for Excellence in Teaching Technical Communication, Frank R. Smith Award for Outstanding Journal Article, and Associate Fellow recognition. Davis serves on the AdCom, IEEE Professional Communication Society, and is a member of ATTW, ASEE, and CPTSC. Davis publishes on such topics as the technical communication profession, accreditation, distance learning, usability, and engineering communication.

ANGELA EATON is an Assistant Professor of Technical Communication and Rhetoric at Texas Tech University. She studies professional and technical communication practice and pedagogy, especially within online environments. Past studies have included evaluating the success of two methods of teaching students to correct formal errors in their work, using both manual and computer-based error location methods. Current research includes a nation-wide genre survey and a quantitative examination of the success of proofreading methods.

BRENTON FABER studies discourse and change at Clarkson University. He is particularly interested in the ideological formation of change and strategies used to implement change. He is the author of *Community Action and Organizational Change* (SIUP, 2002), and is currently working on a second book on discourse technologies and change. Brenton is an open source software user and advocate and is a founding director of PubSoft the Public Software Fund.

HELEN M. GRADY is an Associate Professor in the Department of Technical Communication at Mercer, where she has taught over 200 different technical communication and entry-level engineering courses since 1991. She is also the founding director of Mercer's Center for Excellence in Engineering Education and has been active in educating engineering faculty in instructional technology and active learning strategies. Prior to joining Mercer, she managed a technical publications division for a Fortune 100 corporation in Research Triangle Park, North Carolina, for 10 years. She received a BSc from Queen's University (Kingston, Ontario), an MS from CUNY, and an EdD in Instructional Technology and Distance Education from Nova Southeastern University. She is a member of ASEE, IEEE, AAUW, and a senior member of STC.

TYANNA HERRINGTON is an Associate Professor at The Georgia Institute of Technology. Her first book, *Controlling Voices: Intellectual Property, Humanistic Studies, and the Internet* (SIU Press, 2001), treats issues regarding the inhibiting effects of overly restrictive intellectual property law on free speech and egalitarian participation in national dialogue. Although her second book treats legal issues and many of her publications deal with intellectual property, the first amendment, and the work for hire doctrine, she has also published articles treating ethics and document design. Herrington's Fulbright grant to St. Petersburg, Russia, allowed her to develop the continually expanding Global Classroom Project, a distance learning project in technical communication that electronically links students and faculty in St. Petersburg, Russia and Karlskrona, Sweden with those at Georgia Tech. Her work in networked computer-based classrooms and in other digital projects emphasizes the importance and necessity of contextually based understanding of communication that requires experiential learning for students who face communication challenges and depend on digital connectivity.

ADITYA JOHRI is a doctoral student in the Learning Sciences and Technology Design program at the School of Education, Stanford University. He has a master's degree in Information, Design, and Technology from Georgia Institute of Technology, Atlanta. This chapter is based on research done while he was at Georgia Tech. Prior to graduate studies he worked as a software engineer. His current research interests are in informal learning and learning in distributed work settings. He is currently working on a project that looks at how technology workers distributed across three continents work with one another. More information about him can be found at http://www.stanford.edu/~ajohri.

JOHNDAN JOHNSON-EILOLA works as the Director of the Eastman Kodak Center for Excellence in Communication and Professor of Technical

Communications at Clarkson University, managing a university-wide communication education complex and teaching courses in information architecture, technical communication, and usability. In addition to numerous journal articles and book chapters, he is the author of *Nostalgic Angels* (Ablex/Greenwood), *Central Works: Landmark Essays in Technical Communication* (Oxford University Press, co-edited with Stuart Selber) and *Opening > Writing > New Media* (Utah State University Press, with Anne Wysocki, Cynthia Selfe, and Geoff Sirc) as well as the Web-based textbook *Professional Writing Online* (Longman, with James E. Porter and Patricia Sullivan) and the print textbook *Designing Effective Websites* (Houghton Mifflin). He is currently completing work on *Datacloud: A New Theory of Online Work* (Hampton Press).

SUSAN LANG is an Associate Professor of English and Co-Director of the First-Year Writing Program at Texas Tech University. She is a co-developer of TTU's innovative first-year writing pedagogy, Interactive Composition Online (ICON). Recent publications have appeared in College English, Computers and Composition, and other edited collections. She currently teaches both undergraduate and graduate courses in Technical Communication, Composition and Rhetoric.

REBECCA RICKLY is an Associate Professor at Texas Tech University where she serves as Co-Director of Composition and teaches undergraduate and graduate courses in rhetoric, research, and writing. Her work revolves around rhetoric, but includes such diverse applications as technology, feminisms, methods and methodologies, literacy study, and administration. She has served on the CCCC Committee on Computers and Composition, NCTE's Assembly on Computers in English, and she has chaired NCTE's Instructional Technology Committee. Her publications include *The Online Writing Classroom* (with Susanmarie Harrington and Michael Day), and her work has appeared in several edited collections, as well as *Computers and Composition, CMC Magazine, The ACE Journal,* and *Kairos.*

PHILIP RUBENS teaches in the Technical and Professional Communication programs, Department of English, East Carolina University, Greenville, North Carolina. The graduate programs include a post-baccalaureate online Certificate in Professional Communication, an MA in TPC, available as both online and campus programs, and a Ph.D. in Technical and Professional Discourse, to begin Fall 2004. Before joining the ECU faculty, Rubens taught at RPI for nearly two decades. For over 20 years, he has been involved in various aspects of distance education, including training for corporate audiences. Recently, Routledge published a second edition of his *Science and Technical Writing: A Manual of Style.* He has been involved in developing the Web-based courses used in the post-baccalaureate certificate and masters programs in professional and technical communication.

CAROLYN RUDE, currently Professor of English at Virginia Tech, previously directed the graduate programs in technical communication and rhetoric at Texas Tech University. In that role she led the planning and implementation of the online Master of Arts in Technical Communication and administered the program for five years. She also taught several online classes. Her other pedagogical publication includes the textbook *Technical Editing*. She is past president of the Association of Teachers of Technical Writing (ATTW) and a fellow of both ATTW and the Society for Technical Communication (STC).

SHERRY SOUTHARD teaches in the Technical and Professional Communication programs, Department of English, East Carolina University, Greenville, North Carolina. The graduate programs include a post-baccalaureate online Certificate in Professional Communication, an MA in TPC, available as both online and campus programs, and a Ph.D. in Technical and Professional Discourse, to begin Fall 2004. She serves as Lead Faculty for the certificate and masters programs. Before coming to ECU, she taught at Oklahoma State University for 11 years. She has been involved in developing the Web-based courses used in the post-baccalaureate certificate and masters programs in professional and technical communication.

YURI TRETYAKOV is chair of the St. Petersburg Department of Foreign Languages, Russian Academy of Sciences and Director of the Language Center, The European University at St. Petersburg. His background is linguistics (PH.D., 1982) and his research/teaching experience includes the theory of grammar and communication as well as the history of the English language. In 1996 and 2000 he taught courses in Russian, comparative cultural studies, and technical communication at Georgia Tech. Since 1999, Tretyakov has been actively involved in developing and implementing the Global Classroom Project in intercultural digital communication, which links students in St. Petersburg, Russia, Atlanta, United States, and, since 2003, Karlskrona, Sweden.

BILLIE J. WAHLSTROM is Vive Provost for Distributed Education & Instructional Technology at the University of Minnesota. She is responsible for developing innovative, effective, and cost efficient uses of technology to strengthen the core teaching mission of the University. She is currently working with colleagues on developing teaching and learning strategies for the portal and on the implementation of electronic student portfolios. Billie is also a professor in the Rhetoric Department at the University of Minnesota who teaches courses in information design and whose research interests include instructional technology in higher education and the impact of technology on culture and society.

KRISTIN WALKER directs the Professional Communication Program at Tennessee Technological University, where she is an Assistant Professor. While at the University, she developed one of the first online writing courses for a new statewide online degree program. Drawing upon material produced in her course, Dr. Walker has presented at national conferences and published several articles on online learning and technology. Her research interests include technology and writing, disciplinary writing, activity theory, ethics in the writing classroom, and connecting academic and workplace writing contexts. Currently, she is studying ways conflict can be managed more effectively by students and faculty in online course environments.

MARK ZACHRY is Assistant Professor of English at Utah State University and holds a Ph.D. in Rhetoric and Professional Communication from Iowa State University. His work has appeared in journals such as *JAC: A Journal of Composition Theory* and *The Journal of Business and Technical Communication.* He is co-editor of *Technical Communication Quarterly* and a forthcoming collection, *The Cultural Turn: Perspectives on Communicative Practices in Workplaces and the Professions.* He has taught professional communication courses in online environments since 1995 and in 2003 was named Teacher of the Year in the College of Humanities, Arts, and Social Sciences at Utah State.

Index